ON
THE AIR
IN WORLD WAR II

By the Same Author

JOURNEY INTO WAR: *War and Diplomacy in North Africa*

ON
THE AIR
IN WORLD WAR II

By
John MacVane

WILLIAM MORROW AND COMPANY, INC.
New York   1979

Library of Congress Cataloging in Publication Data

MacVane, John.
  On the air in World War II.

  1. World War, 1939-1945—Europe. 2. World War,
1939-1945—Personal narratives, American. 3. MacVane,
John. 4. World War, 1939-1945—Africa, North.
5. World War, 1939-1945—Journalists. 6. War correspondents—
United States—Biography. I. Title.
D756.3.M32   940.54'21   79-18973
ISBN 0-688-03558-2

Book Design by Michael Mauceri

Printed in the United States of America.

First Edition

1 2 3 4 5 6 7 8 9 10

I dedicate this book to the Allied war correspondents who shared my frustrations, disappointments, and sometimes the fulfillments of World War II, and to Louis Weintraub, whom I first met as a young combat photographer on Omaha Beach, Normandy, France, in June 1941, and whose encouragement has been of great value to me.

List of Maps

Prologue

World War II. There will never be anything like it again. Nuclear catastrophe, perhaps, but never a war involving many millions of people all over the world using conventional weapons for so many years.

World War II officially began at dawn on September 1, 1939, when the armed forces of Germany struck across the frontiers of Poland.

For the next six years, the most powerful nations of the world engaged in a conflict which took an estimated total of 20 million lives. The casualties were considered severe, according to the standards of that time.

It was a war largely conducted by means of ordinary high-explosive bombs and shells, a war in which such archaic military implements as the rifle, the manned aircraft, the naval aircraft carrier, and even the battleship had some importance. Only in the closing days of the worldwide struggle was anything like a modern weapon put to use.

Two crude and, by today's standards, small atomic bombs were dropped on Hiroshima and Nagasaki, destroying only a major part of each city. By their very novelty, however, these primitive prototypes of the infinitely more efficient weapons of today encouraged the Japanese government to surrender.

For the first time in United States history, most Americans relied on an electric medium, radio, for their quickest, most immediate knowledge of happenings around the world which were of vital concern to every American man, woman, and child.

In those days television was still experimental and not yet available to the average person. So the eyewitness radio reporter had his day in the sun. To an even greater degree than his colleagues of the press he served as a personal link between those Americans at home and those who were actually fighting the war.

As such a radio reporter I was in Europe and North Africa for six years during World War II.

I talked to millions of Americans every day from the actual scene of the great developments, the London blitz, the Dieppe raid, the landings in North Africa, D-Day in Normandy, the liberation of

7

Paris, and the meeting of American and Russian soldiers on the Elbe River.

I remember the triumphs and failures of our group of radio reporters, how we succeeded and how we failed. I knew all the great figures of those years of war, Eisenhower and Montgomery, Churchill and De Gaulle.

I was in a position to see the heights and depths of humanity at war, to watch the commanders and statesmen in the fascinating toils of strategy and political maneuver, and to behold the common man and woman confronting terror and sudden death.

The feeling that the remembrance of these things is shared in part by many of my countrymen and the notion that a new generation may gain from my own experiences a fresh view of the background of some of our world leaders and our fellow nations have impelled me to write this book. This is the story of radio at work.

Chapter 1

For several years previous to 1939 many people had felt the inevitability of war. In 1933 Adolf Hitler had become the chancellor of Germany. In the mind of Hitler, psychological currents and complexes which beset the thinking of his countrymen appeared in their most disordered and virulent forms. The frustrated artist of no talent, the connoisseur of cream puffs and Wagnerian music was subject also to wildly exaggerated race nationalism and a cruelty the most sinister characteristic of which was the fact that it was neither felt nor even recognized by the man in its grip.

Hitler first assuaged the national sense of inferiority and united his support by crushing the Jewish German minority. After occupying the Rhineland in 1936 and testing German theories of air warfare through practice in the Spanish Civil War, Hitler annexed Austria in the spring of 1938. In the autumn of that year he forced the chief Western European countries, Britain and France, to acquiesce in Germany's taking over sections of Czechoslovakia inhabited by a German-speaking minority.

To achieve his ends, Hitler menaced the world with war, and against many warnings, the Chamberlain and Daladier governments bowed to Hitler's will. When Hitler eventually imposed his control on the remainder of Czechoslovakia in March 1939, the stage was set for a world conflict which most thinking people understood as to be averted only by a miracle.

In the summer of 1938 my young wife and I arrived in Europe partly on vacation and partly on a quest for more information about the great events which were then in progress. Both of us were somewhat familiar with Europe from previous study and travel.

I had been a reporter on the Brooklyn *Eagle* and the New York *Sun*, two papers now extinct. The near approach of war during what was called the Munich Crisis made my wife and me decide to remain in Europe. I found work as a subeditor on the London *Daily Express* and later worked as editor or reporter on the continental *Daily Mail*, the Exchange Telegraph Agency, and the International News Service in Paris. The latter three news media, British and American, are now defunct.

We were, in fact, living in Paris when the German Army entered Poland. We continued to live there through the uneventful months of what was called the phony war, in the course of which nothing important happened after Germany and Russia absorbed Poland. We were still there on May 10, 1940, when the real war began. German panzers sliced through the Low Countries and cut to bits the French Army, which, until then, had been regarded by American and other foreign military experts as the finest standing army in the world.

By June 10 we had quit Paris on two hours' notice under orders from the New York headquarters of International News. We followed the fleeing French government, first to Tours, then to Bordeaux. When the deputies voted governmental powers to the aged defeatist Marshal Pétain, and Pétain promptly announced negotiations for an armistice, the INS group, including Lucy and me, Quentin Reynolds, Kenneth Downs, Merrill Mueller, and Jacqueline de Mauduit, our French secretary-assistant, made our way to Pointe de Grave at the mouth of the Gironde River. Most of our last night in France we passed lying under some railroad cars while the Germans dropped mines among the nearby shipping. At last, British Navy men put us aboard a Dutch freighter, the *Benekom*. At dawn a German mine exploded near the *Benekom*'s stern. The captain ordered the anchor weighed immediately, and we were off—to a destination we did not know. On June 19 we left France. On June 21 we arrived in the harbor of Falmouth, England.

The British did not know when they were beaten. That much was obvious to the little group of Americans who had spent the last two weeks running away from the invading panzers. It was even obvious to some of the Britons who had accompanied us from Paris, the late Harry McElhone of Harry's New York Bar and John MacAdam, the *Daily Express* sportswriter with the sweeping mustachios, as we consoled ourselves with Scotch whisky until 3:00 A.M. in the Strand Palace Hotel.

Logic demanded that the British understand they were alone, isolated from the Continent by military power such as the world had never seen, about to be invaded and torn to bits by the same savage instrument of war which had just crushed the French. Logic should have required some approach to Hitler for a live-and-let-live agreement such as the aged Marshal Pétain had obtained for the part of France which the Germans had not bothered to occupy.

Fortunately the British were, as always, quite illogical. David Low, the New Zealand cartoonist, expressed their feelings well with a drawing of a British soldier in battle dress, standing on a rock in the angry ocean, shaking his fist at the stormy heavens, and saying, "Alone At Last." The British seemed almost relieved that they would no longer have to worry about their allies, these uncertain foreigners, but could now brace themselves as Britons, all together, to meet the enemy.

At times the complacency of the British in the face of the terror which we refugees knew and they did not seemed infuriating. But it was also magnificent and most reassuring.

For a reporter who had intended to return to America and obtain an Army commission for the struggle he knew must come, the whole situation was so intriguing that when Fred Bate, European director for the National Broadcasting Company, asked me to stay in England in order to cover the German invasion of Britain, the offer was too good to refuse. Lucy and I turned in our return tickets to America, and I hurried over to Denman & Goddard in Sackville Street to be measured for my British Army war correspondent's uniform.

Radio news reporting was just at the beginning of its great influence, and I was lucky enough to be one of those who helped it grow. In the dangerous, exhausting days and nights of the London blitz to come, only six Americans in London were regular broadcasters: Fred Bate and I of NBC, Edward R. Murrow and Larry LeSueur of CBS, the former Chicago *Tribune* bureau chief John Steele, and Arthur Mann of Mutual, who had occasional help from William Hillman.

I might note that back in those days NBC and CBS were the only serious competitors in the news. ABC was an integral part of NBC known as the Blue Network, and I broadcast for NBC's Blue and Red Networks alike. It was only later that the two networks became separated by government antimonopoly order, and the Blue turned into ABC and set up its own news department under the able NBC veteran Thomas Velotta. The Mutual Broadcasting System was a very minor part of the broadcasting picture. Its men abroad mostly did other work as well, and they were never under the stress of the need to be at the scene of action as were the rest of us.

The key men were Ed Murrow and Fred Bate. Early in the war the two—gray-haired, lovable Bate and chain-smoking, sardonic Murrow —agreed that there should be no sensationalism in their war coverage. The war was sensational enough. Instead, they would emphasize calm candid opinion and 100 percent accuracy. When LeSueur and

I joined them, we joyfully adopted their broadcasting philosophy, and so grew a tradition which only now and then was broken, almost always by newcomers from the States.

It had been arranged that I would spend some time watching Fred Bate do his broadcasts, then begin doing occasional broadcasts of my own in preparation for the time when I would be out on the beaches with the British Army and the nine other accredited American correspondents, watching the death struggle with the Nazi invaders.

But I happened to be in the House of Commons on July 4, when Winston Churchill explained how the British Navy had been forced to sink most of the French fleet at Mers-el-Kebir on the Algerian coast, and with only a half hour's notice I was called to do my first broadcast, a full fifteen minutes. I had to sink or swim, and I must have swum. At least I was never afterward worried about my ability to speak into the microphone.

Lucy and I had taken an apartment in a rickety cottage in Devonshire Mews South.

I used to go out each week for a day or two or three with the American and British correspondents of "Sortie W." "Sortie" was the British Army name for a fixed group of war reporters. We covered thousands of miles of territory, inspecting Britain's pitifully inadequate defenses.

The British were completely frank. We could write only what the military censors permitted, but we could see everything. British generals who were later to become famous, Auchinleck, Alexander, and Montgomery, took time for long confidential briefings while they were trying to build a new British Army from the debacle of France. The situation was complicated by the fact that neither we, the correspondents, nor the British Army, nor the German invasion leaders quite knew what kind of military power was needed for offense or defense when, as expected, the Germans attacked across the Channel. Yet we American correspondents must have contributed to making Britain at least seem strong when we wrote or spoke about British readiness to fight to the death. We even became impatient for the invasion, in order that we might see the British Army wipe out the invaders with Boer War rifles and American revolvers collected from arsenals and pawnshops. I am now convinced that if Hitler had known at the time as much about the British lack of defense as we correspondents did, he would have immediately swept across the Channel. There was nothing to stop him.

12

On one section of the coast, I met my most unfortunate hero, unfortunate, that is, if the invasion had ever taken place.

His particular job was to wait until the Germans landed and came up his particular road. At the proper moment he was to set fire to a tank containing a million gallons of gasoline. The idea was that the flaming petrol would cremate all the enemy soldiers in the neighborhood when it exploded. The poor lieutenant who was going to trigger this holocaust had been given, as means of setting off the blast, a Very pistol. He was to point this flare pistol at the gasoline tank and —bingo. But the pistol's accurate range was only 100 yards. For the lieutenant, there was no hiding place.

By August 1940 the Luftwaffe was working on the British airfields, pounding them as an obvious preliminary to invasion. The fields nearest France were already virtually impossible to use except for emergency landings. Once all the aerodromes were eliminated, there could be no real opposition to a German cross-Channel invasion.

This was the heyday of the handful of trained fighter pilots of the Royal Air Force, who, by dint of ability, tenacity, and the machine guns of their Hurricane fighters, with a few Spitfire squadrons later involved, were able to discourage Marshal Göring and cause him to change tactics.

The same month, the first Nazi bombs fell near London, at Croydon, near the airfield, where they wrecked a Bourjois perfume factory and a couple of houses.

I went to Croydon with an outstanding British Broadcasting Corporation broadcaster, Edward Ward, who later became Lord Bangor. The BBC recording machine, carried on a truck, was to be at my disposal. After we had talked to some of the people near the bombing, the sirens wailed again. We expected a new attack, on the airfield, and while we were waiting, we recorded some preliminary impressions so that when the bombs began to fall, we could concentrate on the immediate action. But nothing happened. The all clear blew.

When we returned to London, we listened to our recordings. There was Eddy Ward's voice, calm, natural, and relaxed. But who was this character whose voice shook and quavered with fright? I could not recognize my own voice. The experience was a lesson. There was no shame in being frightened. Everyone I knew was going to be frightened at one time or other. The shameful thing was to show your fright, in your face or in your voice. In all the later broadcasts, although I was often terribly afraid, I do not believe I showed it.

A couple of weeks later Göring switched the weight of his attacks from the airfields to London. This was not bad tactics when we consider how little was known about air warfare at that early period in the war. All the major railroad lines and roads ran through the area of metropolitan London, and if it could have been neutralized entirely as a communications center, no armaments or troops could have been moved from the northern part of England to the area where the invasion was expected, the Channel coast.

The trouble was that neither Göring nor any of the other air generals of that era, including our own Spaatz, LeMay, and company, knew what kinds of bombs or how many were needed to knock out a big city, or even how many were required to halt railroad travel or to make an airfield impossible to use. Like most military air leaders in those days, Göring overestimated the effects of bombing. He could hardly be blamed, because in a peculiar type of war he was one of the pioneers. Even years later, after much trial and error, the bomber generals were saying they could have won the war alone if only they had been given more planes and more bombs. Göring, who at that time commanded the greatest air armada in history, lacked only one element to eliminate London, the atomic bomb.

When Göring turned to strike at London, he had failed to accomplish two necessary preliminary objectives, which were also sine qua non for a successful German invasion: the continuing denial of the airfields near the Channel to the RAF and such heavy attacks on the Channel ports that the Royal Navy would be unable to use them.

Hindsight is a wonderful trait for any correspondent. None of us knew when the Luftwaffe turned the weight of its attack from the airfields to London that Göring had erred. We were convinced that the terror to come was only the preliminary blast for the big invasion.

Chapter 2

The first bombs fell on London proper on a night toward the end of August, striking an office building in the City not far from St. Paul's. I remember going over to the scene the next morning, a Sunday, and poking about in the broken glass and torn brickwork. It was only an incident. Perhaps one or two planes had strayed from their ordinary target or had jettisoned bombs because of pursuit by night fighters.

The next bombs, as I remember, fell on the night of September 5 or 6. This attack was heavier and smashed several small dwellings not far from the Elephant and Castle tube station, south of the Thames.

September 7 was a luxuriously sunny, warm summer day. I did my one o'clock broadcast in the afternoon, heard in America at eight in the morning. Afterward Lucy and I had lunch, then debated how best to enjoy the sun, so often a rarity in England. We talked about going to the outdoor pool at Roehampton outside town to spend the afternoon swimming. But I had a slight attack of conscience about not taking a look at the most recent bomb damage, so we decided to do that first and swim afterward.

That night Lucy wrote a description of what happened:

"Our taxi cruised across Westminster Bridge to the Elephant and Castle. It was a lovely summer afternoon, and I had brought our bathing suits along, hoping there'd be time for a swim when John had finished having a look at the damage done by the Nazi raiders the previous night.

"I waited at the entrance of a closed street while J. made the rounds. Bits of local color were the cat's-meat man, doing a lively trade from his little green pushcart, and a dear old man with white whiskers and gold rings in his ears. J.'s grandfather used to wear rings in his ears, too, when, as a young man, he sailed the Spanish Main.

" 'Wailing Willy' [the siren] had put in its voice by the time we reached the next objective so that an obliging policeman let me through the barricade with J.

Nazi bombers over London in September 7, 1940, daylight raid. German photo. IMPERIAL WAR MUSEUM.

16

"The street we passed down was littered with rubble, and grayish dust choked us. We rounded a corner to find at least four houses in complete ruins. Two Anderson shelters, a bit battered-looking and covered with debris, stood in what had been back gardens.

"According to the policeman, Nazi bombs had found civilian targets after the 'all clear.' A white hen hopped about on top of fallen bricks and timber. Bedding, clothing, and an old piano lay dust-covered in the road.

"As the antiaircraft fire grew intense, the policeman, John, and I took cover in the doorway of a house, empty at that hour of the day . . . probably because its inhabitants had sought shelter . . . though, despite the damage of the night before, we saw one man leaning out of a top-story window. There were many other people at windows and in the streets. We were glad our absent hosts had left their door unlocked as later all three of us had to throw ourselves flat in the hallway, antiaircraft fire and dropping bombs shaking the whole house.

"Mostly we stood in the doorway, though. Three different times we counted more than twenty-five planes overhead. Big gray planes that might have been Nazi bombers. Smaller whiter-looking planes twisting rapidly in and out among the big ones, the Spitfires breaking the German formations. Black and white puffs of antiaircraft shells, behind the planes at first, then as the men on the ground perfected their sights, right amongst the Germans. As one wave of Germans were chased into the clouds by Spitfires and antiaircraft fire, the next would appear in the sky overhead.

"A man on the corner shouted to us that one plane was coming down in flames and that the pilot had bailed out.

"Then 'Ginger' joined us. Another policeman. He had been in the last war and knew what it was all about. Ginger and his colleague had some remarks to make about Baldwin which that worthy gentleman would doubtless not have cared to hear. We felt the bond of sympathy between us and the police escort growing, and we all went around to the local 'pub,' which was 'carrying on,' for a beer.

"On our way, we noticed an immense column of smoke swirling and rising to the east of us . . . and not very far away at that. The beer downed, J. and I set out to find it. People lined the streets or peered from the windows of their houses. The clang of fire engines battered our ears at every crossing. We judged our course by the way the fire engines were going. We passed the junction of Union and Jamaica roads.

"About half a mile along on Union Road, all the windows were smashed . . . out into the street. Ever tried walking on crushed glass? We crunched along to a square. Several houses . . . or what had been houses . . . were smoking. The fires there were already under control.

"Here our ways parted as John was determined to get closer to the big fire and equally determined to send me back to his office with the first story and word of his whereabouts.

"Transportation looked about nil, so I thought I'd phone the office before trying the homeward trip. I picked my way across the street to a public call box. Those of you who visited London in the dear dim days will no doubt remember that street telephone boxes here are made of glass panes on three sides. The panes on two of the sides of my booth were shattered over the floor and over the telephone stand. I thought at first that the phone wasn't going to work at all, but at last I got my call through. It was lucky I didn't have to dip into the return coin box for my two pennies as I noticed that it already contained a needle-thin two-inch splinter of glass.

"As I came out into the street, an ambulance drew up at one side of the square. Three attendants were trying to lift a man inside. He was wrapped in a blanket and was throwing his arms around as if in terrible pain. He made no sound.

"I put my back to the billowing smoke and flames and walked for over a mile before coming across a bus on the move. I hopped it along with three nurses whose heads and shoulders were powdered with dust. I wondered where they had been. They were completely calm and unconcerned.

"I finally reached the office, and it wasn't long before the sirens wailed out their warning again. It was dark, and although London was carefully blacked out, the sky to the southeast glowed a sunset red. The noise of planes passing across the London sky accompanies the tap tap of this typewriter as I wind up another story of Nazi atrocity."

That was how one young American girl saw her first big bombing raid, the first of hundreds she would experience.

The planes were so high that to me they looked like schools of the tiny minnows you see in a stream, now gleaming white in a shaft of sunshine, now dark, now disappearing altogether in the blue depths, to reappear a moment later. They seemed to move steadily in a remorseless procession. I was not quite as confident as Lucy that all the fighters were Spitfires. I reasoned that some must be escorts, for why would the antiaircraft open up when British fighters were overhead?

We know now that 375 bombers and fighters of the Luftwaffe appeared over London in that raid on Black Saturday. It began about five in the afternoon and was over by six.

The huge fire I was following was in the Rotherhithe section, right in the London dockland.

The smoke billowed up in a great black sheet. The eye could see its upper edge, rising and changing shape until it seemed it would spread across the sky. I thought all the docks of London must be burning. When I got closer, I estimated the flames must stretch for a solid mile. It was a fire such as I had never dreamed of, centered in the East Surrey Commercial Docks.

Much of the docks was surrounded by a fence, and I went to the dock office to get directions. There I met an English girl and knew she was a reporter. Somehow one reporter can always spot another. She and I and a photographer, who took off in his car and whom I never saw again, were the only news people in that area. It was a long way from the West End of London, and I suppose the other reporters felt they could see enough from an office or hotel roof to justify anything they could get past the censors.

For me, this was war, and I was in the middle of it, a terrible but gripping experience. The other reporter was Vivien Batcheler, a young cub of perhaps twenty or twenty-one from the *Daily Sketch*.

We walked together toward the blaze. The fire was on a kind of island. We went across a little footbridge. There was a gasworks beside it, and we could smell the gas. I shuddered when I thought that a bomb might hit it and cut off our retreat, for this was the only road to the island. I shuddered more when I was told, down near the fire, that an oil storage plant was also behind me.

My imagination ran riot, and I saw us with a lake of fiery oil and exploding gas behind us and nothing ahead but a wall of flame.

We picked our way among the hoses and talked to the firemen.

One said, "There's housefuls of people behind that fire—and nothing we can do, not one f - - - ing thing we can do."

The blaze had fired the docks, then had spread, and the houses huddled nearby were behind a wall of flame that leaped 100 feet into the air. Oil tankers had caught fire, as had a mass of material piled on the docks. It burned quickly with a roar. The hiss of the hoses seemed slight in comparison, and soon even this died down, for something had happened to the water pressure or the hose con-

London docks set ablaze, September 7, 1940. IMPERIAL WAR MUSEUM.

nections. We could hear nothing above the roar, but it was frightful to know that people we could not see were dying without a chance for life perhaps only fifty yards away. The flame was hot on our faces.

People were being evacuated from the nearby houses. The ambulances were coming down the one narrow street, across the bridge, and picking up women and children. Some of them, wounded, were on stretchers.

We walked back to a little tavern called the Half-Moon and Bullshead, so that Vivien could phone her paper. She stayed on the phone for twenty minutes.

Meanwhile, I had a whisky. When she came away from the telephone, we both had a whisky. She excused herself. She got to the ladies' room and found that that end of the pub had caught fire from blowing sparks. The room was filled with smoke. Vivien nonchalantly went out in the backyard. The fence was burning, but in the circumstances she stayed distant enough to be in no danger of an embarrassing injury. She came back and told the half dozen men, stolidly putting down their pints of bitter, that their haven was on fire. A couple of buckets of water put out the smoldering blaze.

By now it was night. There was no sound but the distant roar of the great fire and an occasional ambulance passing by the pub. We could see other blazes across the river, separate blazes near the docks, but none so large as ours, not nearly, not a tenth as large. Our blaze was a hell such as Dante had never imagined.

We went back a little way down the street, and the sirens blew. We ducked back into a concrete garage, a big one. This was what I had really feared, another raid.

There was only one target for the bombers that night. German pilots could see the flames from the coast 100 miles away. All they had to do was ride in on the glare and let the bombs go. If they could kill the fire fighters and air-raid precaution people and the dockers who were trying to move the ships not yet on fire, they would be able to multiply the daytime damage.

Two foolish reporters, one English and one American, who did not even have to be there, were sitting beside the target, waiting to be hit.

About 200 people of dockland were crowded into the concrete garage. They were waiting for the trucks and ambulances to pick them up and evacuate them. The big garage looked solid to me, and I was glad to be there. Then the bombs started to fall again.

This time there was no antiaircraft fire. It was all bombs. Churchill explained later that those first few nights everything was left to the British night fighters and the guns were quiet so that they could have their opportunity.

The bombs were landing very close. There was no doubt about what constituted the German target—our fire. I thanked my luck I had found the concrete garage. I thought it was too bad that I would not be able to get back to the BBC to give my report, but that was how it was. Maybe by dawn the bombs would stop and I could go home.

I had failed to reckon with the fact that Vivien was a young reporter, eager to make a name for herself. I myself felt at twenty-eight as though I were a thousand years old.

She said, "I'm going to get out of here. I can't report anything from this garage. I'm going to see what is happening."

"Look, Vivien," I said, "I am older than you are. Believe me, it isn't worth it going out and getting blown to pieces just to get a story. Why don't we make ourselves comfortable here? When it calms down, I'll run up to the pub and get us some Scotch."

Vivien waited another five minutes. Then she said, "I've got to see what is happening."

A big bomb fell, and the garage shivered.

I said, "Don't be a damn fool. You're no good to your paper dead. Let's just take it easy for a while. Maybe it will stop." I wanted to stay there desperately.

Vivien was so excited that fright had become a sort of spur to ambition. This was the big story of her short life.

"Well, I'm going out," she said. "I'll drop by later and give you a fill-in if there's anything doing." She started to walk toward the door.

At that moment I hated the girl, hated her deeply and profoundly. I thought: This horrible stupid young bitch is going to get us both killed. What am I doing here with her anyway? I've got one woman to look after in life. I'm not responsible for any others. Let her get someone to stick with her, not me. But that frightful, wonderful, instinctive, inane urge that may be described as sex pride had me in its inevitable grip. If Vivien had not been a nice-looking young girl, the emotion might not have been so strong.

We went out of the garage together, and I felt like a lobster coming out of its shell, all naked and helpless.

Outside there was only the great fire. It made the dockland almost as light as day. Somewhere a fire engine had got a pump into water, and I could hear the beat of the pump. We went down again and took a look at the fire. It was no smaller and no bigger than before. The firemen were silhouetted against the blaze. The roar of the flames was so great that we could not hear bombs falling. When one did fall nearby, it caught us completely unaware. We did not even have time to fall flat.

I said, "Look, this is damn dangerous. We can't hear the goddamn things. We can get knocked off without knowing it. Haven't you seen enough? What's your deadline?"

An ambulance came down and picked up fifteen or twenty people from the garage as we got back to it. Everyone who could be had been evacuated from the area of the blaze itself. Nobody behind the flames was alive anymore.

Another bomb fell, then a string of them. Here we could hear them approaching, and we fell on our faces. The ground under us shook, and we knew they were not far away. If one landed directly on the garage or in the doorway, 200 people would be killed in an instant.

Back at the pub, Vivien phoned in another bulletin. We had a double whisky. Only one or two men were left, one of them an ARP man, his face begrimed with soot. They were still drinking pints of beer.

We started to walk, the bombs coming fast now. About every 100 or 200 yards, we would hear the express train rush of the bomb. We would duck into a doorway. Vivien would lie down, and I would flop on top of her, instinctively. As the sound of falling debris came to our ears, we would pick ourselves up and start moving on. No traffic was in the streets. We were all alone.

This repeated itself, time after time. Down Vivien would go, and I on top. After a while I began to enjoy the sensation, for she was not a small or a skinny girl. A couple of years later, when I met her on another story, she told me she had been black and blue for a week.

We had to walk all the way to London Bridge, a matter of at least three miles, before we saw any cars moving. There by some lucky chance we got a taxi. I put my arm around Vivien and held her close all the way back to her office. For the moment I felt closer to her than to any other woman in the world except Lucy, yet we knew nothing about each other except that we had shared one terrible night of fear together. Through the years that followed we never even became close friends because we did not go around with the same people. But on the odd occasion when we saw each other there was always between us the bond of having looked at the worst of war together.

As I learned later, Vivien on that memorable night got out of the taxi and went into the office of the Sunday paper. The news editor told her he had not used more than a couple of paragraphs that she had phoned in. This was rank stupidity on his part. Vivien wrote out a thousand descriptive words and gave then to him. He put them on the spike—not to be used. White with anger, she took her carbon, walked to Fleet Street, and gave the copy to a rival paper, which used it in full, gratefully. Thus, the scoop of her life appeared in print, even though her name was not on it.

I got back to the BBC exhausted. In the studio were Fred Bate and James Reston of *The New York Times,* who shared Fred's apartment. Jim assisted Fred on an ad hoc basis and, before I arrived, had broadcast occasionally, though he could not use his name because his paper forbade it.

It was ten minutes to one, and we were due on the air at one-fifteen. I slumped in a chair and told Fred Bate I was so tired I could not go on.

"Yes, you can, John," he said. "Jim and I are doing the news. Give me three minutes. Firsthand impression of the attack."

Somehow I dragged myself out of the chair, sat down at a typewriter, and beat out a story.

A week or so later I was told by Ed Beattie of the United Press that the censorship ban on referring to the dockland fires had been taken off just as I went on the air so that my report was the first that America had of the first great air attack of the war in Britain or any other place.

Years later I looked up the broadcast in NBC's London files. I still felt it was something of which I could be proud. I gave the feeling of war, what civilians were experiencing in this first great attack on London.

For me, personally, the event was a baptism of warfare so horrible that nothing again could ever resemble it. I had been frightened to the point where fear itself had lost meaning, and everything else, even D-Day in Normandy, was an anticlimax. But somehow I survived.

Chapter 3

On that first day and night, Saturday, September 7, 1940, 430 Londoners were killed and 1,600 were seriously wounded. Sunday was clear. The fires were still burning, the remains of the nine great conflagrations and the thousand or so lesser blazes. We waited all day for the expected new attack, but it was not until half past seven at night that it came.

I had been having a beer in the Stagshead public house with Ed Murrow. We started to walk up Great Portland Street, and he suggested that Lucy and I spend the evening with his wife, Janet, and him in their flat. Since we were still living in a rickety mews cottage and the Murrows were in a concrete building, I accepted quickly. Neither of us had a broadcast to do that night.

Now we knew what the sirens could bring. That drone, drone, drone of the beating bomber engines became so much a part of our fears that even now, many years later, no matter how often I listen, the first split-second of the sound of heavy propeller engines snaps my mind back. Perhaps anyone who lived through that period will always feel in that instinctive first moment, Here they are again.

The four of us sat in Murrow's apartment with a bottle of Scotch. Each time we heard something dropping in our area, Ed and I would rush to the roof to see what we could see. Down by the river the fires were still burning. New ones were starting. It was plain to see that the bombers were concentrating on the area where they had had their previous success. Then we heard bombs coming with the shriek, changing to an express-train roar, that means they will be very close. We threw ourselves down, and the building shook.

Fires had sprung into being only a block or so away from us. Ed and I went pell-mell down the stairs and into Murrow's car. We were still very new to the bombs. We became much more blasé as the weeks turned into months.

We drove up Devonshire Street, turned toward Marylebone Road, and left the car when broken glass threatened to cut the tires. A gas main had been cut and was burning furiously in the center of the thoroughfare, Marylebone Road. A building right by Madame Tussaud's Waxworks had been knocked about, and flames were licking at it. The auxiliary firemen and the air-raid precautions people were already on the scene. There was nothing we could do to help, so we watched awhile, then returned to Ed's apartment.

The raid continued into the morning. The tally of the 200 bombers that came over was—412 people killed, 747 seriously wounded. And not a single railroad line leading south from London was left in workable condition.

One thing the raids did was to rid me of my police guard. Two or three weeks before the raids began, a high official of the BBC had called me up and asked me to come to his office. Once there I was introduced to an inspector from Scotland Yard, who showed me a copy of a telegram that had come from America to Prime Minister Churchill. The message said:

URGENT GUARD MR. MACVANE WITH INTELLIGENT ENGLISH POLICE. INTERNATIONAL BROADCASTING STUDIO MIDNIGHT UNSEEN DANGER.

If the telegram had come after the night raids began, there would have been a very plain danger anywhere in London at midnight.

I thought it was the work of an eccentric and said so.

"That may very well be," said the Scotland Yard man, "but there's an Irish-sounding name signed to it, and it wasn't so long ago that some of these wild IRA people were putting bombs in postboxes. We've asked America to investigate, but meanwhile, sir, I'm afraid I'll have to assign a constable to keep an eye on you."

I said it sounded pretty silly, but the inspector was firm. So for a time two uniformed policemen hovered near our door. At night one would walk along with me to my office and then to the BBC studios. At first the constable wanted to come with us when Lucy and I went off to a friend's house or to a restaurant in the evening, but he finally compromised by making sure we got a taxi. When we returned, he or his mate would be waiting. Each time we left for the evening we had to tell him where we were going.

Who sent the mysterious message, I never discovered. Presumably the police found it was all a fantasy of some tired brain. When the bombings began, the police were too busy with other matters to bother trailing after an American radio reporter.

On Monday, I went to the War Office and asked to see an anti-aircraft gun site in action. I was given immediate permission.

I hired a car and driver, and as dusk fell, we left London, head-

Aftermath of the September 7th raid. IMPERIAL WAR MUSEUM.

ing down along the Thames. The sirens sounded before we left the city limits.

It was a weird sensation, being out on the flat, swampy land along the Thames, hearing the drone of the bombers overhead, seeing the waving columns of searchlights flicking back and forth, searching the night sky for the incoming raiders, and occasionally seeing the flash of an exploding bomb, light that flared up from the ground, then subsided slowly. Once outside the city I began to see the flicker of the guns, and the sky was studded with the clusters of exploding shells. I felt almost alone on earth, an atom of humanity hung somewhere in darkness with the universe going to bits around me and not able to do anything about it.

At Chatham, near the mouth of the Thames, I found the headquarters of the guns that protected the approaches to the river. A gray-haired captain, winner of the Victoria Cross in World War I, looked at my identification, then told me, "We have orders to show you everything we have to show, and I guess that means everything."

He sent me out to one of the batteries nearby. The battery was already a veteran organization, for it had been doing a great deal of shooting for more than a month. I went to the command post of the battery, then to the gunpits, and finally to the radar station. In those days, it was not called radar, and I have forgotten the technical name the British had for it. The theory of bouncing a radio wave off an object and thereby locating the object on a screen was so new and the equipment so secret that even two or three years later war correspondents were not allowed inside radar finding stations for fear they would disclose some secret gadget in their reports or conversation.

I had never even heard of radar. The British, I learned later, not from officials but from discussing the matter in great secrecy with antiaircraft officers, believed they were far ahead of the Germans in the development of the technique.

The sets in 1940 were primitive compared with what the Allies developed by 1945. For a couple of hours I watched them track each plane as it came in from the Channel, curved over the mouth of the Thames, and headed up the river to London. The little shack whirled around and around as the radar serials followed the planes coming singly or in twos and threes. The noise of the four guns placed around us in an open field was shattering through the flimsy walls. I was fascinated by the wavering green lines on the radar screen, which rose to a peak as the operators twirled their knobs and got a bearing. I learned the theory of how it was done, but I am almost sure I could never have learned the practice.

Later I went to many antiaircraft gun sites to watch the 3.7- and the 4.5-inchers in action. But never again was I allowed inside the radar scanning unit, and when I returned to London, my first guarded inquiries showed me that the whole subject was still top secret. No word of it appeared in the press until years later. So the only people to whom I ever mentioned it were British antiaircraft officers. I am inclined to think that much of the secrecy was uncalled for. The Germans had developed much the same idea. The Americans knew about it and later were able to use the more advanced British ideas to good advantage. Anyway, I can think of no development in the war which did not come to the attention of the regular war correspondents who showed some initiative and energy. We could not help discovering the truth, although it sometimes took us an inconveniently long time to find it.

Three days after the first big attack on London, Londoners were terribly depressed. All we had heard was the noise of enemy planes and enemy bombs. We wondered whether we had any way of combating the menace that bit by bit was blasting London to ruins.

Tuesday, September 10, gave us the answer. The sirens went as usual just at dusk. We heard the drone of the first planes arriving. Then all hell seemed to break loose. British antiaircraft guns opened up from every square in London. Windows broke from the concussion. Nobody could possibly sleep. It sounded like a wild Walpurgis night of noise, so loud that one could hardly hear the engines of the enemy planes, but by listening carefully, one could separate the noises. First was the noise of the nearest antiaircraft batteries. It seemed as though some of the guns must be in the street just outside our windows; actually they were a block or two away in Regent's Park. Next came the sound of bomb explosions. Then came the sound of the guns in the next square or park, slightly fainter, and one's dishes did not rattle. Finally, in the clear intervals, one could hear the fainter sput, sput, sput of the antiaircraft shells exploding 10,000 feet overhead. In addition, whenever a low-flying plane approached, there was the quick bang, bang, bang of the Bofors forty-millimeter guns and, in between, the scream of planes diving to get out of range or occasionally the tearing sound of a falling bomb.

The whole experience was wonderful. We were not just sitting there taking it. We were doing something against the Germans. Churchill has said that he ordered all the guns to open up to build morale. They were to start shooting whenever any German plane came within any possible range.

The whole city came to life. People slapped one another on the back and told funny stories. "By God, we're giving it to them, aren't we?" was the word in the pubs. "Pity a poor Nazi on a night like this."

We grinned continually most of the night, for few of us could sleep. There was a lilt in every voice and a lift to our walk. The next morning the London papers had big headlines, "London Fights Back," and photographs of the night sky lit this time not by the fire of German bombs, but by the flash of British antiaircraft guns. The *Daily Express* headline said, "Shell Curtain Above the Clouds."

Our little mews cottage shook and shimmied every time a gun exploded. The noise of the bits of antiaircraft shells coming down beat a steel tattoo in the streets. I became disquieted by this fact. We had nothing above our heads but a few shingles, and we had learned that Lucy was pregnant.

There was no time of the day or night that we could count on freedom from bombs. Never again was there any big daylight raid such as the raid on Black Saturday, but sirens came and went all day long. There was never any moment that a few Nazi aircraft might not speed over the city to loose their strings of high explosive.

I went to the real estate agent from whom I had rented the mews apartment, explained my situation, and asked him whether I could be excused from my six-month lease. He eagerly told me that he could rent me an apartment in a sturdier building and I need not worry about the lease for the old one, since the eccentric bachelor who owned it lived outside London and was wealthy. The estate agent would fix everything.

We took an apartment in Goodwood Court on Devonshire Street at the top of Portland Place near Regent's Park. It was a third-floor apartment in a five-story concrete and steel building, about as safe as one could be. At least we were under the impression we were quite safe. We lived there during most of the blitz.

In April, just as we were moving around the corner to 88 Portland Place, a friend said, "I've often looked down on the roof of your apartment."

"What do you mean?" Lucy asked.

"Don't you know," said the friend, "you're in a kind of annex or well, separated from the main part of the building? In your section the building is only three floors high."

So, in our fancied security, we were happy. The owner of the mews cottage, wealthy as he was, had the bad taste to sue me for the extra rent. The county court judge decreed that I did owe him the remainder of the rent for the lease, but the judge also said I had been misled by the eager real estate agent. The result was that I paid the mews cottage owner and the estate agent paid me. I doubt that the owner, living happily out of London, ever did rent the mews cottage again, at least while the raids were on. Such frail apartments were not popular in London in those days.

The glorious thing about London was that it continued to function. Ordinary people were braver than their leaders gave them credit for. At one period a battalion of Irish Guards was moved to Hampstead, overlooking the great metropolis so that they might be available to come down and keep order if the people began to riot. This was a lack of faith by someone in charge in the people of the city.

The early raids were concentrated on the East End, the impoverished areas of dockland. Limehouse and East Cheap had many people of foreign origin. Rotherhithe and Bermondsey had no more rich residents than the Bowery. But they took the raids as well as any of the people of the West End.

After a few days' pounding of dockland, the German bombers began dropping their freight on the West End as well, and when a couple of bombs landed in the Buckingham Palace grounds while the king was in the building, the first feeling that only the very poor of dockland were suffering largely disappeared.

London began to clear out. Those who could get out went. Wives and children were evacuated. Some of the children of the poor areas were sent to the country, but usually the wife preferred to stay to look after the man of the family. In the wealthier areas many went off to stay with relatives or took rooms in country hotels. London was a city of 7 or 8 million in September 1939. By the end of September 1940 it was stripped down to the 3 or 4 million people who either had to live there or felt they should.

The fact is that we were never quite free from pressure. I remember one quiet Sunday afternoon. The sky was heavy with cloud, and we hoped the night would be cloudy as well. We dreaded clear nights, especially those with a full moon, a "bomber's moon." Lucy and a girl friend and I decided to go out to the movies. As we stepped out onto the street, we heard the tearing whistle of a bomb. We all fell flat on the pavement. There was no siren. That came two or three minutes later. The bomb blew up a restaurant in the next street. We went on to the movies.

Another time I was shaving, at half past ten of a sunny morning. There had been no warning. Suddenly I heard the familiar crescendo buzz of a bomb falling, then another coming closer toward me, another, very close this time, with the roar that means proximity. My mirror jiggled under the explosions, and I paused with razor in hand. The next was still close, and the fifth farther away. I finished shaving and learned later that I had happened to be in the middle of a string of five bombs of 100 pounds or so apiece. I went out and looked at the results of each explosion. My apartment was just between two of the bombs. The siren, of course, came later.

I do not think any of us really expected to live through the war. Life seemed very tenuous indeed. The worst feature was the constant strain. Unless you have experienced something such as that, a prolonged period in which all your ordinary assurance of living has disappeared and you must face the fact that at any hour of the day or night death may come to you in an instant, I do not think you have obtained full self-knowledge. Most men live their lives without knowing how they would act in an ultimate crisis.

Certainly never before in history had a great city undergo such a mass experience. Courage became the most important, in fact, almost the sole, criterion by which we judged anyone else. It was not being afraid that mattered. Everybody was afraid, or else he was in an asylum oblivious to the world. The real point was that you must not show your fear, for that upset others and added needlessly to the already heavy burdens they had to bear. It was a quick standard of judgment, but there was no appeal from it. We were all together in the same boat, and anyone who could not pull an oar was of no use to any of us.

One of our colleagues, with the best will in the world, was not able to conceal the strain. Even to see his twitching face and body and hear his excited talk rubbed our nerves raw, and we were relieved when he returned to America soon after the blitz began. He was never sent back to Europe.

We clung to the illusion that we all were calm and assured, knowing it was only an illusion, but we had nothing else. The fact that everyone was together in danger developed a mass psychology that otherwise I have seen only in members of infantry rifle companies who have been together in heavy battle for some length of time. Everyone was kind and polite to one another. Three million people went out of their way to talk gently and be helpful to others. The reason was, of course, that the tobacconist or the taxi driver you talked with today might be dead tomorrow. And last night he might have lost his wife or his child, although he would not tell you of it. We helped one another, and we smiled a good deal to show that we all were fellow human beings, staying together in the anguish of the sound and fury that came to us from overhead.

This camaraderie did not extend to those who came to London only during the day and made their escape to the safety of the country before darkness fell. It was strictly reserved for those of us who lived in London the entire twenty-four hours. We were proud to be Londoners. We knew the eyes of the world were on us, and we hoped we could behave with dignity and strength so that the rest of the free world would be proud that they, too, were human beings, sharers of something in common with us.

Day after day and night after night, when we talked with a friend or said good-bye to a wife, we did not know for sure that we would ever see him or her again. When we met someone we had not seen for a while, we added a little extra warmth to our voices and strength to our grips to let him or her know that we were glad they still lived and shared the London air with us.

We shared material possessions as well. One night Lucy and I had a telephone call from a girl named Ann Heffernan. She had once been friendly with an Englishman we knew well, Dunstan Curtis, a Royal Navy hero. It seemed that many of Lucy's best friends had been former fiancées or girl friends or wives of friends of mine.

Ann said, "There's a time bomb in my street, and my windows are gone, and I have no electricity. May I come and spend a night or two with you?"

She came around, and we made a bed for her in the dining room of our three-room apartment. She was still there two or three nights later, when Jerome Willis, the London Irishman who had been Paris correspondent for the London *Evening Standard* and who loved France as much as we did, came ringing at my doorbell. He unloaded an armful of quart beer bottles and said, "My flat is all buggered up. We got one right next door, and my place is unlivable. Can I come and stay a day or two with you and Lucy, Mac?"

We made up the couch for Paddy. We were now as close as peas in a pod. Lucy and I kept the bedroom. Paddy was esconced in the living room, and Ann reigned over the former dining room. We shared one bathroom. I was rather glad, for they were company for

Lucy while I was away. Paddy would drink bottle after bottle of beer from the Mason's Arms next door, and in the morning the dead soldiers were marching in companies and battalions over the living-room carpet.

Even the process of spending an evening quietly talking or reading was sometimes difficult. We would hear the first bomb of a string coming in the distance. By the time of the next we were poised on the floor on our hands and feet, ready to go flat if the close one arrived. No one spoke. We were all listening, trying to judge the fall. If the bombs went beyond us, we would get back in our chairs and take up the conversation or the book.

One night Gault Macgowan of the New York *Sun* came with his wife to dinner. At least a dozen times during the meal we got down on the floor to be out of range of flying glass if the next one landed too close. On one of these occasions we looked at one another and burst into laughter.

"Who ever would have thought," said Gault, "when you were on the *Sun* and we were having dinner out at my apartment in Brooklyn Heights, that we would ever come to this, letting the soup get cold while we tried to dodge a bomb?"

Sometimes there were mild surprises. I hated to go out at night. To get to the BBC studio, I had to walk the length of Portland Place, a quarter of a mile, but very uncomfortable if the bombers and guns were active. After the war I reckoned that more than a dozen high-explosive bombs had fallen within 200 yards of my dwelling. It is surprising that not more people were killed.

Coming back to my apartment about two o'clock one morning, I opened the door to find in my hallway a man capering about in nothing but his shorts, a man, moreover, who did not speak English. Merry peals of girlish laughter rang out from the living room. The youngster was a Polish soldier in the French Foreign Legion whom Ann had met somewhere and invited to the apartment when the bombing became heavy. Lucy and Ann had put him up to meeting me. He was to spend the night in the hallway on a mattress.

We then had Paddy in the living room, Ann in the dining room, Lucy and me in the bedroom, and a French-speaking Pole in the hall. I could not think of anything else we could do except arrange for someone to take space in our kitchen.

The Pole was due to leave the next day. He stayed the next evening for supper and shook our hands heartily, a sad good-bye.

Soon after he left us, the guns and bombs began. In about an hour the doorbell rang. The Pole was there with a broad smile on his face. "The bombs started falling," he said in French, "so I returned. I have brought a present to you."

He handed us a little cardboard box. It contained poisonous-appearing green-frosted cakes that he had bought at a teashop. We smiled and thanked him. There was nothing else we could do. We had to eat the cakes so that his feelings would not be hurt. He said he was leaving on the morrow.

The next night the Pole was back with more green cakes. We grew desperate. He was not a bad youngster, but it was tiresome to have to carry on all our conversations in French, and we were ill from looking at the cakes. We dutifully ate them, however, and we must have made him think we enjoyed them. At any rate he brought us more the following night.

I talked about his unit. Wouldn't his comrades and his officers be worried about his absence? Was he not risking court-martial? Perhaps he was. At least he left on the fourth night, and we never saw him again.

But Ann continued a lively social life. Old Etonians who were now sailors in His Majesty's Navy showed up to use the bathroom for a wash and a shave before taking Ann out to dinner. Or if the bombing was heavy, they stayed for dinner. Sometimes the hallway was three deep in sailors. Paddy was not going to give up the living room. It would not have been respectable if we had urged one or two to move into the dining room with Ann, and I thought: By God, I'm not going to invite them into the bedroom.

As I remember, Paddy stayed six weeks before he found a vacant apartment in our building, Goodwood Court, and Ann stayed eight before she also located a vacancy there.

A very strange collection of people inhabited Goodwood Court. Besides Ann, Paddy, Lucy, and me there was R. T. Clark, the news chief of the BBC, a dry Scotsman with a cigarette eternally drooping from under his scraggly mustache. There were a West Indian Negro rescue worker, a Polish woman in the basement, an intellectual Polish journalist, Swedes, Irish, French, and assorted refugees. Occasionally during a raid we would pool our alcohol and make cocktails while the Polish lady whipped up some tasty mess on her stove to allay our hunger. We would start arguing about the war, its intellectual bases, its possible outcome, and among ten people present we would find ten completely different points of view.

We, the British and those foreigners who counted themselves then as Londoners, were confident we were not going to lose the war. But nobody was quite sure how we were going to win it. The main hope seemed to be that the United States or Russia would enter the war, for then we could start thinking constructively about a counterattack. Meanwhile, all we could do was to sit and take it. And how Britain could take it!

The problem of broadcasting the actual sounds of war was made far more difficult by the fact that we could not make recordings. At that time the U.S. networks insisted all broadcasts be live. When our microphones were open, they received only what was actually happening in the two or three minutes of our broadcast. Time after time Bate, Murrow, LeSueur, and I went up to the BBC roof with our microphones. A few moments before the circuit opened to New York, it might sound as though the doors of hell were being blown off their hinges, but invariably, as soon as New York said, "Go ahead, London," a lull ensued for as long as we were broadcasting. A minute after we finished the guns and bombs might again start bombing loud enough to shatter the eardrums of an engineer across the Atlantic.

We tried every sort of scheme. We broadcast from the basement studio with a microphone open on the roof to pick up sounds. Nothing would be picked up. I would be up on the roof with the BBC spotters and an open microphone and a line to Fred's earphones below ready to warn him when a German bomber approached so that he could switch on the circuit below and pick up the sound. Time after time after time the noises came too early or too late. It was frustrating, for New York kept hearing all about our deafening nights of bombs and guns but never the sounds directly.

London's ordeal was an easy story to write—one could almost have written it by sitting in a basement night and day and reading the papers—but we broadcasters had so identified ourselves with the people of London that we did not feel that we could shirk any of their experiences. We rode with the ambulances, visited gun sites, and watched the firemen at work. Our country was neutral, but we ourselves, for that reason, had to prove to our British colleagues and the people with whom we lived that we were willing to share their lives completely. We felt as though we represented America, and we did not want our countrymen to be ashamed of us, nor did we want the British to have the opportunity of looking down their noses at the United States because the Americans they saw demeaned themselves in any way during the crisis.

Our job was to watch and record what was happening to London, and now, years later, I am satisfied that our small group did the best job of which it was capable, each according to his abilities.

I know that I was glad to be there. After the experience of France, I was ready to admire a people, a city, a person who stood up to tyranny and fought back, and in London there was much to admire. Most of the theaters closed for a time, but not the little Windmill, and now, whenever I go to London, I usually drop into the Windmill to see another of its continuous variety shows, just out of a sort of admiring sentimentality. We picked our restaurants with a view to heavy walls and concrete construction. A favorite was the Lansdowne Restaurant, a converted underground theater, where we often went with Frank Kent, Jr. of the Baltimore *Sun*. We went to movies as usual. I remember going to the Leicester Square cinema and getting out just a few minutes before a bomb landed in the doorway and shattered part of the square. We always seemed to be having close calls, but such incidents were so common that one was almost ashamed to talk of them. Typical British understatement was to call all bomb damage bomb incidents. A fire might rip half of dockland—or a row of houses be blown down with 100 dead—and to the air-raid precautions people each was simply an "incident."

"Where is the site of your incident?" would come the inquiry. Police, firemen, newspapers, everyone, in fact, referred to the "incident." "Catastrophe," "holocaust," "slaughter," and "devastation" were unknown words.

In our first real incident I was fortunately absent. I had called Fred Bate when the sirens sounded and asked him if he needed any assistance, for he was doing the night broadcast.

"Get some rest, John," he said. "I think the girls and I can look after everything. Take the evening off, and I'll see you tomorrow."

Lucy and I spent as quiet an evening at home as was possible. Toward midnight I was in the bathroom when suddenly the whole building shivered. A glass fell off the shelf. Then I heard the cr-r-r-ump that meant a big bomb landing close by.

"I'm glad that one missed us," I shouted.

"The light almost fell over," Lucy called.

When nothing more happened, we went to bed.

The next morning I walked down Portland Place to work. The

end of Portland Place by the BBC was littered with wreckage. All the windows and much of the stonework of the sturdy Langham Hotel, then serving as a BBC annex, had been blown out. The BBC itself was scarred and pitted. Firemen were still going and coming, and hose lines lay in the street. The NBC office at 11 Portland Place was a complete shambles, walls knocked in and doors blown out. Two of the staff, Florence Peart and Mildred Boutwood, were picking their way about the mess trying to gather up papers and the clothing of Fred Bate, who lived in the office.

"You should be glad you missed it, John," Mildred said. "Fred's in the hospital."

The bomb was a parachute "mine" that had drifted over the coping of Broadcasting House. Luckily both girls had been in the BBC basement and escaped the blast. A fire had started inside the building. Firemen had poured masses of water in, and the girls had had to be carried to safety in the firemen's arms.

Fred Bate had been in the office across the street. The blast had caught him, and flying debris had cracked open his head. He had tried to get to the studio, and the girls had found him wandering woozily about, his face and clothes covered with blood, hardly able to speak from the shock that had knocked him out. A number of people had been killed, several of them policemen and wardens who had been in the street or taking cover in doorways.

"Why didn't you call me?" I asked angrily.

"We tried to," said Mildred, "but the phone lines were out, and we were so stunned we couldn't face trying to walk all the way up Portland Place to get you."

The broadcasting lines to our main BBC studios had been cut. Still, somehow some kind of broadcast had had to be made for NBC. Mildred and Florence, with typical initiative, had kidnapped Rooney Pelletier, a Canadian BBC broadcaster, hustled him into a taxi, and taken him down to a studio in the financial district at the main terminal point for the lines connecting London with the overseas transmitters. Rooney had gone on the air to NBC, which must have been somewhat astonished but could not be told the facts of the awful evening.

Fred remained in the hospital for two or three weeks. When he emerged, his doctors told him that for the sake of his health and future working ability, he must get out of the blitz. So he packed a bag and by late December was off to his family in the United States.

I was now the only representative of the National Broadcasting

Company in London, and the worst of the blitz was still to come. Doing two men's jobs was something I did not relish in those circumstances, and I began pleading with New York to send me some assistance. I got many reassuring words, but nothing more.

Chapter 4

My work that autumn was not all bombs and guns. I had early decided that if anything constructive were to come out of the war, if the world in chaos in which I lived were to be rebuilt into some consistent unified pattern, such action would have its beginnings in the free refugee governments of a continent in slavery. I therefore made a point of keeping in close touch with Ambassador Biddle and his assistant Rudy Schoenfeld. They represented the United States to the governments of Norway, Belgium, Holland, Poland, Luxembourg, and later Yugoslavia. Tony Biddle was not allowed to be an official link with the Free French, but in fact, he was the only American diplomat with whom they could have even a friendly conversation since Washington officially recognized only Marshal Pétain's government of puppets in Vichy. I also kept in direct touch constantly with the groups themselves and with the Soviet Embassy through the press attaché there. I never got any news from him, but he always served as a check point for the current official Soviet view of any situation. I talked to the Greeks, the Chinese, and all the rest every now and then to try to keep a finger on the pulse of world diplomacy. Having the benefit of the vast monitoring service of the BBC, I could ring up at any particular time to find out whether any new switches had occurred in German or Russian propaganda or to tap any of the other mainstreams of comment that spewed forth from the world's transmitters night and day. In addition, I had to keep in touch with the British Foreign Office, the Ministry of Economic Warfare, and the press sections of the three services.

Some of the correspondents made the mistake of writing the war as they would a baseball game. They simply kept a box score and noted the bombings and the aerial fighting as though they were unrelated to anything else. I tried to link it all up with the diplomatic background, the struggle of the countries, represented by their governments in London, to create future order out of chaos. Others among the correspondents did the same, people like William Stoneman of the Chicago *Daily News*, James Reston of *The New York*

Times, Frank Kelley of the *Herald Tribune,* and Ed Beattie of the United Press.

The British Foreign Office had placed its entire information staff in the Ministry of Information. Led by the gentle and wise veteran Sir William Ridsdale, the little group performed a difficult task well. They told us the truth, with sufficient background illumination so that Britain would never appear in a poor light. This is a technique of British diplomats that I have encountered and admired for many years. I know how difficult it is, for at one later period I had to do much the same thing for the United States Mission to the United Nations.

One of the information group, I was pleased to learn, was Sylvain Mangeot. After the war he became diplomatic correspondent of Reuters and later the diplomatic editor of the big British counterpart to *Life* magazine, *Picture Post.* Sylvain was a friend of my close friend Dunstan Curtis. We had known each other at Oxford, and I remembered one night we had spent together in the London studio apartment of a man named Rory MacLeod, drinking whisky and reading *Antony and Cleopatra* aloud with Dunstan and Sally Luce of Cleveland, Ohio. Now chance had brought us together again.

Of all the foreign groups in London, to me the most important and interesting were the Free French of General Charles de Gaulle in their headquarters at Carlton Gardens. De Gaulle was the only official of the French government of undersecretary rank to come to freedom in Britain in order to continue the war. His broadcast appeal to all French to join him, the famous statement that "France has lost a battle. She has not lost the war" rang in my ears as representing superb courage in the face of disaster.

I did not realize completely how great was the courage that the general had shown until two years later in North Africa, when I was talking with General Eisenhower, just after Eisenhower had received his third star as a lieutenant general.

General Eisenhower said that he had great sympathy for the French officers who had stayed under Vichy orders. A man brought up in the military tradition was trained to obey orders, he said, especially the orders of a commander in chief, and there was no doubt that Pétain was head of the French government. Therefore, when he called on all French soldiers to lay down their arms, the officers, according to their military tradition, should have done so. It was not part of their function to examine the rights and wrongs of the situation or to make any hairsplitting decisions about acting for the good of France. General Eisenhower said that of course, he was glad to have any possible assistance from Free French forces in the Allied effort in North Africa, but he could not escape the feeling that De Gaulle had acted against the whole world military tradition. In fact, he had thought over how he himself would have acted if the dilemma had confronted him. He believed he might have acted as the Vichy officers did in obedience to orders from the government.

I argued the point with General Eisenhower, whom I always admired greatly as an Allied commander. I said that De Gaulle, a military man all his life, was a better representative of the real France than the old man who was yapping at us from Vichy. The world was divided into right and wrong, and I did not see how the free world could do anything but support the French elements that were fighting for our kind of world and condemn those that were not.

But that was all two years in the future.

In the autumn of 1940 I went out of my way to become acquainted with the men who adhered to De Gaulle. They were a heterogeneous group, some outstanding, some mediocre, some in between, about the same as any cross section of a few thousand men. President Roosevelt, so perspicacious in so many fields, had one blind spot. He believed that by sheer charm he could win the Vichy puppet government in France away from the Germans. Accordingly he saw the De Gaulle group in London as nothing more than an irritant, the uncomfortable stone in the shoe, the sand in the axle grease. The result was that United States officialdom, including the London Embassy, which should have been hand in glove with De Gaulle's men, cold-shouldered the general at every possible opportunity.

I believed that the facts of the Free French should be fully reported to the American public. I therefore took them out to lunch and dinner and had them up to the apartment. I went to their news conferences. I kept in contact with their people by telephone. To me, France was still a big story, and the only France I cared about was represented in Carlton Gardens.

The American diplomats used to say that the little group of people who clung to De Gaulle would never amount to anything after the war, for traditionally refugees did not play a large part in countries later liberated. I believed otherwise, for I thought France would be grateful to the men who represented its fighting qualities through the dark days. It turned out much as I expected. De Gaulle became president and prime minister of France, Rene Pleven, prime

minister, Vincent Auriol, president of France, Hettier de Boislam-
bert, governor-general of the French section of Germany, Maurice
Dejean, ambassador of France. Dozens of others became my good
friends, De Benouville, Diethelm, Boris, Jean Marin, Billotte,
Soustelle. All made great names for themselves later in some form
of service to their country. And when I knew them, I was just about
the only American correspondent who was telling their story, although later Geoffrey Parsons, Jr., of the New York *Herald Tribune*
and Helen Kirkpatrick of the Chicago *Daily News* labored long in
the same vineyard.

The stork-tall general, as *Time* magazine would call him, had had
a strange career. He had written a great deal about armored warfare. He saw a small mobile armored French Army with terrific
firepower as the answer to the *levée en masse*. He believed that given
sufficient armor, firepower and air cooperation, a comparatively
small army could defeat a huge army organized on traditional infantry patterns.

He wrote this, and he argued with his superiors. The arguments
made him persona non grata to the aged French generals. He
struck up a friendship with Paul Reynaud, who tried to expound
De Gaulle's ideas in the Chamber of Deputies. They made no impression on the French General Staff. His writing did impress the
Germans, however, and men like General Heinz Guderian took the
ideas therein contained and used them in forming a new German
Army.

When the German panzers cut through the French Army in
France, they were riding on the strength of De Gaulle's theories.
About eight armored divisions were able to cut up and defeat totally
an army of 3 million. De Gaulle himself, commanding a regiment
of tanks as a colonel, was alone able to meet and defeat the panzers.
He was promoted to brigadier general, youngest in the French Army,
and recalled to Paris. Reynaud, by that time prime minister, wanted
to make him secretary of defense, but the defeatist elements around
Reynaud feared the new young general and persuaded the premier
to list him only as undersecretary.

When the moment of France's downfall came, De Gaulle went
through a typically intellectual exercise on which he based his decision to continue the battle in Britain.

To De Gaulle, the essential France was a strong continuing
stream that flows through history. The kings of France, the Revolu-
tion, Napoleon, the Empire, and the Third Republic were only

transitory political manifestations of a basic reality, France. The people, who rose or fell, suffered or achieved as their leaders were good or bad, then with the leaders who were faithful to them created the moral entity that was France.

This strong sense of the historical continuity of his country was the factor which made it possible for De Gaulle to break with his military training at the moment France became leaderless. Since none of the other representatives of the French government had heeded the call of the underlying eternal France, De Gaulle decided that he and those who followed him became automatically representatives of that France.

As early as July 1940 De Gaulle asked his countrymen a simple question: Would figures such as Joan of Arc, Richelieu, Louis XIV, Carnot, Napoleon, Gambetta, Poincaré, Clemenceau, Foch, Tourville, Montcalm, Bugeaud, or Lyautey have surrendered to the Germans? No, he said, and as they represented France's glory of the past, so the Free French would represent it in the present.

It was late autumn of 1940 when I became the first American correspondent to have a private interview with De Gaulle. London was cold and gray, and every night there were bombs and more buildings blown to bits. My first impression when we were left alone in his Carlton Gardens office was of his extreme height. He smiled shyly and thrust out his hand to greet me. We spoke in French, for although he could speak English, he was much more comfortable in his own language.

I asked when he thought the invasion was coming.

"I do not think the Nazis can now invade Britain," the general said. "They had their opportunity last summer but they have lost that chance. Britain has now been able to restore its defenses."

De Gaulle got up and went to a map on the wall. He explained that what he called the forces of liberty had to realize that two wars were in progress. The war in Europe had been lost for the moment. The war in Africa and the East was still to be fought.

The general said that a new war would begin in the spring, probably in the Balkans with an attack through Yugoslavia. He noted that the Germans now had an overwhelming force of planes and mechanical equipment and would launch their drive in April, as soon as the ground hardened, possibly aiming eventually at Istanbul.

"We must guard the bases at the end of the German rays of attack against this new war," he said. "We must first guard Africa. We must use the help of Turkey and Russia, which are threatened. We must assure ourselves of bases around central Europe strong enough to stop these German drives."

I asked him what he thought about the French colonies in Africa. The general said he thought the people in the colonies favored the Free French, but officials did not, for if the officials changed over, it would constitute an admission that they had been wrong in ceasing to fight.

I asked about General Maxime Weygand, in whom I knew the British and Americans pinned some high hopes, believing that he would hold Africa against the Germans if they attempted an invasion. I knew also that De Gaulle had asked him to assume the leadership of the Free French. I now realized that the approach must have been unsuccessful, for De Gaulle said, with a smile, "I do not believe that Weygand will change. If the Germans invade the so-called unoccupied area of France, there will be a wave of revolt in the colonies, but they will not be fighting under Weygand." He expressed confidence that the majority of the people in the French colonies and in France itself were believers in the Free French movement.

The general went on talking about strategy against the new spring attacks he thought the Germans would make against Eastern Europe. He said that in a year or two the Allies would be able to send an expeditionary force to the Continent. The force, he said, would not have to be very large but would have to be extremely mechanized with a great superiority of mechanized armaments.

"When American aid gives Britain a great air superiority," he said, "this force will be completely protected on its way to the Continent. Continuous bombardment of the Germans and German towns will force the Germans to retire from the East to protect themselves." He believed that under a smashing mechanized attack, Germany would crumble as quickly as France had.

"The hope of freedom in Europe rests in America," De Gaulle told me. "The role of the nations in Europe is fixed by their terrain. Their role is traditional, but America is fresh and does unexpected things outside all tradition."

I asked what message he would like to send to America.

"I would simply emphasize," he replied, "that France is balanced between two forces, a European order run by the Germans and a European order of liberalism, an order of freedom. From certain information that has come to us, the people of France have now chosen freedom—not the German order. Any help that America can give to liberalism and to the order of freedom will be helping France."

He pondered awhile on the kind of Europe that would come out of the war. He said that everyone knew what kind of Europe would emerge if Hitler won.

"If the forces of freedom win," he went on, "they must form a Europe that assures the freedom of the individual but guarantees him a certain basic social security."

The general thought it was wrong to have individualism running riot; people must learn to work and play together. He noted that the Germans and Russians had used mass techniques, the training of people to work and play together, in order to exploit the individual. He said that we must use similar techniques in a highly organized society, but the individual must be helped and protected, not exploited.

"People," he said, "must be taught to like one another's company and like working together."

De Gaulle said after the war there must be close cooperation between the European nations in which rampant nationalism was not allowed.

"You mean a United States of Europe?" I asked.

"No matter what you call it," he answered, "it is a fact that there must be a union in Europe in which people are trained to believe in and to respect liberal ideals and freedom. We cannot map out an exact plan now, but we must be thinking toward such a solution." This interview, I emphasize, took place in 1940.

"What about Germany?" I said. "What's its place in the future Europe?"

De Gaulle said that when the Germans were beaten, they must be trained to believe in the individual and liberty.

"They must be firmly kept from causing trouble in Europe every few years," he asserted, "but even if it takes a hundred years before they are trained out of their present attitudes into believing in the order of freedom and the rights of individuals, one day they will take their part in a European organization that does believe in liberty."

De Gaulle had once served Marshal Pétain as an aide, as Eisenhower had once served under MacArthur. The French general saw no hope that the Vichy leaders would ever take up the fight for liberty. He explained that the driving force in Pétain's soul was the desire for power, a desire that De Gaulle found slightly disgusting in view of Pétain's advanced age. He said Pétain knew he would lose all power if he ever revolted against the Germans, and he predicted that even if unoccupied France were invaded, Pétain would continue to cooperate with the Nazis.

"Yet," he said, "the people of France favor liberty."

And he said that when once the Allies had enough mechanized power to send an expeditionary force to France, they would find support in the people.

I spent about an hour and a half in that first interview discussing the affairs of the world with the general and came away with certain definite impressions. First was the straightforward honesty of the man. Here was a person who would never say the palatable thing because he thought people might like to hear it. His words came not from the lips but from the whole fiber of his being. Second, his courage impressed me. His was a lone voice crying France's glory in the hour of its utter defeat. He had been condemned to death by the government of France recognized by the United States, but beyond his physical courage, his mental and spiritual courage made him outstanding. Finally, De Gaulle had a breadth of intellectual vision which was stimulating. He was already thinking about the unity of Europe, even while the Continent lay prostrate beneath the Germans. And he was already mulling over the problems of integrating Germany into the common European community after it had been defeated.

So honesty, courage, and vision were the characteristics I found in him. I saw him on many other occasions during the next three years until he left for North Africa in June 1943, and I never had occasion to change my estimate of him. He has been called many things by the uninformed. Indeed, an NBC news executive who should have known better once referred to him as a communist and demanded to know why I had publicized such a strong character. Others have called him fascist. Both were completely wrong. He was a man sensitive to the slights cast upon him by governments and people he respected, slights that he felt reflected on the position of his country.

Had the United States government of that day taken the trouble to investigate the man De Gaulle and his movement instead of trying to flog the dead horse of Vichy into life, the future history of Franco-American relations might have been more satisfactory. In fact, the United States need not even have broken with Vichy. It could have developed an unofficial relationship with De Gaulle, helped equip his forces, and recognized his movement for what it was, a rallying point for the Frenchmen of the world who loved liberty. He might then have had some reason for gratitude. As it was, United States government officials were continually issuing criticisms of him, trying to handle French affairs without consulting him, and all in all treating him as a kind of British mercenary. He was anything but that, and the iron burned deep into his soul. It may even be that some of the extreme statements he made in later years were the product of the years of official contempt on the part of the American government.

Well, I felt, I knew something of this man now. I had come to know the youngsters escaping from France in their sports planes or boats. I knew the men who were risking their lives to go back to France and bring De Gaulle word of the Resistance that was springing up in his name. I knew the sounds and the smell from France, and I knew that France defeated would certainly rise again. Meanwhile, this man was the only representative of that arising France, and that was good enough for me. I would cultivate him, and I would tell my countrymen about him, let the United States government do as it wished. In the long run, public opinion makes the American government and who knew what might happen to the seed that at first I alone and then others began to water?

Chapter 5

The autumn had gone on with its constant nightly bombings. In a way we became used to them.

Frank Kent, Baltimore *Sun* reporter, once spent the night at a quiet inn in the country and came back with red eyes. "I couldn't sleep a damn wink," he said. "It's quiet as hell out in the country, and the lack of noise upsets you. I rolled and tossed all night long." But when I was invited to the biggest military maneuvers ever held in England's history, I was delighted to get out of town. Even a couple of nights of respite from bombing would be welcome. I was sorry I could not take Lucy with me.

Forty thousand troops were to work out a plan of attack and defense of southern England on Salisbury Plain. All three "sorties" of war correspondents were to see the maneuver. Clad in our uniforms, with gas masks and helmets and map cases and field glasses and all our paraphernalia, we made quite a parade of military correspondents.

Britain at that time had one armored division, the 1st Armored, and Churchill had taken the extraordinary risk of deciding to send it out to the Western Desert. It served as the attacking force in the maneuvers, a last training measure before the division was shipped overseas. If the Germans then invaded, only a ragtag and bobtail of tanks would be available to try to combat the invaders.

For me the maneuvers were memorable, mainly because I made my first flight in an airplane as the rear gunner of a Royal Air Force Lysander fighter told to shoot at any plane coming down on its tail.

The winter brought the huge fire raid on the financial district which I only observed from the BBC roof. Being alone meant that I was busy all the time. I would read all the morning papers in bed, go to the office about 10:30, make what telephone calls I needed, and write a script for the 1:00 P.M. broadcast, 8:00 in the morning at home. I usually had lunch with some contact or someone I wanted to use in a broadcast. The afternoon I would spend visiting government agencies, the Ministry of Information, an embassy, or a press conference. Unless I had some extra broadcast, I would dine at home, then leave at 10:00 for the office and the midnight or 1:00 A.M. broadcast as the case might be.

When anything terribly important was happening, I had broadcasts at all hours of the day or night. It was tiring, and there was never any letup. The microphone had to be fed, and I was the only one to feed it. When Fred had been there, one of us could occasionally take off most of a day. Fred could play golf, or I could go to a show or get out of town for an afternoon. Now there was not even a piece of a day I could call my own. Wherever I went the office had to know how I could be reached for broadcasts that might be ordered suddenly.

The winter dragged, and we thought it would never end. When our office was destroyed by the "land mine," we took another at 1 Duchess Street, just off Portland Place.

Lucy and I like the looks of the building at 88 Portland Place. When we found an apartment we liked there, we took it in early April. We spent the rest of the war in that building.

On the first weekend after we moved in, and before we had bought all our furniture, I was awakened by a ringing of the doorbell at about seven o'clock on a Sunday morning. Now a Sunday morning at seven is bad anywhere. In London, it was regarded as a most ungodly hour. We had stayed up late Saturday night, and I was half-asleep as I staggered to the door.

Florence Peart was there, without makeup. "John," she said, "Yugoslavia has been invaded. You are on for two minutes at seven-thirty, just twenty minutes from now."

I threw on some clothes and began running the quarter mile to the studio. I ran straight up to the BBC newsroom. I grabbed from one of the subeditors the stuff that had come in about the German invasion of the Balkans and sped down to the basement.

I reflected that the next time I took an apartment I would see that the telephone was installed before I moved in.

In the studio a sleepy censor was already on deck. It was then 7:25. I sat down at the typewriter and wrote an introductory four or five paragraphs. The censor agreed that I could ad-lib the rest from the scattering of material from the BBC wires. London, of course, had nothing at that time of a Sunday morning. Probably Churchill himself had not yet been informed. The news had broken only within the hour. Yet presumably some night-owl Americans at one-thirty or two-thirty of a Sunday morning wanted to hear

London's reaction and whatever news we had. I gave what I had, precious little, then went back to bed. I thought at the time that De Gaulle's prediction to me was now being justified. The Nazis had attacked in the Balkans through Yugoslavia in April, exactly as the French general had said they would.

On the night of Wednesday, April 16, the sirens sounded as usual just about dusk. But it speedily became apparent that this was no usual raid. The bombers seemed to be over us in droves. The bombing was heavy and continual, and the guns set up a racket that made it seem as though most of them would need new linings by morning.

Lucy and I did not go to the basement because we were on the fifth floor of an eight-story concrete building. There was some difference of opinion whether it was better to be in a basement and have the house come down on one or be partway up and come down with debris. We both were satisfied to stay where we were.

The whine of diving planes and the thud of bombs seemed to indicate that the Germans were making their big effort. Perhaps this was the prelude to invasion, after all, we thought.

Some of them were landing close to us. By that late date in the war, April 1941, we were so used to air raids that something extraordinary was needed to excite us. We began to be excited.

It seemed to me that the Germans were concentrating on our part of town. Later I learned that this was the heaviest tonnage of bombs ever dropped on London, and everywhere in the city people were saying the same thing, that the Nazi bombers were concentrating on their particular areas that night.

Our two neighbors from across the hall asked us if we wanted a drink, and we said we were just about to have one and would they join us. They were two charming men, one a blond, good-looking major in the army, the other a dark-haired barrister. They were very close friends. They occasionally had Lucy and me over to intimate little dinners with the best of wine and sparkling crystal and silver and lace tablecloths and food cooked in the best French tradition. They seemed quite self-sufficient together, and we often talked across the back fire escape. They always scintillated in conversation when we had them over for a predinner drink or later, when we had an understanding mixed group of friends. They took the rough with the smooth as the rest of us did, and we liked them for that.

We had just about begun our drinks when the doorbell rang.

Standing in the door were two females, so completely black that I could hardly recognize them. Their clothing was tattered. White teeth gleamed from the slimmer one, and she said in a hurt little-girl voice, "John, will you take us in?"

It was Flo Peart and Mildred Boutwood. A bomb had smashed the houses opposite our office, where the girls lived together. The blast had wrecked the office. A wall had fallen on Mildred. Luckily she had been on the couch, for she had heard the bomb coming, and the wall's weight had been broken by its arms. She had been pinned down but had managed to wriggle free. The fire had blown out into the room and covered both with a heavy coating of soot.

They had staggered out of the debris, their first thought to come to us, up the street. We washed them off, painted their scratches, and filled their glasses with Scotch.

"It's a terrible night," said Mildred. "There are fires everywhere." She said that the firemen were working on the blaze behind the BBC, but it looked as though the whole area were going up in flames.

We heard a few more large ones come down, then in the momentary stillness, a sort of clatter, clatter, clatter that could mean only one thing—incendiaries, either overhead or in the street near us.

The incendiary bomb the Germans used in those days was a two- or three-pound affair that could burn its way through a roof in a very few minutes. Sometimes the Germans mixed in explosive fire bombs so that fire fighters would be blasted while they were trying to extinguish a blaze at its beginning.

I thought I would take a look overhead to see what was happening. Up on the roof were two or three other people, and in a moment there were six or eight. A couple of incendiaries were burning merrily. The technique which all of us knew was to cover them with sandbags and pour water on the sandbags from a stirrup pump.

I got pumping away, with someone else holding the nozzle close to the bomb. In the weird scene, lit by the bombs and by the flashes of antiaircraft overhead, a man carrying a sandbag went by me and dumped it on my bomb. "That'll fix the son of a bitch," he said, and went back for another sandbag.

I was as stunned as though the man had talked Chinese, more stunned, in fact. He was talking pure Brooklynese. I was pumping madly up and down, and as he went by the second time, I said, "You American?"

"Yeah," he replied, "are you?"

"Yeah," I said.

"We get this damn thing out," he said, "I got some coffee, American coffee."

"Come on down to my place," I said, "I got some people there."

"Okay," he said as he came by with another sandbag.

It was only ten minutes or so until both bombs were apparently extinguished and we knew the apartment house was not going up in flames, at least for the moment, though there were plenty of fires around us.

My new friend and I went downstairs together. He stopped in his flat for the coffee.

I found out his name was Meyer "Mike" Ackerman. His father owned a big clothing factory, and I can never walk by Times Square without seeing the name "Simon Ackerman Clothing" and remembering that strange night and wondering where Mike Ackerman might be.

He showed up with two jars in his hand. "Look," he said when he was introduced, "George Washington Instant Coffee."

Mike had gone to Yale. Of all the strange ventures in the world, Mike was engaged in one of the strangest. He was establishing a factory that made men's suits in wartime England. I had no idea why anyone from Brooklyn would want to bring coals to Newcastle or suits to England. I had still less comprehension of doing this strange work in the middle of the blitz. I thought there must have been easier ways to manufacture clothing than to start lugging sandbags about a blazing roof in the middle of London's biggest raid. But Mike seemed unperturbed by the whole thing, and who was I to question?

In five minutes we discovered we had a mutual friend, Elliot Stark, who had captained the New York Lacrosse Club when I played goalie, just after my marriage three years previously. Mike and I became very good friends. In fact, we all became very good friends, our neighbors from across the hall, who in normal times might have thought Mike, with his coffee and his exaggerated tough talk, which I am sure was simply part of a personal act, was a rara avis, and the girls from the office, who liked Mike immediately. They showed good judgment.

We drank cup after cup of coffee. After a while I had to go down to the BBC to broadcast. The blaze near our office was shooting high in the air. The fire pumps were throbbing. I watched it a moment, though it was too good a target, and hurried into the BBC basement.

I did the broadcast but, of course, could not give any complete picture of the raid. Back home the party was still swilling coffee. We all decided to go back to the roof. It was a magnificent spectacle. Twenty or thirty big fires were blazing within a couple of miles of us. There were many smaller blazes. As a bomber came overhead, you would see the pinpoint chains of light spring up as the thousands of incendiaries that each bomber carried hit and began to burn. In between there were the continual swish, swish, swish of falling bombs and the deep explosions, while the guns in the park near us kept up a wild, hysterical banging that slammed our eardrums.

We went downstairs and had more coffee. There was no point in trying to sleep. It would have been completely impossible. We were glad to be together that night.

After a while the noise died down. The all clear sounded. We pulled back the blackout curtains. The dawn had come. Then I heard one of the strangest sounds I had ever heard. After all that frightful racket that had dinned in our heads for hour after hour, we heard the sound of birds. Millions of birds, it seemed, were speaking and caroling and chirruping. They were greeting the dawn just as they did every dawn of spring. They were all around us. It seemed that every bird of England was singing to the sunrise. Suddenly we felt unaccountably happy. We had been through the worst kind of attack that man could deliver. And it did not make any difference to the birds. Life was going on. Nature was still there. Spring was spring, and the dawn was the dawn, no matter what happened. We looked at one another, and there was a smile on every face.

London was exhausted after that raid. You could see it in the faces of everyone you met. Some 450 bombers had been over us. More than 1,000 of us had been killed, and 2,000 or 3,000 wounded. I could figure out how many people lived in London, and if 3,000 were killed or put out of action every night for a year, there would still be a couple of million people left. Yet I knew very well that if repeated raids such as that of April 16 happened for a month running, London still might have a lot of people, but the city could not function as an entity. It seemed to me that where Göring,

British fire fighters extinguish blaze in bomb crater after April 16, 1941, raid. WIDE WORLD.

as head of the Luftwaffe, had made his mistake was in failing to concentrate his attacks. He had been attacking London every night, but he had not continued big mass attacks every night. Mass attacks, I thought, would swamp the fire fighters. The Nazis were keeping our nerves on edge all night, but until the April 16 effort, the number of planes overhead in any particular half hour was relatively small. This gave the guns and night fighters a good chance to combat them. It also gave the air-raid precautions people and the firemen the opportunity to handle the problem. Later in the war we Americans tried the technique of brief huge mass attacks. So did the RAF at night. That way it was all over quickly.

I thought two factors were important; nerves and the physical inability to deal with a raid. The Nazis counted on the first factor. They tried to break our nerves, with their night-long raids. The Americans and British later in the war relied on the second theory, to swamp the defenses with masses of flame and high explosive during a brief period. I am not sure which is the better bombing theory, for the mind is attacked by airpower equally with the material structure of house, railroad, or factory. From the bomber's point of view, the ideal would be to keep up an intense saturation raid for the entire day and night. Fortunately even the overwhelming strength of the Luftwaffe was too weak for such an effort. In his stupidity, Göring dissipated his available strength still further and attacked towns and cities all over the country while he was sending the majority of his bomber squadrons to London.

The bombers came back, 350 this time, in only three days. The casualties were about the same, but Londoners do not remember the second raid with the same sharp recollection as the first. I had been afraid that we would have the same kind of raid on Thursday night and again on Friday and every night thereafter. When this did not happen, I believed that perhaps the Wednesday effort had been a single attempt without great significance. So the raid came on Saturday, and in spite of the thundering strength of the attack, I was not too unhappy. It seemed very probable that after the big Wednesday raid, the Luftwaffe had required three whole days to mount another strong one. If this was the case, and I believed it was, we did not need to fear the Luftwaffe as much as I had expected. London could absorb a couple of raids such as that each week.

Britain, meanwhile, was trying to strike back. Very often a few British bombers flew over Berlin, a feeble effort in comparison with

*Casualty of the April 16th raid—St. George's Roman Catholic Church,
London.* IMPERIAL WAR MUSEUM.

the German raids on London, but enough to show the falsity of Göring's boast that no enemy plane could pierce Berlin's defenses. The British were losing an important number of their available bombers, but they were developing the practices that later proved so successful in their nighttime raids.

Some of the bombers were manned by Poles, always wild men in the air. I heard from a British airman of a bomber, I think it was a Hampden, which had a crew of three Poles and one Englishman. The squadron was training for action, and one day the planes were bombed up and ordered to go out and attack targets over the sea. The Englishman was starting to prepare for the flight when the three Poles came to him and said, "You are very sick today. You are not going with us."

The Englishman asked for an explanation. He was not sick.

One Pole said, "We have decided that since we no longer have any families or any country, we will go bomb Berlin."

The Englishman said, "But our petrol will only carry the aircraft to Berlin. There will not be enough for you to return."

"Who said we would return?" asked one of the Poles. "But you. Today you are sick."

The squadron went out to do its practice bombing. The Englishman did not go. He suddenly became ill. The next day the Berlin radio spoke of a British attempt to attack the capital, an attack that had been frustrated.

Since the RAF had sent no planes to Germany that day, the story was denied. Yet one of the training squadron's planes was missing, no one knew where. Weeks later the Royal Air Force heard from an escaped prisoner what had happened to the Polish manned bomber. Out of nowhere a British Hampden had appeared in Berlin. It had whizzed up and down the streets at 200 feet, machine guns going full blast, bombs falling at intervals, until it was finally shot down just outside the city. The Poles were mad fliers.

We correspondents had been pestering the Air Ministry for most of the winter, asking for an opportunity of going on a bombing raid, preferably against Berlin. We had drawn lots; and three Americans and three British correspondents were to go. I won the choice for American radio. Ed Beattie of UP was to represent the news agencies, and Robert Post of *The New York Times*, the independent papers.

Nothing happened for several weeks. Then one day, May 7, I

was summoned to the Air Ministry. Beattie and Post were there, and our British colleagues.

We all were a little unnaturally gay. It had seemed lately that a very large percentage of the British bombers going over to Germany was not coming home. We did not know whether we were to depart at once or not.

An Air Force official gave us some papers to sign, then told us we were going to have an exhaustive physical examination.

"I don't see how I can pass it," Post said. "My eyes are bad."

"So are mine," I replied hopefully. "Maybe neither of us will get picked."

Beattie said sadly, "My eyes are all right—but I am overweight. Maybe that makes a difference."

We were all half-joking, half-serious.

While we might not have passed a physical examination for flying duties, our eyes and weight really made no difference. It was not we who were going to use the bombsights and do the navigating. We all passed the examinations with flying colors.

We were cautioned to keep complete secrecy and say nothing to our friends. One day we would receive a summons to come to the Air Ministry. We were to report with war correspondents' uniforms and equipment, and if the weather were right, we would soon be on our way to a major target in Germany. We three were very thoughtful as we left the ministry.

That night, in bed, I told Lucy that at any time I might be called away to do a bombing raid on Germany. I cautioned her to say nothing of where I was, but only to say I'd had to leave London for a time on some military maneuvers.

Like a good sport, she said nothing but pressed my hand very hard. Later I heard her writhing silently about in the bed. She was having pains, and evidently the baby was coming.

I got her to a nursing home on the outskirts of London, and later that day our first son was born. We named him Ian Gillies MacVane, Scottish Christian names that were current in the Mac-Vane family 600 years or so ago.

By Saturday, May 10 I was in bad shape from flu. I had heard nothing more from the Air Ministry, and I hoped the summons would not come while I was running a temperature and barely able to drag myself about. For nearly five months during some of the most depressing bombing I had been the only NBC correspondent in London, broadcasting night and day, never having a day in which I was not responsible for covering the news. I was bone tired, and the influenza germs found me an easy victim. My only hope was that Fred Bate was returning any day now and he could take up the burden again. I went to see Lucy and the baby and went to the office. Then I came home to the apartment about six and fell into bed.

About nine or ten the sirens went, but I was too sick and tired to care. Then began a chatter of guns and a thunder of bombs such as I had not heard since April 16. This time most of the bombs seemed to be falling near me. I would hear the rush and roar of a bomb coming close, and I would then roll out of bed onto the floor in case the windows blew in and the roof began to collapse. It was useless to try to sleep. The guns outside in the park were hammering away in a frenzy, and it seemed that the skies had opened to rain bombs on my particular part of London.

Once I got into the elevator and started to go down to the basement. When I was halfway down, the big concrete apartment house shuddered as though in an earthquake, and the elevator stopped. I pressed the down button. Nothing happened. I thought that I was trapped in the elevator shaft. I pressed the up button, and the lift moved up. I got back into the apartment, resolved to stay there.

Fifteen minutes later my doorbell rang. I opened the door, and there was W. B. Mitford, father of my old Oxford University roommate, Frank Mitford. The Mitfords had an apartment at 82 Portland Place, just across Devonshire Street.

"I need a drink, John," Mitford said. He came in and slumped down on the couch. He looked at the gloves he was wearing. They were covered with blood.

I hastily mixed a couple of whiskies.

Mitford said, "I just missed being killed. In all the years I have lived at Eighty-two, I have never gone out the back door. I was alone in the flat, and I suddenly decided to go out to see what was happening. I started for the front door; then for some inexplicable reason I turned and walked out through the back. Just at the moment I would have been walking out the front, a bomb dropped right on the corner. It's right between your block of flats and mine."

"What about the blood on your gloves?" I asked. "Were you hurt?"

"No," said W.B., "that's someone else's blood. The bomb killed some people out there. There was nobody else around, and one

Ludgate Circus, London, after May 10, 1941, raid. IMPERIAL WAR MUSEUM.

of them was still alive, so I dragged him under shelter of the doorway. He's still there. Will you help me get him under cover?"

We bolted our drinks, and I slipped on some trousers and shoes.

The bomb had blown out all the windows on one side of my apartment house. It had chipped the masonry, but the bomb's force had been chiefly upward because it had crashed right down below the street surface before exploding. A huge crater yawned between our two houses—as though workmen had been cutting open the street to excavate sewers or work on conduits.

Three bodies lay in grotesque positions. I looked at one, flung like a limp little bundle of rags against the iron fence. I recognized him. It was the little porter at Goodwood Court, a cheery Irishman with whom I had often had a joke. A woman lay with her skirt askew, her white legs showing. I did not look at her face.

Mitford and I went over to the sidewalk. A stretcher-bearer had arrived, but he was thus far alone. A man lay by his feet. He was breathing great snoring breaths. His head seemed to be badly wounded, and someone had wrapped toweling around it. I recognized him as a friend of mine from the BBC newsroom. We eased him onto the stretcher and took him into the hallway of Number 82. We stayed there until the ambulance arrived, but he did not regain consciousness. He died a few days later. The woman was his wife, whom I had known slightly. They and the porter and another man at Goodwood Court had been standing in the doorway when they saw an incendiary start burning in the street. The bomb would have burned itself out harmlessly, but in those days we believed that bombers aimed at incendiaries, and the little group rushed out in the street to deal with it. At that moment the high explosive crashed down among them.

For five concentrated hours that night some 300 bombers were over us. About 1,500 of us were killed, and another 2,000 seriously wounded. That was the night the House of Commons' chamber was destroyed. Churches and other landmarks all over London showed the effect the next day. Huge fires were started.

At ten o'clock the next morning I was so tired and ill I could hardly get out of bed. I called Lucy at the nursing home to make sure she and the baby were all right. Then I rang the office. Fred Bate's voice greeted me. He had just arrived from America and had spent the night on a train out in the country, a train that could not get to the city because of the station fires and railroad dislocation.

I drew a sigh of relief, as though a great burden had rolled off me.

"Okay, Fred," I said, "you take it from here. I'm going to spend the rest of the day in bed. . . ."

I wondered whether we would have more of the same on the following night. Londoners were very tired, and I questioned how efficiently even a great city like London could function under raids of the size of the April 16 and the May 10 attacks, if they were repeated night after night.

The Luftwaffe could not repeat them, and in any case Hitler was getting ready for the attack on Russia. London had had its last big raid. The blitz was over, and London had survived it very well, battered but unbowed.

We never were called for the British raid on Berlin. The Hampdens and Wellingtons were too small to carry correspondents as extra bodies on the long flight to Germany. The RAF just then was getting some Sterlings and Lancasters, four-engine night bombers, with space for an extra body. At the last moment, I learned later from Ed Beattie, the American Embassy had heard of the plan and protested. Americans were neutral. What would our position be if we were shot down? The embassy, afraid of criticism from American neutralists, made such a fuss that the whole project was canceled. Three big bombers had been earmarked to carry us. On the raid on the night we were to have gone, they were the only aircraft lost. While Beattie and I were in North Africa, and the United States was well in the war, Bob Post went on the first raid that actually carried correspondents. His plane, with all aboard, was shot to bits in the night sky over the German capital. Bob was a fine reporter from an old New York family. If he lived, he would, I believe, have become one of the bright stars on *The New York Times.*

Chapter 6

In June, when we had had quiet days and nights for several weeks, Lucy and I decided to take the baby, Ian, to Scotland. It was the first time Lucy had been out of London since the blitz began.

I had forgotten that Scotland was a restricted area for foreigners in wartime, and it was with some surprise that I answered a rap on our door at the North British Hotel in Edinburgh and found a stalwart Scottish policeman there. "Mr. MacVane? Mr. John Mac-Vane?" he asked.

"What's it all about?" I replied.

"Well, sir," he said, "your travel permits as a war correspondent allow you to go anywhere in Britain, but I'm afraid Mrs. MacVane shouldn't have come here. Scotland is restricted for foreigners."

"This is silly," I said. "There are no secret weapons or maneuvers on Prince's Street. What can I do about it?"

"Perhaps you'll come down to see the inspector," said the policeman.

The inspector at police headquarters was in civilian clothes. He looked at me gravely. "Mrs. MacVane shouldn't have come here," he said.

"Look, Inspector," I replied, "this is a hell of a situation. A Mac-Vane comes back to Scotland for the first time in a hundred and twenty-nine years, and you treat him like a foreigner. Why, do you know one of my ancestors killed thirteen Englishmen at Culloden?"

A big grin split the police inspector's mustache. "Did he, indeed? Too bad he didn't kill the lot."

From that moment we were the best of friends, and he gave Lucy a permit to go anywhere we wanted to go. We knew an English girl, Jill Law, who lived in Edinburgh, and we met her husband, Ramsay, a young Scottish lawyer turned naval officer for the duration. One of Jill's friends was an American girl, the granddaughter of old Andrew Carnegie, happily married to a Scot.

We went on up to Loch Tay and the village of Killin. It was from that part of the world that the MacVanes had originally gone to America, and there were MacVanes buried in the churchyards of the area. Some had been ministers at Killin and at other villages around the loch, and MacVane farms had once existed up in the glens nearby, glens that were now deserted and desolate.

I practiced on the bagpipes while my son lay on his blanket in the sun, chortling with glee. We saw the leafy little island in the Dochart River, Inchbuie, where was buried one of my childhood heroes, Smooth John MacNab. Smooth John was the eldest of twelve sons of a seventeenth-century chief of the clan, the weakest of whom could drive his dirk through a two-inch plank. The MacNabs were engaged in a feud with the MacNishes, whose headquarters was an island on a loch across the mountains. The MacNabs had ordered cases of wine and other Christmas delicacies to be sent from Sterling or Edinburgh, but on the way the MacNishes fell on the caravan and hijacked the MacNab supplies. Came Christmas Eve and The MacNab was sitting at the head of his empty table when his sons trooped into the dining room. "Tonight's the night, if the boys are the boys," MacNab said. Without a word Smooth John and his brothers filed out. All night the old chief sat motionless at his place.

As dawn broke, the twelve sons filed into the room. From under his cloak, Smooth John brought out the head of the MacNish chief and placed it on the board in front of his father. At the same time each of the eleven other brothers brought forth the head of a Mac-Nish.

"Tonight was the night, and the boys are the boys," said Smooth John MacNab. He and his brothers had carried their boat on their shoulders over the mountain pass, launched it on the lake, and rowed to the MacNish stronghold on the island. The MacNishes were celebrating Christmas with the MacNab food and drink.

Smooth John hammered on the door. "Who's there?" said a drunken voice, that of the MacNish chief.

"Whom would you most fear to see?"

"Smooth John MacNab," came the answer.

With that the twelve MacNabs broke down the door and massacred the revelers—a blow from which the MacNish clan did not recover for many years.

We picnicked in the glens, and I caught trout on Loch Tay. Vast armies were locked in a death struggle in Russia, and we were far from the sight and sound of war; but I could not help feeling a certain melancholy. Once the glens had been thick with prosperous farms. A primitive civilization had flourished there and a proud, if primitive, society in which all alike shared prosperity and together weathered adversity. Then had come English laws that supported chieftains and nobles in gaining title to land that was not theirs. Farmlands were turned over to sheep pastures to enrich the few. Finally, with a population withering away and emigrating, millions of acres that had once been tilled became the home of the stag and the grouse, useless for anything but some wealthy English visitor's enjoyment.

Here and there one saw the ruin of a stone house or a bit of wall marking what had once been a home for generation after generation. The Highlander had enriched every corner and country on earth with his blood, but Scotland itself stood disconsolate and impoverished, a romantic dream country in the hearts of men everywhere, the reality of which was as somber as the mists that swirl about its mountain peaks.

London was pleasant when we returned. Without the continual bombing, it was even pleasant to go out at night in the blackout, to dine at a restaurant or visit friends. The pressure was off. Much to the confusion of most of the experts, the Russians had not been beaten in the first three weeks, and it began to look as though Hitler might even need several months to march his troops over the whole of European Russia.

Every day we took Ian out into the little private park at the top of Portland Place. We had a key to get in, and rain or shine, there were always other children playing about on the green grass.

The keeper of the park marked out a tennis court on the perfect turf. All I needed was an opponent. Larry LeSueur, my fellow American broadcaster, admitted he had never played the game. I volunteered to teach him. Larry looked as though he might be an athletic type, and I wanted him to learn the game the hard way, so I took him to a hardware store, and we bought him a racket for ten shillings and sixpence, about two dollars then.

I explained the rules, how he should serve, what the lines meant, and how the game was scored. We played, and I beat him easily 6–0, 6–0, 6–0.

The next day the score was 6–1, 6–2, 6–3, with me winning.

At our third encounter I began to falter slightly. I won, but the score was 6–4, 5–7, 6–3. On the fourth day Larry beat me, and we had some good matches later on the grass. I never told him that two dollars was not the usual price of a good tennis racket.

With Russia in the war, some of the correspondents wanted to be off to Moscow. Larry and Walter Kerr of the New York *Herald*

Tribune went off in the same ship as Paddy Willis. Paddy had become bored with inactivity as a reporter on the London *Standard*, now that the blitz was over. In the First World War, as a boy of seventeen, he had won his air observer wings, and he had been stationed for several months on Russian territory near the Black Sea. He had learned something of the Russian language by methods proper for young RAF gunners and observers who have not reached their twentieth birthday and need something with which to preoccupy themselves so many miles from home.

Paddy sought to join the RAF without much avail until someone noticed that his qualification card bore a notation that he spoke Russian. Almost before he knew it, Paddy was an RAF officer and off to Russia on a secret mission. The British government had decided to ship a squadron of Hurricanes to Russia as the first of many planes that were to help the Soviet Air Force. A squadron of air force men was sent along to teach the Russian fliers how to service and fly the aircraft. Paddy was to be the interpreter and public relations officer for the British airmen up in the frozen airfields near Murmansk. The difficulty was that Paddy had no time to brush up his knowledge of the language, which had rusted almost completely away in the more than twenty years since he had last spoken it.

There was little public relations that he could do, practically isolated on an airfield in an atmosphere so secretive that nobody, including the Russians, was supposed to know the British were there. The Russians disliked having the British teach them anything, and Soviet fliers, after they learned the knobs and switches, would spring into the Hurricanes and take off practically straight up in the air without a warm-up. But they could fly well, apparently, although they seemed to put a great strain, in British opinion, on the aircraft and engines.

I was glad to stay at home in London and watch my little son begin to grow. To me, he seemed the most intelligent baby I had ever seen, and the dearest.

It was then that the greatest sorrow of our lives came to Lucy and me with all the suddenness of a bomb falling from an empty blue sky. One day we noticed a trace of blood in Ian's urine. We took him at once to the only doctor we knew, the obstetrician. That doctor dismissed lightly the symptom that, had we known more, would have sent us rushing to a specialist. We were later told, by doctors who wanted to lighten our sorrow of self-reproach, that it would have made no difference. But I have always felt that had our advice been better, our boy might have had a chance for life. The danger signal did not recur, and we had no further warning, for Ian seemed healthy enough.

That autumn the British Army was holding large-scale anti-invasion maneuvers, and all three "sorties" of the war correspondents were out in the field with them. Theoretically enemy forces had landed in two places and were trying to cut England in half.

I was riding about Oxfordshire and Warwickshire following the operations. Once I stopped in Oxford with a group of correspondents and took them to tea at Elliston and Cavell's.

It had been more than six years since I had gone down from Oxford, but the waitress raised my stock considerably with my fellows by recognizing me. I stopped for a moment at Exeter College and saw the strange sight of a huge static water tank in the middle of the front quadrangle and slit trenches and sandbags in the Fellows' Garden.

That night we were spreading our bedrolls out on the floor of an empty schoolhouse when a message came for me to telephone my wife. I got through to London. Lucy was sobbing as she talked. The baby's abdomen had seemed swollen, and the nurse had suggested getting a doctor to look him over. Lucy had found a good general practitioner. He had looked grave and said that he wanted to consult with a pediatrician. Both had examined Ian and had come to the conclusion that he had a form of malignant growth on the kidney peculiar to children, called a Wilms's tumor. They were having a kidney specialist examine Ian the following day and thought I should be there.

I felt stunned, as though the whole world had suddenly become something quite different which I did not understand. When I had left London three or four days previously, we were a happy family, thinking that the great danger, the bombing, was behind us. Now danger had struck at the being we loved most from a totally unexpected direction. An army car took me to the Reading Station, and I arrived home late that night.

The kidney specialist, the surgeon who would perform the operation, confirmed the diagnosis of his colleagues. They did not beat about the bush in telling us. They said that practically no children attacked by that type of tumor survived. When one did, it was counted a miracle.

68

In the years since then advances in knowledge and treatment have brought a very high percentage of successful operations. In Ian's case the growth was far advanced. The British medical men were the best in England. They would do their best, but from the first they held out no hope. After X rays had revealed the extent of the terrible thing in our baby, the surgeon said that the only chance of making an operation possible would be a series of treatments with powerful deep X rays to reduce its spread to a size with which the knife could cope.

We took him every day in his little carry-cot to the office of a famous radiologist in the London Clinic and stayed with him while he quite happily absorbed X rays of a force that would have immediately made an adult ill after one or two treatments. He was in no pain, and he seemed to thrive on the treatments so that seeing him and not knowing, one would have thought him the healthiest, happiest baby in England.

Lucy and I went about our work in a kind of a daze, thinking of nothing else but Ian, trying to reassure ourselves that because he looked so well, he had a fighting chance for life.

After three weeks or so the radiologist had given him all the treatments he dared give, and a date was set for the final examination and the operation.

It was on Saturday evening, November 6, that Ian began to cry, panting sobs that seemed to shake his little body. We called in Dr. Ripman, the GP, and he left us a sedative to give Ian at intervals. In that awful moment I had to go out to work in the blackout.

We were broadcasting a full half hour live broadcast, a panorama of London at night in wartime. A great deal of work had gone into our production.

One o'clock Sunday morning was eight o'clock at night in America. Fred Bate was in the studio. Robert Montgomery, the film actor, then a navy lieutenant stationed in London, stood in Piccadilly Circus. A Canadian broadcaster was on a gun site where women soldiers helped tend the guns. A BBC man was in an air-raid shelter in Bermondsey where Cockneys sang gay old songs. I was in the press room of the London *Sunday Express* with the roar of the machines in my microphone, and our office manager, Mildred Boutwood, was in the smart Four Hundred Club in Leicester Square, dancing with her brother home on army leave. Everything went off precisely as it was supposed to do. As one bit of description and dialogue faded out, the next came in at precisely the right second.

But the moment my own portion ended, I said good-bye to John Gordon, the *Sunday Express* editor, and rushed out to find a taxi.

It was nearly two in the morning when I got back to our flat. Lucy was torn with grief and fear, for the sedative had not worked, and Ian had been crying constantly, his eyes open but unseeing, and his voice so hoarse that only low tearing sobs could come forth.

I called Dr. Ripman, and he told me that if I came over, I could have some morphine. I ran all the way over to his home and back, and soon the drug put Ian to sleep while we sat by his bed through the night.

The next day the surgeon thought that he had best be operated upon speedily. We took him out to the wartime country section of the Great Ormond Street Children's Hospital at Hemel Hempstead. They kept him under drugs, and I gave them some blood for a transfusion. We asked, in our ignorance, whether it would not be possible for one of us to give him a kidney. We would gladly have given our own lives, or, much as we loved each other, that of the other, for him.

It was no use. We were staying at a rooming house near the hospital. The hospital called us in the middle of the night and told us we had better come. Ian was in an oxygen tent. We were only able to kiss him good-bye before he left us.

He had never recovered sufficiently for the operation to be performed. Walking up the hill toward the rooming house, we felt that the world had ended for us. My old friend Howard Ives, my former Williams College roommate, now a surgeon who had volunteered to help Britain, came to see us. I had asked him to be present at the operation. I told him I would agree to a postmortem, hoping that the knowledge gained might help some other child someday, and I asked him to be present at that. Afterward he told me that although the X rays had performed miracles, there had almost surely never been any real chance.

In London we walked the streets together, Lucy and I. We went to one movie after another to try to keep ourselves from weeping. We tried to sleep and lay sleepless together with our hands clasped, unspeaking.

A few friends came to the flat, W. B. Mitford, Frank's father, and Louise, his sister, the girls from the office, Fred Bate, and Ian's nurse. W.B. had been a Congregational minister in his early days. He said a few words of love and friendship. Fred Bate read the words to the "Skye Boat Song," Ian's lullaby, "Where is the boy who was born to be king. . . . Over the sea to Skye."

That night Lucy and I went alone and left his ashes in the little park where he had spent his happiest hours and where he would always hear the sound of children laughing and playing, in the sunshine under the leaves of the trees he had raised his arms to, and in the soft English rain. There would always be children there.

We took all the money we had and named a bed for him in the Hospital for Sick Children on Great Ormond Street, so that some child will always be able to look up at his bed's head and see the name of Ian Gillies MacVane.

Lucy and I went down to Torquay afterward, to the Imperial Hotel. It was damp and chilly that November on the "English Riviera," but the weather was in keeping with our spirits. Something had died in both of us, and I felt that never again would I be able to know great pain or great fear or great hope. Something had been wrenched out of my inner being that could never be replaced, and I no longer really cared what would happen to me. I would go on living; but the nerve ends at the center had been deadened and cut away, and I knew that I was not the man I had once been, but someone older, a kind of stranger to myself.

We walked along the shore and slept much. Drinking seemed to upset Lucy as it had upset her when she was first carrying Ian, but I drank for both of us. We even danced a little in the evening.

Back in London, I plunged into my work harder than ever, seeing as many people as I could.

Lucy went to the doctor for a checkup, thinking that her grief had upset her physical processes, and discovered that she was nearly three months pregnant.

But the terrible year was not yet over. In December we were sitting alone when the phone rang. A choked voice, hardly recognizable as that of W. B. Mitford, said, "It's Frank. I wanted you to be the first to know."

My best friend, an officer in the Royal Horse Artillery, had been killed by German bombs in the Western Desert when his battery was attacked.

I broke down again and sobbed until I could sob no more. My son, and now my best friend. The war had taken both. I thought of the carefree days Frank Mitford and I had had in Oxford, our trip to Germany, visits he had made to New York, and the times we had spent together in London. That handsome, merry young man had gone without leaving behind him either wife or child who could have loved him, only friends to remember, and some of them had already gone before him in the battle.

I remembered odd things: our competition in the little hotel in the Tyrol to see who could drink a two-quart *Steiffel* of beer the quicker; the night on the Ringstrasse after Dollfuss was assassinated; the night of the jubilee when we had snake-danced up the High Street in Oxford; and the big white-tie-and-tails Balliol Commemoration Ball. I remembered the quiet way he had volunteered after the Germans walked into Czechoslovakia. He told me how pleased he had been when, after he had been commissioned, he was accepted by the Royal Horse Artillery Regiment, a crack body of the Royal Artillery, and the professional colonel interviewing him had asked, "Where did you go to school?" and when Frank had said, "Rugby," the colonel had harrumphed and said, "Thank God, a public school man. Don't know what the artillery is coming to these days. People getting in who came from all sorts of odd schools I never heard of. Some of 'em don't seem to have ever gone to school at all." Frank laughed to himself, but not in front of the colonel.

And now Frank was lying somewhere in the Libyan desert. Frank had been to Greece and escaped that swift Nazi onslaught. I felt numbed with grief all that long winter. The only important thing was that Lucy was there to share it with me and I could work hard at my job.

Chapter 7

December 7, 1941, was as much of a surprise to me as to most other people in Britain. I walked into the office that evening and was told that the BBC had announced the bombing of Pearl Harbor by the Japanese. I was sure that Pearl Harbor was in the Philippines —an attack there, although unlikely, would not have been beyond the bounds of belief—and when Florence Peart said she thought she had heard the announcer say Hawaii, I could not believe it. While we were getting out the atlas, the BBC *Nine o'Clock News* gave us the full story. We were stunned. Most of the correspondents I talked with that night believed that we would shortly be in the war against Hitler as well.

For more than two years we Americans had leaned over backward to be dispassionate and objective—it had become a habit of our broadcasting. It was strange now to think that our own country was one of the combatants fighting for life. For the past year and a half we had not been able to see how the Allies could win the war, although we were all convinced that in the end Britain's cause could not lose. I had believed for some time that eventually the United States *would* be forced by its self-interest to enter the war, but the reports of the isolationist speeches at home, the Lindberghs, the fanatic right-wing isolationist congressmen and senators, men living in a political dreamworld, combined with the reaction of so many Americans that their hearts were with Britain in its most gallant hour, but of course, America couldn't really do anything but stand on the sidelines and cheer, had convinced me it might be years before the United States took the plunge.

Suddenly, at a stroke, Japan had wiped away the indecision. Two days later, when Charles Collingwood of CBS and I did a joint running broadcast of the events in the House of Commons, we knew at last that Britain had declared war on Japan and that the two countries were joined in the task of winning final victory.

From that moment I never had the slightest doubt that victory would be achieved, although as the Japanese swept over Southeast Asia and disaster after disaster struck the Allies, I began to realize how much I had underestimated the Japanese craft and fighting ability.

But for us who were covering the war in Europe and trying to explain it, one war was enough for the moment, and all our attention was riveted on the European-Mediterranean front.

For some time the United States Army and Navy had had an observer group stationed in London at Grosvenor Square, conveniently near the embassy. It had a fluctuating population of officers coming and going, inspecting British training methods and equipment and getting to know the British war planners and commanders. American correspondents naturally kept in touch with the embassy's military attachés, and the office of Colonel Lee, the chief attaché, had swollen to bursting. Finally, American officers in civilian clothes were ensconced in offices all over Grosvenor Square. Once we were in the war, they began to bloom forth in uniform. Many went on to fame and high office during and after the war. But I was able to learn something of military thinking among our own officers from men like Colonel John Dahlquist and Brigadier General Charles Bolte over a congenial highball or at the luncheon table of the restaurant which was so expensive that I frequented it only in the company of ministers plenipotentiary, brigadier generals, and ranks above, the Bon Viveur.

The Bon Viveur in Shepherd Market was, and, for all I know, still is, a luncheon club which served fine food. I suppose one could have obtained a meal there for the dollar or so to which government regulations limited restaurant charges, but I doubt one could ever have been welcomed at a second meal. Usually, when all the extras were added, with wine and a liqueur, the bill for two people removed the best part of fifty dollars with as little trouble as the Twenty-one Club in New York.

For other guests, there was the Écu de France in Jermyn Street, which strove mightily to produce fine meals in spite of the food difficulties and rationing.

My first contact with American combat troops came toward the end of January 1942. I received a telephone call asking me to come to the American military office in Grosvenor Square. There I was told that an opportunity had been provided for a visit to Northern Ireland to see certain military installations, and I was given a pass authorizing me to visit "elements of the U.S. Army forces" in the British Isles. It was numbered eighteen and signed by Colonel Homer Case, who had the title Assistant Chief of Staff, G-2. It seemed obvious that what had been a strictly liaison military mission had been turned into a full-fledged headquarters in the weeks since Pearl Harbor.

I did not know exactly what I was supposed to be visiting, although I knew we had naval installations in Londonderry and there were, of course, rumors that some American troops had been landed in Ulster. But when I boarded the ship to cross the Irish Sea, I knew that something important was afoot, for the vessel was crowded with most of the American correspondents in London. Since the Army was handling the matter, there could be no other logical purpose than witnessing the arrival of the first contingent of American troops.

With Larry Rue of the Chicago *Tribune*, William Stoneman and Helen Kirkpatrick of the Chicago *Daily News,* Joe Evans of the *Herald Tribune*, Drew Middleton of the Associated Press, and the others, I had a fine trip across to Northern Ireland, marred only by the fact that the packet boat had not been provided with supplies for such a hardy group of Americans and the vessel's entire stock of whisky, both Scotch and Irish, had been exhausted before we got to bed.

The Grand Hotel in Belfast was almost entirely filled with correspondents, British and American, and U.S. Army officers, quite a different crowd from the staid North Irish businessmen who usually frequented it, and even the hotel's supply of Irish whiskey failed to last later than about one in the morning, when the bar closed for lack of supply.

The next day the first boatload of American troops landed in Belfast. They were men of a National Guard division from Iowa, the 34th Infantry, led by a general called Scrappy Hartle. They wore the old World War I round type of helmet. They came ashore in overcoats and gaiters, carrying full field equipment. As they marched up the street, they sang "Ioway—Ioway—Out Where the Tall Corn Grows."

I hoped with all my heart that the men who led them knew what they were doing. They still seemed a little dewy behind the ears, almost surprised that they were overseas so far from Iowa, where they might soon have to fight an enemy who wanted to kill them.

I wondered how much training and seasoning they might need before they could properly be called fighting men, comparable with the British Army units that I knew so well. The 34th went through some of the hardest fighting in Africa and Italy, and in time it became one of the finest units in the American or any other army. But seeing them on that first day, I was not reassured. It had been a long time since America had done any fighting. Only a few months previously, many American reservists had been talking of deserting, "going over the hill in October," and they had been supported by isolationist politicians, blinded to all else by their hatred of Roosevelt.

With the British, warfare had been an occurrence in life that one accepted and to some extent prepared for as one did for the changes in the weather. Feeble, wishy-washy politicians such as Chamberlain and Baldwin had not been able to affect the fact that when war broke out, a great number of men in Britain had had World War I experience. Many others had served a term in the Indian Army, or had spent a few years in their twenties in a crack regiment of the British Army, before entering other fields of endeavor. All over Britain there were salesmen, farmers, accountants, lawyers, and factory managers who had spent a period in the Royal Air Force reserve. And there were men who had soldiered in Britain's little wars around the world, a nucleus for the huge expansion that was to take place in the military services. It was not hard for these men to take over the job of creating an army and an air force, and there were millions more who easily followed the British military tradition. Soldiering had been necessary to Britain from the days of Poitiers and Agincourt, and British schools and universities turned out men who naturally took up leadership in war as they normally took up leadership of the empire in peace. To the British, there was nothing extraordinary or cataclysmic about war, so they suffered no shock in changing their way of life.

We Americans, on the other hand, had had a civil war which we had largely forgotten—except as a tradition in the South. We had had a Spanish war that affected us little and a world war in which our share was late and, in comparison with our major allies, small —although fortunately decisive. I was nearly thirty, and war to my generation and those younger was inconceivably remote while we were growing up. The few militant youngsters who joined the Citizens' Military Training Camp or the Reserve Officers Training Corps did so, not because they ever expected to go to war, but because they liked camping out or giving orders or wearing Sam Browne belts. In 1939, I believe, we had only something like 16,000 professional officers in the Army. For the rest, in the huge expansion, we had to rely on men who had no tradition of military leadership, men not at all cut to type like the British, but as varying in their characteristics as was possible to find among men of the same country. They were thrown into a life-and-death struggle for which they had had no real mental and physical preparation.

On the visit to Northern Ireland, Bob Trout was representing the Columbia Broadcasting System, and the first broadcast of the arrival of the troops we did as a joint exercise, so that neither CBS nor NBC had a news beat at the moment the news was released by the military authorities. Bob's wife, Kit, ran with the copy straight from our typewriters to the censorship office and hovered over it until it was released. They were a remarkably attractive young couple, although during their stay of a year or so in England they stayed much by themselves, from choice or natural shyness, and rarely mingled with the other correspondents.

After the first joint effort we did several separate programs, for the arrival of the first American troops was big news in the States. I was about to board the ship for England that evening when a late service message from New York told me to get the first American soldier to step foot onshore and bring him to the microphone for an interview.

I hunted up General Hartle's aide-de-camp, Captain William Darby, later the famous Colonel Bill Darby, commander of the American rangers. Official wheels began turning. The troops had gone off to quarters forty miles from Belfast, and the soldier in question was sound asleep. He was awakened and brought to my studio. I began the interview with him. Then came the big surprise. Somewhere in Iowa, his family, father, mother and girl friend were also in a studio, and he was able to talk to them at four o'clock in the morning Belfast time, nine o'clock at night Iowa time. It was very heartwarming, although the boy was so surprised he didn't have much to say, either to his family or to the nationwide audience of his compatriots. His division was to see some very hard fighting in North Africa, Sicily, and Italy, and I wondered later whether he had come through the war all right.

Interlude I

The Germans, as well as a good many of the Allied military experts, had believed that their army would conquer Russia within a few weeks. They did, in fact, inflict terrible casualties on the Russians and conquer vast expanses of Russian territory. In those first months, Russia was saved by its own vast space and by the weather. Hitler may have been frustrated by the stupidity of his closest international ally, Benito Mussolini, dictator of Fascist Italy.

Mussolini, thinking to win military laurels unaided, had attacked Greece. His campaign bogged down against the stout Greek resistance, and in the spring of 1941 Hitler had to waste precious weeks of fighting weather in campaigns against Yugoslavia, Greece, and Crete in order to rescue his Italian friend from disaster. The German Army's timetable for the attack against Germany's uneasy ally, Russia, was delayed. Winter set in before Moscow could be taken, and the attack of the German military machine, not prepared or equipped for fighting in snow and zero temperatures, ground painfully to a halt.

By the spring of 1942 some of the early damage done to the Soviet forces had been repaired. Hitler's chance for a blitzkrieg victory such as that in France was lost forever, and the armies of Russia and Germany settled down to three more years of deadly struggle.

Russia cried out for aid from its new allies, Britain and the United States. But the weight of the United States forces had not yet been developed or thrown into the combat. Britain's resources were strained by the warfare in the deserts of Egypt and Libya. Only a handful of British soldiers in Britain were ready to strike at a moment's notice against the Germans on the continent of Europe.

Chapter 8

Commando! The word still has a romantic ring in my ears. They were the volunteers of the British Army, specially trained for night fighting and landing on an enemy coast, hitting hard, and escaping before the might of the German Army could be exerted against them. They were never very many, a few companies, perhaps 1,000 men in all at any one time, elite men trained in demolition and silent hand-to-hand combat. They all had the high morale of such small, close-knit units—the Long Range Desert Group in North Africa, which used to spend weeks at a time behind enemy lines; the American rangers, counterpart of and modeled on the commandos; or Popski's Private Army, the British Eighth Army saboteurs, who wreaked destruction far greater than their numbers warranted deep in the enemy's unattended rear. Like all such units, they were eventually submerged, not by enemy action, although, of course, their casualties were always considerable, but by the red tape of headquarters, the envy by more conventional officers of the commandos' dash and devil-may-care disregard of military niceties.

However, they learned and imparted fighting techniques which later extended to all combat units. Much can be said for bringing all infantrymen to such a peak of physical and mental training that any random group can carry out the most difficult raids and infiltrations and other special assignments, for an elite unit used for only the roughest work is bound to suffer heavy losses, and officers of more conventional units, confronted with some difficulty, are apt to rely on the elite unit rather than on their own ingenuity and the courage of their own men. At least this was the theory that resulted in the abolition of commandos and rangers.

But in 1940 Britain, rocked back on its heels, its land forces in contact with the enemy only in distant Africa, knew that the sole way it would ever win victory would be through amphibious warfare, landing on an enemy beach and fighting inland, and as early as July of that year, a retired admiral, Sir Roger Keyes, was appointed by Prime Minister Churchill to form special groups of

British destroyer Campbelltown, *formerly U.S.S.* Buchanan, *pictured before it was exploded and destroyed the important German dry dock at St. Nazaire, France, in March 1942.* IMPERIAL WAR MUSEUM.

amphibious soldiers and train them in conjunction with special naval units.

The commandos made many small raids on occupied Western Europe, hit-and-run attacks.

On one, they and the British Navy cooperated to destroy at St.-Nazaire, on the coast of France, the only Atlantic dry dock which could service such major German vessels as the battleship *Bismarck*. The old former U.S. destroyer *Buchanan*, renamed HMS *Campbeltown*, was loaded with explosive and smashed by night into the gates of the dry dock. Commandos destroyed shore installations and held off fierce German attacks until the work could be completed. The *Campbeltown*'s explosion wrecked the dry dock for the rest of the war.

My personal link with the attack was the fact that my friend from Oxford days Lieutenant Dunstan M. C. Curtis, Royal Navy Volunteer Reserve, won the British Distinguished Service Cross for commanding the motor launch that brought the head of the operation, British Commander R. E. D. Ryder, safely into and out of St.-Nazaire.

At first the only correspondents allowed to go on commando raids —including the big effort against St.-Nazaire and a smaller raid against Boulogne—were the British news agency men, no more than one or two correspondents to a raid, Gordon Holman of the *Exchange Telegraph* or Edward Gilling or Ralph Walling of Reuters. Each time we heard a report of a raid, the thought that we were not along drove us into fits of anger at the British War Office. What was the good of all our training in warfare, we thought, when we were kept from seeing the real thing? We all were much younger then. I should probably not be so eager if it were happening now so many years later, though, I might. So much depends on the atmosphere of the time. At last we got permission for an American agency man, an American radio man, and an American special— that is, a representative of one of the individual papers such as *The New York Times* or the Chicago *Daily News*—to accompany the next raid.

Charles Collingwood of CBS and I were to split the radio berth and do the raids in rotation. Only then did I realize how many attacks that were planned were never carried out. At least twice I went down to one of the ports prepared to land on some spot of the enemy coast with the commandos, and each time, after I waited a day or two, the raid was canceled because of some vagary of weather, tide, or enemy movement. I know that Collingwood had the same experience. Each time, when we returned to London with our gear and no story, the only thing to do was to smile wryly at the other fellow and say, "Hope you have better luck."

On June 12, 1942, my son Myles Angus was born in the Middlesex Hospital, and a few days after Lucy returned to the apartment, I got another of the mysterious cryptic telephone calls that sent me off on another venture. I put on my battle dress, slung my tin hat, gas mask, and typewriter, and reported at the British war correspondents' rendezvous at Cadogan Gardens.

We were taken to the south coast, Southampton, and the Isle of Wight, and I wondered whether the invasion was going to begin. I hardly thought the amount of shipping indicated it, but I knew, by devious information, that consideration was being given to the idea of seizing a piece of ground on the Continent, forming a perimeter defense, and holding it until sufficient forces could be fed into the bastion to take an eventual offensive.

I had met that great and good man General George C. Marshall, the United States Chief of Staff, when he came to London, having blundered into his suite at Claridge's half an hour before a scheduled off-the-record news conference with a picked group of representative American correspondents. He was in his undershirt, just after his shower, and with the greatest informality in the world he made me welcome. I became a rapt listener as he talked about the differences between the American and British publics and the belief of American military men that even with the forces presently at the joint disposal of the two countries, we could carry the war onto the Continent. He, of course, gave me no direct information about his talks with British military men, but knowing his general military philosophy, I could read between the lines and surmise that we were anxious to get onto the Continent to meet the Germans face to face, while the British, who at first had agreed to such a move, were now having second thoughts about it. Later I checked my surmises with other friends in both armies and learned that the Americans were indeed hoping for a speedy invasion.

But I was quickly to learn the real purpose of our journey. We and the troops were now isolated from contact with civilians on Wight. The little group of correspondents, no more than ten altogether, were taken into a frame building that was serving as temporary headquarters and there met Lieutenant Colonel Churchill Mann of the Canadian Army. He looked no older than I at that time, thirty, and he may have been even younger. Behind him was a map of a section of the French coast—Dieppe and its surrounding territory—and under his feet, as he perched on a table, was a relief plan.

Colonel Mann began to explain the operation. For three hours he talked, and when he had finished, we knew as much about the coming action as any officer directly concerned.

Although he did not say so at the time, a good deal of the planning had been done by him personally. He was shortly thereafter promoted to the rank of brigadier, and I have rarely met a staff officer of more clarity of thought or more lucid manner of explaining a coming operation. He was one of Canada's few professional officers. I heard that he left the Army after the war, an action which I would regard as a loss to the Canadian Army.

The story that Colonel Mann told us, sitting there in his shirt sleeves, pointing with a long splinter from a packing box, until two o'clock in the morning was a complicated one.

Briefly, the combat elements of the Canadian 2nd Division under Major General J. H. Roberts were to make a raid on the strongly fortified town of Dieppe. The object of the raid was to test German defenses. Another objective was to test our ability to maneuver a combined force with armor onto an enemy shore and bring it off successfully. Third, we hoped to draw into battle the full strength of the Luftwaffe in Western Europe, strike it a crippling blow, and ascertain how far our estimates of German air strength in the area were borne out by the fighting strength the Germans could throw into actual air combat.

British intelligence had careful estimates of German ground strength in and around Dieppe. But only if we actually tested them by fighting could we know just how accurate our estimates were. Intelligence stood to learn a great deal for future operations from such a test. Indeed, such large-scale raids were almost a necessity if we were later to carry out a full-scale invasion.

The least important objective of the entire raid was the destruction of some elements of the German Army and the blowing up of gun positions and electrical installations and the like.

Dieppe itself was an important little port. It had been chosen for attack because it was within fighter range of Britain's airfields, about 150 miles, and relays of fighters could constantly sweep the air above it. Because most of the French northern coast is rocky and cliffs make landings impossible, there were only certain places where

Correspondents and conducting officer Captain Sir Gerald Boles waiting on board a paddle-wheeler to participate in the raid on Dieppe, France, which was scheduled for July 4, 1942, then canceled, then postponed to August 19, 1942. Author on left, wearing glasses.

troops and vehicles could be landed on flat or slightly sloping beaches. Dieppe was one of these. The Germans knew this as well as we, and they had in consequence fortified it heavily.

About a mile west of Dieppe is a little summer resort, with a beach and a draw, called Pourville. Four miles still farther west on the cliffs is a hamlet called Varengeville, where the Germans had installed a battery of six six-inch howitzers covering Dieppe. A mile or so east of Dieppe along the cliffs is the hamlet of Puys, and between this hamlet and Berneval three or four miles farther was another battery of big German guns.

These guns on the flanks of Dieppe would have to be taken and silenced if the Dieppe expedition were to be successful. A company of British commando troops was assigned to each of these necessary but subsidiary tasks.

The real work of the day was to be done by the Canadian Army. As we looked at Dieppe, the South Saskatchewan Regiment men were to land at Pourville on the right, soon after the attacks against the guns had begun out on the flanks. After the South Saskatchewans had seized the village, the Cameron Highlanders were to come in, cut through the hole in the line that the Saskatchewans had opened, and circle left to enter Dieppe from the rear.

To the left of Dieppe, as viewed from the water, the Royal Regiment of Canada was to assault the cliff village of Puys and block off any attempt by the Germans to fire down onto the main invasion beach at Dieppe itself.

The main assault directly on the town of Dieppe was to be made by the Canadian Essex Scottish Regiment and the Royal Hamilton Light Infantry, with the Calgary Tanks and the Fusiliers Mont-Royal coming onto the beach after them and carrying the ball on into the town itself. I was to be with the Hamiltons.

The complications were introduced by the fact that the force could be landed only when the tide was high because of the sloping but shallow beach and that the attack had to be made in the dark of the moon because of the necessity for surprise.

The only preliminary bombing was to be low-level pinpoint attacks by a couple of squadrons of Boston medium bombers.

I began to worry a little at what seemed to me an absence of adequate bomber preparation and asked Colonel Mann about it.

"We are only coming for a raid," he said. "We don't want to destroy the town uselessly and kill a lot of friendly Frenchmen. We feel that once the tanks get onshore, they'll be able to silence the guns. The destroyers and gunboats with us will act as a kind of mobile artillery to keep the German machine-gun posts which we know are in the cliffs from doing too much damage."

It seemed that every detail had been thought of in advance. I was mightily impressed by the careful estimate of the different factors and the split-second timing of naval, military, and air action.

I spent a couple of pleasant days with the men who were to be my companions, the Hamiltons, and then we boarded the vessel that was to take us to the Dieppe beach.

It was a wooden paddle-wheel steamboat. A more incongruous craft for an invasion, I could hardly imagine. In peacetime, it had been some kind of little river ferry. Now it had been fitted out with small antiaircraft guns on the upper deck and used as an antiaircraft ship against low-level attacks on shipping along the east coast. The ship already claimed one enemy aircraft destroyed and another damaged, but it looked too damned expendable to me, and I could see us sinking if a determined German with a rifle drew a bead on us. Yet aboard were a couple of hundred Canadian soldiers and our little party, Major Wallace of Canadian Army public relations, Bob Bowman of the Canadian Broadcasting Corporation, Bill Stoneman of the Chicago *Daily News*, and Captain Sir Gerald Boles, late of the Seventeenth Lancers and then a British Army public relations officer.

Soon after we came aboard, the troops got their first full briefing and were told where they were to go. They welcomed the plan with enthusiasm.

The attack was due to be made on the Fourth of July. We had come aboard on the first. Life was pleasant with the crew of British Navy reservists who manned the paddle-wheeler. We could buy Scotch at about a dollar and a half a bottle and cigarettes for next to nothing. We studied our maps and operation plans intensively and set up a game of twenty-one that seemed to go on continuously but in which no one ever seemed to win or lose more than five or ten shillings a day. The men were full of expectation and eagerness. They spent much time cleaning their weapons and predicting what they would do when they met the Jerries.

On the third the water where our little fleet was anchored had become so rough that the operation was canceled for the fourth and postponed to the fifth. We were plunged into the depths of despair. At dawn that morning antiaircraft guns opened up, and we woke to the pounding of our own guns. A couple of German planes had come in low just at dawn. One had dropped a bomb in the water, but its companion had sent a bomb right through one of our ships. The only casualties were a couple of wounded sailors, but had the bomb struck slightly lower, it would have sunk the vessel. A. B. Austin, correspondent of the London *Daily Herald*, was peacefully sleeping when the bomb passed through the ship no more than six feet from his head. Sandy Austin—a Scot—was one of the best of correspondents and a good companion of mine later in North Africa. He and another correspondent were killed by a shell from a German tank during the battle for Italy.

On the fourth the attack was postponed until the sixth, the last day possible during the month of July because of tidal conditions. But the rough weather continued, and the whole operation was canceled.

I was terribly disappointed. Six thousand men had been briefed on the operation, and I could not imagine it would ever now be carried out. Probably the next attack would be made at some other point on the French coast, and I would not be with it, for my turn had come and gone. I was sad to think of the waste of all the labor that had gone into the planning and the drop in the morale of the troops.

There was only one chance that I might go on the operation. Stoneman and I went to Major Wallace and got from him a promise that if the operation against Dieppe were ever carried out, we would be invited to participate since we had been briefed and security would seem to dictate taking correspondents who had gone thus far rather than briefing new correspondents and leaving ashore men who knew every intimate detail of the operation as we did. But neither Stoneman nor I ever seriously believed the Dieppe raid would be made, for it was a plain impossibility to explain a secret to 6,000 men, then put them back onshore and expect them to keep the secret so well that no word of the contemplated action would reach German intelligence. And if another raid were made against some other objective, Stoneman and I would lose our turns to Collingwood and the American newspaper correspondent who was next on the list.

We had been issued the shoulder pips of British Army lieutenants before we boarded the ship with the thought that if we ran into Germans ashore, they might regard us as an integral part of the British Army and treat us as such, whereas, if we were wearing our regular war correspondent shoulder badges, they might take a dim view of us and shoot us out of hand, as being in a place where no noncombatant should be.

I took the pips back to London as a souvenir, little thinking I would ever need them again.

Chapter 9

About five weeks after I had returned to London disconsolate, I received another cryptic telephone call from the War Office. This time I was told to be at Waterloo Station, with full field equipment, at eleven o'clock the following day.

I never knew when I left home whether it was a raid or an exercise I was going to attend. This was a little hard on Lucy, who had no way of knowing whether I was merely off for a healthy tramp about the fertile fields of England, with due examination of the fare in country public houses, or whether she might not suddenly pick up her morning paper and learn I had been transported to Norway or France.

I learned later that the War Office had called Stoneman at the Chicago *Daily News* office, but that impatient warrior had become bored with waiting around London and had gone to the Midlands to examine the British industrial effort in the war factories. His secretary asked why the War Office wanted him, and she could not, of course, be told. So the War Office dropped him from the list of correspondents to go on the raid and put the next man on the list in his place.

At Waterloo, Sir Gerald Boles was waiting. He had tickets for Bristol, the west coast port. When I learned that fact, it made Dieppe seem hardly likely, and I wondered why I had been tabbed to go along. When we got in our private compartment, Gerald whispered to me that it was to be Dieppe; the others did not know it as yet, and I was to say nothing about the destination or the operation until all had been briefed by the Canadian authorities. That was why I was going on the raid instead of Collingwood of CBS. I thanked my foresight at having arranged it thus with the Canadian Army press officer, Major Wallace, although Murrow and Collingwood were later to make angry protests.

The number of correspondents to go on the expedition had been doubled. Had we left as scheduled in July, we would have been only ten. But the delay had caused second thoughts among the

Canadian military authorities, and we were now twenty, from Canada, Britain, and the United States.

The appearance of twenty men in battle dress with war correspondent insignia might have aroused some discussion in our Bristol hotel, talk that might have trickled to German agents and caused extra watchfulness. So once again we were issued the shoulder pips of British second lieutenants.

We spent a couple of pleasant days in Bristol before we were mustered in army cars and sped across southern England to Newhaven. On the way we stopped in a field, and under an old oak tree Canadian Major Stewart informed the whole group just where it was going and outlined the operation for us, much as Colonel Mann had explained it to me six weeks previously.

That drive in the afternoon sunshine will always remain with me. I was one of the few who had known where we were going the whole time we had been at Bristol. I had no illusions about the risk of attempting to accomplish a military operation which largely depended on secrecy but every detail of which had been in the possession of more than 6,000 soldiers for more than six weeks. I could not imagine how, if any German intelligence existed in England, it could miss picking up the words of an artilleryman in a pub, the boast of a seaman to his girl, or an officer's chance remark to another in a hotel lobby.

In July I had been buoyed by excitement and certain that our attack was going to be a success. Now I was filled with foreboding and fairly certain that none of us would return from an attack which foreknowledge by the enemy could easily doom.

I then learned something which is often experienced by combat troops going into battle. I looked at the green fields of England as though I could never get enough of looking, as though to engrave them on my mind, for I might never see them again. Every bush, every turn in the road, every song of a bird in a thicket, I saw with the eyes of a child again, something fresh and new that I wished to cling to forever. My soul drank everything in, the voices of friends, the smile of a child on a Newhaven street. I felt like touching these things gently and laying them away in the breast of my tunic so that later I might stroke them with my memory. This is a strange type of experience. I was to feel it again and see it repeated in the eyes of men going from rear positions into an especially bloody battle. Thinking such as this leads men to be especially gentle and considerate to those around them for the period that it lasts, as though they valued human relationships and the sights and sounds of the last peace before battle more highly than they had deemed possible. Indeed, the soldier who believes that he may pass from peace suddenly into battle and his own death may put greater value on such qualities as selflessness, gentleness, and thought of others because at the end, when a man faces death, he wishes to be remembered by what he considers the best within him rather than the worst, which he shares with all other men. And he is often delighted in battle to recognize that other men display evidence of these higher things which, until then, he had not realized even in himself, much less his fellows.

Major Stewart read out to us from a list the number of the landing craft we were to go in and its type, as well as the kind of unit we would accompany and where we were to land. We had no choice in the matter. Most of the correspondents, I among them, were to go over in tank landing craft, the first Britain had made, and land in the center of the battle on the Dieppe beach itself. Four of our number were to go with the subsidiary flank attacks by Number 3 Commando at Berneval and the Royals at Puys on the left side, and by Number 4 Commando at Varengeville and the South Saskats at Pourville.

Captain Gerald Boles had been detailed by the War Office to accompany us only as far as Newhaven, whence he was to return to London. He was irritated at this, for he had been scheduled to go all the way with us in July, and aboard the old paddle-wheeler for nearly a week together, we had become fast friends.

I said, "Gerald, why don't you call your boss at the War Office and tell him they can't do this to you? You'll always regret missing this show."

"I know," Gerald replied, "but they say the Canadians are running the affair, and they don't want any extra bodies along from the War Office."

"Are you a mouse or a Seventeenth Lancer, old boy?" I continued. "Are you going to take orders from the bloody War Office?"

"If I could only think of some logical reason for going that could convince them," he mused. "I have it. There's no one from the War Office DPI going on a major operation in which British troops, the commandos, are involved. What will we do in future all-British operations if we have no firsthand experience with this sort of thing?"

He hastened off to the nearest service telephone and shortly returned, all smiles, looking more than ever like David Niven, the film star.

"It took a hell of a lot of bloody argument," he said, "but I persuaded them to let me go, strictly as an observer, in order to write up a report that may be of use to us in future affairs of this kind."

"Now that you are going, Gerald," I said, "I ought to explain that besides the pleasure of your company, I thought it would be nice to have you along because you carry a pistol and I'm not allowed to as a correspondent. I want you right beside me."

"But frankly, John, I'm not much of a shot with the thing," Boles said. "I've shot it only once or twice for practice in the past three years."

"I'm just joking. Really, I at least know how to fire a Bren or a tommy gun, and if we get in a bad spot, I suppose I'll forget the Geneva Convention and pick up the nearest weapon. Anyway, it's only us who ask our correspondents to go into a fight without any weapon. German correspondents, I'm told, carry sidearms and are given army rank. The Germans probably think we're weird to bother about such matters."

Dusk was settling in on the Newhaven waterfront. Newhaven–Dieppe, cheapest passage across the Channel. I had gone that way when I left the *Daily Express* and we were moving to Paris in 1939. It looked logical—and natural. If you want to go to Dieppe, you go to Newhaven first. But the price might be higher, undoubtedly would be higher this time. If any German planes spotted a flotilla of landing craft coming out of Newhaven Harbor, I hoped they would think of Troms, Gibraltar, or Antwerp as the destination, anywhere but Dieppe.

"These crafty British," the German High Command might say, "mounting an expedition at Newhaven just as though they were going to Dieppe. But we see through their stratagems. They are probably heading for Brest or Oslo." At least that was how I hoped the Germans would react, since they had never been able to fathom how the British would behave under any circumstances.

Moving from boat to boat, Gerald and I at last found the craft that was to take us to Dieppe. With us was another correspondent, Frank Gillard of the BBC. He had just been transferred to London from the west regional branch of the broadcasting corporation at Bristol, and almost as soon as he arrived in the capital, he had to turn around and go back to Bristol, then Newhaven. Frank was still very much the local correspondent, a newcomer to the business of war corresponding and more than a little green. He later had long experience with Montgomery in the desert and became the equal of any of the peerless group of radio men who covered the war for the BBC; but this was his first big assignment, and it might well be his last.

The tank landing craft—at the time of Dieppe called TLC but shortly thereafter LCT—was one of the only dozen or so that existed, prototype of hundreds used later by both Britain and the United States. It was long and narrow. In the stern was a tiny chart room, with the engine room and a tiny gallery. There was a head and a berth for the captain. Presumably the rest of the little crew could also bed down somewhere, but accommodations were so slight that Boles, Gillard, and I spent all our time on deck. The bridge was only half enclosed, and out on the spot of open deck was mounted the craft's one offensive weapon, a twenty-millimeter Oerlikon gun, useful for air or sea battle.

Four-fifths of the ship was a deep open well from the bridge to the bow, which ended in a blunt landing-craft gate that could be let down when we reached shore. The ship would hold three or four medium tanks. In ours, however, were a dozen or more of the vehicles called Bren-gun carriers. These were small tracked vehicles meant to carry a driver and a couple of men with a Bren gun, the Czech-conceived British weapon which was meant to fill the gap between rifle or tommy gun and a light machine gun. The Bren-gun carrier was open on top and protected only by a thin sheet of steel around the sides which was easily penetrable by anything more powerful than a spent bullet.

The dozen carriers were to serve as the division commander's only mobile reserve when he had established headquarters in Dieppe. About a company of the Royal Hamilton Light Infantry was aboard, but I had met none of the men during my July visit to the unit. They had a light machine gun, a Browning automatic rifle, and a number of Bren guns. Until we were ordered ashore, they were to use their weapons to fight off any German planes that attacked us or the other ships. Others of the TLCs bore the Calgary Regiment's tanks.

One by one we pulled away from the wharves and slid out of the harbor just before dark. We blinked our signal lamp to a signal station onshore as we passed into the Channel, where the ships were forming in double line. Through the gloom I could make out a destroyer or two. I knew that minesweepers were ahead of us, clearing a pathway through the minefields the Germans had laid to foul up the Channel and protect the French coast.

No lights were showing, and I could hear no sound but the wind as we crept steadily out toward mid-Channel.

Even in August the Channel wind was chill. I had a light sweater under my battle dress jacket, and I wore a trench coat; but I was still cold. The Canadian soldiers with their vehicles in the well of the ship were protected from the wind, and many of them were sleeping in the carriers or beside them. Others talked in low whispers. We were under orders to make no noise and, of course, show no lights. Boles, Gillard, and I stayed on the bridge deck in order to see as much as possible. Whenever we wanted to smoke a cigarette, we ducked into the cabin, for even a cigarette could show a long way through the blackness. We knew the Channel was patrolled by the fast, hard-hitting E-boats that frequently dueled with our own gunboats and motor launches at night.

As soon as darkness set in, we were a world by ourselves, seemingly out of contact with everyone else. Listening, I could hear the throb of propellers and the slap of the water against the nearby hulls of our companions. Once, while we were making a turn to follow the swept pathway, we came close to the TLC running on a course just parallel to ours. I could just make out the outline from twenty or thirty feet away; then we moved slowly apart again, and once more we were alone.

Frank managed to sleep, but Gerald and I were too excited to close our eyes. Hour followed hour, and I knew that we were more than halfway across the Channel in the area dominated by German planes. I dreaded the thought that suddenly flares from the sky would light up our flotilla filing toward the shore and we would hear the whine of diving bombers and the crash of bombs in our midst.

At about three o'clock in the morning we beheld an unexpected firework display of lights several miles ahead of us.

The first troops, the commandos, were not due to touch the beach until ten minutes to five in the morning, at approximately dawn. This eerie display of lights was therefore completely inexplicable. We could see tracer bullets arching slowly across the sky. Every once in a while there would be a big flare-up as though an exploding bomb had made such a flash that it regretted dying out and leaving the world again in darkness. We peered at the

94

activity through my field glasses but could make out no detail. Once in a while it seemed as though a fire had started, for a flash of white light would take on a reddish cast and continue flaring up and dying down for some minutes. One of the strangest features of the incident was the lack of sound. We might have been watching a silent film, for though we strained our ears, there was nothing but the wind to hear.

"It must be the preliminary bombing," I said to Boles.

"I hadn't heard about anything beginning this early," he replied doubtfully. "Perhaps it's some kind of diversion put on to lure the Germans into thinking that the whole show is just a bombing raid."

We watched for twenty minutes until finally the sky ahead again grew black, and we were left to wonder at the cause of it all. Only the following night did I learn the reason.

The Number 3 Commando had been proceeding ahead of us and making for the subsidiary landing out on the left flank to silence the German battery of artillery between Puys and Berneval. Suddenly their landing craft ran into a number of German E-boats proceeding up the Channel on a routine maneuver, not dreaming of any such encounter.

The commando craft had some protection from a couple of British gunboats, but the E-boats outnumbered them. In the running fight several of our landing craft were sunk or badly damaged, and the whole operation against the Berneval guns was badly crippled. Larry Meier, the International News Service correspondent who was the only reporter assigned to Number 3 Commando, was wounded and shipped back to England before he ever so much as saw the coast of France.

One or two of the landing craft continued on to shore. But by that time the defenses were alert. The remnant of the commando was not able to silence the guns, and the big howitzers fired all day at the ships and the landings at the town of Dieppe. Worst of all, the battalion of Royal Regiment of Canada, which had hoped to scale the cliff at Puys and help silence the guns and clear the whole left flank of mortars and machine guns, ran into defenses that were ready for it. Many of the Royals died without ever getting beyond the beach. Ross Munro, of the Canadian press, landed with the Royals, and he told us the first wave was literally mown down just above the waterline as the men stepped ashore from their landing craft.

Yet there was nothing that could be done at that stage. Six

thousand men were aboard boats heading for France in an intricate operation that, once begun, could not be reversed. On airfields all over southern England, fighter squadrons were ready to take off for France in a great effort to strike a crippling blow at the Luftwaffe.

It was just dawn when we arrived off Dieppe. The sleeping town looked just as I had seen it in peacetime, just as I had seen it on the relief map, and I was able to make out clearly the casino and the low seawall we would have to breach so that the tanks could get into the streets.

There were thirty or forty craft of various kinds slowly milling about together, like sheep under the protection of watchdogs. In this case the watchdogs were the destroyers and gunboats which were circling us and guiding the vessels that were just arriving into position.

We were 600 or 700 yards offshore, and as I watched, the first landing craft headed into the beach. I knew they contained combat engineers with long Bangalore torpedoes to blow gaps in the barbed wire and big explosive charges to blast the concrete seawall to bits. Others had mine detectors to help make a pathway through the minefields we were sure existed on the rocky and gravel beach.

Although I did not know it at the time, Number 4 Commando had landed secretly and successfully far out on our right. Sandy Austin, the *Daily Herald* correspondent, was with them, and at one point he was pressed into action fusing and passing mortar shells. The commando was led by a dashing Highland chief of the Frasers, Lord Lovat, and it successfully attacked the battery of howitzers on our right, ending up with a bayonet charge that gave the commandos possession of the guns, which they promptly blew up.

Nearer the town of Dieppe, but still on our right, the South Saskatchewan men and the Cameron Highlanders of Winnipeg had landed successfully at Pourville against an opposition that was more alert and vigorous than had been hoped by our planners back in England. Wallace Reyburn of the Montreal *Standard* was the correspondent who landed with them.

One battalion commander received a bullet between the eyes just as he stepped out of the landing craft. Yet the attack on Pourville, which was separated from Dieppe proper by the little Scie River, was the most successful operation of the day. The troops landed and sped across the beach and into the village streets with a rush. There they came under mortar fire, and the Germans peppered

96

them with rifle fire from the houses so that the main streets had to be cleared house by house.

But while the South Saskats and the Camerons were separated from Dieppe by the river, the German defenders of the city were safe from any real pressure. A viaduct bridge of concrete crossed the river and offered 200 exposed yards for the German defenders to guard. They had, of course, centered their defenses on the bridge and swept it with a tornado of mortar and machine-gun fire. It was in this heavy fire that Lieutenant Colonel C. C. I. Merritt, commander of the South Saskatchewan battalion, won Canada's first Victoria Cross of World War II, the highest bravery award in the world, for it is given only for tremendous personal bravery under fire, never for outstanding military merit, as our own comparable medal, the Congressional Medal, has sometimes been awarded.

Colonel Merritt discovered his men were held up at the bridge. He said to the men, "Follow me," then calmly strolled across under the heaviest of German fire, twirling his steel helmet in his hand as though he were sauntering down a village lane. The men followed him as he advanced under direct fire from a concrete German blockhouse. During the day he was to stroll back across the bridge six times, giving his men something of his own calm unconcern for danger.

The operation on the right flank, then, was going very well. The big guns were silenced. Merritt and his men had control of Pourville and were in a position to enter the town of Dieppe whenever they were ordered.

The operation on the left flank had failed completely because of the surprise encounter with the German E-boats. The big German guns were being sniped at from a distance by some of the commandos and Royals, but the guns still functioned efficiently. The Royals had sustained heavy losses and were unable to clear the German mortar and machine-gun positions from the cliffs on the left flank. Nor were the Royals able to make any diversionary attacks across the beaches that fronted the center of the city.

Meanwhile, I was in a position to watch the main attack myself and judge how it was succeeding. Just as we approached Dieppe, a little gunboat caught my eye. It was flying the Free French flag, the tricolor with the Cross of Lorraine upon it, and it was covered from stem to stern with Free French soldiers, wearing battle dress like the rest of us, but on their heads, instead of helmets, were the berets and the kepis of their own French regiments. As the little craft dipped and leaped beside us, I wondered how the Frenchmen felt, returning for the first time to their own land, where they, if they were caught, were under sentence of execution by German or Vichy firing squads. I waved at them and called, *"Vive la France,"* and they waved and shouted back as the gunboat picked up speed and shot ahead of us toward the town.

As we fell into position just offshore, a destroyer sped close in to the beach and parallel with it, making smoke. We had seen explosions on and near the beach from several Boston bombers that flew back over the sea as we neared shore.

The first landing craft with the combat engineers went into the smoke, and soon smoke pots on the beach itself were giving some little cover to what was happening there.

I saw a destroyer nose in toward shore and begin firing repeatedly from its bow guns, apparently at the cliff, for I could make out the explosions plainly on the cliff face, although now there were flashes of other explosions closer to the beach. When the screening smoke was blown away for a bit, fires could be seen in some of the buildings that fronted the shore.

At moments, when a shift of wind revealed the beach, the figures of our men could be seen sprinkled along it, and as far as I could see, the low concrete seawall did not appear to have been blown up as we had hoped.

From time to time we would see several landing craft form at the edge of our floating lager of ships. They would then head into shore together and together disappear in the black smoke screen that covered the beach itself. I noticed that of all the craft that went into the smoke screen, only one or two returned at sparse intervals.

As we were watching and waiting for the order to go in, two huge water spouts suddenly rose in the water between us and one of the other craft. The landing craft rocked back and forth, and some spray fell on our deck. In the general noise I had not heard any sound of falling bombs, and I looked overhead; but no planes were near.

Boles swore under his breath. "It's those German guns in the cliff face," he said. "They haven't knocked them out." Nor were they ever knocked out.

It appeared to us as though our main attack had run into much more opposition than had been expected. Our unit of Bren carriers had been scheduled to dart into the battle as soon as the advance divisional headquarters was set up in the town, to act as a mobile

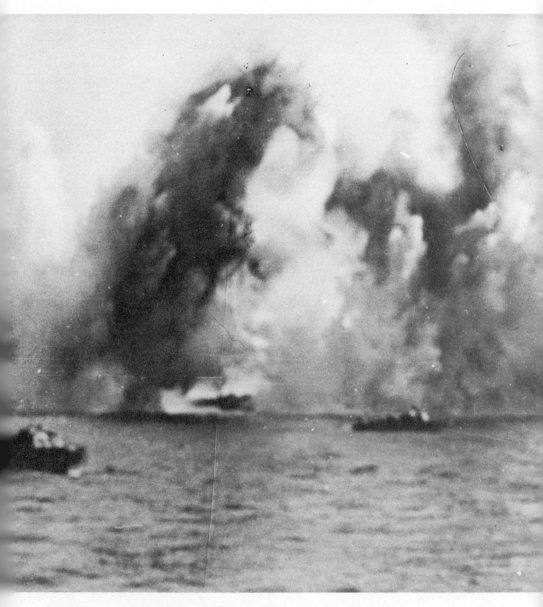

Dieppe, from just offshore. NATIONAL PHOTOGRAPHY COLLECTION, NATIONAL PUBLIC ARCHIVES, CANADA.

Dieppe beach—German guns positioned in cliff in background. German photo. NATIONAL PUBLIC ARCHIVES, CANADA.

reserve to link up with the flanking thrust from Pourville on the right and perhaps to continue out into the country to attack some German installations nearby. It was thought that we would certainly be in the thick of things within, at most, an hour from the first touchdown on the beach. But more than two hours had passed, and still no word for us to come in. I did not know whether any other correspondents had gone onto the beach, and I was getting anxious.

Suddenly the skipper of the TLC, a reserve lieutenant, started up his engines. A thrill of anticipation ran through the troops. I had chosen my place in the first Bren carrier at the head of the line, not from any spirit of daring, but on the canny assumption that as soon as the bow gate opened, I would be ashore and heading across the beach—before the Germans trained their guns on the landing craft.

We headed straight as an arrow for the center beach. I looked behind me. Gerald Boles was in the next carrier, looking tense but cheery, and behind him was Gillard. I gave them the V sign. I could see nothing on either side but the walls of the ship's tank well. Our engines were running, and the driver beside me was hunched over his wheel ready to step on the gas the moment the great gate fell in front of us. The noise of the engines was deafening in the enclosed space. Smoke poured over us. We had entered the smoke screen, and I knew that we were within a few yards of shore. I tensed for the impact of the TLC on the shingle and felt my battle trouser pocket to make sure I had the extra emergency dressing that had been issued to us. I tapped the steel wall of the carrier and hoped it was strong enough to withstand the rifle bullets I fully expected to strike it as soon as the gate was open and we came out of the smoke.

The engines of the TLC stopped their strong beat, and I knew we had gone into neutral, drifting, I thought, to make the touchdown on the shore. The beat of the engines suddenly started up again. I felt the vessel pause in its course. Now, I thought, now. The skipper has put her into reverse so that we won't hit too hard. I waited for the scraping on the shore and hoped the gate mechanism would work. It would be awful to be caught there, a helpless target, unable to get out. I wondered if we could drop over the side or over the gate itself without getting hurt.

The engines continued in reverse, and I could feel the vessel slowly begin to pull away. We came out of the smoke. Quite a way out, the TLC went into forward motion, turning. Someone said, "We're going back out."

End of the line for Canadian Churchill tanks at Dieppe. NATIONAL PUBLIC
ARCHIVES, CANADA.

I got out of the carrier and scrambled up onto the bridge. The skipper explained that at the last moment he had received orders canceling the order to hit the beach. Over the course of the next hour or so, from fragmentary radio reports, I discovered what had happened.

Instead of running into rifle and machine-gun fire, the attack on the center had run into withering fire from seventy-five-millimeter guns and larger, tucked away in positions in the cliffs. The guns would come to the entrance, fire, and wheel quickly back in so that it was almost impossible to hit them. Our tanks had been expected to lumber ashore without difficulty. Instead, the cannon fire had knocked out most of those that had reached shore, as well as the landing craft that had brought them. I could see the inert landing craft lying bow or beam to the beach whenever the smoke cleared momentarily. My unit, the carriers, had been intended to go in with the last squadron of tanks, but at the last moment General Roberts had realized that until the gunfire was stopped, sending any more tanks ashore was only sending them to destruction. It appeared that the operation was never going to get beyond stage one, the possession of the beach.

The squadron of tanks and the Bren carriers that were not yet committed formed the last reserves. The Fusiliers Mont-Royal, the unit of French Canadians, were sent in, but although we were able to get troops into the town, there was no coordinated drive that could clear the guns that were firing from the bluffs right down on the men beneath. The gallantry of the tough Canadians was great indeed, worthy of their World War I tradition, but the task they were called upon to accomplish was too great for the men available in the space of time they had been given. In an ordinary operation a time lag in an amphibious landing is not fatal, but the fact that we were only making a raid, that we had to be particularly careful about our bomber preparation, and the very character of the coast militated against us. At high tide the water was deep enough to bring our craft right up to the beach. But as the tide fell, it went out over a long shelf that was almost flat, so that once the tide started out in earnest, the landing craft inshore were left marooned, and a long stretch of beach separated the undamaged craft offshore from the men who had been landed. Any boat that came too close to the beach on the falling tide risked getting trapped, and the guns in the cliff ensured that eventual escape would be impossible.

That morning of August 19, 1942, was clear, and the sun beat

103

down on the flotilla of ships and landing craft that idled just off-shore. It beat down as well on the men fighting onshore. Air battles were going on in the sky above us. Occasionally German planes would make a run at the mass of shipping, and one could hardly hear their bombs, with such a racket of guns from every craft of the sea.

The Hamiltons on our TLC had mounted their Brens and their machine gun on the narrow catwalks that ran along each side. They would cut loose with full vehemence, as would the Oerlikon on the stern whenever a plane came within sight, even when the aircraft was too high to hit. Sometimes the twisting and diving fighting planes overhead were hard to make out except through my ten-power glasses. At other times they would come scudding into us from over the hills, guns going, or bombs loosed as they slid over the beach. Sometimes an RAF fighter would be right on the Messerschmitt's tail, and the British plane, too, would run into the screen of fire that we all put up.

I will never forget one of the German planes which dropped its bombs just short of us and started to climb as it passed through the tracers from the ships. As it rose, we saw it start to smoke, then falter and explode as it struck the sea a mile or so beyond us. From a thousand throats, including my own, came a shout of joy, a kind of animallike angry joy that welled up from deep inside us, and we shouted, "The bastard. We got the bastard. We got the bastard," at the top of our voices.

I had feared that other correspondents were going ashore, but Major Wallace, going from landing craft to landing craft checking on us, explained that although there had been some thought of sending in the remaining tanks—and the correspondents—somewhat later, the course of the battle had made it impossible to do so without losing the landing craft, the tanks, and incidentally the correspondents. None of us in the center had gone ashore, he assured us, but the reporters who had been with the flank attacks had undoubtedly landed and even now might be dead or captured, although there had been no specific report. He had been to the headquarters destroyer, and conditions onshore were worse than most of us had supposed.

We were angry at—as we thought—missing the battle and made the major promise to try to get a small landing craft so that we could at least go ashore briefly, but as we watched conditions onshore, we understood after a while that happenings there were indeed very

Captured Canadian soldiers being marched through Dieppe streets.
NATIONAL PUBLIC ARCHIVES, CANADA.

grave. I myself had seen many more men go to the beach than ever returned from it.

Meanwhile, the air battles continued overhead, and with the regularity of clockwork, the big howitzer shells from the Berneval battery fell among us.

It seemed as though we had been there for days and days, for we were tense with strain every second of the time; but by one o'clock all who could be evacuated had been evacuated, and the flotilla turned toward the sea. The price had been heavy. Approximately 6,000 men, most of them Canadians, went to Dieppe, and two-thirds of that number were killed, wounded, or taken prisoner. The fighting elements of a division had gone into battle, and in a few short hours only the strength of a regiment was left. We had lost about 100 planes in the air battles that drew in German air strength from all over Western Europe, and we had shot down a somewhat larger number of Germans. One destroyer had been lost, but that was the only important vessel hit, although our losses in the scarce landing craft were so high that it would be a long time before we could mount another such operation.

On the other hand, our planners had learned what to do and what not to do. It had been proved useless, for instance, to make such an attack without proper air bombardment in preparation. And useless also to attack directly when a flank attack could win the day. We had learned something about air, sea, and ground coordination that would prove helpful later. Finally, the Americans had been discouraged from trying to attack France at that early stage in the war. Immediately afterward plans went forward for Operation Torch, the attack on North Africa.

Around midnight, we nosed into the pier at Newhaven and climbed wearily ashore. I had done no running on the beach, but I was bone tired from the strain of the excitement and of being under constant fire. In an officers' mess frequented by Navy officers who covered the Channel in gunboats and motor launches, I had a welcome drink and was able to get a picture of the attack from men who had been with the commandos and the other flanking attacks. Only then did I learn of the unlucky fate of the commando attack on the left flank and the encounter with the E-boats.

We had been told that there would be no release of any of the stories until the following evening, after a conference for all correspondents who had participated. Soon I was in a car bound for

Commandos return to England after the Dieppe raid. IMPERIAL WAR
MUSEUM.

London, and I arrived at my apartment at three or four in the morning.

The next day I was up fairly early. There had been a lot of confusion, owing to the reports by the Germans and a mess-up in the reports by Combined Operations Headquarters. One enterprising American public relations officer who had come into the Army from Hollywood issued a picture of Douglas Fairbanks, Jr., to the press because the screen star had a post in Combined Operations Headquarters, but he had not, I believe, gone anywhere near Dieppe that day. Some American papers had a headline "U. S. Invades France" or "Yanks Land in France," which, since about forty American observers were involved, caused a certain amount of resentment among the Canadians and British.

I felt it was up to me to put the record straight. That night at the release time I went on the air to my American network for fifteen minutes and later did a shortened version for the BBC European service. That night I got the greatest compliment I have ever had in broadcasting when Bob Bowman of the Canadian Broadcasting Corporation, waiting in another studio to go ahead with his own eyewitness report to Canada, came to me afterward and said, "John, your broadcast was so true and so gripping that it made me feel what's the use of my making a report now. You said everything I wanted to say and so much more."

And in Moscow, my old friend and rival broadcaster Larry Le-Sueur, listening with Jim Brown of INS to the report, wired me, "WONDERFUL BROADCAST." When Larry said anything like that, it meant more than somewhat.

The same spring and summer the people of Britain were learning how small the Channel had become through the installation of long-range guns on the French coast near Calais.

The big German rifles could place a shell in the center of Dover, and in fact, they had reduced Dover's importance considerably and made the passing of a convoy through the strait extremely hazardous. When I went down to Dover to do an *Army Hour* broadcast, I was able to see for myself that Dover was still taking it, but it was nonetheless very uncomfortable to have a shell explode in the town out of nowhere and hear the sirens blow only after the first explosion.

Doing the kind of broadcast that the British call an OB, outside broadcast, and we in this country call a remote, meant quite complicated preparations in wartime Britain because we had to produce the broadcast from the appointed spot at the exact time that it went on the air in the United States.

That meant I had to spend a couple of days in Dover finding the people I wanted to participate in the half hour broadcast, interviewing them, and taking notes and at the same time getting all the official permissions for their appearance. It also meant getting the General Post Office to lay the proper lines to the spot I wished to broadcast from, in this case the white cliffs of Dover. Then I had to make sure that BBC engineers and equipment would be ready at the right time.

But first I had to make a trip up to London, write a script that was based on my notes, and get the approval of the BBC censors and the service censors.

Once back in Dover, I had to round up all my cast and get them assembled at the spot from which we were to broadcast, in this case an antiaircraft gun site overlooking the Channel. They included Anne Heffernan, then a British naval WREN stationed in Dover, a British Navy commander of the small minesweepers and other craft that worked out of Dover, civilians from Dover to tell about bombs and shells, an RAF pilot, and a whole battery of antiaircraft gunners of the British Army.

I had obtained permission from the authorities for the antiaircraft battery to fire charges of powder without shells as the climax of the whole broadcast. It was to end with the horn blowing the alarm for the battery, the men rushing to their posts, the sound of the finding and tracking of an enemy plane, the orders to the men on the guns, the slamming of the breeches, and finally the order to fire, followed by shots from the four guns of the half battery.

Three or four minutes before we were due to go on the air, a motorcycle dispatch rider rushed up to the officer in charge. He turned to me in dismay. "Our permission to shoot has been canceled," he said. "A convoy has just entered the Channel, and they're afraid that if we start shooting, the Jerries will come over to see what's happening, and they'll spot the convoy."

"But what can we do?" I asked. "The whole broadcast builds up to your shooting."

"Maybe you could clap your hands near the mike," suggested Mildred Boutwood, our NBC office manager, unhelpfully.

"I know, sir." A sergeant spoke up. "We have some thunderflashes we use in training. I could light them a couple of seconds ahead of time and explode them near the microphone."

Thunderflashes were giant firecrackers tossed around in maneuvers to simulate exploding shells and bullets. There was no help for it. We had to use thunderflashes.

But now it was the BBC engineer's turn to speak. We had the microphone inside a concrete abutment, and the engineer said, "If you have an explosion in here, it may knock the microphone right off the air."

So it was decided that the sergeant would explode the thunderflashes outside the low concrete wall.

The broadcast went off perfectly. Everyone came in at just the right time. Then came the grand climax. Crisp commands barked out. Boots pounded on concrete. Gun breeches slammed shut. And the officer shouted the final command, "FIRE."

Dead silence followed for two or three seconds. The engineer, fearing the explosions of the thunderflashes, had turned down his volume. When the firecrackers exploded on the other side of the concrete wall, the sound going 3,000 miles across the Atlantic, the sound that should have been the mighty voice of 3.7-inch guns, four of them, was only something that sounded on the air like *f-t-t, f-t-t, f-t-t, f-t-t*.

In my conversation afterward with Arthur Feldman, NBC editor, at the other end of the circuit in New York, I got a comment that went something like this: "It was all wonderful, John. Great stuff. But those guns at the end. That engineer must have turned his mike down to zero."

I didn't have the heart to tell Feldman what had actually happened, and in any case I could not have done so at the time because my words would have revealed the presence of the confounded convoy that had caused our permission to shoot to be canceled.

So all I said was, "Well, you know what engineers are, Art. Awfully afraid of their equipment in a case like this."

Interlude II

By the early autumn of 1942 the United States had been at war for ten months without striking any important blow against the Axis in Europe. American fliers had not yet mounted any of the massive raids against Germany which were to become an important factor in the latter part of the struggle. The American Army had sent many administrative officers to London, but no more than two to three divisions of combat troops had arrived in Europe as forerunners of the millions of GIs who would later swarm onto the Continent.

The Dieppe raid by the Canadians was only a pinprick in comparison with the great battles taking place deep in Russia.

Yet there were signs that what Sir Winston Churchill called the "hinge of fate" was beginning to swing. The main German strength began to weaken from the moment Hitler directed the vain assault against Stalingrad on the Volga. The British Eighth Army had repulsed Rommel before Cairo and, at the beginning of November, defeated the Germans and Italians at El Alamein. The pursuit of Rommel's forces began.

Only then did some American combat units, completely untried in warfare, make the first encounter with the veteran German Army, hardened by three years of battle. The first fighting against the European enemies was not staged at the time or place American leaders had desired. But the experience gained in North Africa did help both commanders and troops bridge an important gap—that between the theory and the fact of warfare. By trial and error in Tunisia, the Americans gained the military knowledge that was indispensable for victory in Europe.

Chapter 10

It was in late October 1942 that I kissed Lucy and my four-month-old son, Myles, good-bye and, dressed in a British officer's uniform with war correspondent badges, loaded my bags into a taxi outside 88 Portland Place. There was nothing in such an event to startle the neighbors, for I frequently went off on military exercises with the same paraphernalia.

A telephone call two days earlier had warned me of the time and place to report—Norfolk House in Norfolk Square at 5:00 P.M. During the previous months, ever since Fred Bate had left Britain for New York to run NBC's shortwave operation, I had been broadcasting and at the same time running the business of the office with the aid of the invaluable Mildred Boutwood. Now Robert St. John had been sent over to broadcast also, and only a few days before my departure NBC had appointed a director of the London office. He was a veteran Associated Press man, Stanley Richardson, and his job was not to broadcast at all but to run the business of the office. His coming coincided with one of those periodic shake-ups that affect broadcasting companies. Abe Schechter, the company's news director, who had built our wartime coverage, had had a squabble with someone higher up, and he was out. A new man, William Brooks, a former AP executive, was in the job. He wanted someone he knew to run the London office, so Richardson was appointed.

I might add that during the three years to come, I had all the support from Stan Richardson that any roving correspondent could hope for, and if he relied too much on the gratitude of great companies for both our futures, it was perhaps only because he never understood the jungle war that racks the executive echelons of the broadcasting industry, a war that eventually took off not only Schechter, but later Bate, Richardson, and finally Brooks himself, among many others.

My company had been promised the only broadcasting berth in the first wave of any offensive operation. As soon as I learned that I was to go, Richardson and I got on the telephone to ask other war correspondents of newspapers and agencies who might be expected to be among the first to land also to do some reports and broadcasts for NBC as well as their regular jobs. We knew neither the time, place, nor extent of the coming operation, and we wanted to provide for the eventuality that there might be scattered landings and several expeditions to different places. My hope was to have someone in each group trying to get to a radio transmitter or sending dispatches to NBC.

To our surprise we drew a complete blank. In each case the correspondent's office said that he was out of town for a few days. I had the sudden fear that perhaps in the shuffling around of places, I had lost the berth in the first group that the Army had promised. I had the possibly too-suspicious feeling that Captain Harry Butcher, former CBS vice-president and now General Eisenhower's chief naval aide, might have struck a blow for CBS by suggesting to the expedition's public relations people that there was no need for a broadcaster to land with the first group.

When I found Charles Collingwood of CBS was with me at Norfolk House, I realized that NBC had been paid back for my clean scoop, the eyewitness account of the Dieppe raid.

The first person I saw at Norfolk House was Thomas Watson, the INS correspondent, veteran of the British Rifle Brigade in World War I. Then came Collingwood; Howard Winner, a newsreel cameraman; a BBC engineer named Donovan; and Captain Anthony Leviero, our conducting officer, who after the war was the Pulitzer Prize-winning White House correspondent of *The New York Times.* I had not seen him for six years since he, for the *Times,* and I, for the Brooklyn *Eagle,* had covered the trial in federal court of the two racketeers Gurrah and Lepke.

We were taken by car to an outlying, rarely used station of London and in the rainy darkness clambered aboard a troop train. With only dim blue lights showing, it was impossible to read. The British soldiers were comparatively quiet, for they all suspected that at last they were going off to combat.

We dozed the night through, sitting upright in our seats. Once we managed to get out at some station in the Midlands and got cups of hot tea and buns from wagons that came alongside the train.

There is no excitement quite like the knowledge that one will probably soon be in active combat. It is more excitement than fear, with a lingering sweetness of thought about family and friends and the mystery of what tomorrow may bring. This was my fifth such experience: first, the two times that I had kissed Lucy good-bye believing that by the next dawn I should be with British commandos raiding somewhere on the Continent, only to find after a few days' wait that some vagary of wind, weather, or military intelligence had canceled the expeditions; then the Dieppe raid which had been canceled in July; and finally, the Dieppe raid itself.

This time, because of the presence of the BBC engineer, I suspected that something much larger was in the offing, for unless we were going somewhere to stay for a while, the Army would not be bringing an engineer for a radio recording truck. And I *knew* something bigger was at hand after we had rolled along the bank of the Clyde down to the port of Greenock.

Out in the stream were a dozen or more big troopships, all apparently packed with soldiers, and more soldiers were coming from our own train. I calculated that roughly 40,000 men must be aboard the vessels.

A sailor said, "If you think this convoy is big, you should have seen the one that went out two days ago. Twice as big as this." My heart really sank, for I realized that there must have been correspondents in that convoy, now two days at sea.

Our transport was the Pacific and Orient liner *Stratheden*. Now she was loaded with British and American troops, several thousand, but in the quarters we war correspondents shared with the officers, one could still be comfortable. The white-jacketed Goanese stewards who had served maharajas and British civil servants in peacetime still brought our meals to the grand dining salon and laid them on spotless linen.

There was one immediate shock. No liquor was served aboard, although the ship's stores included plenty of fine wines and liquors. The expedition was under American command, and the order had gone out to make all ships dry, in conformity with practice in the American armed forces.

The steward broke the news to us when we had put our bags in our cabins and foregathered in the smoking room for a refreshing highball after our arduous train trip. "We can serve only orange, lemon, or grapefruit squash, ginger ale, tonic, or ginger beer."

This ghastly news turned pale the faces of the British officers all over the lounge. There was many a piercing cry of "I say" and "Dash it all," "What! No gin with the tonic?"

We correspondents simply sat sipping our lemon squash in numbed silence. That evening we had a drink from the inadequate flask of brandy I had brought aboard, and the next day, from Collingwood's carefully guarded bottle of Scotch, which for the rest of the trip he diminished alone in minute portions.

However, ingenuity is called for in such crises. I soon made the acquaintance of the *Stratheden*'s radio officers, Mr. Horn and Mr. Edmond. They were enthusiastic listeners to the news on the world airways, and they put out the ship's newspaper. One thing led to another, and before I knew it, I was going up to their quarters for a chat and a couple of heartening nips of Scotch or gin and lime before dinner every night. After another day or two I was able to bring my roommate, Tommy Watson, with me, and the officers were kind enough, on our last night aboard, to invite all six of our party to a little cocktail celebration. The ship's officers, of course, did not come under the discipline that ground down the troops, Army officers, and war correspondents.

The officers of the *Stratheden,* especially the radio officers, were very fine men indeed, good exponents of the high quality of the British merchant marine.

The convoy began to move so silently that night that I did not realize it was moving at all until I went on deck in the pitch-darkness and saw the dim shore lights beginning to move past us. In the blackness I could make out the outline of the last point of land. Down the deck a way, a group of American and British soldiers were singing to a tinny piano that someone had brought out on deck. The songs were a kind of symbol of the British-American unity of our new war effort, such songs as "The White Cliffs of Dover," "Annie Laurie," "Rose of Tralee," "The Last Roundup," "Margie," "Tipperary," "I Belong to Glasgow," and "Roll Out the Barrel." I noted the names in my notebook as I watched the phosphorescence break from our passage through the water, felt the throb of the great engines, and wondered, with a lonely, poignant feeling, whether Lucy and Myles were awake or asleep in our apartment. The men were singing as they moved into the unknown, into war, and where were their families tonight? I wondered. Sleeping or waking from Lincolnshire to California 6,000 miles away.

The next day the whole convoy was at sea, guarded by some little destroyers and corvettes. Where we were going was still a mystery. I doubted we would be trying a winter campaign in Norway. That seemed the height of folly. Certainly great ships such as those in our convoy would not be risked near the French coast, so an invasion of France could be ruled out. Leviero laughingly told us he had orders not to reveal our destination until we were four days at sea and asked us to write down our guesses. I wrote "Morocco—Casablanca" with the faint possibility we might be going as far east as Oran. I did not dream we would be going as deep into the Mediterranean as Algiers.

When we eventually learned our destination from Leviero and discovered that other fellow correspondents were on the convoy ahead of us which was to make the initial landings, Collingwood and I cursed Leviero, Colonel Joe Phillips, General Eisenhower and, most of all, the machinations of our press colleagues, who, we were convinced, had maneuvered American radio out of a place in the first convoy.

Our own convoy was still somewhere in the Atlantic when we heard the first radio announcement of the landings on November 8. By that time we knew that General Eisenhower and the commanding staff were at the headquarters of the expedition, Gibraltar. For the next few days all news came from reporters stationed with Eisenhower on the Rock.

The *Stratheden* and the rest of our convoy slid through the Gibraltar Strait by night. On my right I could see the lights of some Moroccan town, on my left the lights of the Spanish city of Algeciras across the bay from Gibraltar. They were the first lights I had seen in any town since war began in September 1939. It seemed odd to me that I should see lights at night again only as I was heading for North Africa and more war.

Even in the Mediterranean, our voyage might have been a peacetime journey—except for the day a corvette dropped a couple of depth charges and the other destroyers and corvettes raced over to the area. But if a German submarine were actually lurking there, it had disappeared. On the morning of November 12 we beheld for the first time the white and tan buildings of Algiers, strewn in artistic profusion against the bowl of land rising from the blue Mediterranean water.

At least seventy sizable vessels crowded Algiers Harbor, and we were forced to wait, fuming in frustration, until early on November 13 before the *Stratheden* was warped into a pier and we could disembark.

A public relations officer, Jack Levien, told us that advance Allied Force Headquarters had been established at the Hôtel St.-Georges and that General Clark, General Eisenhower's deputy commander, was holding a news conference almost immediately. We left our luggage to be sorted out on the pier and hurried to the St.-Georges.

General Eisenhower, Admiral Darlan, General Mark Clark, and Ambassador Robert Murphy confer in Algiers. U.S. ARMY.

It was the first time that I had met General Mark Clark. Some of his military colleagues criticized him for what they believed was too much ambition, wanting to go too far too fast, and they maintained that he had spotted Eisenhower as a man who was sure to rise to high command and had tied his wagon frankly to Eisenhower's star at an early date. Whatever might be the truth in this theory, Clark was now the man who made the decisions in Algiers for the approval or disapproval of General Eisenhower in Gibraltar.

He draped himself loosely across a chair and, talking to the group of reporters rather as though he were musing to himself, began to explain why he had made the decision to recognize Admiral Jean François Darlan, a Vichy French colleague of Marshal Pétain's, as the chief French official in command of the French forces and government in North Africa.

It was not that he had any personal love for Darlan. In fact, the military code word for Darlan in the messages between Clark in Algiers and Eisenhower in Gibraltar was YBSOB, and the meaning of the acronym was flatly "Yellow-Bellied Son of a Bitch." But it had become plain that none of the high officers and administrators would obey General Henri Giraud, who had been handpicked by the Americans for the French command, and even Giraud himself had told Clark that if the Allies wanted cooperation in North Africa, they would have to grant Darlan the supremacy.

It had been unfortunate that Darlan had been there in Algiers at the time of the invasion, said Clark, but there was nothing else we could do from a military point of view, with our own candidate refusing to try to take over the French command. Darlan would grant Giraud the command of the French forces as his own deputy, and Giraud would be the direct contact between Eisenhower and the French civil officials and military leaders.

General Clark gave us a long account of the negotiations with Darlan and an account of the military operations of the landings. This I filled in during the next few days through numerous interviews with others directly concerned in the initial planning and the attack.

In those first hours there was no way to broadcast, so after finding the censors and learning that brief messages would be transmitted by the military to Gibraltar to England, I sent the following radiogram based on the interview with Clark:

BEST INFORMATION HERE INDICATES NEGOTIATIONS LEADING AP-

118

POINTMENT DARLAN CONDUCTED BASIS STRICTEST REALISM VIEW
LOCAL SITUATION. OBSERVERS UNKNOWN REACTIONS FRENCH PEO-
PLE BUT SCALES TILTED HERE BY ATTITUDE VICHY COMMANDERS
NORTH AFRICA AND NECESSITY INSURING COOPERATION LOCAL
FORCES BEFORE ALLIED THRUST EASTWARD POSSIBLE. DARLAN ONLY
MAN WHO COULD ISSUE ORDERS VICHY FORCES HERE WOULD OBEY.
MANY THOUSANDS BRITISH ARRIVED SECOND BIG CONVOY EYE AC-
COMPANIED AND ALLIED NEGOTIATORS HAD DISCARD IDEALISM TO
KEEP BASE PROTECTED BEFORE ATTACKING ROMMEL. INDICATIONS
HERE DECISIONS REACHED STRICTLY POKER BASIS BUT CLARK AL-
WAYS HOLDS ROYAL FLUSH IN LAST DECISIVE HAND.

This last was a reference to the fact that Clark had told us that
should Darlan give any sign of treachery, Clark had sufficient forces
to take him into immediate custody and disarm any French troops
who might try to sabotage the Allied effort on Darlan's orders.

I have often observed that when the men who direct world
affairs start talking about some move dictated by "strict realism," it
usually means that they are trying to excuse to themselves and to
others the ugly truth that what they are doing is unethical. When
they note that "idealism" is all very well but has no place in deciding
international affairs on the grand scale, you can be pretty sure that
the spokesmen's consciences are troubling them or that they are
afraid the reaction of the public will be unfavorable and want to
publicize a quick explanation for doing something questionable.
The United States is inevitably strong in the diplomatic sense when
it acts according to its own best tradition of democratic thinking.
The refusal to agree to the enslavement of weak nations by the
strong; the generosity that leads to help for the underprivileged
peoples; the resolve to make the United Nations a reality—these are
all "idealisms" which have helped increase the world prestige of the
United States. There are rights and wrongs in international policy,
and the right thing to do is usually the wisest course of action. Behind such action stands the whole weight of American public opinion
and the traditional political morality of the nation.

But at times American policy makers, caught in some situation of
uncertainty and weakness, attempt to play Machiavelli and take the
clever rather than the right decision. The result is that those concerned usually wind up by stepping on their own necks and falling
on their faces.

Chapter 11

My first job was to get on the air. Charles Collingwood and I got an introduction to the head of the French broadcasting department of the government. Allied troops had taken over the Algiers transmitter and were using it for some eighteen hours a day for military communications. We would have to make our arrangements directly with the French, now that an armistice was in force.

We were told, after we had passed in and out of half a dozen offices of French officials, that NBC and CBS could make broadcasts to America but not from the studios of Radio Algiers. To have men in Allied uniform going in and out of the radio studios would be a reflection on French independence, so if we could please find an empty room somewhere, French engineers would set up the equipment for us. We finally got a corner in a hotel room of two friends of the U.S. political warfare section of headquarters, Peter Tompkins and George Rehm. Within twenty-four hours we were ready to begin.

Robert Dunnett was the BBC correspondent, and by common consent we gave him first opportunity. Then came Collingwood, then I. I slyly figured that going on the air last would be advantageous. The transmitter was beamed on London, and presumably British engineers were monitoring all the Algiers frequencies night and day. I figured that Dunnett's and Collingwood's broadcasts would give everyone along the line, London, my office there, engineers of the British Radio Terminal and AT&T, and NBC in New York a chance to prepare to receive me. It worked out much as I had expected. Dunnett's broadcast was not heard. The last minute of Collingwood's was picked up, and my own broadcast was received *in toto* by NBC, the first complete broadcast from North Africa.

For many days afterward we did not know whether any of our broadcasts were being received. Fortunately most of them did get through. During air raids the transmitter would go off the air, and sometimes anti-American French engineers would spoil the quality, although the transmitter itself was guarded by a detachment of American soldiers.

But our greatest menace was the curtain of political censorship that had been lowered on us.

In my first broadcast I told how the people of Algiers that day had thronged the streets to watch the 200 members of the Italian Armistice Commission and a few Germans being taken off as military prisoners. I gave some news from an interview I had had with General Kenneth Anderson, commander of the First British Army, which was knifing deep into Tunisia. I told of my trip in the convoy and my impressions of that strangely mixed Arab-French city Algiers.

Then I came to the important part, the first effect of the "deal with Darlan."

I had written: "Aside from the occupation and the push westward, the main news here has been the appointment of Darlan as civil and political boss. Knowing France and the French people who are fighting for liberty so well, I find it difficult to comment on this. It is pointed out as a choice of expediency. We had to have the Vichy officers on our side. The Vichy administration took up control of local affairs again yesterday. One of Darlan's first moves was to arrest hundreds of fighting Frenchmen who have worked against the Axis for the Allies and French freedom. General Clark is keeping his hands strictly off local administration. He said that—in effect —in a statement to the French today. All I know about the local political situation is that many of our friends are paying for it. French honesty and courage aren't getting any rewards in North Africa tonight."

I still have the manuscript of that broadcast with the note of the censor, Delano Ames, "Attention General Clark," beside these statements. General Clark censored the entire paragraph.

This censorship outraged my whole being as a reporter. I could acquiesce and do what most of the reporters did, cover the strictly military events and let it go at that, or I could continue to try to uncover what was happening politically in this, our first encounter with the complexities of occupying foreign territory. Doing this, I would risk disturbing the equanimity of my own government, which was responsible for the policy. But neither Collingwood nor I hesitated in our choice, and day after day we discovered we both were trying to unweave the same tangled political strands for our listeners, although neither of us knew what the other was going to say until we got before the microphone.

But before I could tell the story, I had to find my way through the devious cloud of events, intrigues, personalities, plots, influences, and counterplots that affected every word spoken by any public person and made every decision the result of unimaginable complications.

Robert Murphy, chief of the American diplomatic mission, had been living at the center of the mystery and intrigue for eighteen months. General Eisenhower, weighed down by a thousand military cares, knowing that his slender force in Tunisia could gain victory or be defeated at any hour, was impatient with the political complications and left everything to Murphy.

I had to try to learn in hours matters which had been developing for many months. The good thing from my point of view was that people were ready to talk. I discovered the identities of some of the key people in the group of 377 French patriots who, in the hours before we landed, seized the city of Algiers, guarded by 12,000 Vichy troops, and held it for nearly a day.

Only the fact that the American commander on the first day, General Charles Ryder, cautiously went by the book and hesitated, in order to "consolidate," as the generals say, prevented our troops from walking into the city on the morning of November 8 and ending all resistance immediately. That hesitation and the fact that General Giraud was not brought to Algiers for three days helped pave the way for the deal with Darlan. I met some of the French officers high and low who had helped our landings, men such as Colonel Baril and General Charles Mast.

I talked and talked and learned more and more, weighing each man's account against another's, trying to plumb their motives and their background in order to get the true story. But most of all, I wanted to find the reaction of the people of Algiers to the Darlan return to power. I went about the city trying to find out.

A girl behind a department-store counter said, "You, monsieur, will find real Frenchmen and Frenchwomen here. When you think of France, think of them—not Darlan and his crowd."

In a barbershop a woman manicurist said, "Can you explain to me what the Americans are doing? We believed they were coming to free us from these Chatels and these Darlans—this *canaille* of Vichy. Now we find that everything is to go on as it was before. What does it mean? Is it all a trick, and will you suddenly execute them one night?"

An Arab at a shoeshine stand looked around quickly when I men-

122

tioned Darlan and Chatel, the new-old governor of Algeria. He shook his finger warningly. *"Pas bon. Pas bon,"* he said. ("Not good. Not good.")

In a restaurant a waiter shook his head and made a face when I asked him what he thought of the new government, but he would not reply verbally.

A small businessman said, "I am a republican. These men are all fascists. Yet they say the Americans support them—and they tell us we must now cease collaborating with the Germans and fight on the American side. We have heard these men say many things in the last two years. Do you think anyone will believe them now?"

A Jewish doctor said, "It will not make much difference to me. I welcomed your arrival and tried to help you. Now you are here, I am still not allowed to practice my profession. And the same men who prevented me and forced me to become a day laborer remain in power with the permission of the Americans."

A French Army officer said, "These are the same men who surrendered. You will find the fascists will still hold control of the Army. Beware. One day they may try to use it against you."

A hotel barman said, "They have tricked you. When you entered Algiers, you held it in the palm of your hand. It seems to me the Americans are not very good at politics. Why did you do it?"

The first fruits of our collaboration with Darlan were not hopeful. Jean Darlan had made his way to the top of his profession without ever once commanding a French fighting ship. He played up to politicians and superiors of every category, provided they could help him. I am convinced that he knew of our impending invasion. That was the reason he had gone to North Africa in the first place. He knew, since the entry of the United States into the war, that the dream Hitler had held out to him—the job of being admiral of a combined European navy in a Europe organized and governed by Germany—was becoming less and less of a reality.

After a tour of Africa from Dakar to Morocco to Algiers, he returned to Vichy, talked with Pétain, and gave an interview to a German journalist in which he spoke of Dakar's solidity against any possible attack. But behind him in Algiers, he left his personal staff, and his chief assistant, Admiral Penard, sent him a cable saying that the condition of his son, whom he had left ill with infantile paralysis in Algiers, necessitated his return.

Darlan then destroyed some of his confidential papers and left France secretly, without telling anyone except possibly Pétain. He arrived secretly in Algiers two or three days before our landings—and only five days after he had departed from that city for France in a blaze of publicity.

It all makes sense if you believe that Darlan suddenly discovered the approximate date of the landings. He certainly had entered some kind of negotiations with the Allies through Murphy during the previous month. Darlan was a man who definitely wanted to be on the side of the big battalions. He was willing to make any sort of political pirouette, provided that in the end Jean Darlan came out on top.

One of his early moves after he had tricked the Americans into agreeing to hand over control of the land to him is explicable only if we assume that Darlan hedged every bet that he ever made. After the first day he learned that the battalions on the Allied side were not so large as he had supposed. It may be that he still thought it possible that the Germans would win the war, and he wanted to keep his record of Axis collaboration to the end.

His orders were, to say the least, conflicting. At six-thirty on the evening on Sunday, November 8, Darlan ordered General Alphonse Juin, commander of the Algerian forces, to sign a truce with the American General Ryder. This was nearly five days before the "deal with Darlan" was made on the thirteenth.

But early the next morning Darlan received a cable from Admiral Esteva, the resident general in Tunisia. Esteva had been told by local German officials that they were going to bring German forces by plane to the Tunisian airfields to help defend the area from the Allies. Esteva had sufficient French forces to prevent this—at least for the crucial number of days that the Allied forces would require to move into Tunis and Bizerte. Esteva wavered like a leaf in a storm and besought Darlan for instructions.

Early on the afternoon of November 9, then, Darlan, who had already agreed to the truce in Algeria and was negotiating with Murphy for his future supremacy in a North Africa controlled by the Allies, sent the following message to Admiral Esteva and the Army, Navy, and Air Force commanders in Tunisia: "The Americans, having been the first to invade the soil of Africa, are our enemies, and we must fight them, alone or with outside help."

Under these instructions from Darlan, Esteva welcomed the Germans. The airfields were undefended. The Army commander, unwilling to oppose the orders of Esteva directly, pulled his troops

124

off into western Algeria, whence most of them eventually made their way to join the Allies in Algeria.

There might have been some shadow of excuse for the "deal with Darlan" if by making it, the Allies had with the aid of the Vichy authorities in Tunisia been able to seize the area and strengthen it against the first weak German detachments of troops. But to raise him to power after he had explicitly told Esteva to fight the Americans and accept German aid was something like rewarding a man who already has his knife in your back. It may be fair to say, however, that none of the Allies at that moment probably knew the depths of Darlan's treachery, for the text of the telegram Darlan had sent to Esteva was not generally known until months afterward. The incident affords food for speculation on whether President Roosevelt and Prime Minister Churchill would have been so approving of the outcome of the Darlan-Murphy negotiations if they had known of the admiral's orders to Esteva.

On November 18 Major Kenneth Clark, then chief public relations officer at Allied Force Headquarters, pending the arrival of Lieutenant Colonel Joseph Phillips with Eisenhower from Gibraltar, received a message from the Army in Washington to the effect that MacVane, NBC, was to prepare the *Army Hour* broadcast for the following Sunday. The message gave the times for beginning and ending the broadcast—a whole hour broadcast from Algiers.

I had done half hour broadcasts in my career, but to write, direct, and produce a whole hour program on only four days' notice was a task to test the mettle of the most confident of radio correspondents.

Major Ken Clark and I were immediately in the midst of a furious endeavor. I wanted to give a cross section of all the experiences of the fighting men.

First we had to find the right people, interview them, write scripts, and have the scripts censored and fitted into the overall program. Messages from the chief commanders had to be obtained. Then there was the music. No self-respecting program could be broadcast without music. We raked up some American GIs who could play jazz, organized them into an orchestra, and started them practicing. But at that time the American songwriters' association, ASCAP, was feuding with the networks, and we were not allowed to play any numbers which were not in the public domain. So I had to make sure my GI orchestra played only songs of this category. And I had them learn "God Save the King," "The Star-Spangled Banner," and the "Marseillaise" for a grand finale.

Came the fateful night, eight o'clock or thereabouts, and all fifty of the participants had been successfully assembled, with the right scripts in their hands, in the studio of Radio Algiers, by special order of the commanding general.

Half an hour before we were due on the air, the transmitter was shut down. Frantic calls on the rickety telephone discovered the reason—enemy planes approaching Algiers. The sirens wailed, and we heard the thump of guns and bombs. Luckily I had Captain Jack Beardwood, General Clark's aide, in the studio with me. He was able to obtain orders that the transmitter should be kept on the air, and five minutes or so before the broadcast it was reopened.

I heaved a sigh of relief. The timing was to be done by my wrist-watch, which I had checked a little earlier in the day, but I had no idea how it would all work out in practice. I had typed cue sheets for the army radio engineer, Lieutenant Charles Kibling, who was riding the gain—that is he was in charge of the amplifier—and handling what recorded music we were to use. I had arranged hand signals with the orchestra and with the other participants and had a public relations officer responsible for bringing in each spokesman or group of spokesmen in response to my signal.

At 8:31 I waved my hand, and we began broadcasting a minute of French martial music—the recorded trumpets of the Tirailleurs. As the music faded down, I began:

"This is Algiers—the heart of French North Africa. That music you just heard was the march of the Fifth Regiment of Algerian Tirailleurs—one of the famous French African regiments. Tirailleurs fought in the Battle of France. They are looking forward to fighting again beside the Allies against the Germans.

"Allied troops are in Algiers now. Men from California, Kansas, and Maine. Men from Lancashire, Inverness, and Devon. Hundreds of miles to our east and west, tanks, ships, planes, and guns are on the move . . . to sweep the Germans from North Africa—to finish what Alexander's Eighth Army in Libya began.

"But these boys from our farms and our cities know that the fighting they have done and are doing is just the preliminary—just the last chance to build a combat-hardened army that can thrust into Europe and beat the Axis armies man for man.

"Algiers is the nerve center for this army of French North Africa. Shuttling in and out of its port come great gray transports and

126

warships bristling with guns. Overhead go the squadrons of bombers, off to rip the Germans in Tunisia—sleek fighters soaring to protect a convoy or hunt for enemy bombers. Through Algiers streets rumble tanks made in Detroit and Birmingham—and above the rumble, you will hear the words of half a dozen languages and fifty dialects.

"For this is Africa—and in the streets, you can see the flowing robes of desert Arabs, red fezzes, Bedouins, Berbers, aged Jews in beards and robes rubbing shoulders with officers in kilts, women who might have come from the rue de la Paix—and farm boys from Iowa.

"This is Africa. And this Algiers—this white jewel of a city sprawling in tier after tier from the blue Mediterranean up the sunny hill slope—has known the Phoenicians when the Carthaginian Empire challenged the Roman power. It has known the Vandals from the north. From this blue port, the Barbary Coast pirates used to harry the shipping of most of the civilized world.

"War has come often to Algiers. German bombs have swished down on it these last few nights, and the city has been shaken by hundreds of antiaircraft guns cascading their fire over the bay. But war is not new to Algiers. The Caesars fought in North Africa. Belisarius came this way. The fighting henchmen of the sultans of the Ottoman Empire fought over this strip of green coast, and the French came here with their warships and their guns.

"Behind us lie green fields. And behind them loom the mountains —the mountains of Zab, the mountains of the Ouled-Naïl, the mountains of the Ksours—and behind those mountains is the desert—the Sahara.

"It is night in Algiers. At night Europeans don't go to the Kasbah. For Algiers is really two cities. One might be any city of Europe. The other is the Kasbah—as aged and mysterious as time itself. Twisting miles of streets so narrow that three people might not be able to walk abreast. Shuttered windows. Faces that are always veiled by day. Dirt—squalor. By night you can drive through without seeing a hint of the life behind the high walls and the barred doors—life that has been the same for hundreds of years without change, without a note of interest in the changing life of the European city beneath.

"Europeans don't go there at night. Too many have gone—and disappeared in the twisting warren of streets. But if you were to go tonight, if you could hammer at one of the closed doors and the eyes looking through the slit saw you were a friend, you might find out that inside is life, and hope and love and death. You might, if you were lucky, hear music, and this is the kind of music you might hear, an Arab girl singing a love long to an ancient tune of the desert."

(At this point the Arab song came up for a minute, then faded, and I continued.)

"That is the music of Algiers—of the country that remains the same whether the men in the streets of the European quarter are singing 'Madelon' or 'Tipperary' as they march along.

"For most of the American boys who have heard that music, this strip of French North Africa was the first real fighting they've ever done. They fought well. Some of them died here—because they believed that the rest of the world should have some of the things we Americans take for granted: the right to live, speak, bring up your families as free men in a free country.

"These Americans and these British died also because some French officers could not decide where their duty lay. They had put their trust in men who were tired and old, and when you are tired and old, you do not want to go on fighting anymore. You want to forget and pretend that things are the same as when you were a young man.

"So they gave the orders. Some officers obeyed. And a few of ours were killed, and a few of theirs.

"The old men who gave the orders had lost hope that things would ever be any better. And a few of the younger men had grown old before their time. They had lost hope, too, and all they wanted to do was to help the men who had kicked them down and trampled on them. That was why we lost a few and they lost a few.

"But the men who died and the men who are here tonight have not lost hope. This world can still be made into a good world. Tonight I am going to have you meet some of the young men—and even the older men—who have not lost the belief that this war can make things better, not only for us Americans and us British but for all the nations of the world.

"They are good fighting men. Some of them are sunburned already with the desert wind. They will tell you their stories—and the best thing is that the stories are true."

At this point came Sergeants Charles Bowman and Joseph West, a Yorkshireman and a Londoner, telling how they filmed the American landings east of Algiers and everything that happened. Following them came three Americans from Iowa, Staff Sergeant Paul

128

Tweedy of Unionville, Corporal Dewey Heaberlin of Knoxville, and PFC Keith Shepherd of Atlantic. They told of the landings—how they were welcomed in some places, shot at in others, how they surrounded the city of Algiers, captured the German consul, and marched in next morning after the armistice was signed. Next came the story of an American sailor on the only transport that was torpedoed in the invasion.

At this point the GI orchestra, the Yankee Doodlers, broke in with "Deep in the Heart of Texas" and other traditional American tunes.

A French reserve officer, Lieutenant Maurice Pallet of the Tirailleurs, gave a rousing message on the willingness of French Africans to fight by our side up to the resurrection of France and all the world. Then RAF and U.S. Air Force officers told their part of the grand story.

Wing Commander Tommy Wisdom, a famous racing driver in peacetime, read a message for Air Marshal Welsh, the Air Force commander. A staff officer of General Anderson did the same, and Jack Beardwood read a message from Clark, praising all the forces and promising we would keep on the offensive until we had the Axis licked.

We wound up all standing at attention while the three national anthems were played.

It seemed a huge success, with everything clicking in right on time. Afterward Lieutenant Kibling, veteran New York radio engineer, said to me, "I've heard some good programs in my day, but I'm sure that's the best broadcast I ever helped put on the air."

French reporters had been watching, and the following week one of the papers, a weekly called *Jeunesse Algérienne*, turned over its entire front page to the event. The top of the paper's eight columns gave an account of the atmosphere in the studio, followed by the chief features of the broadcast. There was a big picture of me interviewing Air Force Major Robert Coulter of La Grange, Illinois. Banner headlines said: "In the Midst of the Air Raid—Sunday Night on the Antenna of Radio Algiers—the American Army Spoke Across the Atlantic to Forty Million Listeners." It was a wonderful account, except for the fact that it had overestimated our audience by exactly 39,999,999 people.

Two days after the broadcast Major Ken Clark came to me, a telegram from NBC in his hand. His face looked as though he had lost his last friend.

The wire read something like this: WHY DID YOU FAIL UPCOME SUNDAY WITH FIVE-MINUTE BROADCAST REQUESTED FOR ARMY HOUR. HAD TO FILL FROM HERE. NO TRANSMISSION AT SCHEDULED TIME RE-CEIVED ON RADIO ALGIERS FREQUENCY.

I felt like bursting into tears.

"I investigated," Clark said, "and we got a correction to last week's original telegram asking for the whole hour to be filled. Evidently it was garbled in transmission. They wanted only five minutes."

"And we broke our backs filling a whole hour," I said. "But why didn't they get anything?"

"It appears," Clark went on, "that when the air raid caused the transmitter to be turned off, the engineers here had instructions to come back with a different frequency—in order to fool the Germans. The engineers seem to have fooled the engineers in New York and London as well. Someone must have neglected to give New York the changed frequency, and when we didn't come up on the old one, they couldn't find us."

So all our work had gone for naught—but not quite for naught. Wing Commander Tommy Wisdom of the RAF came up with his face beaming. "The pilot of one of our Spitfires heard our program quite by chance while he was flying a night patrol," Tommy said. "He congratulated me and said he heard the whole thing and it was one of the best programs he had ever listened to."

It should have been. The British and American forces plus J. MacVane and a cast of fifty had combined to put an hour's program on the air for the edification of one British Spitfire pilot. At least, it was nice to know he had liked it. With publicity, the American Army would have appeared ridiculous. And I as well. But we kept the failure a dark secret.

Chapter 12

The political censorship had drawn a curtain of obscurity over political developments in North Africa at that time. I saw General Eisenhower quite often and, like other correspondents, complained to him now and then about the restrictions on our reporting. He was usually sympathetic, and sometimes a corner of the curtain would be lifted, and we could say something about what was happening. But I do not think that he understood our preoccupation with such matters. For him, the fighting in Tunisia, the multitude of uncertainties in the battles to come, blotted out all other interests. When we told him of some new instance of Vichy policy which was affecting the spirits of patriotic North Africans, he was quick to anger and would often order one of his aides to take up the subject immediately with the French.

Yet it took a great deal of pushing by the Americans to get Darlan eventually to release most of the prisoners in desert work camps who had been sent there because of their activity against Vichy or the Axis or their supposed sympathies with De Gaulle or communist Russia.

None of the correspondents held General Eisenhower personally responsible for the rise of Darlan to power or for his abuse of that power. But the general took responsibility as commander in chief for everything his underlings did. He was almost fanatically determined to build and retain the team spirit in the whole military operation.

Our own Army's development had been more on French than on British lines. Some of the top American officers had been to France's École Supérieure de Guerre or to one of the other French war colleges, but few had had any real experience with the British Army. The British officers irritated some of the more rough-cut among our military diamonds, and the fact that the British were in the vast majority in the early days in North Africa and that our battalions, tank platoons, and companies were fed into the battle piecemeal under British command was anathema to our generals, who wanted to get their divisions into the fight as divisions and saw no future for themselves in simply supplying driblets of Americans to the British. Only Eisenhower's spirit and prestige kept the team working as a team, and I used to hear the general say, "If one of my officers gets angry and calls another officer a son of a bitch, that's one thing. But the first officer who calls another officer a 'BRITISH' son of a bitch goes out of this theater on the first boat for home."

My broadcast texts of that period are slashed by the censors of their political content. For instance, I note that on November 25, after first having had the comment censored, I was allowed to say that local authorities had issued an order that Jewish noncommissioned officers and men were to be called up and allowed to fight in the French Army although they had not had that privilege for some time. The censor blue-penciled the news that the PSF, a right-wing party formerly known as the Croix de Feu, had issued an appeal stating that 40 million Frenchmen awaited liberation. Also censored was the news that the proclamation called Darlan "the depository of the thought of Pétain" and ended with the words "Long live Marshal Pétain, long live Admiral Darlan, long live France."

When we made the "deal with Darlan," the chief argument used by the proponents of the idea was that at the right moment Darlan would give the word and our navies would be joined by the French Navy, most of the ships of which were moored in Toulon, Alexandria, or Martinique.

Now the Germans, having occupied the formerly unoccupied area of France, sought to take over the French fleet in Toulon. Soon after we had landed in North Africa, a few of the Toulon ships had started out of the harbor to join the Allied fleets, but they had been recalled. The fleet still had a chance to quit the harbor and make a dash for freedom against German shore guns. Some would have been lost, but we still might have obtained the services of many. Instead, the chief French naval officials took the way of defeatism. They scuttled the ships in the harbor, and the flower of the French fleet went down without firing a shot for France's freedom. Only a few vessels under courageous commanders ran the gauntlet and escaped to North Africa, against the orders of their superiors, but they were chiefly small vessels, submarines, and a destroyer or two.

The loss of the fleet robbed Darlan of any real importance he could conceivably have had. Darlan with the French fleet was somebody. Darlan without the fleet had little or no value. It was another of the anomalies of the situation that only at that moment did Darlan seem to become angry with the Germans. He issued a procla-

132

mation stating that the occupation of all France, the arrest by the Germans of General Weygand, and the disarmament of the Vichy armed forces revealed that Germany aimed to destroy France. Darlan assured the public that he would have no pity for those Frenchmen who were helping the Axis. It was all very fiery, as fiery as the statements De Gaulle himself had been issuing for two and a half years, but it was late—too late. To many it seemed a pity that Darlan had not felt the same way in June 1940 and had then ordered his fleet to join the Allies.

During these first weeks I had made many attempts to tell how Darlan was strengthening his political rule of North Africa. But inevitably I was defeated by the political censorship. As far as the outside world knew, we had made only a military agreement with Darlan and his job remained a military post pure and simple.

At last the censorship allowed one of my political stories, an account of what had actually appeared in Algiers papers, to reach the air. The result was a wave of indignation in both Britain and the United States.

The broadcast, made on December 3, said:

"New details are made public today of the way in which Admiral Darlan is strengthening his grip on French North Africa.

"A decree published today makes it clear that the arrangement between the former Vichyite and the American authorities goes beyond the temporary military arrangement that was first envisaged.

"Darlan announces that he is assuming the prerogatives of a chief of state. He is at the same time commander in chief of the Army, the Navy, and the Air Force and representative of political power. He takes over control of the legal powers in North Africa of the French government.

"To observers here it seems important that the American public should realize that our representatives here are apparently backing Darlan when he announces that he is the depository of French sovereignty. In other words, we are tacitly saying Darlan represents France.

"Today's Algerian papers all publish several pictures of Darlan at yesterday's Allied ceremony in Algiers. He is shown between General Eisenhower and Admiral [Sir Andrew] Cunningham. He is shown saluting. He is shown with French generals.

"Today's proclamation makes it clear that Darlan will continue to control press and censorship here. The local papers never did mention President Roosevelt's comments on the Darlan arrangement. And Mr. Churchill's references the other day to Vichy and General De Gaulle never appeared here.

"As far as is apparent on the surface, the American occupation made hardly a ripple in the control of civil and military affairs in North Africa. The same people that ran the show for Vichy are still flourishing. This still seems puzzling to a good many people of various nationalities.

"The latest Frenchman to jump on the bandwagon is Marcel Peyrouton. Monsieur Peyrouton was a Vichy minister at one time. He was tireless in his activities against those who favored an Allied victory. About the most favorable thing that can be checked up to his credit is that Laval didn't like him. When Laval came in, Peyrouton got out to South America. Today the High Commissariat for French North Africa announced that Monsieur Peyrouton has put himself at the disposition of Admiral Darlan."

This broadcast seemed harmless at the time to me, knowing what was going on, as it seems harmless years later. But the impact on the outside world was, in Hollywood language, terrific. It was the first hint to reach Britain and the United States of the trend of political affairs in Africa.

The BBC picked up my broadcast and put it on all its services. BBC officials had known my work for several years, and they knew that I was reliable, cautious and accurate. The London *Times* reprinted the full broadcast on its chief news page. Other British papers did the same.

The State Department in Washington complained to the Foreign Office in London because the semiofficial BBC had rebroadcast the accounts of "irresponsible American commentators in North Africa."

In Algiers, at Allied Force Headquarters, General Eisenhower, worried about the war, had to explain that Darlan's decree published under banner headlines in all Algerian papers must have been a ghastly mistake. The Americans, said General Eisenhower, had never imagined that Darlan was trying to assume such sweeping political powers. But the report I made was never denied, nor could it have been denied, for it was the truth.

It was about this time in the war that I began to use the words "United Nations," and other correspondents began to think in these terms. The President and Prime Minister Churchill had given us the lead, and agreed that something more than the World War I word "Allies" was required. "Allies" meant nothing but a tem-

134

porary union for a battle or a war. We needed a new term that would explain the feeling in the hearts of so many men of so many countries that the world would have to get together and be united —in peace as well as in war.

The League of Nations had died with its refusal to take action against Mussolini's invasion of Ethiopia and the failure to oppose the German-Italian-Franco attack on the Republican Government of Spain.

I had been a correspondent in Paris when the League of Nations had held its last meeting in Geneva and solemnly expelled Soviet Russia for the attack on Finland. Because of the failure to act against Italy and against Franco Spain, this gesture no longer had any significance. In fact, it was the death rattle of the League, for by that time the world knew that nothing the League did had the backing of the Great Powers, and the Great Powers no longer believed in it.

Nonetheless, by late 1942 those of us who wrote about foreign affairs were thinking continually of the United Nations. I had met too many people from other countries whom I liked and respected ever again to think of the United States as being the only country of major importance to the world. Certainly I was American through and through, and my own country was the first in my heart; but I felt equally at home with many Britons and many Frenchmen. There were men of really good will in every land, and if I were any kind of reporter, I should be able to understand them and their problems.

There was such a thing as a common front against tyranny—a common front among all people against oppression. A human being, whatever his language and his training, was still a human being, with whom an intelligent, sensitive person of another land could get along very well indeed.

But the most important factor in one's thinking about the United Nations was the fact that each country, each person had something different to offer to the common whole. Each nation could be insulted by a particular slight quicker than any other. And in every country there were the influences that opposed all ties that brought their own and other countries closer together. It became a question of whether the differences or the similarities were to win out in the end. For me, in spite of such powerful relics as Mr. McCormick of the Chicago *Tribune* and Mr. Hearst of the Hearst papers, I had no doubt about what influences would in the end become triumphant. I remembered Anne Lindbergh, writing about the wave of the future, as a good wife catering to her husband's admiration of Hitler and Göring, but I thought the wave of the future was not with those who would stifle human beings, but rather with those who believed that there was much in all of us, whatever our countries, that was good and worthy of high regard, and the quicker all of us knew that, the better.

It was because of such thinking as this that I opposed the official line of the United States in North Africa, feeling that I was completely right and that as an American I had the right and duty to speak out against the finagling of our diplomats who were defying our traditional sense of right and wrong. I felt that I had behind me the weight of the people of America and that it was greater than anything those who had arranged the "deal with Darlan" could muster up.

A few days before leaving London for North Africa, I had had dinner in the little Petit Club Français just off St. James's Street with Paul Siriex, my close French friend who later became boss of Madagascar; Paddy Willis of the London *Evening Standard*; and two young French correspondents who had just escaped from North Africa via Tangier, Spain, and Gibraltar. Before the war they had been London correspondents for the chief Paris afternoon paper, *Paris Soir*. Their names were Pierre Gosset and Adelbert de Segonzac. We had a fine evening in the little club, and the two French journalists were able to give me a complete story of conditions in North Africa.

Judge my surprise then when, on my arrival in Algiers, I met a young woman who told me that her name was Renée Gosset and her husband was a journalist. I was able to send word immediately to England that Renée and the two children were well and also to tell Renée that I had seen her husband with De Segonzac only three weeks before.

That done, I considered that my duty had been accomplished. But I was to see a great deal more of Mme. Gosset. Every time two or three correspondents gathered together in one of the Algiers cocktail lounges, the Café de Paris, for instance, Renée would shortly appear. It was not that we minded buying her a drink, but her interest was so specific that I shortly began to wonder whether or not she was an intelligence agent for Vichy, sent to check on the small talk of the American correspondents. Although I had the impression that she understood a good deal, she apparently did not speak much English, and when there were a group of us, Stoneman, say, H. R. Knickerbocker, Collingwood, and I who could understand French, it was boring for us to switch to that language whenever Renée Gosset sooner or later appeared and started asking questions: What did we think of this or that? Whenever the U.S. information people, men like Peter Tompkins or Edmond Taylor arrived, Mme. Gosset would be trailing them.

It was only months later, when I read her book *Algiers 1941–1943*, published by Jonathan Cape in England, that I realized she was one of the most astute of French journalists, for every word we said made up part of her total description of the events of that era. It is probably the definitive book on the political happenings of that time, well worth the study of future Ph.D.s in history.

Renée asked me to write my impressions of the French political scene for her paper, an Algiers weekly called *TAM*.

I said, "Renée, your editor won't like what I am going to write because I am going to be frank."

Renée said, "Write it anyway, and we will print it."

Renée says in her book that I warned her "with a cunning smile" that if a single word in the article were changed, I would forbid its publication.

I wrote the article with one eye on the French censorship, knowing that no Algiers paper could mention the name De Gaulle. I recalled Lucy's and my impressions of the fall of France and how we correspondents all knew of Pétain as a defeatist. I spoke of the handful of French soldiers and sailors who had decorated the Foch statue in London on July 14, 1940. I spoke of my interviews with a French leader in London, without mentioning the name of the general. I recalled French youths who had come to London to fight, after escaping from France in little sports planes. I explained how I had put many of these Frenchmen on the network to America. I told of Oscar Coen of the Eagle Squadron without mentioning his name, of how he had shot up a German munitions train and the explosion had wrecked his plane so that he had had to parachute into France. Oscar had gone to the nearest farm, and when a woman opened the door he had said, "Eat. Eat," pointing to his mouth. The first thing, so I said, Oscar had seen on the wall was a "familiar face," and at that moment knew he was among friends.

It did not need long explanation to impart to North Africans the fact that the "familiar face" was De Gaulle's. I gave some more impressions of Free France at war—Joseph Pierre Koenig at Bir Hakeim and the *mot de Cambronne*, leaders of the Socialist and the PSF parties who had spoken on my microphone in London to America telling our people that France was united behind De Gaulle. But of course, I did not mention the awful name.

In her book, Renée Gosset said this:

> In a hundred and fifty lines, cleverly worded, without once mentioning Fighting France or General de Gaulle by name, he justified the Gaullist movement.
>
> I translated the article. *TAM* accepted it. The American censors—Rehm and Walberg—let it pass with a smile and their blessing. But the French censor almost had an apopleptic fit: "Gaullism in Algiers! Unthinkable! There can be no question of it. . . ."
>
> There was so clearly a question of it that the Office of War Information firmly intervened.
>
> "That is an excellent article. In any case, we cannot allow an American journalist to be supervised by you."
>
> "But it is for a French paper, sir."
>
> "That, sir, is possible, but the author of the article is an American."
>
> Finally, thoroughly nettled, the American censors demanded that the article be printed. They sought decision at the Hôtel Saint-Georges, but there nobody wanted to take the responsibility of settling so scandalous a question. Step by step, General Eisenhower's own Headquarters was reached. By midnight, the unfortunate article at last reached the printers, without any modifications, having won the personal approval of the Commander-in-Chief of the Allied Armies.
>
> And so the first article of Gaullist propaganda to appear officially in North Africa was written by an American journalist, covered by American censorship and imposed by the American High Command, all maliciously united in a kind of joint front against Mr. Murphy, whose anti-Gaullist feelings were well known.

I must say, to temper Mme. Gosset's account, that although I disagreed sharply with Murphy's policy or rather the policy I blamed him for at that time, we were personally on very friendly first-name terms and lunched or dined together every now and then.

I might note also that the British diplomats of that time and place had high respect and regard for his ability. I did not appreciate then that his job was to carry out the policy of President Roosevelt, and as a good career diplomat, a soldier of diplomacy, in fact, he carried out his orders to the utmost of his great capabilities. I never wrote anything against the policy that I had not already expressed to him personally. I once gave a dinner in his honor, a dinner for twenty-four of the top correspondents and officers of three countries with the charming white-haired actress Françoise Rosay and some of the French ladies of Algiers, and it was a pleasure to see how easily he charmed everyone at the table with the warmth of his personality.

The communications in the early weeks were incredibly difficult. It took an average of five days for the dispatches of press correspondents at the Tunisian front to reach Allied Force Headquarters in Algiers and perhaps another day or two for their retransmission to London. Cabled service messages to London usually took several days. We had no means of two-way communication. That is, we could not talk to London or New York to make arrangements but had to send our broadcasts off, never knowing what frequency they were going out on and whether anyone at the other end was tuned into that particular frequency. Another difficulty was with the Army. The signal communications were overburdened, and sometimes when the army engineers broke their regular code transmissions of military traffic to allow us to broadcast, they would find it impossible to get the army transmissions going again for several hours.

At least, in Algiers, we could get all the available news. The correspondents were briefed twice daily by military spokesmen, who described what was happening at the front from the reports from the British First Army. It was at these briefings that the communiqués were also issued. It was one of the sights of the times to see Donald Coe of the United Press, later the dignified director of special events of the American Broadcasting Company, racing Wes Gallagher of the Associated Press, who later as general manager directed all of AP's foreign and domestic operations, and Bob Nixon of the International News Service across the press room to be first at the cable with the communiqués. Eventually the mad scramble ceased when someone thought up the idea of simply putting the communiqué on the cable addressed to all three agencies in turn.

I had been anxious to get to Tunisia with some recording equipment; but weeks went by, and the promised recording equipment

MacVane broadcasting for Allied Force Headquarters in Algiers.

did not arrive. There was nothing to do but wait and view the war from Algiers.

One incident of the early days bore out the old saw about its being a "small world after all." My last night in Tours, during the trek to Bordeaux, I had spent on the grounds of the Château de Cande. It was owned by Charles Bedaux, a Franco-American industrialist, and it was there that the Duke and Duchess of Windsor had been married.

During an air raid I was standing with some other correspondents on a balcony of the Hôtel Aletti in Algiers overlooking the harbor, watching the fountains of antiaircraft fire from the hills and the ships in the harbor as the German bombers made the run from inland down over the shipping. I fell into conversation with a man on the next balcony who spoke with a French accent and invited him to join us for a drink. He showed up with a younger man, his son, and told us he was Charles Bedaux.

At that moment a British lieutenant and a couple of armed soldiers opened the door and demanded to know who had been signaling with flashlights from the next balcony, now empty. Bedaux explained it must have been matches lit for cigarettes and called on us to prove he had not been involved.

A few days later Bedaux was arrested on a charge of espionage. I tried to break the news every few days, but it was not made public for many months. Washington finally released it, and shortly thereafter Bedaux committed suicide on his way to the United States, where he was to be examined and tried.

Chapter 13

Darlan had to die. There was no doubt about that. Alive, he signified that element in the French soul which had surrendered itself to Hitler, and his existence could no longer be borne after France began to purge itself of defeatism. The only question was: Who would perform the deed?

Darlan must have known that sooner or later he would be doomed. Perhaps it was better that he die at the hand of a fellow Frenchman who believed that Darlan's death would help make France new and great with a rebirth of its twenty centuries of history rather than, like Laval, before a firing squad at dawn, or like Pétain, the victor of Verdun, of old age in prison, his name an execration.

I thought when I met Darlan in his villa, high above Algiers, on December 15, that he was an unhappy man. He received about twenty-five of the Allied correspondents. We had seen him many times at public ceremonies, but this was the only time we were to be near enough to talk to him. He was dressed in a brown civilian suit and tie, a short man who looked surprisingly like the cartoons that David Low used to draw of him.

He began by reading us a statement saying in effect that those Frenchmen who had worked for an Allied victory in North Africa had been forgiven and reinstated in their official positions. The statement was translated sentence by sentence by Colonel Joe Phillips. Darlan renounced personal ambition and said that he hoped that after France was free, the French people would select their own leaders.

I had drawn up some questions which I wanted to present to him, but it was announced that everything but the statement would be off the record, so I stuffed the question sheet into my pocket. One journalist did ask Darlan bluntly why he had collaborated with Germany. He said collaboration had been imposed on him by force, that the Germans had had him by the throat.

I am afraid that nobody believed him. Too many pro-Allied

people in North Africa still remained in desert work camps, and his readiness to help the Germans—at the expense of Britain—had been too apparent to the world for his words to ring true.

He was affable to us, but when I chatted with him over the appetizers and champagne, his small blue eyes looked incredibly sad, as though he were convinced that no matter what he did from that time on, nobody would believe him sincere. He had followed one road too long to turn suddenly and take another, too long even for such a master of the art of tracing the correct way through the labyrinth of success.

On December 21 I saw Darlan again at a reception for the Arab notables of Algeria at the Hôtel Aletti. The Arabs, chiefs of tribes and big landowners, were dressed in magnificent flowing robes of many colors. When Darlan left the hotel with them, it was between lines of Zouave troops in scarlet and gray. The crowd waiting outside the hotel to see the show evidenced no feeling of any kind. There were no cheers and no boos, only a kind of watchful silence.

Three days later Darlan was dead, shot to death in his own office.

To understand the deed, we must recall something of the political background, for the act of violence was a true expression of a situation which had been so intensified by the failure of President Roosevelt and Prime Minister Churchill to act in accordance with political reality that pressures built up and built up until they burst forth in the revolver shots that killed the admiral. Given these political pressures and the personalities involved, someone was going to kill Darlan. In fact, correspondents had jokingly referred to the possibility. The only real question was who was to do the deed. Was it to be a communist? Twenty-seven French communist deputies were still in an Algerian jail and had been there since 1939. Was it to be a Gaullist, a patriotic Frenchman disgusted with Darlan's past and present? There was good cause. Was it to be someone nonpolitical, a relative perhaps of some Frenchman in Dachau or Buchenwald who blamed Darlan? Was it to be a fascist Frenchman who considered Darlan a traitor to the Germans or to Pétain? Was it to be an Arab nationalist? A Jew reacting against the racial laws which Darlan still upheld? An official who thought him responsible for France's loss of the French fleet? All these were possibilities. But no one thought of the French monarchists.

In fact, the assassination of Darlan was a "last chance" effort of that element in the French body politic which hoped to see the restoration of order in French society and French politics through

General Giraud, President Roosevelt, General de Gaulle and Prime Minister Churchill confer at Casablanca, Morocco. U.S. ARMY.

the coming to power of the heir of the kings who had ruled France for 1,000 years.

It should not be forgotten that in the years before World War II the monarchist cause had attracted some of France's best minds and purest patriots. A group of young monarchists calling themselves the Camelots du Roi were the moving spirit of the thousands of rioters who tried to attack the Chamber of Deputies in Paris on February 6, 1934. Later young monarchists were among the group that formed the Secret Committees for Revolutionary Action, the Cagoulards or Hooded Men. Their thought, to describe it briefly, was that the republican governments having weakened France by their political maneuvering, the way to restore a strong France was to cut off the rotten parliamentary system and replace it with the monarchy. The royalists were also very strongly represented in the party of Colonel de la Rocque called the PSF and known more familiarly as the Croix de Feu, Cross of Fire.

It was inevitable that these groups should be infiltrated by German agents, Fascist Italian agents, and native French thugs of all social classes so that, in fact, they became a powerful help to Hitler.

When France was occupied by the Germans, the royalists became sharply divided. Some collaborated actively with the Germans, welcoming the German occupation as a necessary means of France's purging itself to regain its own soul. Others simply followed Pétain to the end. Still others realized that the loss of France meant more than any political party or any theory of government; they were among those who fought hardest and took the greatest risks in the struggle for the liberation of France.

In French North Africa monarchy was even stronger than in France itself. Monarchists who had hated the Third Republic had preferred to emigrate to North Africa or serve in the Army's African campaigns rather than adapt themselves to the life of republican France. In army circles, high society, and diplomacy, it was considered smart to be monarchist.

Now many of the royalists were content to go along with the stream of history, hoping that someday France would recognize the value of having a king. But there were others who saw a chance to reinstate the monarchy by establishing it in North Africa, whence it could regain liberated France.

To most foreign students of France, the monarchists seemed to be entangling themselves in a daydream, but the hard core of the monarchists were, in fact, fanatic and dangerous because they moved in influential circles, were intelligent enough to influence others, and were completely ruthless in seeking their objective.

To me, the two most interesting of this group, among those whom I met, were a priest and an aristocrat, the Abbé Cordier and Henri d'Astier de la Vigerie.

The Abbé Cordier was one of those French priests who in time of war take the sword rather than the crucifix. Admiral d'Argenlieu of the Free French Navy, in peacetime the superior of the Carmelite order of monks, was another.

Father Cordier served as a lieutenant in the French Army intelligence branch, the Deuxième Bureau. The Deuxième Bureau, at the moment of the defeat, had begun to organize eventual action against the Germans, or rather some of its members had done so. The *abbé* was one of the officers engaged in the affair from the very beginning. After the fall of France he went to North Africa as a French intelligence officer. There he undertook the weaving of the strange tapestry which was meant to display the monarchy as an inextricable part of the freedom of France. His work was difficult, not only because of the Axis agents in North Africa, but because of the divided loyalties of officialdom, the Army, and even the Deuxième Bureau itself.

The *abbé* was not at all an ordinary man or an ordinary priest. It has been published that one day he learned one of his own agents had informed the authorities against him. Father Cordier, so goes the account, visited the erring member of his secret flock to inform him that he was about to die and that it behooved him to die well shriven.

The unhappy wretch had the grace to make his confession in good order, and the *abbé*, after hearing him and duly giving him assurance that his way into the hereafter was clear and straight, strangled him with his own scarf. The account says that the *abbé* thoughtfully arranged matters so that it would appear that his erstwhile agent had hanged himself on the lock of his window. Such a combination of priestly and military duties had perhaps been unsurpassed since the days of Cardinal Richelieu.

The aristocrat D'Astier could also have stepped out of the pages of Dumas. More of an Aramis than a D'Artagnan, but with elements of both, he came from an ancient family well known in both France and North Africa. For the D'Astiers, life had to be exciting. In another century, Henri would have been a great soldier of fortune, carving out a career with his sword and his intelligence. With his long, thin nose, his dark, glowing eyes, and his high forehead, he would not have looked out of place as another Cesare Borgia in Renaissance Italy.

Henri had two brothers. One, François, was a French Air Force general who had escaped from France only after our invasion of North Africa and had immediately joined General de Gaulle in London. The other was Emmanuel, a great figure in the French Resistance movement, who sought notoriety by going to quite opposite extremes politically. Emmanuel, as a Resistance leader, served briefly as minister of the interior in the French government after the liberation. His particular wave of the future, with which he sought to drown democracy, parliamentarianism, and the rights of man, was communism. It may be that he felt that communism was such an important part of French political life that a D'Astier should lead it. I do not know. At any rate, the D'Astiers were never dull.

Part of Henri's prestige in North Africa came from the fact that everyone in North Africa knew that his brother was an important figure in the Resistance inside France. How this knowledge escaped the notice of the Vichy and German authorities I have never been able to discover.

Henri admitted that he had been a Cagoulard. He had also volunteered at seventeen in the First World War and come out of it with the Légion d'Honneur and the Croix de Guerre.

These two men, Cordier and D'Astier, were generally regarded by those who delved deep enough as being chief among both the monarchists and the anti-Vichy Resistance leaders who had helped pave the way for the Allied invasion.

There were two other men who figured largely in the events of the first months. One was named Lemaigre-Dubreuil, an industrialist who had once been a Cagoulard, then had had the sense to break with the organization as being nothing more than a German stooge. Closely linked with him was a good-looking, dark-haired, somber-eyed young man named Jean Rigault, who was briefly editor of the *Jour-Echo de Paris* newspaper which Lemaigre-Dubreuil published for a short time after the fall of France. Then Lemaigre sent Rigault to North Africa on full salary and expenses to prepare the way for whatever was coming.

Lemaigre, a monarchist, had served as a captain on Giraud's staff during the Battle of France, and it was he whom Murphy sent to sound out Giraud first about the possibility of leading an Allied invasion of North Africa.

Robert Murphy and his diplomatic cohorts were in North Africa to help the Allies by any possible means. The monarchists got in touch with him. It was not difficult, for they moved in the same diplomatic and social circles. Murphy, as a matter of fact, was the center and sole connection between many of the Resistance groups that sprang up throughout North Africa. Even close friends or father and son could be members of the same group without knowing one another's connection with the Resistance.

All those I have mentioned understood the necessity of keeping in close touch with Murphy and, if possible, influencing him in decisions of vital importance. Certainly the idea of uniting North Africa and France under the pretender to the French throne, the affable Comte de Paris, had been suggested to the American. And Murphy is the sort of man who can make anyone talking to him believe that the ideas put forward are the most valid and interesting that he has ever heard. So D'Astier, Cordier, and Lemaigre could not be blamed for thinking that the American envoy would support in Washington the possibility of the Comte de Paris's becoming a kind of Allied high commissioner for North Africa.

The Count of Paris was anything but loath to consider the idea. His followers seem to have believed that once he had been established as high commissioner, working with the Allies, he could move into France at the time of the liberation and win election as president of France. And from the presidency to the throne was the way that one of France's former kings had taken.

The count, a dark-haired, dashing young man, who produced a multitude of children and was barred by law from French territory, had grown up in Belgium. His father, the Duc de Guise, had been a comfortable type of old man whose own ideas were democratic enough to infuriate his own followers. The duke was not the man to take chances, but his son was another type entirely. He wrote books verging on socialism, and I remember reading in the French papers just before the war the story of his illegal visit to France, where he received a group of journalists and dashed away before the police could catch up with him. When war broke out, he tried to join the French Army, and, when he was turned down, joined the French Foreign Legion under an assumed name. Although the authorities must have known his real identity, they turned a blind eye.

At the time of the fall of France, the count retired to his country houses in Spanish Morocco and French Morocco, which legally was not part of France. On at least one occasion he visited Vichy and talked with Pétain, Giraud, and even Laval. Now back in North Africa, he had many powerful friends in the Army and among the rich royalist colonials whose families had settled there a generation or two previously. He came often to Algiers before our invasion and, at the homes of some of the highest aristocracy of France, had met Murphy.

In the small group of men who discussed the invasion with General Clark when he landed from a submarine at Cherchel were at least three avowed royalists: D'Astier, Cordier, and Rigault. The Resistance groups comprised a complete cross section of Algerian society. But in the murky air of secrecy that enshrouded them, a man of positive character could become a leader of men who might have no idea of his essential political ideas. D'Astier was such a man, and in his particular group of patriots were included many who would have been shocked and horrified at the thought of royalism in France was one of the motives.

During the landings one group of young men under Lieutenant Pauphilet, a young Army officer, served as guard for Darlan and Juin. Members of this group suggested at one point during the night that shooting Darlan would solve everything neatly. Murphy was horrified and forbade them to touch even one of Darlan's white hairs. Strangely enough, one of the young men who wanted to shoot Darlan was a twenty-year-old named Bonnier de la Chapelle. Six weeks later he did so.

Young Bonnier was a member of the Chantiers de Jeunesse, a youth organization which was formed at the instigation of Vichy but which helped greatly in our landings, its officials ardently supporting the Allies. Some were Gaullists, some royalists, and the great majority were eager resisters. When Darlan addressed the Chantiers on December 20, Bonnier de la Chapelle was in the uniformed ranks before him.

D'Astier, that magnetic personality, was just the type of man to attract an ardent, idealistic twenty-year-old boy. Like his idol, Bonnier was a royalist. It is not inconceivable that through him Bonnier actually met the Count of Paris and dreamed of France's new greatness after the war under a modern-minded brave and wise monarch.

Bonnier, a Catholic, also knew the Abbé Cordier, Lieutenant Cordier who had helped lead the glorious seizure of the city of Algiers by the youngsters of the Chantiers and the others on the night of the landings. Bonnier must have admired the soldier priest, representing at the same time the unsheathed sword and the cross.

How often must he have heard these older, wiser men, men of such great influence, deplore the tarnish that Darlan had lent to France's glory! What could be done while Darlan lived and schemed against the best interests of his country, occupying the place that royalty should have taken? How often was the casual jest put to Bonnier, "And to think—on that night—you let him go"? How the remembrance must have burned the boy's soul—only a single shot on that night, and all would have been well. Only a shot—and Bonnier would have been responsible for placing his rightful king on the pathway leading to the throne of France.

None of those I talked with later knew young Bonnier well, but one got the impression of a thoughtful boy, quiet, idealistic, a good boy, one of those who in wartime so often take risks for a cause they believe is just.

When the comments of his elders flew back and forth, Bonnier may have asked, "What if somehow someone were to get rid of the admiral?"

One can imagine the answer: "Such a man would have the gratitude of his king and his country." And if it were D'Astier, the head of the Algerian police, who made such a remark, with a wealth of meaning in his lustrous dark eyes, could the boy be blamed for considering that an unspoken pact had been made, a chance offered to serve France and the king, if only one were brave and determined enough?

Bonnier de la Chapelle had some young friends as ardent as he was. He and three of these friends were said to have originally planned a joint action. They would get two cars and follow Darlan on one of his trips. Then, on some lonely road, one car would crash into Darlan's motorcycle outrider, and the second would draw up beside the admiral's limousine. The interior of Darlan's car would be sprayed with bursts from a tommy gun; then both cars would speed away, leaving Darlan and his companions dead.

But after anxious discussion the young men decided that such a scheme would involve too many people. They wanted to kill Darlan but not his innocent bodyguard or whoever happened to be accompanying Darlan in the car.

A new scheme was considered. They would draw lots. One of the four would do the deed alone. The others would sit in the car, waiting to help the escape. But if there were no escape possible, only one would have sacrificed his life, and the others would live to try in turn to achieve the death of the admiral.

Chance gave the honor of the first day to Bonnier. The preparations showed that someone in official power was helping Bonnier and, in advance, trying to throw an investigation off the scent of the monarchists.

An official circular was sent to various branches of the police warning that Gaullists were going to try to assassinate Admiral Darlan on December 24.

Bonnier obtained from the Abbé Cordier, it was reported later, a false identity card, made out in the name of Morand. On the twenty-third, Bonnier went to his friend and confidant Lieutenant Abbé Cordier, made his confession, and asked absolution in advance for what he was about to do. He also needed a car, not easy to come by in Algiers in those days, and obtained a black Peugeot which D'Astier sometimes used.

On the morning of December 24, Bonnier de la Chapelle went to Darlan's office in the Palais d'Été, high up the steep, winding rue Michelet on the heights above the city. He waited for most of the morning; but Darlan was out, and a secretary told him to come back in the afternoon.

That afternoon the black car, with four men in it, stopped by the church near the *palais*. One got out. The car parked by the sidewalk. Bonnier spent some time in the church, then walked into the *palais*, gave his identity card with the name Morand to a secretary, and was told to wait for the admiral, who would be in shortly. Bonnier told the secretary he had personal business with the high commissioner.

It was just before three-thirty when Darlan's car drew up and the admiral, accompanied by his aide Commander Hourcade, entered. Hourcade stepped aside as the admiral arrived at the door of his own office and started to walk away to the adjoining room. Neither of the two men had noticed the quiet young man sitting in the corner of the anteroom. Suddenly Bonnier stepped up to the admiral and, as Darlan turned toward him, fired two shots from a small revolver at point-blank range. Darlan slumped to the floor. Bonnier had stepped up to give him the coup de grâce when Hourcade rushed toward him. Bonnier ran into the admiral's office, then realized he was trapped. He fired twice more, at Hourcade this time, hitting him in the leg and the ear. But Hourcade grappled with him and held him. Other officers and secretaries plunged into the room.

Bonnier made no further struggle but handed over his revolver without a word.

Rear Admiral Battet, one of Darlan's assistants, rushed the high commissioner to the hospital. He had been unconscious since the first shot. Doctors operated, but he died within an hour and without speaking another word.

On that day, I had done my usual 1:00 P.M. broadcast to America, 8:00 P.M. New York time, had lunched, then, exhausted with working sixteen or seventeen hours a day for seven days a week, had lain down in my room at the Aletti Hotel and taken a nap. It was dark when I awoke. I took a bath and walked over to the British correspondents' mess in the Hôtel Regina. Colonel McCormack, chief British public relations officer, said, "Have you heard that Darlan's been shot, John?"

I laughed, thinking the colonel was exhibiting some of his usual wit, and quipped back, "Nothing trifling, I hope."

"Killed instantly," said McCormack.

Well, I could go along with the joke, so I said, "And have Hitler and Mussolini got theirs yet?"

But the colonel wasn't joking. The colonel said not a word would be allowed out about the affair until ten-thirty. Colonel Joe Phillips was keeping in touch with the French authorities and Allied Force Headquarters.

I got no dinner that night. Instead, I started rushing from place to place in Algiers, trying to get all the details of the story I could before the official statements were released. I hurried to the Palais d'Été, to the Hôtel Cornuailles, where our psychological warfare officials were quartered, to the offices and homes of various French officials whom I knew, picking up a bit here and a bit there. This was the story of a lifetime to a newsman, and we all were in that state of jitters which makes most correspondents work better than normal.

We waited until about midnight before the French official spokesman arrived to tell us of the killing and give us the official communiqué. The censors had set up shop in the next room, and we sprang to our typewriters and began pounding out copy, sending it to them sheet by sheet.

In the studio, Collingwood of CBS, Arthur Mann of Mutual, who had only just arrived in Algiers, Bob Dunnett of the BBC, and I matched coins to see who would go on the air first. Eddy Beaudry of the Canadian Broadcasting Corporation, who broadcast in French, said he was content to follow us.

I won the chance to be on the air with the most momentous news since our arrival in North Africa.

I began by spending five minutes calling in the networks. "Hello. To all American networks. Will NBC, CBS, Mutual, the BBC, and the Canadian Broadcasting Corporation, please get ready for a special important broadcast in five minutes? Please get ready to break into all programs. I have an important announcement from Allied Force Headquarters in North Africa. This is John MacVane, NBC correspondent in North Africa. Will the GPO in England, the BBC, and AT&T get ready to relay an important broadcast to all American networks? Please tell NBC, CBS, and Mutual to get ready to break into all broadcasts for an important broadcast. This is MacVane in North Africa. I will read an important communiqué in just four minutes. Then I will broadcast for NBC, and I will be followed by Collingwood of CBS and Mann of Mutual and Dunnett of the BBC in order. Please get ready to pass on a live broadcast onto the NBC network and break all programs. This is important. I repeat. This is very important."

The editor on the NBC news desk was Burroughs Prince. I had not come up in the news period just finished with my usual broadcast, and Prince was wondering why. An office party on the night before Christmas was already under way.

Suddenly the telephone rang. It was RCA Communications. "MacVane is doing a talk up from Algiers. Says he has an important story. Wants you to break into the net to put it out."

Buck Prince lost his languor. "Okay, okay," he snapped. "Tell engineering to put it through the school desk."

He ran the few feet to the school desk, the communications center from which he could bring in overseas points, cut them out, or switch on the microphone beside the desk.

Prince put on the earphones and began listening to me. From the urgency in my voice and my message, he knew something of tremendous consequence was afoot. He yelled for an announcer who was in the act of lifting a paper cup with some of the Christmas bourbon in it.

"Come here. I need an announcer."

He thought for a moment. Who was on the air? He switched on the program going out on the network. A big commercial show.

Bob Hope. Buck grinned. If my story wasn't good, his head would be served on a platter next morning, but he would show them how damn little newsmen cared about their comedy when big news was breaking.

He heard me saying, "I am going ahead in thirty seconds from now. I am going ahead in just twenty-five seconds. In twenty seconds."

Buck nodded at the announcer. "Interrupt program. Special broadcast North Africa."

The announcer's smooth tones went out as Buck pressed the button that cut our news microphone into all programs all over the country.

"We regret that we must interrupt this program momentarily for a special news broadcast directly from Allied Headquarters in North Africa."

Buck pressed another button and flipped a switch. Onto the network went the words "This is John MacVane at Allied Force Headquarters in North Africa. . . . Admiral Darlan, high commissioner for North Africa, was shot to death today. He was killed shortly after three o'clock this afternoon at the entrance to his office in Algiers. . . ."

And I went on to tell the story of the killing.

After I had finished, Collingwood came to the microphone and gave the story to CBS, then Mann to MBS and Dunnett to the BBC. Because of the usual communications difficulties, the news agency reports did not reach New York until hours after we had finished our broadcasts, so I was the first to give the outside world the story.

Prince went home happy to supper and bed. He knew his head would not be served up on a platter next morning.

It was about one-thirty in the morning in London. Lucy, who had been nursing our baby boy, Myles, was asleep. The telephone rang. Lucy answered half asleep.

"This is the BBC censor," said an excited voice. "Has the broadcast John MacVane just made from Algiers been passed by censorship? Is there any stop on the story?"

"What's that? What's that?" said Lucy sleepily.

"Isn't this the National Broadcasting Company office?"

"No. This is Mr. MacVane's home." And she gave the office number. "What's it all about? What happened?"

"It's important news," said the censor. "I'm afraid I can't tell you now. Hear it on the BBC eight o'clock morning broadcast."

The censor rang off. Lucy lay back on the bed, wondering drowsily what could have caused the excitement. The only thing that might have caused such a stir would be news that Darlan had been assassinated. That must be it. She went back to sleep.

Chapter 14

By the next morning, Christmas, everyone knew that Darlan had been killed. I had never seen happier faces in Algiers than on that day. It is said, *De mortuis nil nisi bonum*, but the plain, self-evident truth was that Algiers seemed pleased that the admiral no longer existed.

It was incredible, therefore, to read in the official communiqué that general indignation had been caused by the event. If anyone was indignant, I did not meet him, and I combed the city looking for reactions and information.

Even harder to understand was President Roosevelt's statement back in Washington, which condemned the deed as "murder in the first degree." We asked ourselves how the President could prejudge the case with such finality. It might certainly be murder— but there had been no trial, no verdict by a court. There might well be extenuating circumstances. There was more of hero than criminal in the boy who had done this thing.

I quickly found out the name of the killer but was not permitted to broadcast it for what were called "reasons of national security."

In my 1:00 P.M. broadcast I pointed out the great interest everywhere in the identity of the young man who had shot Darlan, although the official communiqué had not yet been printed in Algiers papers. I noted Darlan's death would not affect French cooperation with us.

I said: "The sudden reality of a revolver shot has again underlined the feeling that diplomats—like college professors—are often removed from the passions, the mistakes, the loves and hatred of the common people. The professor sometimes believes that history can be tied up in paragraphs and explained by logic.

"The diplomat, living for the most part with other diplomats, sometimes falls into the error of neglecting the violent surge of feeling that underruns so many of the historical facts.

"A diplomat can arrange, negotiate, and build an imposing

structure on sand—without realizing that beneath the sand runs a river of vitality that may spurt up and smash the structure to bits."

I went on to say: "Until we can know the mind of the young man who brooded until he felt he must shoot Darlan, we can't understand this event of yesterday. Charlotte Corday, Ravaillac—both sprang from a particular set of circumstances at a particular time in history. It will take an understanding of the whole background in France and the French colonies since the armistice two and a half years ago to comprehend this sudden flash of a bullet from a revolver. Yet to some correspondents here, the tide of feeling was plain—as it must be plain in France, in Norway, or in the other occupied countries. Whether the tide would spurt through the sand was something none of us could guess."

During Christmas Day I heard a rumor that Bonnier was to be rushed quickly before a firing squad without public trial.

I wrote the script for my evening broadcast on the theme that since the Vichy government had laid aside the right of public trial, it would be a good test of the new administration in North Africa if the man who had killed Darlan were given a fair trial so that the rights and wrongs could be fairly examined in the democratic way. I noted that the killer had not been accused of espionage but merely of a crime of murder that could be tried in the open courts.

The Allied military censors refused to pass my script for broadcast. They killed it on the grounds that my charge that an attempt was being made to rush through Bonnier's execution was an unjust accusation against French government justice.

That evening we were called to another official conference. The correspondents were told that an official French communiqué was being issued stating that Bonnier was to be executed next morning at dawn, only thirty-eight hours after he had committed his crime.

We all were badly shaken by the news. We did not know the boy or at the time his motives or who was behind him. But our ideas of impartial justice were outraged. The man was being railroaded without a fair public trial, and the right of public opinion to know the reasons had been flouted. Many of us were old police reporters. We immediately asked one another: Whom are the authorities trying to cover up?

Bonnier had been subjected to a so-called court-martial during the late afternoon and early evening, his lawyer the only outside person allowed in the room with him and the military judges. The coffin was actually ordered before the trial began so that there would be no delay in carrying out the execution.

Bonnier himself was calm. He seemed to think that the trial was only a formality and that before long he would be released. Even the verdict of guilty did not upset him—he remained confident that he would not have to suffer the penalty. He even mentioned a "pretense of execution," and the story in Algiers later was that he expected the firing squad to use blank shells to carry out the pretended execution, following which he would be liberated.

But as the hour of dawn approached, he asked the prison chaplain for a sheet of paper. He perhaps realized that his mysterious protector would never come. The chaplain had no paper, so Bonnier pulled a visiting card from his pocket and on it, it is alleged, wrote a confession.

He admitted that there was a royalist plot to kill Darlan, and he named those who had suggested that Darlan be killed so that the Count of Paris might come to the throne of France. The visiting card was the card of Henri d'Astier de la Vigerie, secretary-general of police.

At about the same time we broadcasters sat down in the studio, the bedroom of Lieutenant Charlie Kibling, the engineer, in Allied Force Headquarters. He had decorated it with a little Christmas tree, with bits of tinfoil from cigarette packages hanging on the branches.

Feeling anything but Christmasy in spirit, we solemnly flipped coins. Again I won first turn at the microphone; then came Mann of Mutual, Collingwood of CBS, and Dunnett of the BBC.

For the second time in two nights I was, by sheer luck, the first person to give important news to the outside world.

I said, after warning all networks to stand by for big news: "Tonight I have to announce a communiqué. It says that a French court-martial condemned the assassin of Admiral Darlan to death and sentence will be carried out tomorrow morning. The communiqué says the assassin, caught in the act, made a complete confession. He insisted he acted without accomplices. It is stated that his name is being kept secret for reasons of national security and that he was of French nationality.

"Any comment on this communiqué is strictly limited. We can never know from the young man who killed Darlan the motives that inspired him. There is no chance we can find out in the few hours between now and dawn.

"He dies before the firing squad only about thirty-eight hours after Darlan's death. There has never been any indication that he was in any way implicated in espionage. He—a Frenchman—killed another Frenchman. That is the whole story. We can examine the history of Darlan. There is no secret about that. Only the history of the young man is veiled in mystery. It will remain veiled in mystery because he can never tell the public. He had no time. There is no time for talking of such things—not now.

"Yet someday there will be time. That will help us little to clear this mystery. The sentence that was so quickly and easily decided will have been carried out a few hours from now—in the cold Algerian dawn before the firing squad.

"Yet there will be questions—questions that will remain."

In the broadcast following mine, Arthur Mann was also moved and somber. He said at the end that the "unknown assassin" of this war might someday rank with the "unknown soldier of the last," the implication being that a French patriot was about to die —for a deed that the Allies and France itself should have welcomed.

Collingwood followed Mann. Then Dunnett carried out our general theme.

We dispersed each to our own rooms with hardly a word. My stroke of professional luck in being first to broadcast such important events to the outside world was no comfort at all.

Even the kudos for that was in the end denied. Months later I received a copy of *Time* magazine with a large article in it stating that Collingwood of CBS had received a broadcasting award of which I had never heard, a Peabody prize given by some southern school of journalism. He won the honor, said the account, because he had been first to broadcast to America the news of the death of Darlan and the news of the execution of the assassin.

It was something that my friend Charles Collingwood would never have claimed for himself, and he knew as little about it as I did. I sent a reproachful telegram to NBC asking the reasons for my own "beat" being credited to another. NBC ruefully explained that the CBS publicity department must have been smarter than NBC's. We had the news on the air first, but nobody at NBC ever thought about claiming any honors for this fact. Then and there I lost my respect for broadcasting awards. I was only able to solace myself after the war with the knowledge that never in five years of covering top foreign and diplomatic news for radio was I ever beaten on the air by a competitor, with one single exception, which

I will describe later. The Darlan story was no credit to me. I had only won a toss of the coin. But when we were out on our own, making our arrangements and getting the big stories on the air, NBC was always first.

The North African Imperial Council met on the day after Christmas to choose a successor to Darlan.

Meanwhile, the Count of Paris and his close associates were busy. They had been counting more on Darlan's stepping down in favor of the count than on this sudden change of situation. They held endless meetings to discuss the supposed feelings of the Imperial Council. The aides believed that the count could count on a majority. But when he saw Giraud, he was disillusioned. From a reliable source, I heard that Giraud had expressed his personal esteem for the count and said that while he, personally, believed a king might be the means of achieving French unity, he could not advise or approve any attempt by the count to assume power in North Africa.

"Be patient," Giraud told the count. "When all France is liberated will be time enough to see whether monarchy can again return to our country."

Murphy sent a message to the State Department to the effect that a movement was on foot to name the Count of Paris to the post of high commissioner. The State Department sent a decisive reply that the entry of the Count of Paris into politics would mess up the whole situation and might affect French support for the armies of General Eisenhower.

From that moment Murphy's backing was assured for the election of Giraud. The Imperial Council named him unanimously once Auguste Noguès had withdrawn.

The one thought of the majority of the members of the council was that they must unite behind Giraud to prevent De Gaulle from obtaining control of North Africa. The Count of Paris, thunderstruck at the election of Giraud, remained a few days longer in Algiers, then departed to his Moroccan farm. The attempt had failed, and monarchy as a solution for France's problems had vanished into limbo.

Chapter 15

Through January I explained carefully where I thought our policy toward the French had been in error. The whole story was fresh to the American public, for almost nothing had come out about it previously.

There were still many hundreds of people in prison camps in North Africa, for no other reason than that they were suspected of favoring De Gaulle or the Allies or were Jews or political refugees from Franco Spain.

President Roosevelt made a speech in early January, and for almost the first time since June 1940 extracts from it were broadcast over the Algiers radio.

I said: "The President spoke of the people moving forward in their might and power. This is not a new idea for Americans. It is not a new idea for many people of Europe and Africa. But there were listeners tonight all over the world who didn't agree with the President's statement.

"I'd like to talk about this because the whole business of believing in the common people, believing that the ideas that you and I and the other fellow have are important, has an effect on the future of the world.

"When you are a kid in America, you take it for granted that democracy—believing in the common people, believing in ourselves —is the way the rest of the world lives. Then you grow up, and you find that there are many people both in your own country and out of it who don't think like that.

"If your business happens to be international affairs, and you start looking at international politics, you find that in almost any country you can tell the ones who think the ordinary people are all right and the ones who don't think so.

"I don't think I'm wrong in saying that most American correspondents feel the same way about it. After all, we're brought up that way. So whenever our government talks about democracy and doesn't back it up with action, the correspondents, and a good many millions beside, feel disappointed. The people *are* moving forward in their might and power. And tonight there will be men in concentration camps from Algeria to Poland who will approve the President's every word."

I had been trying for some time to get an exclusive interview with General Giraud, through his chief aide, my good friend Major André Bauffre.

One night Bauffre sent me a message that he wanted to see me. When I reached his office, he told me that Giraud, before departing for Dakar on a visit, had left a written exclusive statement for me.

The statement seemed to leave the door open for the unification of the French forces under Giraud and those under De Gaulle. In one passage he said, "More than all else, we wish the union of all forces that can participate in the war. From various sides, hands are stretched toward us. We are ready to clasp them without any second thoughts, knowing well that all truly French wills, wherever they may be, must be reunited to assure the total liberation of France. It suffices that each one bring to this work his faith without self-interest."

This union between De Gaulle and Giraud became the chief underlying political theme. Some Algerian papers were even allowed to print the fact that Free French forces were fighting with Montgomery and driving Rommel backward, and men like De Larminat, Catroux, and others of De Gaulle's lieutenants could be mentioned.

Possibly because each time we correspondents met him or Murphy we asked what was being done about freeing the prisoners in North African prison camps, General Eisenhower ordered formation of a committee to inspect the conditions of political prisoners in North and West Africa and to urge their release on the French authorities. The committee was to be made up of the American and British consul generals in Algiers, three representatives of Eisenhower's staff, and a representative of the French administration.

It was at least a beginning, although, as Eddy Beaudry of the Canadian Broadcasting Corporation asked Rigault one day, "Why, in the name of the liberty we are here to fight for, should men still remain in prison for their political beliefs?"

In explaining at length so much that was political, I hope I have not given the impression that the war itself had no place on the airwaves from Algiers.

Since the Allied forces had failed to reach Tunis in the autumn, there had been little fighting of an important nature. In the cold mud of the Tunisian valleys and among the djebels, as the hills are called, neither side could strike a decisive blow. There was bitter fighting for this hill or that which might be necessary when a big attack took place, but we had lost our chance to win the war quickly, and it was to be a slow, slogging matter until the very end.

I wanted to go to Tunisia, but I was alone with no one to leave at the transmitter, whence alone I could broadcast my messages. At length I got my old Paris friend and Aletti Hotel roommate, Merrill Mueller of *Newsweek* magazine, to agree to do some broadcasting, and I prepared to leave for Tunisia with the newly arrived BBC recorder.

I had heard a rumor from a friend momentarily in town from Tunisia that something big was getting under way there shortly.

As it turned out, something big was getting under way 1,000 miles west of us in Morocco. Just as I was about to head for Tunisia, I was told to report to Maison Blanche airfield with toilet articles and sleeping stuff in my musette bag, but no bedroll. Just that and nothing more.

We were not even told why, but the dozen of us in the C-47 learned that our destination was Casablanca. Correspondents had been called in mysteriously and flown to Algiers from all over the front. Only Bill Stoneman of the Chicago *News* had refused to come. He told public relations loftily that he had a war to cover and had no time to gallivant off to Algiers to get briefed by some bigwig who didn't know what he was talking about. He was going to stay and write the war in Tunisia. No officer would tell him the real reason for the trip. So he missed Casablanca, as he had been unlucky enough to miss Dieppe.

The trip was marred by a tragedy. The pilot who brought the second load of correspondents from Algiers mistook the airfield at Larache in Spanish Morocco for that of Port Lyautey in French Morocco forty or fifty miles farther south along the Atlantic coast. He started to come into the airfield to pick up some gasoline. As the unarmed transport was circling the field slowly at only a couple of hundred feet altitude, Spanish machine gunners opened up on it. Bullets spurted through the floor and one hit Eddy Beaudry of Canadian Broadcasting between the eyes. He died instantly. The pilot of the American plane sped his aircraft away, and no more were killed, but Franco's hatred of us could have cost the lives of all those aboard.

Eddy was a fine man, quick to understand what was going on in

North Africa, a warmhearted man. He was given a military funeral at Port Lyautey and laid to rest with the Americans killed at the time of the landings.

At Casablanca I immediately found out from Sammy Shulman, a photographer friend, that President Roosevelt and Prime Minister Churchill were there conferring and that General Giraud and General de Gaulle were also there.

We correspondents had nothing to do for a few days except see the countryside, visit Rabat to meet General Noguès, and generally twiddle our thumbs. At the close of the conference we all met the President and Churchill on the lawn in front of the President's villa. I had never realized that the President had to be carried by one of his bodyguards from place to place until I saw him being brought from the villa to his chair on the lawn. That was the moment when the President first made the statement about "unconditional surrender." Roosevelt told us, as we sat about the lawn at his feet, that the only reasonable assurance of world peace lay in the unconditional surrender of Germany, Italy, and Japan. He made it clear that the destruction of the populaces of these countries was not proposed but only the destruction of their philosophies based on the conquest and subjugation of other peoples.

It was a beautiful setting for the statesmen to talk to us, the white villa, green lawn with palm trees and purple red bougainvillaea flowers climbing over the terrace.

We learned precious little of the real decisions taken at the meeting, but there was one incident that even Churchill did not seem to have heard about, an incident that delayed the unity of the French effort for several months.

When General de Gaulle arrived, ready to cooperate with Giraud, his first words to Giraud were: "Good day, General." Giraud replied, "Good day, De Gaulle." It was the reply of a five-star general to a two-star general, an indication that Giraud felt De Gaulle to be in the inferior position. Giraud may not have known what he was doing. If he had only replied, "Good day, General," it would have been an indication that Giraud considered they were meeting as equals. But to have Giraud use to him the same phrase a general might use to a young officer burned De Gaulle's soul. After all, he alone had rallied the French people to continue the war on the side of the Allies. Giraud had entered the scene very late in the day and then only as Darlan's subordinate. As equals they might negotiate, but as superior and subordinate, never.

164

De Gaulle believed, after he left the Casablanca Conference, that he had achieved very good relations with the President. He was ready to forgive and forget the past slights that Roosevelt had put upon him. When later he learned that the President was still as stubbornly set against him, criticizing him in conversation, it was an unexpected blow to his pride and a very personal hurt.

We wrote out long accounts of the meeting and had them censored. One copy we sent with Colonel Phillips to Gibraltar, whence it would be flown to London for transmission. The other copy we took back with us to Algiers for broadcast. We could not give out the news until a certain period after all the Allied leaders had left Casablanca.

On the night of the broadcast Collingwood, Mann, and I were in the studio, ready to begin, when the air-raid signal sounded. The Algiers transmitter went off the air, and for hours we sat there during the raid, unable to put out a single word about the big story. Luckily London was able to send on most of what I had written, so my company did not suffer.

The bombs dropped. Our studio building, the St.-Georges Hotel, shook, and it was nearly dawn before we all went home to bed, three completely frustrated broadcasters.

Chapter 16

I managed to get up to Tunisia several times during the winter to see the fighting, with both American and British forces. On these occasions I had Merrill Mueller of *Newsweek* substitute for me in Algiers.

In late March and early April I received a series of dispatches by telegram and airplane by Grant Parr, NBC's Cairo correspondent who had come up to the Eighth Army in Tunisia. Day by day the eyewitness accounts of Montgomery's attacks—the Mareth Line and the Wadi Zigazou, the Gabès Gap and the Wadi Akarit—came in. They were gripping human stories, among the best accounts that I have read of military operations and I gave as much of them as I could in my allotted time. Finally, when Montgomery's army had cleared the coast and the Germans were penned in the mountain semicircle of northeastern Tunisia, Parr flew over to Algiers.

Since November I had been pleading with NBC for some assistance. Now I had plenty. Ralph Howard Peterson arrived from New York about the same time that Parr came from the Eighth Army. After I had introduced them to the proper sources in Algiers and started them broadcasting, I hurried back to the front to be in for the kill. I went to the British Army, for I was well aware that the big story would be the taking of Tunis, and the British were going to do that chore.

I think that the average war correspondent who was there looks back with a certain nostalgia on that final campaign in Tunisia. It was such a small war that practically everywhere you went you found people in the British and American divisions whom you had known at some time or other. The divisions and even the regiments meant something to us, for we had seen them and written and spoken about them. Later in France and Germany the operations were on such a vast scale that no reporter could know much beyond his own particular army, and even in that one army there were many units that he could not visit or know much about.

The American II Corps, which had been in the south, was brought secretly up to the north. When the final offensive began

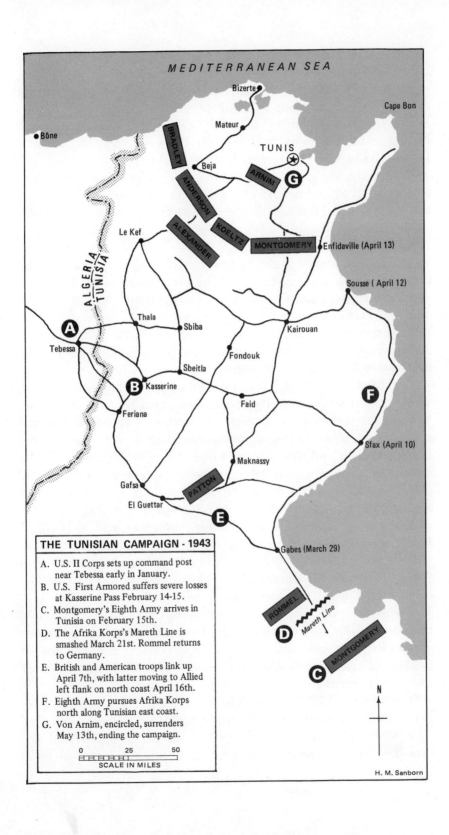

MEDITERRANEAN SEA

Cape Bon

Bizerte

• Bône

Mateur

TUNIS ✪

Beja

Le Kef

BRADLEY

ANDERSON

ALEXANDER

KOELTZ

ARNIM

MONTGOMERY

G

Enfidaville (April 13)

ALGERIA
TUNISIA

Sousse (April 12)

Thala

Sbiba

Kairouan

A

Tebessa

Fondouk

Sbeitla

B Kasserine

Faid

Feriana

F

Maknassy

Sfax (April 10)

Gafsa

PATTON

El Guettar

E

Gabes (March 29)

THE TUNISIAN CAMPAIGN - 1943

A. U.S. II Corps sets up command post
   near Tebessa early in January.
B. U.S. First Armored suffers severe losses
   at Kasserine Pass February 14-15.
C. Montgomery's Eighth Army arrives in
   Tunisia on February 15th.
D. The Afrika Korps's Mareth Line is
   smashed March 21st. Rommel returns
   to Germany.
E. British and American troops link up
   April 7th, with latter moving to Allied
   left flank on north coast April 16th.
F. Eighth Army pursues Afrika Korps
   north along Tunisian east coast.
G. Von Arnim, encircled, surrenders
   May 13th, ending the campaign.

ROMMEL

D Mareth Line

C MONTGOMERY

N

0   25   50
SCALE IN MILES

H. M. Sanborn

about April 23, the front was a half circle or slightly more. In the north on the left was the Corps Franc of the French in impassable brush-and-hill country. Around the curve was the American II Corps, the 1st, 9th, and 34th Infantry divisions and the 1st Armored Division. Then, to the south, were the British First Army, the 1st, 4th, 46th, and 78th Infantry divisions, the 6th Armored Division, and the 1st Armored Division, brought over from the Eighth Army, the same division over which I had flown with Bob Cooper in 1940 in England on maneuvers. Next, to the south, was the rather weak French XIX Corps, and finally, as the stopper in the bottle and extending to the coast on the right, was Montgomery's Eighth Army.

The Eighth Army, for the first time, had met the Germans in the same mountain country through which the First Army had been fighting all winter and had come to a jarring stop.

The situation as the last offensive began was very interesting. The actual numbers of troops on our side and on the German side were about equal. The Germans had the best positions, but we had the greater weight of armor and guns and planes.

The British press camp was established in an orchard near the Thibar monastery, where the monks continued tending their vines and making their wine as though war were very far away. Many of my old friends among the correspondents were there, Drew Middleton, Ed Beattie, and Bill Stoneman, together with the British. Major Arthur Pilkington was in charge of all, and among the other conducting officers were Captain Sir Gerald Boles, my colleague at Dieppe; Captain David Heneker; and Major Nigel Dugdale.

A new face showed up among the conducting officers, Captain Dudley Forwood, of the sweeping mustache, who had once been an aide-de-camp to the Prince of Wales. He brought with him a Soviet Tass correspondent named Solodovnik and some correspondents of the Eighth Army whom I had not seen for years: Alan Moorehead of the London *Daily Express*; Alexander Clifford of the London *Daily Mail*, who, with Moorehead, was one of the two outstanding correspondents with the Desert Army; and Christopher Buckley of the London *Daily Telegraph*, who always looked more like a professor than a correspondent.

We correspondents always teamed up, two or three to a car, with a driver and sometimes a conducting officer. One whom I now often went with was Ward Price of the London *Daily Mail*. Ward was very much the right-winger, and in our evening dinner sessions in the dining tent or hotel, he used to bait Philip Jordan of the *News Chronicle* unmercifully. Philip, who later served Prime Minister Clement Attlee as press spokesman for 10 Downing Street, was a typical liberal, intense and outspoken. Price was far older than any of us, certainly thirty years my senior. He had been the confidant of the first Lord Rothermere, publisher of the *Daily Mail*, when that gentleman believed that cooperation with Hitler and Mussolini might benefit Britain. For many years, Ward Price, monocle in his eye, had been the liaison when Hitler or Mussolini wanted to get a friendly story in the British press or to fly a trial balloon. He had had exclusive interviews by the score with both, and he wrote an apologia for them called *I Know These Dictators*. He was at the same time one of the most cynical men in the world when it came to his profession.

"I have always operated on the theory since my youth in Fleet Street," he once said to me, "that the way to advancement in journalism is to know the big story and to make sure that you are covering that particular story, from the inside, if possible.

"I might frankly say that sometimes the dictators revolted me," he went on, "but like it or not, between the two wars they and their thoughts and actions determined the future of the world. I felt the only way to cover them properly was to get to know them personally and intimately. I did that successfully so that from the very moment they came to power, I was indispensable to the *Daily Mail*. When the dictators had some big story to leak, they leaked it to me. Jordan, for instance, would never have done that. He feels his liberalism too keenly. But Rothermere's policy was to develop relations with these people in the thought that they might be persuaded not to use their power against England. A good many politicians in England felt the same way. I could not criticize them and remain in their confidence, so I simply recorded what they had to say to me and left the judgment on it to others."

And Price said, "You are still a young journalist, John [I was then only thirty], and I think you will go far, but you must remember. People will not forget you if you are always where the big story is happening and can write about it."

That was an understandable point of view. I could not agree with Price's view of journalism, but I could at least respect the cynic. It was a point of view quite different from a few of the only semi-intelligent right-wing journalists in America who actually believed some of the nonsense they wrote in their columns.

If Ward Price had erred, he was doing penance for it in North Africa. He did not need to come out to live the hard life in the field, for he could have remained in London in any job he chose. He may have felt that as a patriotic Englishman he ought to suffer the risks and hardships of campaigning as his way of paying for some of the stories he had written about Hitler and Mussolini.

I admired his courage, and I liked him personally. Together we jolted over the dusty roads, shared foxholes under bombing or shelling, and climbed up and down hills.

I remember one incident that concerned Ward Price, Keith Hooper of the Australian Truth papers, and me. In the final offensive, for the first time in North Africa, we had gained control of the sky. But every now and then a Messerschmitt or two would slip over to bomb or machine-gun our units. One day we three were riding down a country road. Hooper was spotting for airplanes, with his head out the roof. Suddenly about 100 feet ahead of us I saw some fiery red balls bouncing off the hard road surface. So unexpected was the display that for a second I simply gaped at it. The sensation was almost as though you were strolling down your front walk in January when Fourth of July Roman candle lights began to spring out of the pavement at your feet. I yelled. The car skidded to a stop, and we leaped for the side of the road. Only when we were twenty yards out and down on our faces did we all completely realize what had happened. Hooper had seen nothing. But flying off overhead, with antiaircraft bursts exploding around it, was a German fighter. The pilot had been cruising along when he saw a lone army vehicle on the road he was about to fly over. He had dipped down, given us a squirt from his guns, then, as the nearby antiaircraft opened up, made off without pressing the matter. What we had seen was the Messerschmitt's tracer shells. Through it all, Price's monocle remained glued to his eye.

The original plan had been for the Eighth Army to attack in the Enfidaville area near the east coast. The Germans, presumably, would become alarmed at the advance of the redoubtable Montgomery and would rush reinforcements to that front. Then the First Army would crash through its weakened front to Tunis.

The First Army attack began on the morning of April 23 before dawn. Americans and British troops both made advances of from two to five miles.

We were at the time just about twenty-five miles from Tunis. The approach lay through two valleys. Roads through the valleys joined, and the two became one wide valley at a point the British called Peter's Corner. While the Germans held the hills, we could not send tanks and trucks down the valleys without getting them shot to pieces. The question then was how quickly we could take the hills, huge chunks of granite lightly covered in places with grass. In them the Germans, as I was able to discover when I examined them later, had prepared elaborate emplacements, some blasted into solid rock.

The most famous of the early battles in the preliminary drive was the Battle of Longstop. That was the lower of three hills which were utmost in tactical importance, Tongoush, Heidous, and Longstop, or, to give it its Arab name, the Djebel Ahmera. From Longstop the Germans had a balcony seat on the Medjerda Valley and could direct artillery fire from the hills behind onto anything that moved. The mortars on Longstop itself could cover the road directly below.

The name "Longstop" comes from a position in English village cricket, the man who stands behind the wicketkeeper to recover balls that he misses. In children's baseball, it would be the boy who stands behind the catcher so that the balls he misses won't go out of the field. The Englishman who named it felt it was the last hill blocking the way to Tunis.

The Germans on Longstop were as safe as anyone could be, unless a shell happened to land directly at the door of their rock-and-concrete dugouts.

The attack on Longstop opened with a heavy shelling of the position by the British artillery. The Royal West Kent Regiment was sent in during the darkness before dawn. They were shot to pieces, but they re-formed at the bottom of the hill and tried again. The remnant was unable to do anything.

I reached the area in early afternoon and, from an elevation some distance away, watched the Argyle and Sutherland Highlanders, bagpipes playing, try again for Longstop. They were supported by Churchill tanks and preceded by a creeping artillery barrage. The valley was green, overlaid with purple and white spring flowers. On the lower slopes of Longstop itself, immense beds of crimson poppies looked like gouts of blood.

At first the whole hill was smoking with the artillery barrage. Through the afternoon the barrage lifted higher and higher as the Highland infantrymen advanced. At the end of the afternoon only one little corner was puffing with white bursts of smoke, for that was the corner on which the Germans were making their last stand.

One of the Churchill tanks was flaming on the hillside, and a nearby village was burning with fires set by some stray bombs or shells.

By evening the last point was still untaken, and I had to get back to First Army Headquarters near Thibar to find out what had happened elsewhere on the front.

It appeared that the British had been fighting all day on Heidous and had surrounded Tongoush. The two British armored divisions were fighting in and near the adjoining Goubellat Valley.

The brigadier who briefed the correspondents at night felt that the Germans were putting everything they had into a desperate effort. And the effort continued to be intense, for the Germans counterattacked that very night near Medjez-el-Bab, and only the pale moon served to distinguish friend from foe. On the following day, April 24, progress slowed down under rain and low cloud as the Germans poured everything they had into the defense. They were still holding out on the two high hills and even on the last pimple of Longstop.

Captain Gerald Boles and I wangled a car for ourselves and went off together. We were very close friends and had been so ever since our Dieppe experience. Gerald was a second baronet, the son, I believe, of some prominent West Country political figure. He had gone through Sandhurst, spent some time in the 17th Lancers, and wore on his cap their badge, a death's-head with the words "Or Glory" underneath. He had lived a pleasant life administering his farms and estates, and he had a flat on Park Lane in London. His wife and son had gone to America for the war period, so Gerald had nothing to worry about but the Army. He was a dear friend, and he was later killed in Italy. Sometimes it seemed to me afterward that most of the men I liked best were killed. I sometimes wished that I could have seen their wives and children if they had any, but then it seemed that there was not much that one could say to people who were so much closer to them, except that I also had liked them and had had a good time whenever we were together.

On this day we were driving up a back road to a hill overlooking the Goubellat Valley when, with a sudden zing-smack like a whiplash, a German eighty-eight-millimeter shell landed about fifty feet from us. We leaped from the car and dispersed into the field to wait for the next one.

If it came close, we would know someone was observing us and would get going just as quickly over the ridge. Nothing happened, and we slowly got back into the car and in a minute or so found ourselves in the midst of about 100 British artillery pieces of all types. They were tucked into the folds and flat spaces among the hills. We climbed onto a bare knoll above the guns and lay down so the Germans would not notice us. For most of the afternoon we lay fascinated, watching Allied guns firing from three directions on the Germans. The whole front echoed with the cannonade, and we could hear the British shells from behind us rustling over our heads and see them exploding in puffs of white smoke across the valley. British infantry were advancing up the valley slowly, and from time to time we would watch Messerschmitts in pairs come up and dump bombs on them. In other parts of the valley the German aircraft were attacking in fours and sixes. It seemed obvious that the Germans were making an all-out effort to hold the valley, carpeted as it was with what looked like deep green plush daubed with smears of white and scarlet flowers.

That Goubellat Valley was a bloody one. Between the twenty-second and the twenty-sixth of that month, it was later estimated, the British armor had drawn the full strength of the 10th, 15th, and 21st Panzer divisions onto the plain, there to be hammered to bits by our tanks and artillery. We—that is, the British divisions—suffered losses, but we could afford them better than the Germans, for we had replacements. The Germans had none.

The next day Gerald Boles and I went up to see the Americans to the north. I knew the 1st Division would be in the thick of things, and I found General Terry Allen in a little white stone hut shattered by bombs and shellfire. The 1st had just made a night attack on Kef el Goraa, the highest hill in the vicinity.

Terry seemed glad to see me and told Gerald and me about that action: first, 3,100 shells laid down on the comparatively small hill within the half hour between two and two-thirty in the morning; then the sudden attack, with rifles and hand grenades. The hill was ours by four-thirty on Easter Sunday morning. The 1st now had the highest hill, and German resistance on the range of lower peaks leading toward Mateur crumbled, the Germans retreating so fast that the Americans lost touch with them while I was there with Allen.

The next obstacle on the road to Bizerte was Hill 609, which the British had tried to take months earlier and had been unable with the forces at hand to seize. Now the 34th Division, just moving up from reserve, was going to work, and take it they did.

Generals Theodore Roosevelt, Jr., Terry Allen, and George Patton share a foxhole under shelling at El Guettar, Tunisia. WIDE WORLD.

It was only on Monday, April 26, that the final 200 Germans on Longstop surrendered. They had been badly shaken by the artillery pounding, but if every 200 Germans had fought as hard, we might still be trying to take Tunis.

After Longstop and the two higher hills came the Bou Aoukaz, called by the British the Bou Feature. It had been taken and re-taken, taken and retaken a half dozen times. I remember that on the day of the first British attack on the hill I went into the valley nearby looking for a friend, Lieutenant Desmond Fitzgerald of the First Battalion Irish Guards.*

On that first day the roads in the valley were only narrow dust trails with paths through the minefields. Captain David Heneker and I were in his little Simca. Each time an enemy plane came overhead, we had to get out and walk slowly and inconspicuously down the road, hoping a Messerschmitt would not waste bullets on a tiny French car and two frightened men in battle dress. The Guards had just taken the area, and just off the road we saw two dead British soldiers.

Brigade headquarters was in a fold of uneven ground, and a headquarters officer told me that Fitzgerald was in good health and that in fifteen minutes his battalion would be attacking a point about a mile ahead of us. Around us British twenty-five-pounders and heavier guns were shelling spasmodically. I saw no point as a non-weapon-carrying participant in getting involved in an advance infantry attack, so we returned to the rear.

After the campaign ended, I heard Desmond had been killed, and for several days I felt terribly low in spirits, wondering how I could break the news to his wife until I learned that there were three Desmond Fitzgeralds in that battalion and the one who had been killed was not my friend. The 1st Battalion was badly shot up. Reorganized, it went to Anzio, where it was so badly decimated that it never functioned again during the war. I believe my Desmond Fitzgerald was almost the only officer neither killed nor wounded in the two campaigns.

* One of my best friends at Oxford had been Rawle Knox, son of E. V. Knox, editor of *Punch*. Rawle had been taken prisoner by the Japanese at Singapore. His young sister, Penelope, known to her friends as Mops, was married to Desmond Fitzgerald by Monsignor Ronald Knox, her uncle. Monsignor Ronald and E.V. "Evoe" were sons of an Anglican bishop of Bradford, an extraordinary family. In 1978, Penelope Fitzgerald's book *The Two Knoxes* about her father and uncle was published in the United States. For years they did not know what had become of Rawle, and when the first card came through, I believe I was one of the first people Penelope and E.V. called by telephone to say that he was still alive.

In the campaign on that short front I kept running into people I knew. At one point, I discovered Dunstan Curtis, lieutenant commander in the British Navy, camped with a conglomeration of military characters in a pasture.

What Dunstan, the theater manager turned hero of St.-Nazaire, was doing in a Tunisian pasture was beyond my comprehension until I learned he was a member of what was called S-Force, a mobile group trained to rush ahead of the Army, seize intelligence documents, stop the Germans from blowing up wharves, and all that sort of thing.

On April 28, after trying to figure out what might happen, I tacked a notice on my daily dispatch to the effect that I believed Tunis would fall on May 7 and New York and Algiers should get ready for special broadcasts to mark the event. This was just guessing on my part, based on some close observation; but New York complied, and NBC had, I believe, a world beat in consequence, for it was ready for the first flash of news.

April 29 was my thirty-first birthday, and I remember that I spent the morning doing a "think-piece" in the orchard of Thibar and feeling old and decrepit. I had lived, then, enough years for anyone twenty years my senior. A letter was delivered to me from a girl I had never met but who had written me once or twice from the NBC office in Hollywood. She said she had been listening every day to the broadcasts and wished me well. Her letter bucked me up. I always wished I had written to thank her; but I never had the time, and when I thought of it, I had lost her letter and her name.

I thought of myself so far away from Lucy and my son, Myles, and I wondered whether I would live through the rest of the campaign. It was a sad few hours, until I went to the evening briefing at First Army Headquarters, wrote my story, and had more than my allotment of Scotch whisky without telling anyone it was my birthday.

General Alexander at this point decided that he would strengthen the British First Army with units from the Eighth and crash through to Tunis on the First Army front. He ordered over the 7th Armored Division and the 4th Indian Division. They came with their thousands of vehicles still painted a desert yellow, but the Germans did not spot the transfer, for our air forces kept the skies clear during the operation.

Gerald Boles and I again went north to see the Americans and the French Corps Franc d'Afrique. The Americans were circling

In Tunisia, MacVane with A. B. "Sandy" Austin, correspondent of the London Daily Herald, *later killed in Italy.* IMPERIAL WAR MUSEUM.

and isolating two important hills on the Sedjenane–Mateur road, Green and Bald hills. Supplies had to be dropped to the most advanced units by parachute, for the terrain was next to impassable. We saw the Corps Franc and admired their spirit as they drove the enemy through the brush so fast where one could not see a yard ahead that Americans spoke of them as kindling again the torch of French military glory.

We bathed on the Tabarka beach with a couple of hundred British troops, plus Dan DeLuce of the Associated Press and Roderick Macdonald of the Sydney *Morning Herald*, who happened by. Then we spent the evening at an American field hospital, drinking with the doctors and nurses, until we said good night and went down the road and rolled into our blankets in the bushes.

At last came the moment for the final plunge that would rip open the German front. For a long time the British had been putting a great deal of their armored strength into the Goubellat Valley, and that was where the Germans expected the main attack. Instead, Alexander was going to strike down the Medjerda Valley with everything he had.

The thrust was to be made by four divisions—hitting on approximately a two-mile front—to the right of the Bou Feature and to the left of the main road. Other divisions were to protect the flanks of the corridor of attack.

Five hundred and fifty tanks would strike in that narrow space, and 400 artillery pieces, which could be switched quickly from objective to objective by a senior artillery officer in an advanced position, were brought into readiness. These guns would rain between 1,000 and 2,000 shells each minute on the German defenses. Air forces, half American, half British, were on nearby fields, to bomb and strafe objectives just ahead of the advance.

As before, my conducting officer was David Heneker, son of a British general and himself a Sandhurst graduate who had served for some years in the professional Army until he decided he liked songwriting and innkeeping better. He had written hits for London shows. When war broke out, he joined up immediately as a volunteer, and here he was conducting correspondents around the front. Lucy and I knew David and his wife, Gwenol, in London, and it was a great pleasure to have a man of his experience and courage with me.

With us were Will Lang, correspondent for *Time* magazine, and Robert Raymond, correspondent of the *Echo* of Algiers. I had known

178

Robert slightly in Algiers. He had been touring the front all alone when his car broke down, and he showed up with his bedroll in my tent one night. He had no official accreditation, but he was so likable that Major Pilkington allowed him to stay as a sort of *entente cordiale* gesture. His fund of humorous stories and comments on life and love kept us laughing, although sometimes the laughter was delayed for translation.

The offensive was to begin with a preliminary attack late in the afternoon of May 5 on the Bou Feature. The big offensive would begin with the 400-gun barrage at three o'clock on the morning of May 6. We four—Heneker, Lang, Raymond, and I—decided to go out to the valley that night to see the offensive begin.

A major at corps headquarters invited us to go with him to the top of Grenadier Hill. He had helped prepare the gun concentration and wanted to see the show. In the valley, all we would have seen would have been the nearest gun flashes. Now we could see the whole sweep of the attack.

We waited outside in the car until the major was ready to leave at about two o'clock in the morning. Robert, whose family had lived in North Africa since his grandfather was sent there in 1851 as a man of undesirable republican sentiments, wrapped himself in his oilskin jacket, lay on the ground, and went to sleep. We shivered in the biting wind, and someone said, "May fifth in Africa."

At last we stopped by a hill and started to climb. I had two full bottles of Scotch whisky in my trench coat pockets in case of need. The major set a brisk pace. I stumbled along behind him, up a path so sheer that one had to work one's toes into the side of the hill and steady one's self to keep from slipping backward. The bottles became heavier and heavier. I wanted to fall beside the path to rest, but I dared not, for fear the bottles would break. I was gasping and almost felt like vomiting when I reached the top. I flopped down on the ground for half an hour, but at least I had made the summit. When I saw the hill in daylight, rising sheer above the plain, I knew I would never even have attempted in the light of the sun what I had accomplished in the pitch-blackness. The strange thing was that the bottles were unopened when we got back to camp next day. What happened next was too interesting even to take time out for a drink.

We were on a hill that had been skillfully entrenched by the Germans, and when dawn came, we could see their holes and ditches all over the summit. But at three o'clock, just as we reached the top, the whole valley before us became a heaving sea of flame. The fires twinkled and winked and jumped, and each flash meant a load of destruction. The huge barrage—that is, relatively huge, for it was the biggest thing of its kind any of us, including the officers, had yet seen—opened up just as the Germans counterattacked against the Bou Feature. They must have thought they were walking through the gates of hell.

The noise on the valley floor must have been incredible, but to us it sounded as though thousands of doors along a tunnel were being slammed. Sometimes it reminded us of a drummer banging with incomprehensible speed against a slack-headed bass drum.

Just below our hill we could hear the hundreds of tanks clanking into position. The two divisions, Indian and British, raced down the valley together. Something like one division of Germans with eighty-five tanks was opposing them.

We on the hill were chilled to the bone when dawn came. The fire of the guns, now shooting at more distant objectives, was as fierce as ever, but we saw it through a pall of dust. Over a dozen roads and trails plumes of powder dust rose from the columns of vehicles. A strange sight met our eyes, a quarter circle of rainbow arching down through the hills on the opposite side of the valley, although we had had not a drop of rain.

Then, at quarter to six, a dozen of our planes arrived, medium bombers, sweeping in stately formation over the front, returning, then going back to drop their bombs. As the black columns of smoke cut through the dust, the bombers turned finally toward home.

Others were coming as they left, twelve, eighteen, twenty-four, and after the first half hour we stopped counting. The predicted rate of bombing had been twelve to eighteen bombers over the front bombing every seven minutes. A German prisoner I talked with later, a man who had fought two years in Russia, said it was the most impressive display of air power he had ever seen. It was certainly better than anything I had ever seen, and I had seen plenty.

Once the infantry took the first objectives, the two armored divisions were let loose. They raced so fast that some of our bomb attacks had to be canceled, so that the air forces would not bomb our own men.

We climbed down from the hill and went, much farther than we expected, to find the headquarters of the 4th Indian Division. They were fine-looking men. Gurkhas from Nepal, they fought for fun at home and by tradition fought for pay and fun in the British

180

Army and were about as cocky as any army men I have ever seen. They could fight with rifles and guns, but they especially liked to fight at night with their big knives, the kukris. They liked to slip behind hostile positions in the dark, come on them from behind, and decapitate the enemy with one swift stroke. Two blows to cut a man's head off was considered something for women and children, not for the proud fighting men from Nepal. I remember hearing of a raid by Gurkhas of the Eighth Army in the desert when they cut the heads from the twelve men in an outpost without a sound and left them planted on stakes for the relieving forces to find in the morning. This was considered a very fine joke on the Germans.

Division headquarters was ahead of the guns, the first time that a British officer with the division could remember such a circumstance. They barked away all the time we were there, and only once or twice did we hear the explosion of the incoming mail from the German position. By nightfall the British were on high ground north and south of Massicault, fifteen miles from Tunis, and the American 9th Division to the north was only twelve miles from Bizerte. We were back in Thibar, sleeping for the first time in two nights.

Chapter 17

That morning of May 7, we four debated whether or not to take our bedrolls, for we knew we were not going home until we had been in Tunis. We decided that we would sleep in the city that night no matter what happened, and we left the bedrolls in camp.

The main road from Medjez-el-Bab is a good hard-surfaced road. It formed the extreme right flank of our attack, which had all been to the left of the road. We considered for a while whether it was better to be all safe and go down the dusty plain to the left of the road in the midst of the corridor our forces were taking or to be half safe and go down the road and miss most of the dust. We chose the latter route.

We passed Peter's Corner, where the previous night German troops had been reported. About half an hour after we went by the corner, a British officer from London on a special mission, an officer who had stayed at our Thibar camp, was driving down the same road. Suddenly some German soldiers fired an antitank gun at him and blew off his leg. He crawled painfully out of his wrecked car, and the three German soldiers came up asking him to accept their surrender. They had been sitting in their hole all morning, seen dozens of cars go by, and suddenly for no particular reason opened fire on this particular automobile. The officer cursed them and, after he had made them tie up his leg, told them to go to a military policeman when they surrendered and explain his plight. But he was 50 or 100 feet from the road, and by the time he was picked up he had lost too much blood. He died the next day.

Along the road we kept seeing the wrecks of cars and tanks destroyed in one battle or another.

A sign told us we had reached the end of the section of the road that was cleared of mines. We stopped, and as we were discussing further progress, an armored reconnaissance car came up the road toward us. The driver said he had been a few miles down the road and had not hit any minefields or seen any Germans, so we continued, watching the macadam carefully for the splotches where mine holes had been dug.

182

David Heneker stopped the car when we saw some military police-men who, he knew, were attached to the 6th Armored Division. He believed the 6th Armored would be among the first into Tunis, and if we stayed with it, we would have a good chance of being ahead of the other correspondents. Two soldiers came by, sweeping the edge of the road for mines. They circled around us and continued toward Tunis. We were happily eating bully beef by the roadside.

Two or three minutes later we saw the two stop and dig a couple of mines out of the shoulder of the road. We were uncomfortable, for we had been tramping around the shoulder, not noticing where we were walking. We turned the car very carefully back onto the road and headed for Tunis.

Some other cars with correspondents aboard passed us while we were eating lunch, and it became evident that we would have to get ahead of the 6th Armored Division people if we wanted to get quickly into Tunis.

After a while we saw a company of infantry in a field on our right. One of the officers said there were Germans in the hills and his brigade had just been ordered to attack them. We knew the main body of British troops were somewhere on our left, but we could not see them. At Massicault, fifteen miles from Tunis, some French people waved and cheered at us. We drank some wine with them. From a water tower we could see tanks moving down the right of the road.

A light drizzle began to fall, and our driver had disappeared. He showed up after we had been waiting half an hour. He was loaded with toilet kits and bedbug powder he had found in a German quartermaster's store. We cursed him roundly, for we feared the other correspondents would beat us.

At St.-Cyprien, less than ten miles from Tunis, we found most of the other correspondents. Through field glasses we all watched a tank battle in progress. Looking like toys, the tanks would go to the brow of a hill, and suddenly shells would fall among them in white puffs. The tanks would shoot and dodge back behind the crest. We saw one tank hit. It stopped, and white smoke poured out of it. In the village was a German military cemetery, and on its edge a German tank was burning. We went toward it, thinking that we might be able to pull someone out, but it was blazing fiercely inside. We could smell the burned flesh. We got away for fear of exploding ammunition.

Some reconnaissance cars and tanks cut into the road from the left ahead of us, and we stayed with them. Just before we reached the outskirts of the city of Tunis, we got into a close-packed line of tanks and armored cars. We heard some firing ahead and saw some other reporters coming back. Alan Morehead of the *Daily Express* was one of them. He said, "Two blocks down the street, they're fighting with machine guns and hand grenades. It's bloody awful. Nobody can get in any further." A block or so along we hit a sign saying TUNIS. We were on the edge of the city itself.

The other reporters said they were going back to Massicault to send their stories and spend the night.

We kept moving on slowly. At a crossroads we met some other reporters we knew. About 400 German prisoners were being marched out through the gateway of a big mansion, which, we learned, was one of the palaces of the bey of Tunis. We left the car and walked over to the gate. A policeman in red fez and sky blue uniform said, "Come quickly. I will show you where four or five more are hiding. My brother officer just called on them to surrender, and one of them shot him in the stomach with a machine gun." David found a British tank officer and told him the situation. A few minutes later a Sherman tank, looking very formidable, lumbered into the gardens. A few minutes more, and some more prisoners came out, holding up their hands.

Prisoners were swarming at the crossroads. Five came up and tried to surrender to us. We waved them on to a British tank officer.

We heard some more firing down the street, so we went on to investigate. It was at this point that the remaining correspondents turned and went back. We were still only in the outskirts of Tunis, technically part of the city but not really it.

A few Germans were holding out in a house up on the right side of the road, and we had a chance to see a typical squad attack. Some British soldiers lying behind a bank that ran beside the sidewalk were spraying the house with rifle fire and bursts from their Bren gun. A young British lieutenant was directing the operation. David Heneker felt his army blood surging and paced up and down in view of the house, while the rest of us kept prudently concealed behind a corner.

The lieutenant was about to lead a flanking assault, and David said, "You chaps wait here. I'm going to help in this attack."

I said, "David, don't be a god-awful fool. It won't help us. Your job is to go with us into Tunis. We've got a chance to be the first correspondents into the city, and you want to go off and get yourself knocked off in some goddamn attack on a house that doesn't mean a damn thing."

David cooled down and said he would go with us.

The firing from the house stopped. A figure started in from the side, and the soldiers in the street began shooting frantically at it. Someone yelled, "Stop that shooting, you bloody fools. It's one of ours."

At the nearby fork in the road we had to decide which of the two ways to go. It was then past four in the afternoon. A French civilian told us that he had seen two tanks go down the left-hand road; but nothing had gone to the right, and he had heard there were Germans in that direction. We took the road to the left and in two or three minutes met the two British Sherman tanks returning. We assumed they had been on reconnaissance, but they made so much noise on the hard street that we could not talk to them.

We moved slowly and cautiously, always ready for trouble but not finding any. By the time we reached the gates that mark the beginning of the city of Tunis itself people had begun to cheer us. No other correspondents had been within a mile of the Tunis gates. I carefully checked a French guidebook later, and only the area inside the gates was shown in color on the street plan and marked as Tunis. Outside, the areas were given other names and marked in white.

The next day, when Lang and I heard that other correspondents had sent stories datelined Tunis and saying they were in Tunis that day, we thought they might have said the "outskirts of Tunis" or "suburbs of Tunis" or some such phrase. At least we had the satisfaction of knowing we were the only Allied correspondents in Tunis on that day of May 7.

Crowds lining the sidewalks kept cheering us: *"Vivent les alliés,"* *"Vive la France,"* *"Vive De Gaulle."* They rushed up to wring our hands and climbed over the car. They kept asking where the Allies were and what was happening outside the city. We learned that we were the first men in Allied uniform any of them had seen. We imagined that the tanks must have gone in to take the city by some other road.

Robert Raymond was ecstatically happy and popped his head through the sliding roof to bow gravely at the homage of the city. Montgomery and Alexander could not have done it with more aplomb. We all were saluting with, we hoped, the same sort of gracious politeness conquering field marshals and bored royalty evince. Our uniforms puzzled them. Robert was wearing a beret, riding trousers, and a jacket with the insignia of the Chantiers de Jeunesse. Will was in ordinary American field outfit. David and I were in British tropical uniform, David with a British officer's cap, Will and I in the knitted caps that were used under American helmets.

The multitude kept asking us whether we were English, American, or French, and we yelled to them that we were all three nations. This always brought delighted cheers from the crowd. The audience was easy to please. We told the crowd that they need fear no longer, for we were there to protect them from the *boches*.

As we drove slowly down the street through the crowd, we kept hearing explosions. We discovered only the next day that the noise was Germans blowing up with hand grenades the vehicles and garages along the street.

One young man running beside the car kept exclaiming that now the Tunisians at last could see American films, Robert Taylor and Greta Garbo. I promised him in our running conversation that I would do more than that. I would grant him the right to view Clark Gable, Mickey Mouse—and Myrna Loy as well.

"Vivent les vedettes de cinéma," yelled the young Tunisian in frenzied delight. "They too are fighting the *boches*."

Robert knew Tunis well. As a matter of fact, a month or two earlier in the campaign, he had sneaked into the city and spent several days there. He told us the Hôtel Majestic was the best hotel. We arrived at about quarter to five, and 200 or 300 of our admiring followers streamed in with us and filled the lobby.

This quick change must have surprised the hotel clerks, for as they told us only the next day, ten minutes before our arrival two German officers drinking in the bar had suddenly downed their drinks and left in a hurry.

The questions we got inside and outside the hotel were the same. What was happening outside the city? When were the Allies going to arrive?

"Do not fear," we said grandly. "The Allies are here. We are the proof. They have taken the city, and you are safe."

Yet even then it seemed a little odd that no other correspondents or officers were at the Majestic. It was the kind of hotel that both categories immediately head for when a city is captured. We assumed that the combat men were at work cleaning up in other parts and their officers had not had time to reach the Majestic Bar.

So numerous and persistent were our well-wishers that it took us half an hour to sign the register and another half hour to park the car in a neighboring garage. En route we had to kiss babies, mothers, grandmothers, and even men. Some tried to pull us away to their houses for a visit.

By the time we went to our rooms and washed it was nearly dinnertime.

We were happy and at peace with the world. Our triumphal welcome had deeply affected us, and the joy of the people had stirred us to the heart. We had thought we would have to dodge German snipers and Italian grenades, and instead, we had had a welcome that Caesar returning from the wars might have envied.

Robert was in seventh heaven and let it be known, with due modesty, that although we had not won the war single-handedly, it had been a rare day that Eisenhower and Alexander had made a decision without consulting us in advance.

The rosy cloud on which we walked would have evaporated quickly had we known that at that moment we were the only 5 men in Allied uniform inside Tunis and that some 8,000 German troops still remained inside the city proper.

What had happened was this. The British Army had not wanted to get involved in street fighting with night coming on. Instead, the combat troops had gone to the edge of the city and ringed it to guard against possible counterattack. The British armor had gone off in pursuit of the remnants of the German panzers, at that moment heading out toward the Cape Bon peninsula.

A special combat force to clear the city was waiting on the outskirts and came into the city at dawn. With them was the S-Force, the special group to take the major installations and to handle the administration of the capital.

The leader of S-Force was Lieutenant Colonel David Strangeways. He was to be administrator and military ruler of the city. Strangeways himself came into the city that evening of May 7, sometime after we did, and spent the night inside the city limits. So during the night of May 7–8, there were just six Allies in the city, Strangeways, Heneker, Lang, Raymond, I, and our driver, Reed.

It was Colonel Strangeways who, surprised at where we told him we had spent the night, informed us the next day of the exact situation. Had we known it that night, we would undoubtedly have barricaded ourselves behind the Majestic Bar and prepared to sell our lives dearly with David Heneker's revolver and Reed's carbine for our protection. Instead, we were supremely confident that the

British troops had taken over all the main positions in the city and were probably even then killing off the last opposition.

When we entered the Majestic dining room, Robert told us some French people wanted us to be their guests. The meal was lengthy and excellent. High Axis officers had been staying at the Majestic, and to judge by the fare we had, they must have been eating very well.

Our new French friends told us that the Germans and Italians in Tunis had not appeared to sense their danger until that very morning. Even then, it was sometime later that firing was heard on the city outskirts and the Axis troops began to get panicky. Some changed to civilian clothing.

The previous night, we discovered, Admiral Esteva, the regent who had helped the Germans arrive in Tunisia, had been dragged from his bed at three o'clock in the morning and hastily flown off to Italy.

The meal was a happy one, and a dozen times someone proposed the health of the Allies, America, England, France, Eisenhower, victory, De Gaulle, Roosevelt, Churchill, Alexander, the liberation of France, and even our modest selves.

After dinner we accepted an invitation to go to the house of one of the Frenchmen for a little party. We stepped forth, unaware that several thousand Germans were at large. We did not want to wander about the streets in an unknown city after dark, for fear of snipers, but we felt that taking a short stroll with a party of Frenchmen and Frenchwomen would not be too dangerous. The streets were deserted. People were staying indoors as a precaution. No streetlights showed, and we had to move in the blackness by a kind of instinct and by sound.

David was a natural entertainer and an expert pianist. We three had a little repertoire to entertain our new French friends. For the past two or three days we had been singing two songs that David had composed but had not yet published. One was a little ditty in French called "Simone," and the opening words were something like *"Au clair de la lune, je pense à toi, je pense à toi, Simone. Au clair de la lune, je rêve de toi, je rêve de toi, Simone."* The other, in English, was titled "I'll Remember to Forget." I never heard the song again after that night, so I presume it was not published. The tune stays with me, however, and I sometimes find myself whistling it or humming it in my mind; but the words have gone, and all I can remember is the phrase "your smile—And in a little while, my pet, I'll remember to forget." We learned those and a third song Robert taught us, the famous old French student song "Les Pères de St. Bernardin," and we used to roar the chorus about *"la vie— la vie—la vie, chérie—aha."* We sang the songs so much driving along in the car that we were quite adept, and after we had sung the first two, the French people joined in for St. Bernardin. We sang many other songs, English and French, and a Frenchman named Bob told funny stories that I translated after a fashion.

Now and then we heard rifle shots, which we imagined were either snipers or Frenchmen shooting off rifles for sheer pleasure.

As we were walking back to the hotel with one or two of the Frenchmen who lived there, we heard shots just ahead of us. We pressed against the wall at a street corner.

Two cars came roaring past the corner at sixty miles an hour or better in the blackout. The car behind was firing at the car ahead, just as in a gangster movie. Someone was shouting what Lang understood to be German. They appeared and disappeared almost simultaneously, a rush of motion in the blackout. Later we discovered that some Germans and Italians had been rushing around Tunis that night, firing at anything they fancied, a kind of last fling before giving themselves up, venting their anger at the defeat. Also, some of the French patriots may have been settling scores with the Germans or with pro-Axis Frenchmen.

At the hotel we decided on a last toast, in champagne, but the clerk said the wine cellar was locked. Robert got very angry and snapped at the clerk that if German officers the previous night had asked him for champagne, he would have produced it quickly enough.

When the clerk still said, "Impossible," Robert said that we were not just visitors. We had just conquered Tunis and wanted champagne. To emphasize his words, he took out a revolver and laid it on the counter.

I told the clerk confidentially that Robert would probably rather shoot him and the proprietor than eat. In any case Robert had just that day killed many Germans and Italians and felt his day was not complete because he had failed to kill any pro-German Frenchmen. I begged the clerk to hurry and get the champagne so that we might distract Robert from his announced intention of putting a peanut on the clerk's head and playing William Tell with his revolver. Three minutes later the clerk returned with two well-iced bottles of champagne.

May 8, Saturday, was a town holiday. The crowds kept cheering

The happy people of Tunis welcome the Allied liberators of the city,
May 1943. U.S. ARMY.

A British tankman gets a personal welcome in Tunis on liberation day. British Newsreel Picture. WIDE WORLD.

us and asking us whether French troops were coming. We assured them that in a while they would see plenty of troops, but at that moment the British, French, and Americans were busy killing off Germans. Over the city, Spitfires were diving and climbing and turning for pleasure. The populace cheered them, and we were so much in the mood that we did also. Some British Army cameramen arrived about nine, and since we were about the only people in Allied uniform in the vicinity, they took pictures of us. I have always wished I had thought to ask them to send me some prints. We began to see a few soldiers on the streets, and hundreds of people crowded about each one. We ourselves went to the balcony of a newspaper office. People below saw us and began cheering. It was the moment for a speech; but none of us felt up to it, so we only gave the V sign and smiled, and that seemed enough.

British, American, and Soviet flags, hidden for months, now began to appear. Communists organized a parade of Italians bearing the signs, in Italian, Down with Mussolini, Down with fascism, Long Live America, Britain, and the Soviet Union.

I remember the days before the war when Mussolini was trying to frighten the French and the rest of the world by organizing student demonstrations calling for "Nice, Corsica, and Tunisia" to be handed over to Italy. In this new parade some of the participants were Italian soldiers still in uniform. Everyone kept shouting, "Hurrah for democracy and the Allies," and "Vive De Gaulle" was on every lip. In the two days and night we were in Tunis, none of us ever heard anyone shout, "Vive Giraud."

We discovered the office of Colonel Strangeways, and when we learned that he and our little group had been the only Allies in Tunis during the night, we felt very pleased, now it was all over, and nicknamed ourselves Heneker's Spearforce with the slogan Where we go, the tanks will follow.

I had sent off messages by dispatch rider from the edge of the city on the previous day. Now I sent another, briefly telling of the situation and saying that I was going to try to broadcast from Tunis. But the Germans had wrecked the electric power plant so that at night in the hotel we had only candles, and I discovered they had tossed hand grenades into the radio transmitter. Fixing it might take weeks. The prisoners were being gathered up by the thousand, although all had had orders to fight to the last man. If they had fought, they might have held out in Tunis for another week or two, but they very sensibly decided to quit since no good military purpose would be served by further resistance.

Here and there outside the city the fight continued a little longer. Some units were out of communication and did not receive word of what was happening for several days.

On Saturday we took our own pet prisoner, a man from Silesia who had once served six years in the French Foreign Legion. He boasted that in his own village the Gestapo ranked him as pro-Ally suspect number three, but they had drafted him the previous spring. The Silesian brought with him a Frenchman who vouched for the fact that the German had been heard to express anti-Nazi opinions in Tunis. We found a military policeman who took him away.

On the road near Alouine Airport we saw hundreds of prisoners. Some had formed themselves into ranks and were marching to give themselves up to their captors. They could see dozens of their own wrecked planes on the airfield.

The next day, Sunday, we went out to the outer port of Tunis, near ancient Carthage. The effects of our bombing were evident all around the docks, as had been the case in the inner harbor. But it was very peaceful. A single soldier shooting at a tin can in the water was the only martial note.

I ran into my friend Lieutenant Commander Dunstan Curtis, DSC, of the Royal Naval Volunteer Reserve. Across the bay at Hammam-Lif, where the British First Army was finishing off the resistance on Cape Bon, we could see British troops moving near the water, and we could also see our artillery shells landing near the distant docks.

It had been thought that some of the Germans might try to escape in small boats. But Dunstan, with a smile, assured me that the Royal Navy had the situation well in hand.

As we passed through the city again, there were many Allied troops of all kinds in the streets. Nobody cheered us anymore, and we decided that it was time we said good-bye to the lovely, tranquil city of Tunis. But as we went out of the city gate on the road back to Thibar, and to Algiers, a few people, weary from their joy, still gave us the V sign for victory.

Interlude III

With Africa entirely freed of Axis forces, the Allies paused before the next move. I believed, as did some well-informed Allied officers, that the long-awaited invasion of France would take place in the summer of 1943. As we now know, that was originally the plan. So I hurried back to England to be ready to move in what I felt sure was to be the great and final Allied invasion.

However, the British were able to have their way when they pointed to the difficulties of mounting an attack on France at that time and the comparative ease of attacking across the Mediterranean into Sicily and the mainland of Italy.

With Britain's best strategist, General Alexander, doing the military thinking for most of the operation, and the American generals Bradley, Patton, and Clark and the British General Montgomery in tactical command, the Allied forces struck across the narrow sea. But in spite of the crumbling of Mussolini's regime and the official surrender of the Italian forces, it was to be a whole year before the Allies entered Rome, and until the end, the German Army held northern Italy.

Meanwhile, I spent the year in England, waiting impatiently for the big invasion. The winter passed slowly. At times I envied colleagues who were with the armies in Italy. Yet I always felt that Italy was the sideshow. Soon the band would strike up, and the main performance take place, and I wanted to be there. By the end of the winter signs multiplied that the effort we all expected was indeed under way. The moment was coming for which all else had been preparation, a moment history would always remember—I would be able to see it for myself.

Chapter 18

When I learned that the 1st Infantry Division had arrived in England, I knew that England was in fact going to be the springboard for the main endeavor, for it was inconceivable that the 1st would be used in any sideshow. I went down to the division headquarters in southern England, had dinner with the new general, Clarence Huebner and his staff, and spent the night with some of my old friends in the division. One whose acquaintance I first made then was Captain Quentin Roosevelt, son of General Teddy, who had earlier been deputy commander of the division. Quentin Roosevelt was one of the nicest men I have ever known. He had been wounded when his battery was bombed during the Battle of Kasserine Pass and invalided home to the United States. After he got out of the hospital, he was told he could be passed only for limited duty, which meant a desk in Washington or elsewhere in the United States. Somehow he had wangled his way to England to rejoin the 1st Division, for he was anxious to go into combat with his fellows on the biggest exploit of all.

"Q" was given a title, something like Inspector of Artillery or Artillery Liaison Officer for division headquarters, and became, in fact, a general all-around handyman for General Huebner and division headquarters.

The new commanding general was an interesting man. He had enlisted as a cook's helper in the 1st Division many years before, and he had moved through every rank and position in the division except one, brigadier general and deputy commander. He had been successively PFC, corporal, sergeant, second lieutenant, first lieutenant, captain, major, lieutenant colonel, and colonel, all with the 1st Division.

When the division had finished the Tunisian campaign, it was sent back to the spot where it had first landed in Africa, Arzew near Oran. Bereft of the delights of Algiers, the men roistered and fought and let off steam, with the approval of General Allen. Then they went into more hard fighting in Sicily. Higher headquarters then decided that the 1st, although it always fought magnificently, was so convinced of its superiority over any other American combat aggregation that it had to be taken down a peg. The 1st did not have the American ideal, the old team spirit. It believed its commander was the best general in the whole damn Army, bar none, and the 1st was the best division, and by God, if headquarters and the other divisions would just get out of the goddam way, the 1st would win the goddamn war for them. I am convinced that the 1st Division had good reason for this belief, but higher headquarters got tired of a division which believed that possibly only the British Guards were of sufficient military caliber for the 1st even to acknowledge being in the same war with it. General Patton clashed with Allen, but General Bradley said that he himself was responsible for the ultimate decision to remove both General Allen and his deputy commander, Brigadier General Teddy Roosevelt. When the two men were on the way back to headquarters to be told the news after days of bitter combat at the front, they were stopped by MPs and told they were improperly dressed, Terry for riding in the jeep without wearing his helmet and Roosevelt for wearing his stocking cap instead of his helmet.

Both men were sent back to the States next day, Allen to build and command the 104th Division, which he made into a fine outfit, and Roosevelt to command a regiment in the 4th Division.

The new commander had had no combat experience in World War II; but he knew the division, and he himself was tough enough to show the hard-bitten combat unit who was boss. He set the division at practicing close-order drill when it was pulled out of the line. This was a supreme insult to men who had been fighting and dying for months, but Huebner's spit and polish proved to them at least their new commander had a mind of his own.

When I first saw the division in England, the men talked longingly of Terry and Teddy. They obeyed General Huebner, but he was still very much on trial and would remain so until he proved his ability in combat. When he did, the division learned to believe in him, and when he finally left the unit, his departure was a matter of great regret to all the men.

With the announcement that the Supreme Commander was to be Eisenhower and his deputy was to be Montgomery, the pace in England quickened. I went more and more often on maneuvers, which now largely consisted of invasion tactics. Indeed, the 29th Division and the V Corps staff of the U.S. Army, which had not yet

196

been in combat, must have a record of getting in and out of boats more often than any other.

They practiced with frenzied activity, climbing into barges, dashing out of them onto beaches, and rushing inland while charges of high explosive banged around them and machine-gun bullets were shot over their heads. For these were realistic maneuvers, adapted from those patterned by the British commandos, and often men were killed or badly injured in the effort to give them combat hardening without the actual combat. Such tactics are now routine training, but in those days it was all new.

Early in December a friend of mine in British military intelligence, knowing that Lucy was pregnant, suggested that I get her out of London before Christmas. He told me of a new German horror weapon, giant rockets that Hitler was believed to be preparing to rain on London sometime during Christmas or the New Year. He said the weight and frequency of the rockets might well make life practically unlivable in London.

I talked it over with Lucy and decided that she should stay until something more definite developed. As a matter of fact, the attack on Peenemünde had delayed the rockets considerably, and it was not for several months that they arrived, and then in far less numbers and striking power than British intelligence had first predicted.

But in March, for the first time in two years and ten months, there was again real war in the sky over London. The Germans began to send fifty or sixty bombers over a night in a kind of little blitz. It was nowhere as bad as the real blitz, but it was a nuisance to us who had forgotten what going to the shelters was.

Lucy and I had taken an apartment on the next to the top floor of 88 Portland Place, and Googie Withers, a most charming and intelligent screen actress, had taken over our old smaller apartment halfway up the building.

Our son, Myles, was then a year and nine months old. At first we took him down to the basement whenever a raid began. But it meant waking him up, dressing him in something, and then interrupting his sleep for perhaps a couple of hours in the cold, drafty corridor of the basement with two or three dozen people milling around.

Then we devised the idea of waiting before we waked him. We would turn out the lights, open the curtains, and watch the anti-aircraft fire. If it seemed as though the attack were concentrated on some other part of the city and our own antiaircraft guns in Regent's Park did not bellow out, we would wait there, letting him sleep. If we beheld the lights of the antiaircraft explosions coming across the sky in our direction, we would whisk him out of bed and down to the basement.

The raids were noisy, for there were many guns in London, but they were not particularly terrifying in comparison with those we had experienced so often in 1940 and 1941. Yet the presence of our son made us again aware of the fact that both of us dreaded much more the thought of anything happening to him than to either of us. Myles himself never appeared worried by the noise and played happily in the basement with the other children.

Another complication was my having to broadcast each night. I would have to leave home about ten o'clock at night, knowing that I would not be back until some time after one in the morning. When raids happened in those three hours, I could not be with Lucy and Myles.

Only three American broadcasters were ever permitted to broadcast live without censorship during air raids on London: Fred Bate of NBC, Ed Murrow of CBS, and I. When Fred left London, there were only the two of us.

The British military and civil authorities considered that our knowledge of censorship regulations and our good judgment of such matters, proved in the past, was sufficient to allow us an open line to the United States. The British knew that we would not give vital military secrets away even unwittingly, for we knew the censorship regulations as well as most of the experienced censors did.

It was judged unfeasible to set up facilities for such broadcasts on the roof of Broadcasting House, where our little studio was. But on a BBC building two or three blocks away on Oxford Street, a microphone and a headphone were secreted. The plan was that I should go there if a raid began, and inform the duty officer of the building, who would have BBC Master Control, the engineering center, put the New York circuit through to me on the roof, so that I could both broadcast from that point and hear the New York feedback—that is, the editor sitting at the NBC schooldesk in the New York newsroom.

Sometimes the raid alarm would sound and the raid would be over before I went to work. Sometimes it would come early in the morning. But for some reason or other it never seemed to come at precisely the right time.

198

Then, on March 23, 1944, Lucy went to the Middlesex Hospital and had our daughter, Sara Ann Andrew. On her first evening, a nurse came up to her and said, "Oh, Mrs. MacVane, I knew you were here because among the babies I saw one that reminded me so much of your other one, so I came looking for you."

Mary Smith, the faithful cook from South Africa who had worked for us during the whole war serving ambassadors and generals the same good food made out of nothing as she served privates and newspapermen, came to stay at the apartment during the two weeks Lucy was in the hospital. I had great confidence in her judgment. Her husband was a prisoner of war, and she loved the children as though they were her own.

Each night the nurses took the mothers and their babies down to the basement so that if a bomb hit the hospital during the night, each mother would have her baby beside her bed. They brought them up to the sunny ward in the morning.

It was two or three nights after Sara was born. I was just entering Broadcasting House when I heard the sirens wail. My broadcast was only about five minutes or so away, and I had my script in my hand. I turned and ran down the street to the annex on Oxford Street. I found the duty officer, told him I would broadcast from the roof, and raced up the stairs.

I got the microphone and the earphone, one in each hand, then found I had no hand to hold my sheets of script, which in any case were not censored. I put the sheets down and placed a foot on them. Then I discovered, of course, that I was on an open roof where no light could be shown. It was pitch-dark, and I had no flashlight anyway. There was one minute to go when I heard New York in my earphone, and they heard me calling them. I did not even have a watch with me, so I told New York to give me a "go ahead."

But since the sirens had sounded, nothing had happened, absolutely nothing. I looked over toward the Middlesex Hospital, half a mile away, where Lucy and Sara were lying.

I looked behind me to where, a quarter of a mile or so away, I knew my son, Myles, was probably in the basement with Mary. I looked ahead of me to where I could see faint streaks in the sky from antiaircraft fire, and I said, "I hope, I hope, I hope there isn't a raid. But if there has to be a raid tonight, let it happen now and may nothing drop to my left or behind me. I don't want a raid at all tonight—but if it has to come, let it come while I am on the air."

In my disturbed condition I lifted my foot, and the cold wind blew the pages of my script away across the roof. So there I was with no raid and no broadcast script, and the voice from New York said, "Go ahead, John."

I started to talk to fill my three allotted minutes. I have no idea what I said. But all I could see was the low flashes of antiaircraft fire and bombs on the edge of London, and I could hear nothing. I was terribly disturbed by my personal fears and my predicament. I was about to halt when I thought my three minutes were up, but a voice said in my earphone, "Keep talking, John. This is good stuff. Keep talking." I kept talking for another minute or two, and the voice said, "You're coming in fine, John. Keep it up. We're washing out the rest of the spots. Keep talking, John. You have all the time you want. Keep talking. Don't stop."

With that I dropped the earphone, kept talking for the best part of fifteen minutes, and signed off. When I picked up the earphones, I heard someone, perhaps Buck Prince or Joe Myers back in New York, say, "Swell show tonight, John. Swell show." But nothing at all had happened.

Chapter 19

One day Stanley Richardson said to me that I should decide what I wanted to do on the invasion. He said, "You have earned the right to any job you want and it's yours, Supreme Headquarters or Army Group or London or anything."

I said, "Stan, since I was kicked out of France by the Germans, there is just one thing I have wanted to do—go back to France with the first combat troops to hit the beach."

It was not in any spirit of bravado that I picked the assignment; it was simply that that was the job I wanted to do. It was what my whole war correspondent career had been building toward, and I would leave the rest of the job to others.

We were quite a large group of NBC correspondents by this time. Some months previously Richardson had told me he was thinking of hiring Merrill Mueller of *Newsweek*. He said I knew him better than anyone else in NBC, and his being hired would depend on my recommendation. I told Richardson I thought Red was a good newsman and could learn broadcasting, for he had done a good deal for me in Africa, and I recommended him wholeheartedly. So Mueller showed up in London. So did W. W. Chaplin from the United States, an old INS ace reporter. Then came Wright Bryan of the *Atlanta Journal*. He was then managing editor of the *Journal*, later editor of the *Journal* and of the Cleveland *Plain Dealer*, but the only way it appeared he could get an early look at the invasion was through accreditation as an NBC correspondent because the station his paper owned was an NBC affiliate. There was Ed Haaker from the New York newsroom, and we also had a young man from another NBC station who had done little broadcasting but was a relative of a high executive. He, too, became one of our band. Finally, one of the top New York newsroom editors, Frank McCall, complete with an engineer and a tape recorder developed by the Navy, arrived.

In informing the Army that I was to be NBC representative with the first troops, I specified that I wanted to be with the 1st Division. If I were to be killed, I wanted to be killed in good company, and I

A month before D-Day, MacVane and Royal Air Force Officer Jerome Willis drink to coming success at the Dover Castle Public House in Devonshire Mews, London.

figured that with the experienced 1st Division I would be as safe as anyone could be on an enemy beach. At least I knew what it would do; it would not cut and run when German panzers hit. With a new, untried division, I could not be sure, and I believed in taking as little chance as was humanly possible under the circumstances.

We correspondents, with Lucy, Myles, Sara in a carriage, and Mildred Boutwood, Florence Peart, and Jean Smith from the office, used to meet at noon on Sunday in Devonshire Mews, where the pub called the Dover Castle provided us with sustenance. Usually Jerome Willis and a couple of dozen other people from the neighborhood would be there. We would stand out in the mews with our beer or sit on the bench in the sun and talk and drink until two o'clock, when we all would separate for Sunday dinner. It was very festive, for we knew that sooner or later the mews would be half vacant some Sunday, and we would be off for the invasion.

When, during the first week in May, I got secret orders to report with my equipment at our London rendezvous, I again kissed Lucy good-bye and set off for what I thought was the invasion at last.

Instead, we were loaded in cars, twenty of us, American and British, and driven to one of two London stations, Euston or King's Cross. This was to be a maneuver to deceive German spies, who, it was known, were keeping watch on the stations. The theory was that they would see a group of prominent war correspondents leaving the station with all their gear and assume the invasion was just about to begin. Also, the authorities wanted to have us stop writing and broadcasting for a few days, so that when the real time came and we did do just that, the Germans would not automatically assume it indicated the imminence of the invasion.

We all were taken to Dundonal, an amphibious and commando training camp at Troon, in Ayrshire on the Scottish coast. Most of us selected were scheduled to go with the first invading forces. We were given a week of lectures on amphibious warfare at Dundonal, coupled with practical demonstrations of landing craft and vehicle waterproofing. The waterproofing was one of the marvels of the invasion, and it always amazed me to see a tank plowing along entirely underwater except for the very top of its turret. The waterproofing of each vehicle took three days for trained men to accomplish, and I hesitate to judge the millions of man-hours used in this work, for every one of the thousands of vehicles which landed during the first few days in France had been waterproofed. Jeeps, guns, tanks, and trucks slid down the landing-craft ramps and went ashore with perhaps only the tops of the hoods or the windshields above water.

During that week we correspondents drank somewhat more in the officers' mess than might have been the case in other circumstances. We knew we were to be the first of the reporters, some with airborne, some with assault divisions, to step ashore on the fortified coast of France. We knew the time must be near because the commando school had finished training for the European invasion, and the young naval officers we met there were already being prepared for amphibious operations against Japan.

May was a lovely month, especially sweet to Lucy and me because we knew it might be brief. Any time she left the flat to go shopping, I might be gone on the great adventure by the time she returned.

I thought I should see General Eisenhower alone before I went off on the assault. I had gone to the one or two news conferences he had held and had been present at major exercises on at least two occasions when he had been present. One of those I remember was Exercise Fox in March. Both Montgomery and Eisenhower had been there for the two or three days of the maneuver. At one stage, I remember, I rode in a 2nd Armored Division tank while the artillery shot airburst shells at us. Buttoned down inside the Sherman, I could hear nothing except the rumble of the machinery, but correspondents outside said the shelling sounded as though hell were breaking loose. We were quite safe, of course, for the fragments of the high-explosive shells could not penetrate or even damage the heavy tank armor. Watching our progress through the periscope, I understood some of the difficulties that confronted driver and gunner. Ground that looked completely flat to me would dip and rise so our tank would dip and rock until I had trouble keeping my feet. I began to appreciate how tank gunners can miss seeing foe that might seem in plain sight to anyone outside the tank.

When I got out to Widewing, Eisenhower's headquarters at Kingston, and passed under the mound of camouflage netting that made the whole group of buildings look like a brown and green hill, Captain Harry Butcher led me in to the general, then left us.

Among the four or five books on Eisenhower's desk I noticed my own, which I had autographed and sent him. He shook hands, then said, "You were certainly a little rough on me in your book, John."

This surprised me and I replied, "I don't think I was, General. I thought I explained how much we all thought of you and how much we admired what you did during the campaign."

"I mean the political stuff," he said, "the Darlan appointment. I felt it meant a saving of lives and would make our rear secure so we wouldn't have to keep troops to guard Algeria, troops we needed in Tunisia."

"Well, I did disagree with that, as you know," I replied, "but I thought I had made it clear that Bob Murphy and Clark made the Darlan deal."

"Nevertheless," Eisenhower went on, "the responsibility was mine, and I had to approve anything political or military which happened in my theater of operations. No. Mine was the responsibility, and criticism of policy and the subordinates who acted under my orders was criticism of me."

I explained that I had never meant to criticize him. I thought he was sensitive to criticism and somewhat quixotic in his assumption of criticisms aimed at Murphy. Murphy was a tough, experienced diplomat, tough enough to give as good as he got and to remain unmoved by the fulminations of newsmen unless he saw some positive value in them as expressions of American public opinion. But General Eisenhower was another sort of man. He did not care for the niceties of political maneuver and always thought of himself as a straightforward simple soldier. Yet his reaction showed that his skin was extremely tender to adverse political comment.

He told me that his thought was that American troops should not go into France in order to set up any particular government, De Gaulle's or anyone else's. He seemed to believe that his political officers would work with any local authorities favorable to the Allies in any particular area, and only after all France was liberated would a national government be chosen by free vote.

I said I thought he would find that most of the French wanted De Gaulle and the Free French would take over automatically.

We talked for perhaps half an hour about the course of the war and the gigantic effort that was about to be made. I told General Eisenhower I wanted to go with the 1st Division, and he said that if I did, he was sure I would see plenty of action. He wished me luck and said that probably the next time we met, we would be on the other side of the Channel.

General Montgomery, sometime after this interview, received a large group of Allied correspondents and officers in the auditorium of St. Paul's School in London, his headquarters.

He held his audience spellbound. We knew he was to lead the ground forces of both countries in the invasion itself, and I must say it gave me some comfort when he said, "I know Rommel. I know how Rommel thinks. He's a good commander—but limited. I can outthink him, and I will. I study these German generals. I know how their minds work. Most of them have no imagination. That's why they lose wars. And they're going to lose this one. I beat Rommel every time I meet him. I shall continue that habit, and Rommel knows it. He's half-beaten before we start. I will hit Rommel where he doesn't expect it and when he doesn't expect it, and then I will hit him again before he knows what has happened."

I thought that Montgomery was certainly cocky, but cocky in a nice way. When his appointment had first been announced, I had broadcast an analysis of his fighting abilities. I said that he was a very sure commander and an excellent leader, but he had one great weakness, his caution. This caution was more than justified in the desert, where his supply lines ran several thousand miles from England around the Cape of Good Hope to Suez, then across 1,000 miles of desert. In the desert one false, incautious move could have cost him his army. But would he remain as cautious when his supply lines ran only across the English Channel? Would he be prepared to take chances when the odds were in his favor and a temporary defeat would not be a decisive defeat, while a gamble might win resounding victories? I thought that if he could unlearn the experience in the desert and learn to gamble now and then, he might become the greatest military genius of World War II. As it developed, Montgomery did not gamble in the campaigns in Europe. He remained as sure of hand and judgment as ever, but he still was the commander of the set piece, the carefully prepared offensive, and his careful, tidy mind was not best at developing the fighting according to the situation once the objectives he had in mind were achieved. He was more apt to leash his war dogs quickly, once the task he had ordered was performed, than let them slip through the unforeseen opening to worry the quarry from the unexpected angle. He treated the vast forces now under his command as he did the handful of divisions in his Eighth Army, attempting to keep them all where he could make decisions for them and control their every move. His offensives were likely to follow a pattern of much heavier preparation by artillery and air than most other commanders were accustomed to, followed by an advance to the objectives in overwhelming force, followed by a pause for what Montgomery called "tidying up the front," a phrase I heard him use many times. Montgomery, I thought, would never lose a war, perhaps hardly lose a battle, but he would, on the other hand, never win a quick victory.

A basic difference between American and British temperament may have been responsible. The British commander, whether of platoon or army, tended to fight by the book. Told to take a hill, the British would take the hill by direct assault, no matter how few were left to win the summit. When the same orders were given to Americans, there was much less certainty in the result.

The American inclination was to try to figure out how the hill could be taken with as little pain as possible. They might surround it and take it from behind, or they might ask the Air Force to work on it, or they might take another hill from which the first hill could be dominated, or they might sneak up at night and take it before the defenders knew what was happening. Or they might leave the hill entirely and go on and take the next four hills, and eventually the first hill would surrender anyway. It was very pragmatic and American.

When the final call came, it came suddenly. The telephone woke me at eight o'clock one morning. I was told to report with full equipment at half past nine. I sprang from bed and hastily began to get together odd bits of gear I thought I wanted at the last minute. At nine o'clock the telephone rang again, and the voice said, "Forget the order to report at nine-thirty. Report at one o'clock instead."

I was still in a rush. I had had everything ready, but there were always last-minute thoughts—perhaps more Players cigarettes, for who knew how long it would be before I could get Players again, or any other cigarettes, for that matter, in France? A roll of adhesive tape to help waterproof my typewriter. Had I enough notebooks to last until I could get more? Such thoughts as these kept me adding little extras to my duffel bag or musette bag.

I reported at the London headquarters of the First U.S. Army Group, which, for some reason, had been changed to the Twelfth U.S. Army Group, and Lieutenant Colonel Howard Nussbaum of Public Relations gave me a little slip of paper to paste onto my adjutant general's office identity card, saying, with a smile, "Here is your overseas visa."

Nobody mentioned the horrid word "invasion." Instead, everyone at the group headquarters spoke self-consciously of "the exercise." But the little white slip of paper meant to me that this at last was the real thing.

A French correspondent, looking strange and unhappy in civilian clothes, was sitting in the office when I arrived. He left with an officer, and Nussbaum said, "We don't know what to do with Rabache. He arrived here without any equipment. He says he hasn't any. We can't let him go around London collecting any. Nobody can leave this building until you are sent off to your destinations. We'll have to keep Rabache under guard somewhere. He may never get to go on the exercise."

I waited two hours in the office, then, with other correspondents, some of them old friends, was driven to a correspondents' training camp near Bristol, where the public relations officers and the new correspondents had been learning what to do in the field. Some other reporters were already there, and we were put into tents under the wet pine trees. At the mess hall that night, rain swirled and drummed hideously on the roof. Some of the correspondents in the mess were new to me. Times had changed since the early days of the war when we all knew one another. So many correspondents had arrived from America and so many new ones had been assigned to war reporting by the British papers that we had never even seen the faces of several.

After dinner we were told to draw special equipment. Each of us received five boxes of K rations, concentrated food in waterproof boxes. We were given waterproofed matchboxes, pills to purify drinking water, extra cigarettes, pills for seasickness, and even the means to make love safe and sanitary, which were also useful for waterproofing small articles in our pockets.

We were about twenty-five or thirty in all, but not all of us were going with the assault troops. Ernie Pyle, for instance, was to be with Bradley at First Army Headquarters, which would probably not reach France for a couple of days after the invasion. Others would be with naval command ships and might never get onshore at all. Four or five of the reporters had taken the special quick course in parachute jumping. They were going with the airborne divisions, which would be dropped before the landings. I did not envy them, nor did I want to take the parachute course which was a prerequisite for covering the airborne men. I had never felt happy in any kind of flying, although I had had to do a lot of it since that first flight of mine so long ago in the rear gunner's seat of the Lysander. I never felt, nor have I yet felt, safe in the air. By comparison, I have never felt in danger at sea. With the sea or solid land under me, I have felt I could face anything.

The next day we were sent in groups by jeep to the units we were to accompany to France. I arrived at Blandford, not far from Dorchester, and discovered with pleasure that I really was going to be with the 1st Infantry Division.

The division headquarters were in the same country mansion I had previously visited.

With me were three other reporters and two photographers. They were John H. "Jack" Thompson of the Chicago *Tribune,* Don Whitehead of the Associated Press, John "Tex" O'Reilly of the New York *Herald Tribune,* Bob Capa, *Life* magazine photographer, and Bert Brandt of Acme News Pictures.

O'Reilly left us almost immediately. He had been assigned to the division artillery headquarters of Brigadier General Clift Andrus, and the artillery would not be coming into the beach until very late on D-Day. Then the photographers left to get some pictures of the loading of troops and join the units to which they had been assigned. My impression is that Brandt went to the 26th Regiment or First Army Headquarters and did not get in at all on D-Day. Capa did get ashore early on D-Day, snapped roll after roll of pictures, and hopped a boat back to England with them in midmorning. When he arrived, a technician in the *Life* magazine developing room spoiled practically every picture he had taken. Only six photographs survived the technical error, and they were almost the only picture record we had of D-Day morning. Some GIs splashing into the water from a landing craft was one, and a group huddled around a German obstacle on the beach was another that became famous and has been republished often through the years.

So there were only three of us, Thompson, Whitehead, and I, with our old friends of the 1st Division.

I knew many of the officers sleeping and eating at the mansion with us, among them Quentin Roosevelt; Major Paul Gale; Captain Max Zera, the division's public relations officer; Major Peters, commander of the headquarters company; and others. Lieutenant Colonel Kenneth Lord, a brilliant young officer who used to spend his summers at Port Clyde, Maine, in a cottage not far from Lucy's, was G-3, the operations officer of the division.

Now the best technical brains of two countries had been working out plans for the press and radio coverage of the invasion. This was meant to be the best-covered landing that American troops had ever made. Thousands of man-hours had been spent on all the details. The net result was that practically nothing worked.

Before I left London, I had asked Richardson to get details of just how I was going to cover the assault landings. Was I going to have recording equipment? Was I going to have priority on radio circuits? Who was to transmit my broadcasts? How were they going to be received? Where would I find the proper equipment? Should it not all be planned ahead of time? But headquarters replied to each query that everything was arranged, and it all would be revealed to me at the proper time. In a whisper, it was stated that Colonel David Sarnoff himself was in charge of such preparations, Sarnoff, president of RCA.

I now queried the 1st Division to find out where the recording equipment might be. No one had ever heard of any. Nobody had delivered anything for me. In fact, nobody knew anything.

I began to have a suspicion that as in Dieppe and North Africa, the radio coverage of the invasion was to be all mucked up. After my lengthy conversations with the division signal officer and his conversations by telephone with other field units, he at length traced a portable wire recorder and had it sent over to Blandford. It was a huge affair, army equipment, slung on the back by a harness over the shoulders—it must have weighed fifty pounds or more. I could barely walk with it. The power was an array of batteries. Nobody knew how much it had been used. There was no way of listening to what one recorded with it, for there was no playback equipment anywhere available, either in the set or outside it. I knew the BBC had light portable tape-recording equipment, but I supposed someone considered it would have been a slight on American ingenuity and industry to employ British recording machines.

I also inquired as to what broadcasting facilities I would have when I reached the beach. Nobody at the division knew, but the signal officer said I could have the use of any of the division's four radio transmitters, which were being taken to the beachhead by DUKW.

With my big allegedly portable wire recorder, I arranged for a jeep ride down to the coast. The beach at Weymouth shone white under a hazy sky. At the water's edge, the sand showed the gouges left by snub-nosed landing craft. One or two of these were maneuvering inshore. A few hundred yards out, the harbor was covered with boats and ships of various sizes and appearances.

Barbed wire in accordion rolls separated the beach from the town. Next to the barbed wire was a sidewalk. Between the sidewalk and the adjacent road were two or three strands of barbed wire. On them was a sign, Do Not Communicate with Troops.

This second line of wire was not a formidable barrier. One could step over it or brush it aside, but on the day in question it represented a dividing line more definite than the widest river. For the sidewalk was reserved exclusively for the troops of the 1st Division. A file of soldiers dressed in their assault jackets and helmets stood on the walk. But civilians shared the road with majestic gestures. A bus conductress rang her bell, and the bus jerked ahead with the grinding of gears. Greengrocers put vegetables in shopping baskets and clipped ration coupons. In the corner pub, two commercial travelers finished their glasses of bitter and hurried to their next appointments.

Separated by only the slight strands of wire from the life of the civilians, the American soldiers felt as though they were aboard a speeding train which had lost its engineer and was heading for a concrete wall in the near distance. There was no possibility of stopping the train, and the time left before impact could be easily calculated. The only questions now which provoked interest were the thickness of the concrete obstacle and how many passengers might survive the smash.

It was evident from the self-conscious looks the townsfolk gave the young strangers in uniform that the civilians shared their knowledge. There was a look of musing on the faces of the soldiers, the look one sometimes sees in the faces of members of a football team just before a big game. From time to time, when the line moved or some chance sight or sound forced itself upon them, the men came back to an awareness of their surroundings. They would shrug their shoulders into a more comfortable position beneath the load of equipment which hung like Christmas tree ornaments on each man, or they would talk to the next men in line or throw a joke at a passing English girl.

The line was passing through a tent erected over a section of the sidewalk. The tent was a miniature Bar of Heaven with three or four officers and sergeants as recording angels. As each man stepped in front of a high desk, he spoke his name loudly and clearly. A sergeant repeated it, and the men walked quickly past the desk and out of the tent. The company commander stood watching, but making no comment.

"Ray—Regan—Roberts—Ruggiero." Names followed each other in quick succession. Until the tent was reached, some miracle might happen. He might break a leg, catch smallpox, or faint, and doctors would discover he had an ailment that should have barred him from the Army entirely; but once he was out of the tent, this theoretical last chance of staying behind no longer existed, and the man became part of a boatload of men whose immediate future was mapped out for them with painstaking exactitude by mysterious higher authorities. All over England, other men and vehicles were on the move toward the ports. These were the assault troops, but behind them were coming corps headquarters, mechanized cavalry, armor, artillery, trucks, and every manner of manpower and matériel the Army possessed.

Each unit of the assault combat teams went to its boats on the beach at Weymouth or nearby Portland, and each had its quota of maps, water, gasoline, trucks, mess kits, seasickness pills, shells, bullets, spoons, typewriters, nuts, bulldozers, bazookas, flamethrowers, toilet paper, road markers, radios, telephone cables, thumbtacks, crayons, map cases, detective stories, chewing gum, grenades, gas ointments, and the thousand other articles that a company must have to function.

An American chief boatswain's mate with a voice like a brass trumpet bellowed orders on a wharf. Landing craft of two navies moved into the wharf by twos and threes. The troops standing on the dock dropped into the craft in their allotted order. The boats slid away, and other boats took their places in the constant shuttle back and forth from the shore to the vessels out in the harbor.

"Come on in, Number Thirty," the petty officer would yell through his megaphone. "Come on in with Number Twenty-two and Fourteen. What's the matter out there? Hurry it up."

The 1st Division looked confident and capable in spite of the fact that the Germans had for four years tried to make France impregnable to attack. In the men's minds, the attack had been prepared for so long, talked about so much that most had become convinced that whether the result was success or failure, at least the battle would be epic.

These were experienced men, and they knew fear, for the uncertainty of the battle, the unknown quantity of resistance ahead,

212

and the remembrance of past battles all affect the mind of the experienced combat soldier. One could see it in the preoccupied look and the tightness of the cheeks. This was not the exhilaration that sometimes sweeps over inexperienced troops before their first battle. But the confidence surmounted fear, and when they stepped ashore, training, experience, unit spirit, and what can best be described as combat wisdom would govern their actions.

General Huebner, the commander, and General Willard Wyman, the assistant commander of the 1st Division, were on the hard concrete docks slanting down to the water where tank landing craft nosed up with lowered ramps to receive cars, tanks, guns, and trucks in the order opposite to the way they would leave the ship.

Huebner, dressed in trench coat and helmet, was joking with officers and men. But he was the loneliest man in Weymouth, for under him he had 36,000 men, and he alone was responsible for their lives. In a few hours his whole career could be made or broken; if he made a mistake in judgment, the lives of those who died in failure would be his responsibility alone. He knew that chance could disrupt all the plans, and the essence of his generalship must be to be able to scrap all plans in a moment and replace them with others as the battle developed.

Lugging my recorder on my back, I interviewed the generals. I described the scenes around the docks, held my microphone up to the commands of naval officers on the hards, the roll call of the troops going through the tents, the rumble of tanks and trucks. In two days of hard work that left great red weals across my back from the recorder shoulder straps, I must have recorded the voices of at least 100 of the troops departing for the great invasion.

I sent the reels of wire up to London for censorship. They were to be released for broadcast as soon as the D-Day announcement was made. Many days later I learned that the batteries of the recording machine had run down so that at the slow speed the wire moved, my voice and all the others were practically unintelligible, not at all fit for broadcast purposes. So all the work went for nothing.

Back at the headquarters at Blandford, "Q" Roosevelt was spending his spare time with his bride of a few weeks, a Red Cross girl. But on one of our last nights, Whitehead, Thompson, Major Paul Gale, Captain Max Zera, and I spent the evening at a modernistic upstairs bar in Bournemouth, the British seashore resort. The proprietress welcomed her 1st Division friends with open arms. Her clientele was changing rapidly. Only a few swaggering short-sleeved

1st Division men now mingled with a horde of newcomers in smartly pressed uniform blouses. These were the newcomers who themselves would be combat veterans after the invasion began.

We five linked arm in arm around the circles and drained our glasses in the "blood-brother" rite.

On an impulse we left Bournemouth and roared across country to another bar in some tiny village known to the men of the 1st. There we stayed on and on after the closing hour, dancing with the middle-aged proprietress in turn and drinking luck to ourselves in the days to come.

We arrived back at Blandford some time before dawn, singing every song we could remember, because we knew we were going into danger together and we might not have the opportunity to drink or sing together again.

Chapter 20

On Saturday morning, June 3, 1944, we lined up in jeeps in the driveway of the mansion and set out in convoy, led by Major Peters, commander of the headquarters company. Our building had already been taken over by a new unit, a corps headquarters. It would stay there a few days, then follow us into France. I suppose when the corps left, some other unit was ready to step into the building, and someone after it, and so on.

At the dock out on Portland Bill, we separated. General Huebner, Colonel Stanley Mason, his chief of staff, and the head of every staff section, G-1, G-2, G-3, and G-4, as well as the chief signal officer and the rest, went to the nerve center of our operation, the *Ancon*. This vessel was for the time being the headquarters of not only the division but of the V Corps' commander, General Gerow, as well. The *Ancon* had a vastly complicated system of communications, and it bristled with radio antennas so that the vessel could keep in constant touch with First Army, Army Group, and Eisenhower's Supreme Headquarters in England, as well as with the units which would be onshore.

We three correspondents went to another vessel, the Coast Guard ship *Samuel Chase*. An alternative headquarters had been set up on this ship so that if the *Ancon* were sunk, General Wyman could immediately take over the direction of the battle. With him he had the assistant chief of each section. Also on board was the headquarters of the primary assault regiment, the 16th Infantry, and a full battalion of that regiment.

The division and its regiments had been so strengthened for the assault that 10,000 men were included in the 16th Regiment and its reinforcing units.

If the *Ancon* were not sunk and all went well, General Wyman's group would become the advance divisional command post in France.

When we were aboard, Major Gale said to us, "We don't think you three reporters should go ashore together. If your boat were sunk, and it may well be sunk, the division would lose all its reporters together."

He then informed us that I was assigned to the advance divisional headquarters group, Thompson to the 16th Infantry headquarters, and Whitehead to a roving assignment in the personnel boat of General Wyman.

Whitehead and I were assigned beds in the hospital ward of the *Chase*. A sign on our lavatory door said, For Venereal Cases Only, and during our stay on the vessel sad-eyed young men in bathrobes drifted back and forth through our quarters, concerned much more with their personal problem than with any such thing as an invasion. We were told they used only one of the two cubbyholes in our lavatory, but we had conflicting reports on which of the two it was. I remember thinking how ironic it would be if I had to go on an invasion of France to catch syphilis from an unclean toilet seat.

Equipped with maps, we went into "Q" Roosevelt's tiny cabin, and he and Gale gave us our first detailed briefing on the coming operation.

It is worth explaining because it was the largest invasion ever undertaken across water and it was unique. The invention of first the atom bomb and later the hydrogen bomb ended the possibility of a repetition of such an invasion ever again in history.

Every road in southern England was lined with stacks of ammunition in boxes, shells, and bullets. On every road, lines of army vehicles streamed toward the masses of shipping concentrated in a few ports. Troops were concentrated in 1,200 camps. Some 144,000 tons of supplies were all loaded and waiting in the ships, and 2.5 million more tons were in dumps waiting for the support of the invasion. And 4,100 vessels and craft of all types were necessarily concentrated in the huge convoys that would move through the mineswept lanes to the coast of France.

In the light of our later knowledge, three atom bombs could have wiped out our forces in the ports, or on the way, or in the three comparatively small stretches where landings were concentrated over a total length of about forty miles of French coastline. One hydrogen bomb would have ended the invasion and destroyed it utterly. It could happen only once, because of man's scientific ingenuity, that such an operation across sea could take place, yet even at the moment it was launched, the form of attack was becoming obsolescent because of the activity of scientists in laboratories at Columbia University, the University of Chicago, and Los Alamos, men who had never heard a gun fired in anger or seen an ordinary bomb explode.

216

Yanks embarking in England for the Normandy landings. WIDE WORLD.

The first task of Allied intelligence had been to discover what forces the Germans had protecting the coastal areas of France.

On and behind the coast of Britanny and Normandy, where our invasion was to be made—that is, between the Seine and the Loire rivers—the Germans had eighteen divisions in readiness. Three were armored, seven were first-class mobile infantry divisions, and eight were what was regarded as limited infantry divisions, with equipment sufficient for static defense but not with the transport or armor necessary to move quickly and strike a smashing blow.

Just to the north of the Seine at Le Havre and continuing up the Channel coast to the border of Holland were twenty-one more divisions. These were all of the German Fifteenth Army, as were two of the armored divisions and one of the infantry divisions south of the Seine. The greatest concentration of these units was in and behind the Pas de Calais, where the Germans feared an Allied landing across the narrow twenty miles that separate Calais from Dover. But the divisions that were in a position to act against us immediately on our landing or within twenty-four hours were seven in number, six infantry and one armored. The two other armored divisions could swing quickly into action. Furthermore, the Allied planners figured that with no interference to the German road and rail transport, Rommel could bring eighteen to twenty divisions, including eight armored divisions, into the Normandy assault area by three days after our landings. We at that point were scheduled to have onshore thirteen divisions, including elements of two armored divisions.

Our assault was to be made in this fashion: During the night the 82nd Airborne Division, followed by the 101st Airborne, was to be dropped or landed in gliders on the neck of the Cherbourg peninsula to prevent troops from that peninsula from swinging down to hit our landings. A brigade of the British 6th Airborne Division would be dropped beyond the beach defenses on the left flank of our invading forces to secure the bridges over the Orne River between the city of Caen and the sea.

On the beaches behind them and to our left would be the British 50th and the British 3rd divisions and the Canadian 3rd Division. The U.S. 1st Division, strengthened by the 116th Regiment of the 29th Division so that it had a total of 36,000 men, would attack the center—that is, Omaha Beach—while on the right wing the American 4th Division would attack Utah Beach.

On both Omaha and Utah beaches, some 55,000 men were in the

American contingents. During the first day some 150,000 men could be expected to pile onshore in the whole Allied operation if all went as expected. Behind them would come the follow-up units with orderly speed.

As we listened to Roosevelt and Gale, we three correspondents began to realize the tremendously detailed planning that had gone into the coming assault.

Thirteen hundred British night bombers were to plaster the whole shore area of the invasion. Then at dawn American heavy bombers were to drop 13,000 bombs on the coast. Finally, just before the time of the landings, medium bombers and fighter bombers were to attack specific batteries of German guns. For the forty minutes before the troops first touched ground, the battleships *Texas* and *Arkansas*, with three cruisers and eight destroyers, would be showering the shoreline with shells. The naval barrage would be supported by landing craft bearing howitzers or tanks, which would add their fire to the general attack. Nine landing craft to be stationed less than two miles offshore would drench the beaches with 9,000 rockets when the first troops reached a point 300 or 400 yards from land. The 1,000 rockets, which in their elevated firing tubes covered most of the deck space of each landing craft, had to be fired in sections. Otherwise, the blast of all 1,000 rockets going off simultaneously would probably sink the boat or fry the crew alive.

First to land onshore were to be the combat engineers. During past months every type of German beach defense had been photographed and studied. Replicas had been faithfully reconstructed in lonely parts of Scotland, and our engineers had experimented with various sizes of explosive charges powerful enough to blow them up.

On a typical stretch of Omaha Beach, we would probably find some 250 yards out in the water from the high-tide mark a Belgian invention called Element C which the Germans had adopted. It looked like a heavy steel gate some ten feet high, fixed on a solid base and supported by steel girders slanting down to the rear of the base. Land mines were lashed to the top of the uprights, and the whole contraption was sturdy enough to hang up even a good-sized landing craft and blow its bottom out.

The next band of obstacles some fifty yards nearer shore consisted of heavy, pointed logs driven deep into the sand so that the points, on which mines hung, slanted toward the sea. Other log obstacles were also mined, and when a landing craft came down on one, just under the surface of the water, the logs pierced the bottom, and sometimes the mine wrecked the craft. There were other types of obstacles as well. Quite a bit nearer the shore were what were called hedgehogs, steel girders crisscrossed like jackstraws, anchored in cement, and festooned with mines.

Finally, on the shore itself were rows of barbed wire and irregularly placed minefields, some of the mines worked by a trip wire, others of the type a man had to step on to explode.

Up and down the beach and on the bluffs above were concrete blockhouses whose cannon could command broad stretches of the beach. Besides the blockhouses, there were smaller pillboxes, open positions for guns, and firing trenches, all surrounded by minefields and wire.

Fire from various points overlapped so that knocking out one position was rarely enough to grant any safety to a stretch of the shoreline. Gun positions farther in the rear and machine guns as well could command the beach by shooting on fixed lines of fire.

Inland also there were rocket pits, each fitted to fire four thirty-two-centimeter rockets. Rifle pits, machine-gun emplacements, and trenches were along the brow of the bluffs that rose just behind the beach from 100 to nearly 200 feet high. Omaha Beach in all was about five miles long, and about four miles of it were suitable for landing in any way. The tide rose and fell about eighteen feet so that if we landed at low water, we would have a 300-yard stretch of open beach before we could reach the high-water mark. It was this which determined the planners to make the initial landings as near the time of high tide as possible during a period when the tides were at flood.

From photographs and dangerous reconnaissances made chiefly by British naval intelligence men slipping quietly in during the night, it appeared that the tides had scored deep runnels in the sand paralleling the shore, so that the danger was that landing craft would get hung up on some high ridges of sand and men springing from it might go into water over their heads.

On the five-mile area of Omaha the Germans had sited some sixty artillery pieces. Those low down on the beach itself were screened by concrete from the sea so that they could be fired along the beach without their flashes being observed by attacking navy craft.

Cutting the five-mile length of bluffs were five "draws," indentations or old beds of streams, some with footpaths or little roads leading off the beach. These, of course, were heavily fortified with concrete pillboxes and other defenses. They were the natural beach exits.

Most dangerous to the ships of the Allied navies involved were six 155-millimeter, that is, about six-inch, howitzers thought to be mounted partly in casemates. They could cover both Omaha and Utah beaches from the high cliff of Pointe du Hoe. At the other end of the beach, in the British sector, were known to be heavy guns guarding Port-en-Bessin which would rake Omaha from a distance. The British were to deal with these latter guns. A detachment of American rangers were to climb the cliff at Pointe du Hoe by means of rope ladders and seize the big howitzers there, if any remained unscathed by the bombing and the naval shelling.

The combat engineers, who were to land first of all to blow up obstacles and clear pathways through the wire and minefields, had a great deal of special equipment. Some were to land in special tanks, which could throw a huge charge of explosive, called the Flying Dustbin, to blow up the minefields. The tanks could also roll up to an obstacle, place a charge, and move back to wait for the explosion without the engineers ever having to get outside the tank. Other special tanks were equipped with flaillike rollers so that they could beat paths through the minefields ahead of the troops. The individual engineers themselves carried strange equipment such as Bangalore torpedoes, long tubes of explosive to be shoved through a wire barricade and exploded to create a pathway. Some engineers bore necklaces of high explosive which were fashioned exactly to deal with the dragon's teeth and the other types of German obstacles we would find ahead of us.

I was pleased at the thought of the intensive and meticulous preparation that our forces had made. But I had had enough experience with war not to be altogether convinced by it. It had been my experience that things rarely worked out as the planners ordered.

Our advance division command post, some hundred of us in all, was to land on a section of the beach called Easy Red for identification purposes. The sector was on the beach between points roughly opposite St.-Laurent and Colleville villages, which were a little way inland.

I was fascinated by the sight of the model of our beach shown on a table in the forward hold of the *Chase*. On it was a little white house, of course, a German blockhouse. A steep ridge rose behind the beach. The ridge dipped at the green-wooded bed of a dry river.

221

A little narrow dirt path rose behind the house, ran up beside the edge of the bluff, and disappeared along the gulch.

Lieutenant Colonel Kunin, the division chemical officer, was to command our party. He assigned us, half to one landing craft, half to another.

Kunin said, "Every man will get ashore as quick as he can. I don't need to tell you to move fast. H-Hour is six-thirty in the morning. We will arrive at H plus one hundred and ten—that is, at eight-twenty A.M. We expect the beach will be clear at that time, but it will probably be under fire.

"If we are separated, we will all make for the hill near the road. There we will wait. The hill should give us some shelter. At that point, whoever is senior officer will send a reconnaissance party up the path to see what the situation is and decide where to establish the command post."

Colonel Kunin was a small man with glasses and a mustache. He seemed quite positive in his statements, and I thought they made sense—especially the part about hurrying across the beach and getting under the shelter of the hill. But we all were also thinking seriously about the possibility that we might never get to the beach or at least across it.

For somewhere on those cliffs and slopes would be Germans firing at us, ripping up the beach with their machine guns. The thought was very sobering.

I judged I would be about as safe as anyone could be and still land with assault troops and see the fighting. If the beach were cleared, I thought we would have a good chance of coming through. I had no desire to be the first soldier ashore. I would settle for being the first war correspondent on the beach, for it was not my job to blow up mines and attack barbed wire. I carried no weapon but my typewriter, and weapons more lethal than the typewriter were required to crack through Hitler's Atlantic Wall.

Thinking of the future, I began to wonder why I had got myself into such a predicament, for it was as though a music critic had to go into the orchestra and sit beside the kettledrummer all evening in order to write his review of the symphony.

But I also thought of Shakespeare's Henry V at Agincourt saying:

> *And Crispin Crispian shall ne'er go by,*
> *From this day to the ending of the world,*
> *But we in it shall be remembered;*

We few, we happy few, we band of brothers;
For he today that sheds his blood with me
Shall be my brother; be he ne'er so vile
This day shall gentle his condition:
And gentlemen in England, now abed
Shall think themselves accursed they were not here
And hold their manhoods cheap whiles any speaks
That fought with us upon Saint Crispin's day.

I felt that way strongly, and so did many others before that D-Day "exercise."

Chapter 21

One of my first concerns was to find out how I was going to broadcast from the beach in France. I had my big pack recording machine, for I did not yet know that the weakening of the batteries had made it useless. I could send spools of wire back to London for censorship and transmission on the air, but I was chiefly interested in finding out just how my voice was to get from France to London, where it could be relayed on to America.

The whole operation had been conducted in such fantastic secrecy with all the great radio brains of the Army, both professional and temporary, involved that nobody had thought to call in and ask my advice and that of the two or three other radio reporters with practical field experience at amphibious warfare and campaigning.

Now I hunted up the signal officer of our advance command post on the *Chase*. He knew nothing about what arrangements could be made and only looked blank when I asked him what frequency—among the hundreds in use by the Army—would be used for voice broadcasts from the field of battle. He suggested I go to division headquarters on the ship *Ancon*, headquarters for both the division and the V Corps. Perhaps it would have the list of all the wavelengths which would be in use and could tell me which one was the proper one for any transmitter I might use to send voice broadcasts.

After a while I got one of the little launches used for communication to take me to the *Ancon*. There Lieutenant Colonel Pickett, chief signal officer of the 1st Division, indicated he had no idea what frequency had been allotted. But he got out the V Corps signal book. Only one listing looked promising—a wavelength labeled "First Army News Service." I copied down the wavelength on a slip of scrap paper and with that in my pocket, carefully buttoned, returned with more hope to the *Chase* than when I had left it. The results of this will be described shortly, among other grandeurs and miseries of war.

Most of Saturday I spent getting briefed and studying the models and maps of the coming invasion. But life on the ship was pleasant, and our tension relaxed. We had enough duties to occupy ourselves, but nothing seemed urgent any longer. All decisions had been taken from us. We had made the step from which there could be no return. Home, family, even the land a few hundred yards away seemed separated from us by centuries of time and light-years of space. Hundreds of boats and ships were in the harbors of Weymouth and Portland around us, warships, transports, tank landing craft, tank landing ships, special craft of many varieties.

The little ones bucked and rolled in the choppy water, and we pitied the men crowded into the smaller vessels, knowing that some had boarded their craft as long as two weeks previously. The food aboard the *Samuel Chase* was excellent. No liquor was served; but every man had been issued a novel or a book of short stories, and books were swapped so that everyone could read as much as he wished. After dinner every night the officers had a motion picture in the mess hall. I remember that the night before we left, we saw some film starring Gary Cooper and Barbara Stanwyck. I read a lot and enjoyed the Gilpatric stories of old Glencannon, the Scots engineer, more than ever before or since.

For us nothing existed but the present. The past and the future were alike unreal. Only the ship was real, the good food, the familiar faces, the cigarette smoke in the cabins and in the hold, and the wind that swept across the deck. The boat became almost a kind of home and family to us. Leaving it would be as painful a process as birth itself.

On Sunday, June 4, the wind had whipped up whitecaps as far as we could see. The *Chase* rocked at her anchor. Gray clouds scudded across the sky with occasional bursts of rain. The weather was so rough that a tank landing craft, a good-sized craft capable of ocean travel under almost any conditions, rolled over on her beam ends and sank. She had been overloaded, and although the men aboard were saved, her tanks were a total loss. The thought of a tank landing craft capsizing in the harbor made us speculate what the weather must be out in mid-Channel.

The invasion had been set for Monday, June 5, and we waited for the order to depart. Then came the signal "Postponed for twenty-four hours."

We waited eagerly for Monday, hoping we would see an improvement in the weather. But on Monday, the harbor surface was still frothing with whitecaps.

At Widewing General Eisenhower made the fateful decision, and by midafternoon the order reached us to the effect that we were to start off at 4:00 P.M. The anchor came up at the appointed time, and we were under way.

The sky was laden with heavy clouds and the Channel ahead was dark. Just as we started out of the harbor, a soldier leaning on the rail beside me said, "My God, it looks like we're really going to have some help."

Across the gray, churning waste of water where sea and sky blended into each other without perceptible horizon, the stately superstructure of a battleship mounted into sight. Behind it came another, and another, and more and more warships of various sizes. They moved majestically eastward on a course parallel to ours. Specialists in land warfare that we were, we could recognize the mighty gunpower that we beheld in the distance, our shield across the Channel, our artillery when we got ashore.

The deputy commander of the 1st Division, Brigadier General Willard Wyman, a Maine man from Damariscotta, was on the top deck, watching the wind lash the sea. A bank of ominous black cloud drove across the sky above us. We thought of the frail landing craft hanging in our davits. In such a sea, it seemed to me from my years around Casco Bay, such unwieldy craft, heavily loaded, might not survive. I could imagine the waves battering the Normandy beaches.

General Wyman said, "I hope those weathermen know what they're doing." Then, more quietly, as though to himself, he added, "They *must* know. They *must* know it will be all right on the beaches tomorrow."

Thompson, Whitehead, and I asked him whether we could wear the Big Red One of the 1st Division on our tunics when we landed. We were so proud to be with the division that after thinking it over, he gave us permission.

I was excited and nervous. An officer asked me to read messages from General Eisenhower and General Montgomery over the ship's loudspeaker system. Used to broadcasting as I was, my voice shook a little when I read General Eisenhower's famous order of the day: "Soldiers, sailors and airmen of the Allied Expeditionary Force.

"You are about to embark upon the great crusade toward which we have striven these many months. The eyes of the world are upon you. The hopes and prayers of liberty-loving people everywhere march with you.

"In company with our brave allies and brothers in arms on other fronts, you will bring about the destruction of the German war machine, the elimination of Nazi tyranny over the oppressed peoples of Europe and security for ourselves in a free world.

"Your task will not be an easy one. Your enemy is well-trained, well-equipped and battle-hardened. He will fight savagely.

"But this is the year 1944. Much has happened since the Nazi triumphs of 1940–41. The United Nations have inflicted upon the Germans great defeats in open battle, man to man.

"Our air offensive has seriously reduced their strength in the air and their capacity to wage war on the ground.

"Our home fronts have given us an overwhelming superiority in weapons and munitions of war and placed at our disposal great reserves of trained fighting men. The tide has turned. The free men of the world are marching together to victory.

"I have full confidence in your courage, devotion to duty and skill in battle. We will accept nothing less than full victory.

"Good luck. And let us beseech the blessing of Almighty God upon this great and noble undertaking."

I felt the words so deeply at the time, and his reference to the "great crusade" upon which we had embarked, that many years later when some clever politician wrote the same phrase for General Eisenhower's use in the presidential campaign, I was not amused and felt that the use of the phrase to describe a political battle with rights and wrongs on both sides was somewhat of an insult to my memory of what happened the following day in Normandy.

Around us as we moved out of the harbor, all the other ships were on the move. Between us and the English coast was a line of tank landing craft, guarded by a couple of lean destroyers. Outside us were the fighting ships of three navies.

We were heading up the Channel on a course that would take us to the Pas de Calais, target of our heaviest bombing. This was part of the complicated movement of deception. Over the past weeks, many movements of ships had taken place to confuse the Germans as to exactly where and when we would strike. The Germans could not be sure at this particular time that the invasion was actually beginning, and afterward we discovered that they believed the weather was too bad to permit such an operation.

We ate early. It was a fairly serious meal. Afterward I looked over my equipment once again to make sure that I had packed everything as economically as possible. My sleeping bag and duffel bag were labeled and packed with the division equipment. When I went in on the morrow, I would take only what I could conveniently and lightly carry.

I went out on deck and stood for a while in the darkness, until I was chilled to the bone by the Channel wind. It reminded me of that other cold dark night when I had headed for Dieppe. I knew that with the darkness, our whole convoy would turn and head toward Normandy, while other craft pretended with special devices to fool the German radar that a big flotilla was approaching Calais.

Since we had to get up so early, I thought it was time for bed. But as I stepped out of the darkness of the deck into the light of the companionway, I met one of the ship's Coast Guard officers. The *Chase* was manned by coast guardsmen, and we were lucky to have them next day, with their experience navigating small boats in rough weather.

The Coast Guard officer said, "How about a drink? I've got some good Bacardi."

This was an unexpected boon from heaven, I felt, and I replied, "It's pretty chilly. I could do with one."

In his cabin I sat with other officers. We talked about the fact that the *Chase* had survived three invasions without once being hit, while a white-coated mess attendant brought ice and soda for our Bacardis. The ship's officers lived very comfortably, as was their due, for they had to make their home on the *Chase* for months on end. They did not subscribe to U.S. Navy prohibition regulations. We sipped the nectar from Cuba the entire evening until, much too late, I went to bed.

I got out of bed about three o'clock in the morning. My headache convinced me that I had been mistaken to stay up so late. The *Chase* was rolling. I wondered whether it would be too rough for the landing craft, whether many would be swamped, and whether my own craft would be one of them.

Breakfast was served at three-thirty—three hours before the first landing. On each plate was a luxury, a large orange. I cursed the pleasant company of the previous night and the necessity of eating a breakfast I did not want, but I decided it was better to have food in my stomach. I did not know when I would eat again or even whether I would ever eat again. I finished everything, including the orange.

We had halted somewhere in the darkness, and the vessel was pitching and rolling worse than ever. We had come about 100 miles

228

in our voyage to a point where the transports were to stay 23,000 or 24,000 yards off the Normandy coast, between 12 and 13 miles at sea. This was the point at which German aircraft a night or two later attacked the ships and from which George Hicks of ABC on the *Ancon* made his famous recorded broadcast of the air raid.

It was still dark, and once again I went over my equipment, discarding still more of it, with the thought that the sea was so rough I might have to swim for it. I wrapped my little Swiss Hermes typewriter, bought secondhand from an Australian woman in London, with my paper and carbons in a waterproof cover and slung them in an old gas mask case. I had my folding shovel, the entrenching tool, my water bottle, and first-aid kit on my belt and my special assault gas mask in its rubber case over one shoulder.

Even then, the load was heavy. The light typewriter seemed to weigh fifty pounds.

I discarded my trench coat, although the morning air blew cold. I had a pullover and a leather vest under my battle dress jacket, and I hoped that would be enough. I could not imagine how the assault infantry could carry guns, ammunition, and grenades and special paraphernalia and still move quickly. I thought they must be in wonderful physical condition. As for myself, a year in England with exercise confined to walks between home and office had not prepared me in any way for an invasion.

Up on deck, gray dawn was showing before five o'clock on that morning of June 6. The sea was kicking up wildly, and the water looked cold and wintry. Heavy banks of low, menacing clouds covered the sky.

The first assault troops were already loading. They climbed into their landing craft and were rapidly lowered into the water. The landing craft circled the *Chase*, rocking and smacking down into the sea with their flat bottoms until, their formation complete, they plowed off together toward the French coast. We were twelve to fourteen miles at sea, but visibility was limited to half that distance.

I took my recording machine onto the bridge of the ship, hoping to record the sound of the huge naval barrage that was to open up at half past five and continue until ten minutes past six. But the battleships, cruisers, and destroyers were somewhere nearer shore, and I could hear only a faint rumbling through the strident wind.

I knew the American and British air forces were exerting all their mighty power with a tornado of bombs against France. I would have been less happy had I known that the bombers, because of the heavy

The armada of crowded landing craft stretched to the horizon. WIDE
WORLD.

cloud, had left the beach practically untouched and dropped their bombs on the fields inland.

At length came the turn of our group. We climbed into three boats slung in davits beside the deck, two larger craft and one small thirty-foot LCVP—that is, landing craft for vehicles and personnel. I was in the LCVP with "Q" Roosevelt, Lieutenant Colonel Kunin, and Lieutenant Colonel Grant. An LCVP can carry about thirty men with their equipment comfortably, but we were somewhat more than that, perhaps forty. It was six o'clock in the morning, thirty minutes before H-Hour, and the beach was a dozen miles ahead of us, too far for us to see it.

We all had assault lifesavers strapped around our waists. These could be blown up by mouth or simply by breaking a built-in capsule of compressed air.

The water was terribly rough with waves I judged to be six to eight feet high, which slapped the boat hard and set it rolling and pitching. I judged it to be a kind of chop that would have made swordfishing impossible on Georges Bank. The type of roughness was no danger to a large vessel, but it was just the water that could catch a small craft and flip it over before you knew what was happening. I was glad I had not tried to bring the recording set, for laden with that, I could not have swum a stroke. I wondered about the men in the special DD tanks, rigged with propellers and canvas on steel struts to make them amphibious, that I knew were being launched somewhere in the sea around us. The tanks were sealed watertight. They sank as they splashed down their ships' ramps; but the crews had oxygen masks with ten minutes' supply of oxygen, and in practice the tanks had bobbed up again in good time. Later I found that the rough water had wrecked the tanks' swimming equipment, and only two or three of the sixty-four tanks, ever reached the beach. The wind and waves smashed the others as far as two or three miles from shore, and they sank like stones.

Foolishly I had stood near the bow of the LCVP. My theory was that it was better to be one of the first out of the boat when the ramp dropped on the beach, for any German gunners would have less chance of hitting me if I sprang out and raced up the beach among the first, while the extra few seconds it took the others to get out might mean the Germans had a chance to adjust their sights. But now, as the flat bow spanked into the seas, they broke high above our heads, and solid sheets of water rained down on us. In ten minutes I was drenched to the skin and chilled by the wind.

We took off in formation with our assault wave.

I knew we would be going through narrow mine-free lanes swept through the German marine minefields. Stake boats were anchored in the swept paths to give us directions or tell us news, for they were linked by radio with both the Navy and the Army.

The coxswain and the skipper of our little craft were coast guardsmen. As we plowed through or smashed into the waves, the craft jumped like a frightened horse. My stomach began to feel a little uneasy, and I began to regret having eaten breakfast and more than ever to regret the previous night's Bacardis. I thought I could control myself in any case. Just then a thin boy standing next to me turned white. He started to try to push through the tight-packed group to reach the rail, but he vomited just before he reached it. The high wind whipped some of his sour vomit across my face. I wiped the stuff off and hastily took one of the seasickness pills we had been issued. The boat continued to pitch. I lifted my face gratefully toward the icy waves that were splashing over the rail, but I began to get hot and cold. I had been to sea too often not to know what was coming. I too edged to the rail, and up came the sour orange I had eaten with the rest of my breakfast.

Nobody laughed. The moment was too serious. About a dozen of the forty men were sick. In some landing craft all the men aboard were sick. In others, none was affected. In most, I imagine, the number ran from 20 to 50 percent seasick, at least in the little LCVPs. We joked a little among ourselves, then vomited some more. I continued to be wet and sick and cold for most of the next four hours.

Weak as I was from vomiting, I wondered how the fighting men could handle their equipment when they reached the beach. As a matter of fact, the battle with the rough water decreased their efficiency terribly. They could not lift equipment they ordinarily had no difficulty in carrying. They had to drag their equipment across the sand. Others found they could not walk and had to crawl across the beach instead of proceeding on the double. I did not hear of any who felt fit after being buffeted by the sea. Some of the boats sank before they ever got within sight of the shore, and we occasionally saw floating debris or men in inflated life preservers. But the landing craft were moving on an exact timetable and could not stop for rescue work. That was the Navy's job, among so many others.

I knew that we had begun the attack by a huge air bombardment, but all I saw for the whole early part of the morning was a couple of our medium bombers flying back toward England under the lowering cloud banks.

The whole scene, as we among hundreds of other boats headed for shore, could have been a study in gray by El Greco, weird streaks of black and light gray, gray seas with frothing peaks. It was a wild, dark, and oppressive scene. The wind and the spume beat at my face. I felt almost hypnotized by the rise of the bow upon which I stood and the smacking against the waves.

Several thousand boats and ships were used in the whole invasion. I myself must have seen at least 1,000 craft at one time or another. They ranged from battleships down to the little LCVPs like my own and included the strange-looking Rhino Ferries, square craft, their lower decks entirely awash, carrying various types of machines. They must have been the most ungainly craft that ever went to sea and crossed the Channel. They were around us, dotting the gray sea like bugs on a millpond.

At last, dimly seen through the mist and spume, came the beach. Its cliffs looked much higher than we had imagined from the scale models, looming up black against the streaked sky.

Visibility was so poor that we had to go in to about half a mile from shore before we could make out enough detail to realize that we had not come into the place where we had expected to be. Colonel Kunin and the Coast Guard officers consulted and looked at their maps, and the coast guardsmen decided that the current had carried us east of our expected position, so we crawled along just offshore until we spotted the right landmarks. I was glad that the decision had not been up to me, for by that time I felt so weak and seasick that any responsibility would have been intolerable.

Finally, we could see the line of white beach and the house that had appeared on the photographs and the model, with the dip in the line of bluffs that gave evidence of the draw.

As we came in, we could see explosions on the beach. There were two columns of black smoke rising to meet the cloud layer, and other fires were sending white smoke up that was mixing with the mist.

The wind was blowing toward the beach, and waves four or five feet high were breaking on the sand.

My watch said it was 8:15 A.M., and we were exactly on time for a landing five minutes later. I was thankful, for I wanted to get anywhere on land to be away from the boat and the sea. I thanked God for the privilege of feeling land under my feet and knowing that my seasickness was ended.

GIs GOING ASHORE ON OMAHA BEACH

The view from the sea. U.S. ARMY.

The view from the beach. U.S. ARMY.

We nosed slowly in toward the beach. It was then nearly half tide. The beach should have been comparatively clear, with our men well inland; instead, the beach was covered with men lying down flat. I could not tell whether they were alive or dead. The wind was blowing from almost behind us, and we could barely hear the explosions from the beach.

Most of us in the bow were so seasick that we had lost interest in what was happening. It took a conscious effort for me to keep looking around to mark our progress for my future use.

Something had gone terribly wrong, for the men on the beach were not moving, except for those who were wriggling on their stomachs from the sand to the bed of flat rocks that formed the only protection of any kind from the fire that was being directed against the landing area from the bluffs.

At first we could not find an entrance between the rows of iron obstacles that rose with wicked mine-tipped picket points out of the water and were spaced all the way up the beach to the stones. We tried one place and had to back out before we collided with one of the obstacles. We wondered whether others were even now beneath our bottom and at any moment an explosion might crush our little craft.

To our right, I could see some craft that seemed to have been hit. There were bodies of men floating in the shallow water. Another boat was broadside the beach, and the four- or five-foot waves were beating it remorselessly against the sand.

One boat, almost beside us, was half sunk, bumping again and again against an obstacle. I could not see any men in it, and I wondered whether they had been drowned or had managed to make shore. Perhaps it was a boat sunk after it had landed its contingent of infantry.

At last the coxswain found a narrow pathway through the obstacles that looked feasible. We moved in. Three or four other boats were ahead of us against the shore, filling the point where we would have to disembark.

The engines idled while we waited for them to clear a place for us. When we drifted sideways toward one of the obstacles, the coast guard steersman would start up the engines and we would move slowly back into the cleared area. But it was very narrow.

The light had an eerie, unearthly quality, streaking through the smoke and the heavy gray clouds that were hurrying across the sky. I was leaning over the starboard side of the bow when only a few yards away I saw the water suddenly beaten to a frothy white, as though someone were flogging it with a gigantic cat-o'-nine-tails. It happened once, and again and again, and again, farther off. I could not understand what it was, for with the wind in my ears I could hear nothing. Then all at once the sickening understanding swept over me that these were machine-gun bursts coming from somewhere onshore. The fact that I could not hear the bullets made it somehow unreal, and I felt as though I were seeing someone else go through the experience.

I saw dead men floating by us in their inflated life belts. One was near where the sea had just been whipped up to a froth by the machine gun, and I wondered in a dispassionate way whether the bullets had killed him or whether they had hit his dead body.

Other men were swimming between the obstacles toward shore, and I wondered what had happened to their landing craft and how far out they had been hit.

At that point we heard the peculiar whine of mortar shells. Three exploded near us in quick succession, sending huge jets of water and sand into the air, to the right of us, then to the left, then in front of us.

We felt hemmed in, like rats in a narrow corridor. We could not go forward without being driven by the rolling waves onto the craft that were trying to land their men on the beach. We could not go to one side or the other without hitting the evil mines dripping from the iron prongs above the surface of the water.

Colonel Kunin wiped his glasses, salt-fogged from the spume, and said, "We don't want to lose the command post at this stage of the game. We'll go out a way." I remember wondering to myself what kind of target we appeared from shore, how big we looked to the German mortarmen. They had bracketed us closely, without damaging us. But I knew that one shell in that tightly packed group of men would have killed most, if not all, of us.

The LCVP started backing slowly out through the clear lane, then turned around. As we went, other mortar bursts followed us, to the right and the left again and behind us.

One of the GIs near me said, "Son of a bitch. Son of a bitch. Son of a bitch," over and over, with a pause between each word.

One of the officers said, "Not very pleasant. Let's get to hell out and decide what to do." We all knew that something had gone wrong.

It was then about a quarter to nine. Even when we had been

Survivors of sunken LCVP make it to Omaha on a rubber raft on D-Day.
LOUIS WEINTRAUB. U.S. ARMY.

First aid to buddies on a Normandy beach. LOUIS WEINTRAUB. U.S. ARMY.

239

practically on the beach itself, the noise of the battle had been faint.

The wind was coming from the sea, driving our boats against the shore, and I was reminded then that it takes an artillery barrage or a bombing to make the sounds that are the average person's imaginary picture of battle, not an infantry firefight when you are a few hundreds yards away from it.

We were hovering offshore perhaps half a mile, trying to decide what to do, when I saw a remarkably heartening sight. As far as we could tell, the invasion was two hours at least behind schedule. The obstacles had not been destroyed. The infantrymen were crowded on the beach, with more and more coming in and getting shot up. In spite of what had been planned as a huge air bombardment and naval shelling, most of the Germans had not been killed. We learned later that the German reserve division in our particular area had been moved up to the beach on maneuvers, so that we struck much heavier resistance on Omaha those first few hours than anyone had anticipated.

Colonel George Taylor of the 16th Regiment had arrived on the beach at about the same time as we were trying to land. He found that the only protection the men had was the ridge of flat stones a few feet high running just above the high-water mark. A man could dig in with his elbows and his knees and get slight protection, but too many were getting killed, packed closely side by side, by the streams of machine-gun and mortar fire that raked back and forth across the beach.

I now saw some men get up from their stomachs and start walking forward toward the hill and up. They went through the mines and the wire in a kind of wavering line, with each one finding his way. I saw some disappear in explosions and some fall. But there was still a line going up the hill, now dark green, meeting the lighter color of the sky.

I saw some of the tiny figures silhouetted black against the gray sky. They disappeared. They were over the edge.

Men were still coming in, and so was matériel, held up for hours, being kept waiting until room could be made on the beach still black with men. Over our heads warships were still firing at German positions. But I knew that some of us were now at least inland, and that was a wonderful thing to know.

I believe that it was at about that moment that Colonel Taylor on the beach stood up and said, "The only people staying on this beach are the dead and those who are going to die. Come ahead."

240

I may have seen the group around him at that moment, but I also may have been looking at men who went ahead up the bluff without any orders whenever a sergeant or a lieutenant decided that it was better for his men to be killed on their feet than on their bellies. It happened at many places that morning, and slowly the men began infiltrating the German defenses, and I had been there to see it. And I thought again of Shakespeare: ". . . gentlemen in England, now abed/Shall think themselves accursed they were not here."

Our LCVP went out to sea. We had gone, I judged, two or three miles and were coming up to a stake boat for information when we saw a line of landing craft coming in. A colonel shouted to Lieutenant Colonel Kunin, and I believe he was the colonel of the 18th Regiment, coming in with his forward battalion in support. Two of his battalions were very much delayed, but I believe that he himself came in fairly early and on time.

Kunin yelled at the regimental commander that the men of the 16th were stuck on the beach and needed help, and the full colonel yelled back, "Okay. We're going in now."

We tied up to the stake boat. At first I was so weak I could hardly clamber aboard it. Kunin, Grant, and Roosevelt talked with the officer commanding, reported to division headquarters ten miles farther out at sea on the *Ancon* what they had seen on the beach, and listened to the messages from the men on the beach, such as they were, for there were practically no communications available on Omaha. The rest of us took off some clothing and tried to get warm near the ship's boilers.

We stayed there about half an hour, and I began to feel a little better. But much too soon we were on our way in again. Once again we searched for a way through the obstacles. The tide was higher now, a little short of high tide, and the time was somewhere between ten and ten-thirty.

The boat jarred to a stop. The ramp let down, and we jumped into water that reached our thighs. Shells were still landing on the beach, and occasional bursts of machine-gun fire. A bulldozer was onshore digging a road through the sand so that some of the equipment now crowded on the beach could be brought inland. Soldiers were putting metal netting down to help the vehicles, the tanks in particular, get off the sand, where they seemed to be stuck. But at least I was onshore, and for that I was thankful.

Chapter 22

I was one of the first off the landing craft. The coldness of the water was a shock, but by that time I felt numb all over and dead tired. I weaved and staggered as I moved through the water, and I felt that if I fell, I might never get up. The typewriter and my entrenching tool felt as heavy as though they were made of lead, and the water had soaked into my uniform so that it seemed to drag me down.

I had a fleeting thought of the men who had to go in with rifles, Brownings, mortars and ammunition, and grenades. What must they have struggled against? Afterward I was told that the seasickness and the chilling effect of the cold water had slowed down all movement of the first units by at least 50 percent. Men who could ordinarily run with certain burdens now could only walk step by painful step. Men who could ordinarily carry heavy equipment at a brisk march now had to drag it across the sand with the help of one or two of their companions.

I wanted to trot across the sand and stones toward the bluff ahead of me, but I could hardly walk, slogging along, looking ahead. The beach was littered with everything an army uses. Boxes of one kind or another from wrecked ships had floated ashore. The beach was covered with discarded combat life belts.

Wrecked landing craft and tanks half covered with water were dotted here and there. The dead lay rolling in the incoming tide at the water's edge, and some still floated on the sea.

Somewhere to my left I could hear automatic fire hammering, and there were the figures of men lying on flat ground. I did not know whether they were also dead or whether they were still trying to fight their way inland. To my right, in the direction of what we now know as Les Moulins draw, where a Frenchwoman in a tiny shop near the war memorial sells postcards marked "Omaha Beach," there was the loud thump of artillery.

But for the five minutes it took us to go from the landing craft to the beach exit, there was no firing on our particular stretch of ground.

We went past the German camouflaged blockhouse that had been ripped open by our naval fire. About 150 yards inland, a concrete blockhouse had guarded the exit. A long-barreled antitank gun stuck out from a narrow slit facing the beach. The concrete had not been shattered, but our infantry, coming from behind, I heard later, had killed the Germans manning the post.

Just outside this gun position, two-thirds of the way down the bluff, we established the advance division command post. Signal Corps men started laying wires. General Wyman, the division's deputy commander, began conferring with other officers on plans for moving units to deal with the resistance that continued on and near the beach.

I did not pay much attention to what went on around me for the first hour or so. I moved out a little way from the blockhouse and began digging a foxhole in the sandy bank. I found the traces of that particular foxhole remaining ten years later. I dug so hard with the entrenching tool that soon sweat was streaming off me. I had only one thought, to get as deep into the ground as I could, and only when I was down far enough would I look around to see where all the noise of artillery and machine guns was coming from.

I did not know or care who was in the next hole or what was happening to the war or what the situation was. I could think of nothing but the movement of my shovel. I cursed whenever some sand ran into the hole and made me dig an extra few shovelfuls to clear it away.

When the hole was about up to my armpits and wide enough for me to crouch down into it without difficulty, I began to take an interest in my surroundings.

Across the draw on the other bank some of our men were moving in to attack among bushes and trees. I could hear fierce bursts of rifle and machine-gun fire and some of our own tanks or artillery pieces shooting. I judged that we were clearing up some gun positions or some German infantry that were making trouble farther up the draw.

But right in front of me on the beach, I watched the unfolding of a grand and terrible martial spectacle.

We had not, of course, expected anything like the opposition we received at the very beach itself. Instead of being deep inland by noon or one o'clock, we were still fighting to hold sections of the beach, and nowhere was the penetration greater than a few hundred yards by scattered units, which found themselves often attacked from the rear harder than from the front as they sought to move south. The reason was apparent next day when Intelligence discovered that, as stated, instead of a regiment holding the beach areas, we had run into a whole extra division, the 352nd, which, ordinarily stationed miles inland, had been moved up to the beach protective positions on maneuvers. Thus the unit we expected to hit us twenty-four to forty-eight hours after D-Day we met at the very moment of landing.

This German 352nd Division had four battalions of artillery, and these were the guns which had been shelling the beach and continued to shell it as I watched.

The German machine-gun fire against the beach seemed to have stopped, although I could hear it just behind me over the hill. The German artillery and mortars continued to hit it with unerring aim. The explosions seemed to dance up and down among the boats and the men who crowded the shoreline. They came in bursts of two and four shells together along the 300 to 400 yards of beach under my direct observation. Occasionally a single shell would crash upon the beach, but usually the shelling appeared to be the work of batteries or half batteries. Of course, shelling the beach was the standard problem for all German artillery within five miles around, and every gunner knew the correct range.

The target was perfect. Hundreds of boats were bringing in masses of men and machinery, trucks, cars, and bulldozers. The 18th Infantry Regiment had begun to come ashore. The men formed up in ordered ranks on the beach, waiting to get their directions and move up the draw. Shells landed among them, causing great gaps. But the men closed up the line and moved forward with superb military discipline. The wounded were given first aid on the beach and placed aboard landing craft to take them back to England so that many of them saw no more than a stretch of French beach for a few minutes before they were out of the war. The dead, none had time to look after. Two days later the beach was still lined with the dead, who were later buried in the beautiful St.-Laurent Cemetery on the bluff.

I saw landing craft, hit and broken, go up in flames. Others were sunk 100 yards at sea and never reached the beach. Occasionally a gasoline truck would be hit and go up in one flowerlike burst of orange flame.

Vehicles and men were packed on the beach because there was only one cleared path through the minefields, up the narrow little road that ran beside the blockhouse. Thus far there had been no movement out of the Les Moulins draw to our right, where we heard heavy fighting was still taking place, or to our left, the E-3 Colleville draw, where the Germans were still stubbornly blocking our passage.

The beach itself became a kind of inferno of artillery. I was in the position of someone sitting in the first balcony of a theater. The German shells could rake the second balcony, the bluff above my head, and their shells could range at will through any section of the orchestra, the beach at my feet, but as Colonel Kumin and Colonel Evans had figured, the trajectory of the shells would not permit them to shell the side of the bank, the first balcony, where I crouched with just my head sticking out of my hole. Bursts were landing on the bluff, 50 yards above me. They may have been shells that fell short, or they may have been shells directed at some of our infantry who were doing I know not what on the high flat ground. The rest of the shells landed on the flat ground 150 or 100 yards in front of me.

When a truck carrying ammunition or an ammunition barge received a direct hit, there would be a flash and a roaring explosion which seemed almost to tear the beach to bits. A great column of black smoke writhed into the sky from one of these. Then another was hit, and another column of black smoke sprang upward and flattened out into a great cloud, a small forerunner of the shape of the atom bomb explosions more than a year later. Up and down the beach ammunition trucks continued to burn and send out occasional explosions for an hour or two after they were hit.

At one time white smoke drifted across my foxhole, so thick that I felt alone in an impenetrable acrid fog. I could not see the next foxhole four feet away. It bit my eyes, and the pain became unbearable. I put on my gas goggles, but they gave me no relief. Then a sudden shift in the wind blew it in another direction, and I could see the beach again.

Men and matériel were still moving across the flat and up the road. As far as one could see, more landing craft, guns, tanks, and trucks were coming in. I got an impression of our huge power. A destroyer, so near the beach that it looked almost aground, was banging shell after shell into a German gun post to my left. Another was doing the same thing. Two big French cruisers, the *Georges Leygues* and the *Montcalm,* were moving calmly athwart the beach a few hundred yards out, their French flags fluttering proudly in the wind. An American battleship, the *Texas*, I believe, had come closer to shore than I ever believed possible for such a huge mighty engine of war. Disdaining the minefields, it was sending broadsides against German targets far inland. The mustard yellow blaze of its guns brought smoke that almost hid the great ship from my eyes.

The German shelling went on like this for most of the afternoon. Even the next day occasional shells continued to hit the beach.

It stays light very late in Normandy during June. It must have been six or seven o'clock when General Huebner, the division commander, arrived, and after a time he moved the division command post a mile or so inland. Our advance troops were fighting a short distance farther in, as well as on our flanks at the villages of St.-Laurent and Colleville. The Les Moulins exit had not yet been taken, and the 116th Regiment of the 29th Division had a hard baptism of fire.

John O'Reilly of the New York *Herald Tribune* had come into the beach when the division artillery and tanks began to arrive in force, in late afternoon. He, Jack Thompson, Don Whitehead, and I had a reunion. Bob Capa, the photographer, had gone back to England in midmorning. (Capa was killed a few days short of ten years later in the Indochina War.) If there is ever a D-Day-on-Omaha Correspondents Association formed, the members would be the four of us, the correspondent of a Baltimore paper who was over on our right with the 116th Regiment, Lou Azrael, I believe, and, as I learned years later, Warren Kennett of the Newark *News,* who covered one New Jersey cavalry unit attached to V Corps for the invasion. If U.S. colleges and universities were ever to match correspondents on D-Day, Williams College with Jack Thompson and me had twice as many as any other American institution of higher learning.

In the brush and in specially built camouflaged holes in orchards and fields, our advancing troops had missed many German machine guns and snipers. There was fighting in front of us, behind us, and all around us. All of us were fired at many times that evening. On one occasion, I remember, I was standing talking to an officer beside an armored car when a bullet struck the car between us and bounced off with a ringing clang. We were both surprised but both tried to appear nonchalant as we strolled around to the other side of the car to continue our talk.

246

At times a machine gun would start clattering in the woods, and one would see leaves and branches clipped above one's head. As soon as a few shots had been fired in any particular place, signs would be posted, Sniper Up This Road. Dead Germans at various points showed where the fighting had been fiercest. Sometimes the bodies of Americans would be lying nearby. When a machine gun started firing, the nearest American unit would start looking for it, so that there were little battles all around us. There was no real front at this time, only groups of American troops in various places fighting little battles and then trying to move on.

Lieutenant Sam Brightman showed up in the late afternoon. He was the only Army public relations officer on Omaha that day. All the vast public relations preparations, and only Brightman, a lieutenant, there to help us. He had no means of communication, but when we all wrote short dispatches, he volunteered to take them to the beach and give them to some Navy officer in the hope of passing them along by hand to England. We entrusted our messages to Sam, but none of them ever arrived in London. Brightman, years later, became managing editor of the Democratic party magazine.

I thought I had arranged things well for my broadcasting from the beach, but Lieutenant Colonel Pickett, the division signal officer, told me that all four of the radios he expected to have had been sunk before they reached shore.

I was very discouraged. It was dusk, about eleven o'clock at night, when I bumped into my old friend Colonel Cleaves, signal officer of V Corps.

The advance corps headquarters had just arrived and was establishing itself in a long trench dug by the Germans as a defense post in the hard clay soil.

Cleaves was from Maine originally, and there was even a Cleaves landing on Long Island in Casco Bay. I believe he must have been descended from the Cleaves of Cleaves and Tucker, who first started the settlement of Portland.

"Hello, John," he said. "I'm glad you got through it all right."

"Same to you, Colonel," I replied. "How's chances of sleeping in your new little home?"

"Go right ahead," he said. "Some of your sidekicks are up at the end of the ditch." The colonel meant Thompson, Whitehead, and O'Reilly, whom I had lost track of as I wandered around in the darkness.

"I'm depressed," I said. "No way of communication. No radio."

"Don't let that trouble you," Colonel Cleaves replied. "I'll have some ashore tomorrow, and as soon as I can spare one, you can use it for your broadcasts."

The corps had no information on anything, and I was completely exhausted, so I dropped into the trench beside my fellow correspondents. Some of our field guns began to fire nearby. I was cold, chilled to the bone, soaking wet, and I had no blanket. The trench was too narrow for me to lie on my back, so I lay on my side. Yet I was completely happy because I was thankful to be alive. I think most of the men onshore that day must have felt the same way.

After what we had seen and experienced, we became a kind of little martial aristocracy. Later, when other correspondents or soldiers asked any of us, "How was it on D-Day at Omaha?" we were apt to say, "Pretty rough," and leave the rest modestly unspoken.

By that night we had partially occupied and subdued a strip of ground no more than a mile and a half inland from the beach at its deepest and considerably less in some places. We had not made contact with the British at the designated spot, Port-en-Bessin, on our left flank. We expected a strong counterattack the next day which might wrench from us some of the ground we had so hardly won.

But I could not worry about the next day. I was so exhausted that even in the narrow trench, lying on my side on ground which felt as unyielding as concrete, I fell asleep.

I had hardly got to sleep before the machine guns woke me. I looked up, and the air above the trench was filled with tracers. I thought the German counterattack had begun, but the way I felt the Germans were welcome to come and take me. I had no weapon of any kind.

The bullets seemed to be coming in a flat trajectory from the woods beyond us. I did not raise my head, for the bullets were hitting the bushes and trees in our hedgerow and bits of branches were falling down in the trench. Our own automatic weapons opened up, and I could see the tracers going both ways over my head. I was very unhappy to be caught between two machine-gun positions, both going full blast. But after a while the firing became spasmodic, then died out altogether, and I came to the conclusion that I was not going to be killed by the Germans, at least that night. When all became quiet again, I fell asleep and stayed dead to the world and the beachhead until morning.

Chapter 23

The next morning we breakfasted on K rations sitting beside our trench. It was to be our headquarters for the next day and a half. During the day some other correspondents appeared, among them, Bunny Austin, a New Zealander accredited to the Americans.

We had no transport. It was too precious for war correspondents to acquire any. So we walked everywhere, over to 1st Division headquarters, back to the beach to watch the 2nd Division coming ashore, around to any other units we could find. Each of us must have covered many miles. But Lieutenant Brightman still had no means of communication, except to take our dispatches down to some landing craft and ask a Navy man to pass them on to England. He said he had found a broken radio, and he thought he could get a Signal Corps engineer to fix it sometime.

All this while the news of the invasion consisted of the scanty reports available back at SHAEF, General Eisenhower's headquarters in England. None of it came from the highly frustrated correspondents on the beach.

It was nearly dark when I again met Colonel Cleaves of V Corps and asked him whether he had yet received his 399 radio.

"Yes," he said. "I have one ashore. It's in a DUKW."

He gave me directions to find an assistant of his who knew the exact spot where the DUKW had been laid up for the night. By the time I discovered the assistant darkness had fallen. In my pocket I had the script of a broadcast already censored, for one of our army censors was on shore doing his job on the edge of our trench.

"You go down this road," said the signal officer, "and in the third pasture on the right, you'll find the three ninety-nine."

I walked down the road. It was overhung with trees and lined with hedgerows on both sides, one of those Normandy roads that are in deep shadow at noon on a summer day. Now there was no sound except my footsteps and no visibility at all, so that at times I walked off the side of the road. I wondered whether it had been mined by the Germans, as most roads seemed to have been.

I had to feel, rather than see, the openings in the hedge. At the

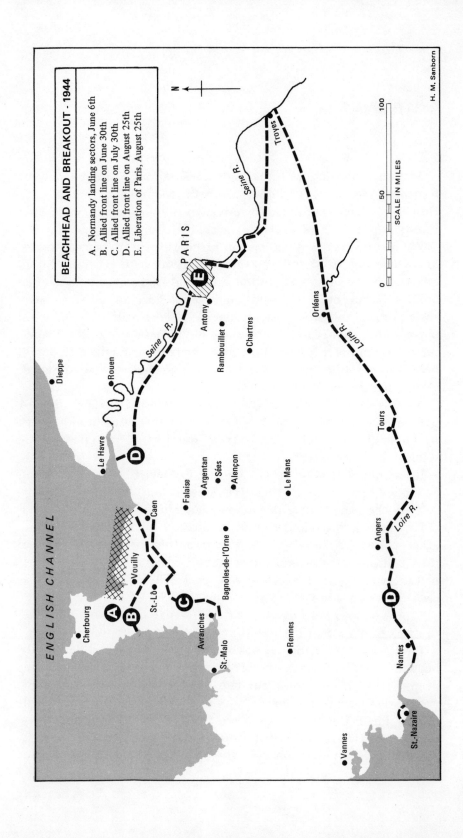

BEACHHEAD AND BREAKOUT · 1944

A. Normandy landing sectors, June 6th
B. Allied front line on June 30th
C. Allied front line on July 30th
D. Allied front line on August 25th
E. Liberation of Paris, August 25th

N

ENGLISH CHANNEL

Dieppe

Le Havre

Rouen

Seine R.

PARIS

E

Antony

Chartres

Rambouillet

Cherbourg

A

B

St.-Lô

Vouilly

Caen

Falaise

Argentan

Sées

Alençon

Le Mans

Avranches

C

Bagnoles-de-l'Orne

St.-Malo

Rennes

Angers

Loire R.

Tours

Orléans

Loire R.

Troyes

Seine R.

Nantes

D

St.-Nazaire

Vannes

SCALE IN MILES

0   50   100

H. M. Sanborn

third opening I heard the distant high-pitched, broken whine of a radio transmitter sending code. I turned and was about to enter the orchard when, almost beside me, I heard the click of a rifle bolt. I stopped stock-still. With snipers still all about us and the front no farther than a few hundred yards away, nobody could be sure who was friend or foe in the pitch-blackness.

I said in a steady voice, "I am John MacVane, radio war correspondent. I don't know the password, but Colonel Cleaves of Fifth Corps sent me to find the corps' three ninety-nine."

For a long minute there was still no sound. Then a voice said, "Okay. Over in the corner of the orchard."

I blundered into the DUKW, climbed up the side, and was admitted by the operator, a sergeant. I explained my mission, and he said it would be all right after he had finished his messages. At about one o'clock in the morning he switched from code to voice transmission on the frequency I gave him, the "Army News Service." I talked up for fifteen minutes, then sent my broadcast, three times repeated. But the operator told me electrical conditions were bad, and he had no means of knowing whether London had been able to receive the broadcast.

As I got back to my home trench, a German plane flew over the fleet of ships. The antiaircraft opened up in fountains from both shore and sea, and I thought I saw a distant flash of the plane going down.

The next day, Thursday, D plus 2, I went over to 1st Division headquarters for a hot lunch, knowing that the Big Red One prided itself on feeding its men hot meals in circumstances in which ordinary divisions would be scraping by on cold K rations.

Afterward Lieutenant Colonel Pickett, the signal officer, detached a captain with one of his 399s on a truck which had just arrived that day to try to get a broadcast over to England. We went to the edge of the bluff overlooking the beach, so there would be no obstacles between us and the far shore. I started talking up on the only frequency I knew, and after fifteen minutes, with atmospheric conditions good, I began my broadcast, first giving the name and number of the censor who had censored the script.

Now in London, elaborate preparations for broadcasting from Normandy had been planned, all unknown to me, the one most closely concerned with such things, unknown as well to my CBS colleague Larry LeSueur over on Utah Beach. The plan was to have an American broadcaster do the first broadcast from the British sector of Normandy about three weeks after the landings, when all arrangements had been perfected. This was hands-across-the-sea stuff, which in ordinary times I might have approved, but I had not risked my life on Omaha to be frustrated about broadcasting for any longer than the time it took me to find and use a transmitter.

In London there was a big U.S. Army relay station, meant to pick up our broadcasts from the BBC and boost them along to our networks in New York. I had timed my broadcast to coincide with NBC's morning broadcast.

In the NBC London office at 2 Manfield Street, the telephone rang. It was Roy Trouncer, one of the BBC censors, saying, "We're getting John from the beachhead. It's coming in fine, and we're sending it right along to the army transmitter."

The NBC London office was overjoyed, first, to know that I was still alive and, second, to think that we had obtained the scoop of the war, the first broadcast from Normandy—or vice versa.

It was only later that disillusionment set in. In the Army Signal Corps installation in London, a bunch of bureaucratic desk officers were warming their capacious rears on cushioned swivel chairs. "A broadcast—from the beachhead," they said. "Impossible. No broadcast is expected for at least three weeks."

They examined further and discovered the broadcast was not arriving on any of the frequencies they had allotted for such matters, allotted in such deep secrecy that no correspondent knew the secret.

Whoever was in charge said, "This is on an unauthorized frequency. It must not be sent on to New York. This is breaking all the rules. We'll fix the bastard. We won't retransmit his broadcast."

That was what happened. The broadcast went to London perfectly, but nobody outside the BBC and the Army Signal Corps ever heard it. When I got back to London, Roy Trouncer told me the sad story, and we had a drink to bemoan the great scoop, the first broadcast from Omaha Beach, the broadcast that would have startled America.

Two or three weeks later, when I was in England, I heard Bill Downs of CBS give the first broadcast from Normandy, all in order, all arranged, from the British sector. I was not happy.

After I had successfully, as I thought, completed my broadcast, I went back down to the beach. It was still littered with wreckage, ships, landing craft, tanks. Dead men still lay here and there along the shore. Around them were letters, toilet articles, pictures, souvenirs that had fallen from their pockets or drifted in from wrecked ships on the tide.

But now great masses of our men and machines were landing. At 1st Division, General Huebner told me that he had been worried about counterattacks. "Now," he said, "they can counterattack and be damned. We are in Normandy, in France to stay."

In late afternoon, dog tired from all my tramping about, I met Captain Max Zera in the 1st Division area.

He said, "Let's go to Colleville and look for some Calvados. Then we can take a bottle or two up to one of the advance battalions. They'll appreciate it about now."

I was exhausted, but I had not had a drink, except my tiny flask of brandy on the first day, and I agreed.

We were in a pasture and, to get to the road, had to jump across a hedgerow ditch, from which the Germans had been driven only the previous day. Some of their equipment was still there. Max jumped, and I tried to follow. My foot slipped, and in an instant I was rolling in agony at the bottom of the ditch. My ankle, even with the heavy British field boot protecting it, felt as though it had been torn off.

Max and some other soldiers unlaced the boot. The ankle was already beginning to swell, and in a few moments it was so puffed up that I could no longer put my shoe on. Even touching my foot to the ground caused frightful pain.

Max and the others carried me to a section of the ditch where some soldiers were preparing to spend the night, and Max sent to division headquarters for my bedroll, which had come ashore with those of the division officers that day. He said he would get a doctor to look at me next morning.

I spent the night in the ditch, hardly sleeping at all. Near morning I dozed off, and when I awoke, it was broad daylight. The soldiers who had shared the ditch with me were gone. I could hear firing in the distance, and I hoped no counterattack was beginning.

I felt all alone, stuck in a ditch with no means of getting anywhere. As an immobile correspondent with no transport, I was useless. My leg looked three times its normal size.

I opened some K rations and ate, and by that time Max was back with the doctor. The doctor took a swift look and said, "You're not going anywhere for some time with that leg. You may have broken it, but I can't tell without an X ray."

As a cripple, I could not continue with the 1st Division, so the doctor wrote out a medical order transferring me to the casualty clearing station for examination and disposition. I got the doctor to agree to send me first to the press headquarters in Colleville. There I could decide my future.

The correspondents were headquartered in an old farm or château. Capa was there, and Thompson and some others. I sat watching them work for a while, feeling very despondent. For all my great hopes, here I was without communication and immobilized by a bad leg. The leg was still as painful as ever, and I could not hope to walk on it.

Finally, after getting a sergeant to promise to pick up my bedroll and put it with the press headquarters equipment, I got a ride with an Air Force public relations officer to the casualty station.

This was about half a mile from the beach. It was crowded with the wounded. Blood transfusions were being given. Doctors were operating. Everyone was extremely busy with the badly wounded, and there was little time for a mere broken ankle.

At length a doctor took a swift look and said, "With that leg, you've got to go back to England."

"If it's got to be England," I replied, "make it London because I've got to broadcast."

"Okay," he said, and wrote out an order for me to report to the army station hospital in London on my arrival in England. Then he sent me to the nearby airstrip, on the bluff overlooking the beach. It was here that transport planes were expected to fly out patients as soon as all the mines had been cleared away and a landing strip prepared. From D plus 1 on, it had been used as a possible crash landing ground for fighters.

On duty at the strip were two captains, a doctor and a dentist. They seemed pleased to see me. They had only four or five other patients awaiting air evacuation. The badly wounded were going back on ships, for no one knew when the air evacuation would begin.

The doctor clucked sympathetically when he examined the leg. "There may be a broken bone in that ankle," he said. "You need a cast."

He was delighted to get to work on me.

"I've been in the Army eighteen months," he said, "and this is the first time I've had a chance to put a cast on. Usually it's just ingrown toenails or a dose of clap."

He slapped on the plaster with enthusiasm, making a cast that went halfway to my knee.

"We have been waiting for crashes; but there haven't been any, and life is pretty dull," he said. "No air opposition, so no fighters shot up, so no crashes on our little airstrip. A fellow ran out of gas and came down here yesterday, but he landed pretty as anything."

"I can understand your being here," I said, and I turned to the dentist. "But what about you, Doctor? I don't see many teeth to fill here."

"The theory of the Air Force," he replied, "is that since I am a dentist and have a certain specialized knowledge of the face and jaws, I should be on hand so that when fighter pilots smash their faces against their control board on crack-ups, I will help patch them together."

Then he added, "As a matter of fact, all I do is help the doctor, if we get so many cases that he can't look after them all."

They were a nice pair of officers. The captain dentist tried to teach me to play gin rummy. But after he had taken five dollars from me, he said, "You do know this is a game of skill, don't you?"

I replied, "It seems all luck to me."

"I thought so. I might inform you that it is a matter of skill, and a good player will always beat a bad player." He explained just why, and that was the last time I ever played gin rummy. If it was skill at cards, I wanted no part of it.

That evening, as I was lying on my cot, the doctor poked his head in the tent and said, "How would you like to join us for a cocktail before dinner?"

I hastily scrambled onto the crutches the clearing station had given me and followed him.

The drinks were ice-cold. They tasted like gin and grapefruit juice. A dozen officers were there from units scattered a mile around.

"How do you do it?" I asked in awe and grateful appreciation.

Then the doctor told me the story. When he had landed on Omaha on D plus 1, he had noticed that his jeep's gasoline supply was running low. The doctor told his driver to fill it up.

The driver looked downcast. "I can't, Captain," he said.

The doctor tapped one of the five-gallon cans of gasoline that were standard jeep equipment.

"Fill it up from this," he ordered.

The driver looked even gloomier. "I did fill that can before we left England—with your medical alcohol."

"Well, what about this other can, then?" retorted the doctor.

The driver answered, "I filled that one up with five gallons of grapefruit juice. I thought you might want a drink sometime."

"So," ended the doctor, "I bawled him out, but he meant well, and here I am with five gallons of alcohol, two hundred proof, and five gallons of grapefruit juice. We mix it fifty-fifty."

"But what about the ice?" I asked. "I didn't know there was a piece of ice in all Normandy."

The doctor waved airily. "Well, you see, they fly penicillin in from England to this airstrip. It's packed in ice. I take out the ice and send the penicillin right down the road to the casualty station. It doesn't inconvenience them because they use every bit of penicillin they get right up and they don't need to refrigerate it. And when the doctors there can, they drop over here for a drink. It's a very satisfactory arrangement."

I thought so, too. The drinks were so potent that none of us paid any attention to an air raid that started the guns banging around us and out to sea, and later, when we all went outside to relieve ourselves in a ditch, two of us almost fell in. With his five gallons of alcohol, the doctor had the equivalent of more than fifty bottles of gin.

On Sunday, D plus 5, I thought I was going to get off the beachhead. A P-47 fighter landed on our little airstrip, and out stepped Major General Elwood Quesada, known to all his underlings and to the correspondents as Pete.

Quesada was a young, black-haired, good-looking man who will always be young, black-haired, and good-looking. At least when I saw him ten years later in Normandy, he looked about the same as I remembered him. But he was one of the Air Force veterans. I believe he was one of those three officers—another was General Carl Spaatz—who set an endurance flying record back in the twenties or early thirties.

Pete commanded the Ninth Air Force, the tactical air force the job of which was to be the spearhead of our armies in Europe.

I met him when he landed. I had met him several times previously, and seeing my plight, he said, "If I go back to England this afternoon, I'll take you with me in the forty-seven. We can crowd in together somehow."

He dashed off to his headquarters near Grandcamp. An hour or two later he was back with the word that he had to attend some conferences in the British sector and wasn't going right back to

Generals Bradley, Marshall, and Arnold meet in Normandy on D-Day plus 6. U.S. ARMY.

England. I gave him a message for NBC in London, telling them I had to come back and asking them to send a substitute. Quesada said he would send it at the first possible opportunity.

Pete, who could have been Air Chief of Staff, became a casualty years later in the internecine warfare of the Air Force. His crime was that he was too successful in his arguments for a balanced air force.

Now, let us admit it, no nation in the world had ever had a balanced air force. The Royal Air Force had developed according to the geography of Britain. It had an excellent protective fighter force. It had an excellent long-range night bomber force. But its Army cooperation squadrons were pitiable. Britain's armies had never been important, so Britain's air force problem was twofold—to protect the homeland with fighters and to strike deep into Europe with the long-range bombers. Thus the Royal Air Force was developed.

On the other hand, the Germans and the Russians had developed air-army cooperation into a powerful instrument of war. Ahead of their tanks, their planes formed the long-range artillery, and coordination was extremely good. But neither air force had a long-range bombing arm that was worthy of the name. Nor had their military men developed the established theory of long-range bombing in a sound manner. The Germans had attempted long-range bombing against England. To us on the ground, it had appeared horrendous, but there had been no consistent pattern of attack behind it, and the whole effort petered out into nothingness. The point is that both the Germans and the Russians are land animals. Their problem was to cover vast spaces with their armies. Their air forces were never basically anything more than auxiliaries to the millions of soldiers they pushed over the face of Europe.

The United States Air Force effort was different. The leaders of our Air Force were men who had spent most of their professional lives fighting off an inferiority complex. They were convinced that air power was important and that long-range bombing—longer-range than any American Army leader imagined—was the answer to the problem of how America could exert its power against enemies across the seas. However, Army leaders paid little attention to the cries of the Air Force. In their minds the Air Force was not basically important. This failure in Army understanding caused the handful of professional Air Force officers to become so partisan, so embittered that they made extravagant claims that they seriously believed, for example, that bombing from afar could win World War II. As we now know, this was a myth. Men could live and work under a rain of bombs far greater than anything that even our own Air Force men had ever imagined in the thirties and early forties.

And just at the moment that General Spaatz and the other officers of the Eighth Air Force in particular were undertaking to prove that daylight mass bombing could win the war, they saw vast amounts of American military energy being expended not only in a vast land force to invade France but also in the creation of the Ninth Tactical Air Force, a force the chief purpose of which was to act in close cooperation with the Army as a kind of long-range artillery and sky cover.

Worse than that, the air chiefs realized that this new air force under General Quesada was so brilliantly successful that it might nullify in Washington the importance of their own pet project, the mass destruction of the enemy from afar. To some of the strategic bombing advocates, every plane, every bomb, every success of the Ninth Air Force were bitter disappointments since potentially they robbed the strategic air army of men and funds which would otherwise enhance the all-important work of destroying Germany's production centers.

Quesada did train and send into action a marvelously competent air weapon, bearing a large share of the responsibility for the success of the ground forces. The strategic air force at one point tried to prove its own ability to carpet enemy positions from on high with a devastating layer of bombs. This was at the time of the St.-Lô breakthrough. But high-level pinpoint bombing did not prove effective, and the chief result was the killing of U.S. General Leslie McNair in his observer's foxhole, along with many others of our own men.

Years after the war the bitter opposition of the top Air Force men to the needs of a balanced air force shunted General Quesada from the candidacy for the highest position of all, Air Chief of Staff. He, in fact, resigned from the Air Force when it became apparent that its heads intended to create a lopsided air army, without the fighter and the medium-bomber units necessary to cooperate with ground forces.

It was Monday, D plus 6, when I got a ride back to England in one of the first transports using the little airstrip. On my return to London I found that Quesada's aide had telephoned my office and that Mildred and Florence already knew my plight. Don Whitehead had filed a brief Associated Press dispatch on the irony of my escaping death by rifle, machine gun, grenade, mortar, and shell on D-Day only to succumb to a broken ankle. W. W. Chaplin had already been sent to take my place. Before I went to the hospital in London, I broadcast a fifteen-minute account of the invasion, which, I was told, was the first full account, because of the poor communications, to reach the United States from an eyewitness of the stirring events of D-Day.

Chapter 24

I had continued to hear rumors from people who should have known that Hitler was about to launch his big rocket attack on London at any moment. So before I left for D-Day, I had arranged for Lucy, Myles, and baby Sara Ann to go to a house in Amersham, some fifteen or twenty miles outside the city. There they had several rooms and the use of the kitchen.

When I returned unexpectedly from France, however, Lucy had been forewarned and was already back in the apartment at Portland Place.

On the day after my broadcast I reported at the American Army hospital. My leg above the cast was a ghastly yellow and purple. Since the station hospital thus far had not received many casualties from France, I was still something of a novelty. The doctors X-rayed the leg, discovered I had broken an ankle bone, and immediately swathed me in a cast that ran up to my hip. I was put to bed and told it would probably be weeks before I could leave the hospital.

Two or three days later the director of the hospital came to see me. He said that he thought he was bound to give me a Purple Heart. I protested that I had broken an ankle, not been shot, and when he sent a stenographer to take down my statement, I made it quite clear that my mishap had been from my own clumsiness, not from an enemy bullet. But in due course the director presented me with the decoration. He had read the regulations carefully. I deserved the decoration, and I was going to get it willy-nilly.

I reflected that I could have been killed or wounded some hundreds of times on Omaha Beach. I reflected also that I had heard of a colonel getting the Purple Heart for jamming his fingers in a jeep door, and I accepted the medal with as much grace as possible in remembrance of all the bullets that had not hit me. Who was I to say that I was too proud to abide by Army regulations in such matters?

I went into the hospital on a Tuesday, and on the following Saturday night London had an air raid. We were moved downstairs into the hospital shelter. The guns sounded as loud as ever, and I could hear planes above the roar; but to an ear as accustomed as mine to such things, there was something quite different in the hideous din. Something mysterious. Something I had not known in the past.

It was next morning before we discovered that the Germans that night had launched their V-1 pilotless ramjet planes against London. The urgent buzz, buzz, buzz of their jets was the new sound in the London night, ominous, appalling, in fact, for what good were guns against a machine without a pilot, an automaton bringing us death in spite of anything we could do?

Sunday morning was sunny and beautiful. From our big windows in the ward, we could look across a large open space which seemed as big as a couple of football fields, a space edged with houses and trees. Then the buzz bombs started coming again, in broad daylight. We could hear the panting of their jets, then the terrible silence when their engines cut out, and finally the crash of the explosion.

Suddenly we saw one heading for us. The engine stopped. Within a twinkling, I was on the floor, cast and all. Almost everyone else in the ward had done the same thing. One man was seriously ill and delirious. I saw a nearby nurse rush to him and throw her body across his to screen him from the blast we expected.

But the V-1, instead of continuing its long glide, which would have brought it practically into our window, curved backward and struck pointing away from us just at the edge of the open space. Something must have gone wrong with its steering apparatus. There was a tremendous explosion. The windows shook, and one or two panes went; but we were unhurt. I saw it had struck a house. Black smoke was rising from the debris.

A few minutes later another came in low, to one side of the hospital, and cut out just beyond us. Another great explosion sounded. I discovered a few days later that the second great explosion had been the bomb which struck the Guards Chapel while it was filled with worshipers. Most of those inside had been killed, among them a girl from the Ministry of Information whom I had known well for years.

From then on the buzz bombs came at all times of the day and night, in such profusion that a day or two later the colonel who directed the hospital told me that all the less serious cases were to be evacuated to another hospital near Oxford. In my case, however, since I had a family and could find refuge outside London, I was free to go home. Lucy and the children had stayed in London during the first few days. Now we speedily moved again out to Amersham.

Amersham might have been a desirable place had German marksmanship with the V-1s been more accurate. In fact, many of the little pilotless planes bearing their load of explosive grunted their way right across London to the countryside beyond, and we were often in their track. It was frightening at night, when all was still except for the distant hoot of an owl or the chirping of a cricket, to hear that beat, beat, beat of the ramjet approaching across the empty fields and woods. The silence was even more frightening, for by then we could never tell how far the bombs would glide since the Nazis experimented with many settings of fuel and directive gear. Suddenly would come the crump of the explosion.

When a buzz bomb came over in the daytime and we heard the engine cut out, we would seize Myles and wall him up in a corner behind an armchair or a couch so that he would not be hit by any flying glass. Sara we would place on the couch or in her carriage and cover with cushions or our bodies as the occasion and time might warrant.

For the four or five weeks I stayed in Amersham, reporting weekly for inspection to the hospital in London, I did nothing but listen to news broadcasts on the BBC and drink beer at the local public house. At last came the day when I was able to discard my crutches and cast and hobble about with the aid of a shooting stick.

A day or two later I was back at the First Army press camp, established in the orchard of a little château at Vouilly, and W. W. Chaplin could return to London.

Lucy stayed only a few more weeks at Amersham. She had invited out to stay with her Mrs. Gerald Marks, who had been little Ian's nurse. Now married, she had her own little redheaded daughter about Sara's age.

Greta was a German Jewess who had come to England before the war. She had been our dear friend in the saddest moment of our lives, and Lucy wanted to get her and her baby out of London. She stayed with Lucy for several weeks, until, I believe, she went to live with relatives. But during that time the retired Indian civil servant and his wife who owned the Amersham house made several obvious and noticeable anti-Semitic remarks. This so infuriated Lucy that she wrote me she would not remain longer in the house.

Luckily an American woman who had heard my early broadcasts from London had written me that she was now living in Carnforth in Lancashire and asked whether she could look after my family during the buzz-bomb period. She was Mrs. Ruth Jackson, wife of an English doctor, and we have always been grateful to her for her hospitality to Lucy and the children.

I had arrived back with First Army at a lucky moment, July 26, two days after the Army had broken the German hold on St.-Lô It was the beginning of the spectacular run around the end of the German Army by General Patton's Third Army. And while the Third Army was romping around the periphery of the German forces, drawing them into a giant bag, the First Army was constricting that bag, slowly chewing the German divisions to bits and keeping their commanders so occupied that they had no time to flee or to fight the unsuspected menace from the Third.

We correspondents lived in tents in the orchard of the Vouilly château. Our press briefing and writing room and the censorship room were inside the château. Ten years later the white-haired madame who owned the château still proudly kept on her wall signs marking the old press room.

Our broadcasts at that time were made from a mobile 399 radio constructed by Hallicrafters for the Army. It was mounted in a truck and was supposed to have a reliable voice broadcast range of 75 miles. This particular set was called Jig Easy Sugar Queen from its call letters JESQ, and it was manned by a Signal Corps lieutenant, James Rugg. He had been a university student and an ardent radio "ham" in private life and was so skillful in increasing the power and range of his set that it reached London easily from the beachhead, a distance of some 200 miles. Later it often spanned as much as 500 miles from positions deep in the heart of Germany. In contrast, Tom Treanor, NBC and Los Angeles *Times* correspondent with the Third Army, broadcasting on an identical set some 50 miles farther away, was almost never able to reach London successfully.

The press correspondents used a Press Wireless transmitter. In spite of all the grandiose communications plans for press and radio, it was only by an accident that the press people were able to communicate with any regularity to New York. The Press Wireless set came ashore several weeks before it was supposed to arrive. Army authorities wanted to send the set immediately back to England. They were dissuaded only by a combined front of correspondents, who pointed out that without the Press Wireless set they might as well start sending their copy back by carrier pigeon or Channel swimmer.

From that time on the Press Wireless men sent many thousands of words a day by radio beam.

But the PW company was not authorized to send voice broadcasts, and it took weeks of demands, tears, pressure, and threats against the SHAEF authorities in London before the networks obtained permission to use the transmitter. Thus the communications plans for correspondents, which undoubtedly won those most closely concerned great kudos from the Army and from industry, were successful only because they were not put into operation. Instead, the accident of having an interested radio ham fiddling with his little regulation army transmitter and the other accident of an individual company, Press Wireless, landing its transmitter several weeks ahead of schedule made the information of radio and press correspondents at the First Army available to their countrymen in America.

The other radio correspondents with the First Army were Larry LeSueur of CBS and George Hicks and Gordon Fraser of ABC, which by that time had become separated from NBC. Johnny Johnstone and Tom Velotta, who headed ABC's news division, had tried the experiment of sending as correspondents men who were trained announcers and special events men but who had not had the newspaper and news agency background of the rest of us. I may say it worked very well indeed. George Hicks was able to make the only usable recording of an air raid on the invasion fleet, and being intelligent, both men rapidly learned the techniques of the news business.

The routine of our days went something like this: We were up and had breakfast by eight-thirty or nine. At ten we would have a briefing based on the dawn reports from the various units. This briefing was usually given by Colonel Monk Dickson, intelligence chief of the First Army, or one of his assistants. Another briefing was given in late afternoon. One could have filed quite respectable reports from these briefings alone and never have left the press camp. Such a procedure, however, was never indulged in by any of the first-class reporters. Usually, after the morning briefing, we teamed up, took jeeps, and started off to find the most likely spot of battle.

My regular broadcast schedule called for a broadcast at about one o'clock in the afternoon and another at midnight to fit into NBC's two main news roundups, eight in the morning and seven-fifteen at night New York time.

This was perfectly all right as long as the armies were holding static positions. I could go to one unit at the front in the morning, return for my 1:00 P.M. broadcast, then visit another sector after lunch and be back by dinnertime to write my spot and put it on the air at midnight.

But once Patton's Third Army began to slip down along the coastal corridor, I felt duty-bound to follow the spearheads, even though NBC did have a correspondent with the Third Army.

I got Wright Bryan, covering the Canadian forces for NBC and the Atlanta *Journal*, to become assigned to the First Army. Wright would attend the morning briefing with me. Then he would go to some nearby unit and be back with an eyewitness report for the 1:00 P.M. session at Jig Easy Sugar Queen. I would have taken off with one of the press correspondents, often Hal Boyle of the Associated Press or some special newspaper correspondent, and I would have all day to follow Patton's drive, then return and make my night broadcast. Bryan, meanwhile, was free in the afternoon to go where he wanted and pick up information for his nightly cables to his Atlanta paper. Should startling news warrant it, we could call for special broadcast times, but usually the two-a-day schedule was the one we followed.

My memories of the month between the breakthrough at St.-Lô and the taking of Paris are chiefly recollections of moving all the time. General Bradley had taken over control of both the First and Third armies at his Twelfth Army Group headquarters. General Courtney Hodges, a white-haired, soft-spoken Southerner, now commanded the First Army. Hodges was as good a general as any I have ever met; but since he did not have Patton's personality, he was overshadowed by the latter in the public estimation. Other generals and the correspondents who watched him closely realized his value. His First Army did most of the fighting against the German forces in Normandy, while Patton's men in reality had the benefit of not battle, but pursuit; nonetheless Hodges's army was the first to enter Germany, the first across the Rhine, the first to meet the Russians. It destroyed more German divisions than any other Allied army. It also suffered greater casualties, had more days of combat, and took more prisoners than the others.

Yet how could correspondents of the First Army have possibly glamorized this southern gentleman whom his own staff had nick-named Auntie? Who could put "Auntie" Hodges beside "Old Blood and Guts" Patton in the battle? Yet I am not alone in be-lieving that Hodges was the sounder and more reliable commander. Patton had dash and personality, yet at times he took great risks that might have ended in tragedy. Fate was indeed with him when he took "Lucky" as the code word for the Third Army headquarters. Hodges had picked the code word "Master" for the First Army, and he was truly a master of the military art.

I tried to stay with the leading tanks in the push down the coast. After we had seized Coutances, the forces headed south. The first day we reached Bréhal. The second day we arrived in the coastal resort of Granville, later Eisenhower's first headquarters in France. There I met Major Paul Gale of the 1st Division, who had spent part of a night rocketing around the city in his jeep before the army entered, shooting up any Germans he saw, and escaping when all the German soldiers were buzzing around like hornets in con-fusion. Granville was not in 1st Division territory, and to this day I have wondered just what Gale was doing there.

The third day we reached Sartilly and Avranches. Travel with armored divisions being what it was, it took all day to get down to the spearheads and back to Vouilly for my broadcast. Our First Army press camp moved slowly with the First Army headquarters, for the bulk of the army was meeting ferocious resistance at every point.

The press camp went from Vouilly to a field near Littry, where we lived under canvas. Then we moved to an orchard near a somewhat wrecked château not far from Canisy. But by that time Third Army spearheads were far away, and at times I could not make the First Army press camp by night, so had to stop at the press camp of the Third to do my broadcast. Strangely, although Tom Treanor had been unable to get on the air, by some freak of atmospherics I usually was lucky enough to reach London on the two or three occasions I used the Third Army transmitter.

The Third Army slipped down through Montorson and St.-James, threw one column toward Rennes and another toward Brest in the Brittany peninsula. Patton had certainly stamped his personality on his army. Practically all the commanders of the armored divisions under him wore shiny boots like his, talked roughly as he did, swaggered as he did, and even told his jokes.

The correspondents of the Third Army were filled with frustration. They were not even allowed to mention Patton's name or reveal that the army had landed in France, although one would have thought the Germans might have been aware of that fact already. As a result, they were always bickering among themselves. The correspondents from the major papers, as well as the news agency and radio correspondents, had gone with the First Army to France. They were chiefly experienced men. The Third Army had, with some notable exceptions such as Joe Driscoll of the *Herald Tribune* and Pierre Huss of INS, many second-string correspondents and reporters from smaller papers getting their first war experience. There always seemed to be a press camp crisis or open war between correspondents and press officers whenever I visited the Third Army reporters at this time, although later the situation improved greatly.

As we streamed down the narrow coastal corridor on only a couple of roads, we were in a terribly vulnerable condition. Troops, machines, fuel were so concentrated that it was almost impossible to make any speed up or down the line. The most vulnerable points were the river crossings at Avranches, Pontaubault, and St.-Hilaire du Harcouët. Why, in those early days, the Germans did not realize their danger and risk some bombers to cut the bridges or drop some determined parachutists to blow them up, I have never known. Perhaps the reason was sheer German ignorance of the threat that had developed. If they had attacked the bridges successfully and steadily enough, they could have relieved themselves of the danger from the great trap and could have held up our progress for many weeks.

On the occasions I saw Patton at his forward headquarters near Folligny and he strode up and down with his bull terrier in front of his tent, talking to me, he also expressed wonderment at why the Germans had not attacked him at his vulnerable heels and cut off the supply of his armored columns beginning to fan out south of the Cotentin peninsula. He spoke highly of the French Resistance forces. When one column was going toward Rennes and another toward Brest, he said to me, "Hell, I haven't got any real flanking protection. I'm just shooting them out and telling them to cover ground like hell. But the French Resistance boys are pinning the Germans down on our flanks and spotting them when they move for us. Doing a great job."

The pursuit was exhilarating. The tank columns would pass through territory which they did not take time to clear up. The tanks took the roads, and the Germans lurked in the weeds and brush between the roads until the FFI boys found them.

Following the tanks was dangerous sport, for one was never certain just which ground was ours and which the enemy's. Bill Stringer, a young American correspondent with Reuters, the British news agency, was killed in that manner. Later Gault Macgowan of the New York *Sun* was taken prisoner in similar fashion, escaping later only by jumping from a moving railroad train that was taking him to Germany. The commanders themselves were uncertain just where their leading tank columns were at any particular moment. I often met Third Army Signal Corps officers laying their wire far behind the spearheads who confessed that neither corps nor army was able to get reports from the leading units. Even division headquarters sometimes failed to know the latest movements.

In circumstances like these, the only thing a correspondent could do was to see for himself what was happening. General Patton felt the same way. I often saw him dashing along in his command car far from his own headquarters hunting for some errant division, so that he could pinpoint its movement and give it a nudge if he felt it was moving too slowly.

On one occasion, I remember, I had heard from a corps headquarters that Rennes had been taken. I hurried down in a jeep. I was moving at forty miles an hour a couple of miles outside the city, for I knew that three French correspondents, Rabache, Gosset, and another, were just ahead of me, and I did not relish the thought of being second to them in reaching the city. Suddenly, from the corner of my eye, I noticed a soldier wave at me and shout. We stopped and went back.

"What is it? What's the matter?" I asked.

"The Germans are two hundred yards up the road. They have a strongpoint on this hill."

"But there was a car, with correspondents, just ahead of me."

"Yeah," said the GI. "They went past here at full speed in a sedan with the windows closed. They didn't hear us shout. They must have been killed or captured."

The next day I found that their car had been brought to a halt by a burst of machine-gun fire. I saw it wrecked and riddled. Somehow the three men were unhurt when they were taken prisoner.

But on the day in question I had a wire recorder with me. The generator for the recording machine was housed on a trailer and was run by a gasoline motor. I ran into a nearby pasture just off the road where some of our tanks were scattered along the hedges that separated the fields. I learned from one of the officers that a summons to surrender had been sent the German unit between us and Rennes and a deadline of noon had been set for the reply.

Noon came and went, and there was no reply. A couple of airburst shells exploded over our pasture. Jim Rugg and I then picked ourselves up from under the tank whose protection we had sought in simultaneous dives and started the motor of the generator sputtering and banging so that we could record any further sounds of battle.

Immediately the lieutenant colonel commanding the tank detachment came up shouting "Shut that — — thing off. The krauts are in the next field. They — — didn't know we were here until you turned that — thing on."

Since the krauts in question had just been dropping shells over us as though they did know we were in that particular pasture, I could not understand why the colonel thought they were so ignorant, but in the circumstances I forbore to ask him for explanations. Besides, Rugg had already turned the motor off. Such were the difficulties of front-line recording without decent equipment. The BBC correspondents, on the other hand, had portable disc recorders that worked beautifully, and they were able to cover the war in a way which was made impossible for us because of the earlier mentioned aversion of our networks, in those long ago days, to recordings of any kind.

The next morning, when I came down the same road, the strongpoint had been overcome, and our troops had moved into Rennes soon after dawn.

My first concern at Rennes, as in other places where I knew radio transmitters were located, was to find the transmitter in the hope of being first to use it. Had I ever discovered one in working order, it would have given us a forward base of operations which would have eliminated the many miles of driving from the front to the press camp each day.

We took the road to the south, I believe the one through St. Jacques and La Potière, where we were told we could find the Rennes radio transmitter. It was a lonely road, and ours was the only car. I wanted to ask someone whether the Germans were still holding the territory, for we did not know where our tanks had gone. I saw a farmer plowing his field. When I yelled at him, he deliberately turned and started in the other direction. Some people were walking along the road 100 yards ahead of us. When we

270

reached the spot, they had disappeared into the hedges. In a village I saw some women and children on their doorsteps. When we arrived, not a soul was visible, and all doors were closed.

Finally I reached the village where I believed the transmitter was to be found. I discovered one man on foot and shouted so loudly that he could not ignore me. I could not understand the stupidity of the local population, the way they seemed to shun us.

"We are Americans," I said. "Where is the radio station?"

"Americans?" he replied, with a stupid look on his face. "I don't know."

Some more people came up. "Americans?"

"Yes," I said. "What is all this about? You people act stupid. Everyone seems afraid of us."

A young Frenchman suddenly said in English, "Where do you come from, and what do you want to know?"

I answered him in the same language, and he said to his colleagues, in French, "Yes. They are Americans."

At his words the whole atmosphere changed. A hundred people crowded around our car. They tried to force us to drink wine and cider. Everyone was talking at the same time. They shook our hands and kissed us.

"We thought you were Germans," someone said. "You are the first Americans we have ever seen."

That was it. We had come through territory which our tanks had not yet entered. The peasants had never seen American uniforms, so we had, for a brief time, been treated as German soldiers were treated, with hostility and contempt.

A crowd accompanied us to the building that housed the transmitter. A nun had collected six little girls together. They stood in a line by our jeep, waving French flags, and they sang the "Marseillaise" to us. It was a thrilling moment.

Unfortunately the Germans had blown the Rennes transmitter to bits. We had hoped to find enough material to put it together in a day or two, but Jim Rugg said it would take months of rebuilding to make the set workable.

As we left the village, the little girls stood in line, waving good-bye to us with their little flags.

Only once did the Germans try seriously to break out of the big bag we were drawing around them. They launched a strong attack meant to break through to the sea and cut our supply lines, at the same time reestablishing their own position, for their left wing was, as the saying goes, up in the air and vulnerable to attack. The stroke was aimed at Mortain, but the 30th Division stood firm and repelled it while the pincers closed even tighter on the German Army.

I had blithely gone to visit the 1st Division on the northwest shoulder of the bag, somewhat above the main German thrust. I was moving on small back roads, and it was some time before I noticed that nothing was moving. Usually one would run into cars or trucks transporting supplies. In one village all was as quiet as a tomb. Around the corner of a building stepped a GI, with a bazooka aimed at me. He lowered it, and I asked what he was doing.

"They just put me here, sir, and told me to shoot at any German tanks I saw," the GI replied.

At the 1st Division headquarters, the map showed German armor appearing all over the place, mostly places where no Germans were expected.

An intelligence officer asked, "What road did you come down?"

I told him, and he said, "Well, at least we know that road was clear when you came along it."

Even while we talked, we heard the sound of shooting. A German tank had bobbed up near the command post, and some cooks or Signal Corps men had picked up rifles and bazookas and driven it off. I did not greatly relish wandering about in my jeep when no one knew where the German tanks were, and I also wanted more information. So I performed a quick strategic withdrawal to corps, being careful to take exactly the same road on which I had come. It was only late in the day, from the Army briefing, that I realized the extent of the German attack.

I remember some of the rides we took, trying to keep up with the fighting, down through Avranches and Fougères to Mayenne. But there the Germans were still fighting, and we knew the tanks were still moving east of us, so we sideslipped down to Laval and over for the entry into Le Mans. For Le Mans, the attack went north as the drawstring of the bag closed. General Jacques Leclerc's 2nd French Armored Division, an American armored division, and two American infantry divisions battered their way up through Alençon, Sées, and Argentan. At one point on the road, I saw where five or six of the French Sherman tanks had been burned out within a road space of a couple of hundred yards when they had run into some powerful German antitank guns.

I found the headquarters of the French division in Argentan in a grove behind the prefecture. Jacques Keyser, later a leading editorial writer on *Le Monde*, showed me around. In the Deuxième Bureau section, a German colonel, in full ceremonial dress, with gloves, decorations, and shining boots, was being questioned. I have always been amazed at how much German colonels resembled Erich von Stroheim, the actor. The German looked somewhat stunned.

A French officer named Boris, cousin of the distinguished journalist and diplomat Georges Boris, whom I had known in London, said, "These Germans are always surprised to find that the troops who take them prisoner are French. They seem to think there is something unfair about it."

The Americans and the French division were held still, a little north of Argentan, while Montgomery's forces tried to close the bag from the north at Falaise. But Günther von Kluge, the German commander, was able to hold the British and Canadians back, and although the German units were hammered by our guns and planes as they passed through, and some of the Nazi units were wiped out completely on the roads, the greater part escaped in the mob rush to the Seine. The inside of the former gap, when we saw it later, was littered with German bodies, burned-out vehicles and tanks, dead horses, and destroyed carts which reminded those who remembered it of the First World War.

Wright Bryan and I were sitting in a café in a little French village having lunch when an American major, somewhat the worse for cognac, told us Tom Treanor had been killed, his jeep crushed by a skidding tank as he tried to keep up with the first of Patton's armor to reach the Seine.

We hurried to the crossroads where the accident had taken place, both of us terribly depressed at the loss of a good friend and an able correspondent. There was nothing to be learned from the wrecked jeep, and we had to go to Dreux to see Joe Driscoll of the *Herald Tribune* before we learned the whole story. Tom was a lovable, lively man who had hitchhiked into battles without authorization so long that he was quite surprised to find himself ashore in Normandy accredited to the Third Army.

Afterward in Portland, Maine, I attended the launching of a Liberty ship christened the *Tom Treanor* by Mrs. Treanor, and I had the chance to meet Tom's very attractive boys.

Chapter 25

Chance is as determining a factor in a battle involving millions of people as it is in the individual human life. By chance, the closest I came to death was many miles behind the front.

I was riding along the broad highway from St.-Lô to Bayeux to see Bob Cooper of the *Times* of London, Alan Moorehead of the *Daily Express,* and some of my British officer friends in order to get a better picture of what was happening on the British front. My jeep driver was bowling along at fifty or sixty miles an hour, more or less in the center of the road, when a huge American Army truck came tearing up behind us, going a good deal faster than we were. I thought my driver had seen the truck, but he was driving in a daydream and failed to pull over as the truck started to pass us. I could see the first of its ten wheels creeping up on our flank as my driver moved neither to right nor left.

Suddenly the truck spurted, and I thought it would get past. I started to shout at my driver, and at that instant the side of the truck flicked the side of the jeep. To this day I do not know whether the truck driver did it on purpose, to frighten what seemed to be an officer and driver hogging the road.

Our jeep shot off the road into a dense screen of bushes and trees, going more than fifty miles an hour. I thought my last moment had come. I had no time to think more than that this was the end and how strange it was going to be when I felt the bushes raking my face and I put my arms up to take the shock.

Before I knew what had happened, we were through the bushes. I was flying through the air, and so was the jeep, rolling over and over and down toward me. We struck the bottom of a steep twenty-foot embankment at almost the same time. I had only a split second to worry about being crushed by the jeep as it bounded down toward me, and then it was past.

I slowly collected myself. The jeep lay on its side nearby. The driver was picking himself up not far away. We did not speak for a moment as we felt ourselves and I made sure no bones were broken. It hardly seemed possible that neither of us had been killed. I looked to the top of the bank. We had careered through some trees. If we had struck one head-on, there would have been little left of us or the jeep. My heavy metal pocket flask was twisted out of shape. I had lost my glasses, scraped off my face in the bushes, but after a five-minute hunt I discovered them unbroken.

If we had been injured, we might have lain there for a long time undiscovered, for one could not see the road through the bushes. I saw a distant figure on the other side of the field, and I waved and shouted; but he did not come across the field to see us. It must have been ten minutes later when a French peasant poked his head through the bushes.

"I saw your accident, monsieur," he said, "Are you hurt?"

"No," I replied, "but why didn't you come across the field?"

"Not me, monsieur," he said. "You are on the edge of a German minefield. You had better climb up here right away and not walk around. I lost one of my cows in that field last week."

We picked our gear up carefully and, as carefully, climbed back on the road to get a ride to Bayeux. There was no sign of the truck that had done the damage. It had not stopped.

The taking of Paris was an example of how chance affects the course of armies.

General Bradley did not intend to take Paris at the time he did take it. His objective was the Germans fleeing northeast from the Falaise gap. From a military point of view, Paris was of no use to him then. Far better, he thought, to outflank it, go around it and keep on chasing the Germans without the bother of fighting for the metropolis.

General Bradley told us that at a night conference at Twelfth Army Group headquarters near Laval on August 20. I stayed on that night in Laval in order to record a speech of General de Gaulle, who was arriving in the city, and to do a description of his reception.

I got back to the First Army press camp, in a resort hotel at Bagnoles-de-l'Orne, on the evening of August 21. The next day we had our surprise. Colonel Dickson came over from First Army headquarters, just across the park from us, to give us our daily briefing on the battle. He went through his usual explanations with maps. Then he paused, smiled, and said quietly, "We may be in Paris tomorrow."

A bursting grenade could have caused no greater excitement among the correspondents.

Dickson explained that an emissary from the French Resistance in Paris had come to Bradley's headquarters and told the general that the Germans had asked the FFI, the Resistance, for an armistice to permit them to extricate the bulk of their troops holding positions south of Paris. These troops could no longer escape on either side of Paris, and the German commander, General Dietrich von Choltitz, wanted to get the FFI to allow them to go through Paris and northward without interruption.

The FFI had agreed.

Now emissaries from the FFI and the brother of the Swedish consul in Paris had come to ask General Bradley to take Paris. The FFI officer declared that fighting had stopped and that we could move into Paris at the expiration of the armistice, noon on August 23. In fact, fighting had broken out again between the Resistance and the Germans, and the German Army had not passed through Paris northward; but the situation seemed too good to be missed. The Swedish consul had sent a hint that Von Choltitz might surrender to a regular army but that he would fight to the end against the FFI.

The emissaries saw Bradley the same morning that Colonel Dickson broke the news to us correspondents. Bradley immediately made the decision to enter Paris and ordered General Leclerc's French division, then attached to the First Army, to carry out the mission. Leclerc's tanks were based at Sées, between Alençon and Argentan. The American 4th Division was to sweep across Fontainebleau, outside Paris on the east. But the first troops Parisians would see would be their own Frenchmen, the Free French, many of whom had fought their way all the distance from Lake Chad in Central Africa to Tunisia, then on to their homeland.

Bradley did not want to wreck Paris. He gave Leclerc orders that if he could not get into Paris without a major battle, he was not to move in. Instead, he was to wait until the city had been surrounded and could be taken without a fight.

As soon as Colonel Dickson finished his account, every correspondent began packing his equipment for an early-morning start.

Charles Collingwood of CBS had joined the First Army correspondents only a few days previously. He was one of the only two reporters I ever saw wearing a smartly tailored battle dress. The other was Ed Murrow of the same company and Charles's boss.

Collingwood was so sure that we would be in Paris next day that he made a recording on the basis of the information G-2 had given us. He put a "hold for release" on the record, and it was flown to London. Someone in London's official army circles interpreted it as having been made inside Paris. A slip in censorship let it out, and in a matter of minutes, the whole world thought Paris had been liberated on August 23.

Actually on August 23, Collingwood was starting out with the rest of us from Bagnoles and the Germans still held Paris with something like 10,000 troops.

Rain was falling that morning as we set out, Wright Bryan; a public relations lieutenant named Jack Hansen; our driver, Ray Kokoska from Chicago; and I. We had our wire recorder in a trailer. Our destination was Rambouillet twenty-odd miles outside Paris. It was there that Leclerc's troops were to wait for the armistice deadline—noon.

We had arranged for the censors to follow us quickly, and the Press Wireless and the Jig Easy Sugar Queen transmitters as well.

We met some of the Leclerc division vehicles on the roads. I thought that Bradley had given the division a tremendous distance to move because from Sées to Rambouillet was a good 100 miles. That is not far in a car, but for a column of military vehicles it is a very long way indeed.

By midmorning we were in Chartres. We could find no one who had seen the Leclerc division go by. Nor did anybody seem to know where the Germans were or whether the road to Rambouillet was clear.

We took the main road leading east; but there was no military traffic of any kind, and the road stretched flat and deserted ahead of us. I was always suspicious of empty roads. Correspondents got blown up, shot at, ambushed, or even killed when they traveled on such roads too often.

The Germans had blown a bridge, and we wondered whether they might not be waiting beyond it on the main road, so we turned off and picked our way across country on the byways toward Rambouillet, passing through such hamlets as St. Symphorien, Ecrosnes, Orphin, and Orcemont. In some of the villages we were told that we were the first Americans the people had seen.

When we reached Rambouillet, other correspondents were already there, waiting on the main street leading into town. Investigation disclosed that we were the only Allies in Rambouillet, a crowd of reporters and photographers that got bigger and bigger by the minute. The Germans were reported to be just beyond the outskirts of town. We left our jeeps under the shade trees and crowded into the Grand Veneur Restaurant. There was nothing to do but wait.

A lieutenant of the Leclerc division arrived to go on reconnaissance. He had got only a short distance out of Rambouillet when he ran into an ambush. One of his men was killed, and the lieutenant came back, looking very angry, with a bullet in his arm. This incident discouraged us from trying to lead the division into Paris.

At last, Leclerc's tanks began to roll into town. They did not roll far. Most lined up along the road or dispersed in the parks.

A column of cars containing a mixed lot of American officers came whizzing through the center of Rambouillet and zipped out on the Route Nationale. Wright and I immediately followed them. A half mile on the other side of town, we found the column halted. It was a group of psychological warfare experts from the Twelfth Army Group who had been told the way to Paris was open. We told them they would run into Germans a short way up the road. French soldiers confirming this, the column of psychological warriors sadly returned to Rambouillet.

More and more correspondents filled the restaurant. They seemed to be coming from every unit in France, through all the doors and windows. As usual, we all became impatient and started to argue. Then someone proposed we beard Leclerc himself and ask him why he did not start off at once for Paris. We reporters did not have all day to wait.

We must have looked like an invading army as we tramped into the park to see General Leclerc. He met us in the open, playing with his cane and poking it into the ground as he talked with us.

What he said made sense. The distance had been so great that his division was all strung out over the roads and not ready to go into battle. The armistice had not been agreed. In fact, it had been broken, and it appeared that the Germans were going to fight. Leclerc did not want to move on until he was ready. He was a little supercilious, but he did promise to meet us the next day and tell us his plans for entering Paris.

We returned to the Grand Veneur.

One of the figures in Rambouillet was Ernest Hemingway. I had grown up admiring his early novels, and I thought that *A Farewell to Arms* was as good as anything done by an American in our century. Hemingway had affected the writing of a whole generation of American authors so that half the college English majors could not put together a short story without sounding as though they were copying Hemingway, as, in fact, they were doing. But Hemingway was always better than any of his imitators.

Sometimes to admire the art is to be disillusioned by the artist, and I must admit I felt that disillusion at meeting Hemingway for the first time. He had come rather late to our campaigning. In the spring, driving in the London blackout, he had crashed into a static water tank. The result: concussion of the brain and a long spell in the hospital which had delayed his arrival in France.

Hemingway was telling all and sundry that he had spent several days in Rambouillet. He told us that he and some adulatory young French boys who clustered around him armed with pistols and ancient rifles had alone defended Rambouillet against the Germans. Since there was no conceivable reason for any Germans to try to take Rambouillet, this sort of talk made something less than a sensation among Hemingway's rather cynical audience. The only enthusiast he seemed to have was an OSS colonel, David Bruce, who later became American ambassador to Paris.

Hemingway would yell at one of his boys to "go out and check the Germans" on such-and-such a road. The boy would nod or salute with a *"Oui, mon colonel"* and leap onto his bicycle.

Hemingway was draped in pistols. Since he rated as a correspondent, he, like the rest of us, was strictly forbidden to carry arms, for the U.S. Army obeyed the Geneva Convention, no matter what the correspondents thought about it. We felt that the novelist was not quite playing the game, but it was, in fact, a kind of game that he was playing.

He would pound the table at the Grand Veneur and say, "This is my headquarters. This is my GHQ. We fought 'em off for days. Now the Army can take over. They have to have my men to tell them the enemy strength."

In spite of his gray beard, he seemed like a small boy, playing soldiers with other boys, swaggering about and taking himself as seriously as though he were commanding the legions of Rome. He was posing, like an actor, and the reality of the man did not gibe at all with some of the fine work of his that I had read.

A disillusioned old Chicago reporter, with a deeply lined face, having stood about as much of Hemingway as he could stand after a flock of brandy and sodas, finally said, "Look, Hemingway, why don't you stop trying to be a chickenshit general with your chicken-shit little army? You're just making a chickenshit spectacle of your-self. Come on down to earth, and act normal."

I have rarely seen a man get as angry as Hemingway. He grew red in the face. The cords on his neck stood out. He swelled his chest and clenched his fists until I feared he might have a stroke.

Another reporter and I got between them.

"I'll beat the bastard's brains in. He can't say that to me," said Hemingway, shaking his arms and shoulders like a prizefighter. "I'll kill the bastard."

Since the other man was a good fifteen years older and perhaps 100 pounds lighter than Hemingway, the match did not look like a promising one.

The old reporter continued to sit at the outdoor table in the Grand Veneur garden, sipping his cognac. After a minute or two he looked Hemingway up and down and said, "Horseshit, Heming-way. Go play with your little soldier boys." And the novelist, al-though he still scowled and flexed his muscles, permitted us to lead him away on the plea that some of his Frenchmen had important information for him.

That night Wright Bryan and I slept at the home of a butcher and his wife whom we had met by chance on the street. We had asked them where we could find a hotel, and nothing would do but that we should stay with them. When we arrived that night, we found that they had turned their only bedroom over to us and that both were sleeping on couches in their living room. But they refused to swap places with us, and we passed the night in their big double bed under a comforter.

As I went to sleep, I still kept thinking about Hemingway. Here was an artist of the first order. That was admitted. But why should the undoubted artist appear as bully and braggart?

Why should such a writer strike that particular pose? It had been my experience that the best fighter, the most courageous soldier, the man who was sure of his own ability did not ordinarily shout about his toughness and pick fights. Jack Dempsey did not go about cleaning out barrooms and yelling that he could lick any man in the house. Nor did Terry Allen spend his time boasting to his friends of his victories and praising his own ability as a tactician. Still, I thought, perhaps we all want to be something we are not. Hemingway might have cherished the desire to be a prizefighter or a military man instead of a writer, and this was the way the suppressed desire demonstrated itself. For all I knew, Dempsey may have always wanted to be a painter, and he might bore his friends by boasting of his watercolors instead of his conquests of Carpentier and Firpo. And Terry Allen, in the intervals between battles, might have dreamed of being a poet and infuriated his friends by reading them his imitations of Shelley. Most humans, such is our perversity, wish themselves to be something they are not. Nor was I myself exempt from this failing, I thought as I went to sleep, for between waking and dreaming I could see myself as the writer of the great novel of the century, ambassador to the Court of St. James's, skipper of a Gloucester fishing schooner at the turn of the century, great Shakespearean actor, or the finest bagpipe player the world had seen since MacCrimmon. Instead, I was a radio reporter, which is a little of almost anything you can think of. And perhaps Hemingway, sober, was quite a reasonable fellow. At least he later married Mary Welsh, the former London *Daily Express* reporter, who had a sensible head on her shoulders and was not likely to be entranced by bluff and bluster in a man.

The next morning, August 24, Wright Bryan and I were up early. We learned that during the night German patrols had come as close as two miles to Rambouillet. A light rain was falling, and down at the Grand Veneur the whole scribble of correspondents were still arguing, fretting, and waiting for their meeting with General Leclerc.

I suggested to Bryan that we go out on the road. We picked up Jack Hansen and Kokoska and took the jeep. Just outside Rambouillet we found a column of Leclerc's tank-destroyer guns on the move. They were on the road leading east, and we kept up with them. When they halted, we went on to pick up some more of Leclerc's moving vehicles. Kokoska, who had labeled his jeep "Chicago Kid," was a skillful driver. He could keep the jeep on the move, dodging in and out of a column whenever he got the chance. Our technique was to pick out the vehicle that looked like the leader of any particular unit and hang just behind it for as long as the column kept on the move. When the line stopped and we could see anything else moving, either ahead or on one of the roads beside us, we would swing out and join the mobile group.

The column went as far as Cernay, then switched to the right. We could see other armored vehicles moving on a parallel road. I followed our course on my road map and checked off the hamlets through which we passed, obscure crossroads with a few houses and a name. For the sake of any military student who may wish to follow the course of the Deuxième Division Blinde, we passed through Pecqueuse, Limours, Forges-les-Bains, Briis-sous-Forges. As I followed the column on the map, I could see that we were not heading toward Paris, but taking a line parallel to the main German defenses of the city. These were centered in a series of strongpoints some ten miles southwest of Paris between Fort Trappes and Fort Palaiseau. The bulk of the German troops still held these strongpoints, and Leclerc was outflanking Fort Palaiseau. For he now turned his columns and began to work toward Paris through the country byways, where the Germans would least expect him.

The first place of any size which we reached was Longjumeau, and it was there that we met our first resistance.

Wright Bryan and I were with some artillery at the time. The column halted. Guns dispersed in the fields and began firing. The Germans had a strongpoint there with antitank guns and mortars. We waited a little while in the rain with guns. The Germans lobbed over a few shells, none landed near us.

We began edging the jeep along slowly, ready to jump into a ditch at the slightest excuse. I struck up a conversation with the commander of one of the batteries. When I told him I was an American war correspondent, he seemed surprised but cordial, and he confirmed the fact that Leclerc intended to reach Paris that very day.

Ahead of us two German tanks had been hit and were burning. They had set fire to a haystack. Off to the left of the road some of the French Shermans were nosing toward the strongpoint, while our artillery banged shell after shell at it. French infantrymen came walking back across the field.

We continued down the road between a long line of trees. Our jeep passed through the smoke of a small German tank, which was burning furiously. An antitank gun was a twisted wreck beside the road.

We hurried on. A little farther on a car drew up beside us. In it was a French naval officer, Jean Marin. Jean, of an aristocratic Breton family, was a reporter who had joined the BBC in London after the fall of France. He took the name Jean Marin, "John Sailor," as a *nom de guerre* for the broadcasting he did for the BBC French service. He became renowned under his new name, a voice of hope to the millions of his countrymen in bondage, just as Maurice Schumann, speaking anonymously as the voice of Free France, became famous.

Not long before the invasion Jean poured his six feet six inches or thereabouts into a Free French Navy uniform and served in motor-torpedo boats in the dangerous Channel fighting. I had not seen him in several months. The last time had been in London at the house of Pierre Brossolette, the underground leader who committed suicide rather than give away the secrets of the coming invasion to a Nazi torture chamber.

Now Marin and I shook hands with great warmth. I asked him if he had seen any other British or American correspondents.

"No," he replied. "We're right at the head of the column. No other correspondent has come here. I'm glad you're with us. You deserve to be in at the end."

We chatted a moment or two, and Jean said, "Did you see De Gaulle back there? He was standing in that group of men with Leclerc and Billotte. Billotte's commanding this combat command."

I thought it must be quite a thrill for Billotte. He was the son of a French general killed in an auto accident when the Germans attacked in May 1940. As a captain in the tanks he had been taken prisoner in June 1940. He had escaped from a German prison camp to Russia, where he had been held prisoner for a time.

Released after Hitler attacked the Soviet Union, Billotte, still a captain, had come to London. I had put him on the air to tell his story to America a few days after he reached England, on the day De Gaulle had promoted him to major. His obvious intelligence had made him head of De Gaulle's personal military staff. He had gone to Africa, and I had lost sight of him. Now he was a full colonel, heading one of Leclerc's regiments.

We were getting close to Paris now. You could feel it in the way the French boys looked and talked. In the halts I talked with some colonial infantrymen in the truck ahead of us. One boy came from Oran in Algeria. He had never seen Paris. But when he spoke the word "Paris," his face lighted up.

This march on Paris was an achievement for all the 20,000 men under Leclerc, whether they were Frenchmen, Spaniards, Berbers, or Americans. Perfect achievement is rare in life, but at this moment it was possible for men who had dreamed of nothing but the liberation of Paris during the years they had lived in Equatorial Africa, in London, in the United States, in North Africa, in Syria, in Madagascar, in Tahiti, or wherever else they had passed their exile. With

Paris in German hands, all Frenchmen were in exile. For me, the coming again to Paris would also be an achievement, a rounding out of my career, for I had a personal resentment at having had my life twisted out of shape by German force. I had begun the war in Paris. I knew I could not be sure that we would win the war until once again I walked the streets and boulevards of the French capital.

We were held up again only six or seven miles from our goal. At Fresnes the Germans had placed tree barricades across the street, and from several points their antitank guns swept the roadway.

The road was mined, and we halted our jeep some fifty yards from the barricade. Snipers fired at us when we exposed ourselves between the houses. We waited beside a little empty shop.

One of the strangest duels of the war was taking place in the street just in front of us. A German antitank gun had been emplaced in a sewer. It was firing from ground level, from under the pavement. The gun was so low and so well protected that it was almost impossible to hit.

A French Sherman tank would rumble a few yards down the street until it reached a position just opposite the sewer. From fifty or sixty feet away, the tank would pour stream after stream of flaming machine-gun bullets into the German gun position. The tank could not depress its big gun low enough to aim at the sewer. Then the German antitank gun would fire. A cloud of smoke from the direct hit would cover the tank. But the German gun was not powerful enough to pierce the tank's armor. The tank would lumber back a few yards to reach cover. Some minutes later the whole procedure would begin again. Eventually, I was told, the German gun was knocked out by some infantrymen who found a back way into the sewer and eliminated the crew with hand grenades. But it was an amazing fight to watch from fifty feet away. I hope I shall never see a battle at any closer range.

Mortar shells fell on the road near the crossing. We munched K rations and waited. Some shells were falling on the road, perhaps 100, perhaps 50 yards away. We could not tell whether it was our own artillery hitting the Germans or German shells fired from somewhere behind us. We knew Germans were both in front and behind us.

Jean Marin came up to us again. He and Wright Bryan loomed up to about the same height. I thought that with three more of such altitude, I could challenge CCNY to a basketball game. Jean said the French troops were about to blow up a miniature German tank, a

284

Goliath. These were curious little weapons, a load of high explosives on treads which could be directed into enemy positions and blown up by remote control. We thought the window glass in the shops might fly, so we moved back out of the way. When the Goliath was exploded, we did not notice it among all the other explosions of the moment.

The people of the suburb were so happy that they seemed incapable of staying out of the way of the battle. They could not comprehend that their homes and their streets were the front line. One shell passed just over our heads, knocked off the top of a tree, and landed in the street. It killed two French children and wounded several more civilians. I do not know how many more French civilians were killed that afternoon, but the number must have been considerable.

At last we moved on, and I thought we would reach Paris. But once again the column was held up, at Antony, only five miles from the capital.

Paris seemed to hang before our eyes like a ripe fruit ready for plucking, but the Germans were still fighting at the Croix de Berny in a prison and a stadium.

A crowd collected around our jeep as we waited. Mothers put their babies up to kiss us, and we gave them candy.

One middle-aged woman was known among her neighbors as L'Américaine. She had been in love with an American boy killed at Château-Thierry in World War I. Ever since that remote day of her lover's death, she had been more American than the Americans, more royal than the king, and all her neighbors knew the reason therefor. L'Américaine wept when she first saw us and realized we were Americans. In fact, most of the French men and women paid more attention to us than to the men of the Leclerc division, for we were an oddity, Americans with the Deuxième Division.

Two women in particular were extremely kind to us. One owned a butcher shop and was conducting the business while her husband was a prisoner in Germany. The other woman lived with her husband in a tiny apartment over the same butcher shop. They invited us to stay for supper, but we replied regretfully that we had to hurry on to Paris.

War seems to be nine-tenths waiting for something to happen, and that afternoon was no exception. We waited and waited. Meanwhile, one after another would come columns of trucks or tanks, not knowing of the bottleneck ahead, rolling full tilt as though their drivers feared they might be late for the triumphal entry into Paris. We would watch them through binoculars and a half mile or more down the road they would slow to a stop and add to the mess of vehicles.

Once Maurice Schumann, later foreign minister of France, but then the Free French radio spokesman and a *sous-lieutenant* in the French Army, came racing past in a jeep, one hand holding his kepi on his head as though he were rushing to a fire. But after a time he also came back, much more slowly. He was an old friend of mine, and I tried to yell at him; but he was past before I could speak.

General Leclerc himself was easy to recognize. Like Schumann, he wore a kepi instead of a helmet. He kept dashing down the road to direct the attack against the Germans, then dashing back to send out flanking attacks on each side of us to clear the surrounding territory.

As far as we knew, the only ground we held was the road over which we had come. We knew there were German tanks in the neighborhood, and the main body of Germans defending Paris was already behind us and on our flank.

As the hours dragged by, I realized that it was very unlikely that we would reach Paris that night. We were with the leading troops of the division that was to enter Paris, and it would be a foolish gesture to try to send it into the city by night, for many Germans remained there. French officers confirmed to me that the troops were going to spend the night where they were. As a matter of fact, one squadron of tanks did enter Paris during the night by a roundabout way. But we did not know that fact until the following day, and the exploit was a reconnaissance in force rather than a victorious entry.

Our artillery somewhere behind us began shelling the German strongpoint. The shells, as usual, rushed over us with a rustle like silk and exploded in the gathering darkness ahead.

The woman who owned the butcher shop once again invited us to spend the night. We stretched out our sleeping bags on the floor of the butcher shop and the kitchen. We brought in our own rations, cooked them, and invited half a dozen of our new friends to supper.

We were about to eat when an explosion shook the house. I thought for a moment that the building had been hit. Wright and I rushed into the street to discover that a mortar shell had hit the house two doors down from us. When more shells fell in the street and another house was struck, we moved our food down into the cellar.

After dinner one of the men sang French songs, and we reciprocated with some American tunes like "Old Black Joe," "Yankee

286

Doodle," and "Dixie." Wright, a southerner, bellowed out "Dixie" with great fervor.

The French people were amazed when we told them that the United States had been torn by a civil war and that, only eighty years before, some of Wright's relatives and some of mine were probably shooting at one another.

"*Ça. Alors,*" said one of the Frenchwomen, "*une vraie guerre civile aux États-Unis? Incroyable!*"

"But we are good friends, now," said I after our little "Dixie" duet. But I did not, remembering *Gone With the Wind*, push friendship as far as asking Wright to join me in "Marching Through Georgia."

Chapter 26

The next morning, August 25, we were up before dawn. By the time we had rolled our bedrolls and stowed them in the jeep our kind French hostess had made us coffee. Neighbors came in their dressing gowns to say good-bye.

In the street the French soldiers were beginning to stir. The shelling had stopped sometime during the night.

We waited until the first tanks moved. They rolled around the corner, off the main road, to a little side road a half mile away. The time was just after dawn. A heavy ground mist blotted out the landscape a few hundred yards away. We bumped into an American liaison officer, a Lieutenant Colonel Zimmerman.

We passed the time of day, and he said, "The weather looks lousy, doesn't it? We can't hope for much air support with this mist." He told us that a company of Leclerc's men had penetrated Paris to the Hôtel de Ville during the night but that no Americans had accompanied them, and we could still hope to be the first Americans in Paris.

We went northward by small roads. Before eight we were in Gentilly. Crowds lined the streets, cheering us as we swept through. They pressed in on us, offering everything they had—wine, champagne, apples, bread, even cigarettes. The women must have swept their larders clean to give us the food.

A colonial infantryman in the truck ahead of us was so intoxicated with joy that he tried to shake the hand of everybody nearby while his vehicle was moving at twenty-five miles an hour. People darted out to touch his hand, and we almost ran over several of them.

I kept yelling, "Attention. Attention," in my loudest voice. But it did little good.

We reached Paris itself, the university, at just ten minutes past eight by my watch. I felt like pinching myself. It was hard to believe I was back in Paris once again.

Suddenly a fusillade of bullets spattered on the street. The whole column came to a quick stop. We leaped out and crouched beside the jeep. FFI men started blazing away at something over our heads.

288

Men in the dozen vehicles ahead of us began firing at something—the tower of the university.

Germans in the tower were firing on the column. I saw the stonework blasted off in white flakes as Leclerc's men kept it under continuous fire.

We were also being fired on from a nearby house. Some FFI men, with Leclerc's troops, got cover near the building, then rushed through the door and up the stairs. I heard the explosion of a grenade—and the firing stopped.

After about half an hour the tower of the university fell silent, and the column moved on.

Twice again the column was held up in similar fashion. One moment the streets would be filled with people. At the first volley of shots they would scatter to the doorways. FFI men with ancient pistols and captured German rifles would start firing at what they thought was the source of the attack.

Whenever the trouble seemed serious, Leclerc's men would loose a few bursts of machine-gun fire from the weapons mounted on the trunks. Or a light tank would stop at a street corner and streams of tracers would spout out of it to cover our advance. We felt terribly unprotected in the jeep, and the noise of the bullets singing past us was most unpleasant.

Just as the column began moving again, a civilian in a black homburg jumped onto the jeep. I told him roughly to get off.

The civilian grinned and told me in good but accented English that he was an American OSS agent who had been in Paris for three months preparing for our entry. He was French by birth but naturalized American. We let him ride with us down the boulevard Jourdain and through the porte d'Orléans. In the rue St.-Jacques he jumped off with a "thanks very much," smiled, and disappeared as mysteriously as he had come.

We passed across the bridge that led directly to the square between Notre Dame Cathedral and the Prefecture of Police. In the sunshine Paris had never looked more beautiful. It was then just a quarter to nine.

The vehicles just ahead of us rolled into the square and parked, and we parked the jeep with them. Kokoska switched off the motor. We looked up at the lovely towers of Notre Dame, and someone said, "Well, that's that. The fight is all over now."

As he finished speaking, the air crackled into life with bullets, hissing and whining all over the square. The French light tanks be-

A jubilant Paris welcomes Americans entering the city on August 25, 1944. U.S. ARMY.

gan firing over our heads at some Germans just across the Seine. Germans were also shooting from Notre Dame and from nearby houses. For twenty-five minutes Wright, Jack Hansen, Kokoska, and I lay on our stomachs crouched beside the jeep. We could see no likely shelter of any kind. There was so much shooting that we could hardly hear one another speak. Guns, machine guns, rifles—everything was going off together in one great earsplitting, crackling inferno of sound.

The wounded were carried across the square by girls and doctors in Red Cross uniforms. They waved Red Cross flags.

The shooting sputtered, then died down, and finally burst out with new fury before it ceased. The air was strangely quiet. I could see the sun glint on the white marks where the bullets had struck Notre Dame.

A new sound broke the hush of that Thursday morning—the bells of Notre Dame. Someone began ringing them. They pealed over Paris as they had for so many hundreds of years, a song of triumph that Paris was once again free.

The sound crossed the Seine. It went to the Tuileries Gardens, where German tanks were then concentrating. It went to the people of Paris, who were even then opening the barricades they had laid to permit the entry of Leclerc's tanks. The sound of the bells made me think of Sunday mornings in peacetime, the chapel bells at Williamstown, Massachusetts, the bells of Oxford, and the old Sunday bell of St. Stephen's Church in Portland.

"We've got to get this," I yelled. Jack Hansen started up the generator for the wire recorder. I switched on the microphone and began taking the sound of the bells. A crowd collected, and I cried to them, "Are you happy? *Êtes-vous contents?*"

"*Oui,*" they shouted back. I described the scene and spoke with one or two who knew some English before I switched off the recorder.

There were some strange incidents in that square. Two men dressed in the helmets and uniforms of Paris firemen came up to me and, speaking in unmistakable American, said, "Are you guys Americans?"

"Sure," I replied, "but what in hell are you guys doing in that getup?"

One of them, whose name I took down, reported to the authorities at his request, then promptly lost, said, "He and I are Eighth Air Force. I'm a pilot. He's a navigator. We got shot down, and the

French underground took charge of us. We been in Paris for a month attached to this fire department unit. We have a hell of a time at night, going around fighting fires and killing Germans when we get the chance. I wouldn't have missed this for the world."

"Do you speak French?" I asked.

"Not a damn word," said the bomber pilot. "One of the firemen speaks a little English, and he does all the translating. We get into a house of some collaborator that is burning, and we bust up the whole inside before we put the fire out. Or maybe we just let it all burn down."

When he left us, the pilot said, "Hell of a thing to have to go back to flying—after all this fun."

In the crowd was a well-dressed man with the long face and luminescent pale skin of one of El Greco's subjects. He said with a kind of sad eagerness, "When are the Spaniards coming?"

"Spaniards?" I replied in some puzzlement. "These troops are French, not Spanish."

Then I suddenly understood that he was talking about the anti-Franco Spaniards serving with Leclerc.

"You will find them just behind us," I said, "in tanks marked 'Teruel' and 'Guadalajara.'"

It was true that fascism had won the victory in Spain. But was it not also true that the republican Spaniards were fighting that same fascism in the ranks of Leclerc's Deuxième Division Blindé? It was German planes that had helped defeat democracy in Spain. Nazi fliers and Italian *fascisti* troops were responsible for the death of the Spanish Republic. And who had greater right than the republican Spaniards to be in at the death of German Nazism?

I walked across the square and into the prefecture. Almost the first people I saw were Rabache and Gosset, the two French correspondents whose enthusiasm had caused them to try to crash full tilt into Rennes before it was taken by our forces.

They explained that they had escaped from their German captors, put on civilian clothes, and bicycled calmly into Paris by night. They introduced me to Jean Guignebert, who had been in charge of the Resistance information activities.

Guignebert beamed. "Here is your radio, at your disposal for your broadcasts. Go right ahead. We have been in touch with London and New York all morning."

It was the chance of a lifetime, the opportunity to make a broadcast from Paris before it had actually been cleared of its German garrison, the opportunity to send the first eyewitness description of the Allied entry into the city to the outside world.

Yet it was an opportunity I could not accept. As a war correspondent I had signed a pledge that all my broadcasts and messages would be passed through army censorship. And I had no censor. The censor who had promised to follow us closely had not arrived. Until he did, I could not go before the microphone and still keep my written pledge. The choice was a hard one, but I had to refuse Guignebert's offer. At least, I thought, no other American can broadcast before I do.

After a while our little party proceeded to the rue de Rivoli, where Leclerc's tanks were making slow progress. The last German tanks inside the city were mostly concentrated in and around the Tuileries Gardens, and for some hours a tank duel and an infantry firefight were in progress. Wright and I took turns in recording the fighting, opening the recorder when the battle flared up, turning it off in the periods of quiet waiting. It was a strange spectacle, the elegant Parisian women in their bright dresses and high-piled coiffures stepping unconcernedly among the fighting tanks, manned by the sweating khaki-clad soldiers. By sheer chance, the wire recorder did not break down, and the whole description from the pealing of the bells of Notre Dame until the last shot was fired was censored in London and put on the air the next day.

I can conceive of no more incredible sight than that of the half dozen French Sherman tanks wheeling into position in line abreast before the colonnaded facade of the luxurious Hôtel Crillon facing the place de la Concorde.

Then the tanks opened up with their big guns and their machine guns as well, spitting tracers into the front of the building where General von Choltitz, the German commander of Paris, and his staff were still ensconced.

One shell knocked down a column, and we were quick to notice it was the fifth column in the line. Finally the fighting died away, and we heard that Von Choltitz had surrendered, that he was being taken to Leclerc's headquarters in the Prefecture of Police.

I only hoped that Von Choltitz could contact all his units scattered in and around Paris, for we heard that fighting was still going on beyond the Étoile.

It was midafternoon by this time. We turned the jeep up the

rue de la Paix, making slow progress among the crowds of civilians who thronged the sidewalk and the street itself.

Suddenly in the crowd I saw a familiar face. It was Jacqueline de Mauduit, the former INS secretary who had left France with Lucy and me on that memorable night at Pointe de Grave in June 1940. She had returned to France after her husband, Alain, had been released by the Germans who had netted his army unit in the drive through France.

We rushed toward each other and embraced with kisses and, on her part and almost on mine, tears.

Jacqueline climbed into the jeep with us and rode to the Hôtel Scribe, which had been designated in advance as headquarters for the war correspondents. Before long the hotel was crawling with us, each recounting his adventures, each boasting he had been the first correspondent in Paris.

Wright Bryan and I were certain that we had been the first American correspondents to enter Paris, and we are still convinced of that fact; but it was useless to try to convince 100 other correspondents good and true that they all were mistaken.

Of one thing I was going to be certain, that my broadcast script, which I had been writing at intervals between the fighting, was going to be the first dispatch censored in Paris. I camped on the censorship doorstep until the censors finally reached the hotel after dark. Mine was the first dispatch that received a censor's stamp.

I seized it and with Wright and Jacqueline tore off into the night aboard the jeep. Jacqueline took us first to an official of the police, who gave us the address of the clandestine radio which had been operating in Paris under the noses of the Germans. The studios were on the rue de Grenelle.

It was pitch-dark, no stars or moon showing, and no streetlights either, as we drove slowly down the long street. I got out and lit a match to see the number on a door.

A rifle banged, and the shot splattered on the building not far from my hand. I hastily blew out the match. We drove a little farther, and again I went to a door and lit a match. *Spang* went the rifle of my unseen sniper. Three more times we stopped, and three more times the rifle sounded when I lit my match.

At last, to my great relief, we found the right door.

Inside, all was light and excitement. The clandestine radio was now out in the open. But I received a shock at seeing that the studios

294

were also crowded with British and American broadcasters.

Well, I thought, at least my own will be the first broadcast unless a censor has shown up here in the studios rather than over at the Scribe.

While awaiting the signal to go before the microphone, I began reading the script aloud. My first words were: "This is the first broadcast from liberated Paris."

An American colleague happened to walk past while I was reading. He said, "I made a broadcast an hour ago. Y—— did one about five o'clock, and Z—— has done two or three since seven o'clock this evening."

"But that's impossible," I replied. "My script was the first through the censorship. I know because I looked at the censor's log."

"Censorship," my colleague commented contemptuously. "Who cares about censorship tonight? We have been putting them through without censorship. Who cares about that now?"

There was no disguising the fact that I had been beaten on a big story, the only time during my whole career as a war correspondent. But at least I had the cold comfort of moral satisfaction. The mass breaking of the rule resulted only in a fortnight's suspension of their activities by the Army. Most figured the act had been more than worth the penalty, and they spent a happy two weeks in Paris or London without working, as a kind of vacation.

After Wright and I had done our broadcasts, we all returned to the Scribe. We stood with Jacqueline at an open window and heard the crowd outside sing the "Marseillaise." It was a moment of great emotion. But my trials for the night were not yet over. Sleeping in the fields, I had picked up a plague of fleas. My clothes were crawling with them. I stripped off my uniform and underwear and, since the Scribe had no hot water, forced myself to immerse in a tub of cold water. It was a terrible ordeal, but it got rid of the fleas.

The next morning Lieutenant Rugg and the faithful Jig Easy Sugar Queen were set up in the Tuileries Gardens, beside the pond which is near the little Arch of the Carroussel. The Tuileries were littered with about a dozen burned-out German tanks. From some came the sickish odor of burned flesh. There was also a wrecked French Sherman or two in and near the gardens, testimony to the last fight for Paris which we had watched on the previous afternoon.

I made my broadcast, and in the afternoon a correspondent from the Chicago *Times*, Jacqueline de Mauduit (as she was then, for she

*Welcoming shouts, signs, and smiles greet General de Gaulle as he enters
the liberated city the next day (August 26).* U.S. ARMY.

But the crowds scattered when enemy snipers started shooting. U.S. ARMY.

is now the wife of Dr. René Deupes de Perpessac), Bob Cooper of the London *Times* and I, all jeeped up to the Arc de Triomphe to watch the triumphal parade of General de Gaulle.

There was no question now that De Gaulle was in charge of France. President Roosevelt's theory, which had been voiced by General Eisenhower—that each liberated locality of France would pick its local officials, and later France would decide who should run the country—had been swept into oblivion. All the local Resistance people who took over civil government turned out to be ardent Gaullists who immediately pledged support to the general. The Leclerc division served De Gaulle, as did all other organized fighting units of the French Army. The cheers of the populace told the story. De Gaulle, the leader of Free France, was the undisputed chief of the new French government.

We drove down the Champs-Élysées in the procession of Resistance leaders and Army men following De Gaulle, down to the square by Notre Dame. We were somewhere in the middle of the square and De Gaulle was in the act of entering the cathedral when the square suddenly sputtered in a cacophony of shots.

Someone, it later appeared, had fired on the crowd, perhaps some embittered French fascists, perhaps some Germans, from the nearby rooftops. We were out of the jeep and stretched on the cobblestones within the first split second after the shooting began. The whole crowd in the square was down as well. Crouching FFI men had their guns out and were spattering all the nearby upper stories and roofs with their fire. The general himself, I was told, never batted an eye, looked calmly around, and walked unhurriedly into the cathedral, although the shooting probably had been an ill-prepared attempt to assassinate him.

I had flung myself on top of Jacqueline in what had now become my usual chivalrous gesture at such moments. I may have been influenced by the fact that the cobbles were very hard and Jacqueline made a fine cushion. After we had picked ourselves up, Jacqueline said, "When I was down there with you on top of me, I kept thinking, John still hasn't learned much since that night under the freight car on Pointe de Grave when we were leaving France. Why doesn't the old so-and-so learn to cover my legs when all these bullets are flying around?"

Police and Leclerc's men blocked nearby streets while they searched the houses for the perpetrators. There was some shooting in other parts of the city as well. It may have been an attempt by

298

Generals de Gaulle, Leclerc, and Koenig lead a Free French victory march to the tomb of the French Unknown Soldier. U.S. ARMY.

collaborators to assassinate De Gaulle and cause chaos in the city, which might have profited the escaping Germans.

Our first thought was to find out just what was happening, whether this attack was a serious threat to the liberated city or whether it was only the final gesture of the Germans and collaborationist Frenchmen.

There is a gripping photographic record of Paris under the Germans, a book called À Paris, sous la Botte des Nazis, which traces life in Paris from the entrance of the Germans to the day of De Gaulle's triumph, August 26, 1944. Four pages from the end is the picture that some French photographer took of our jeep while a Paris policeman was pointing out a street in which some fighting was still taking place. Driving the jeep is James Wellard, then of the Chicago *Times*, and in the back seat are Cooper of the London *Times* and I, chewing my thumb in my anxiety of the moment.

After we all had relaxed for a time in a convenient bistro, the fighting had ended everywhere throughout the city, and we were able to get back to the Scribe without running the danger of ricocheting bullets, either from our enemies, the Germans and traitor French, or our friends, the FFI.

The most unhappy correspondents of all were George Hicks and Gordon Fraser of the American Broadcasting Company, who were the only radio reporters who had their tape recorders present at the shooting. The tape broke at the crucial moment so that they were unable to obtain the lively record of the shooting and the description of the scene. The BBC men made the only actual on-the-spot recording.

Chapter 27

That fall and winter I spent chiefly covering General Eisenhower's headquarters in Paris, SHAEF, broadcasting from the excellent studios constructed in the Scribe Hotel by Lieutenant Colonel Walter Brown and Major Arthur "Bill" Perry, formerly NBC and ABC engineers. There were brief visits of a few days to one or another of the armies in the field and a welcome Christmas stay in London. But I was anxious to get back to my friends in the First Army for good, and when a replacement came in March, I was able to drive from Paris to Germany to do so.

There were many familiar faces among the twenty-five or thirty-five First Army correspondents. There was bearded Jack Thompson of the Chicago *Tribune*, my fellow alumnus. There were Whitehead of AP, Hal Boyle with his broad smiling Irish face, Chris Cunningham of United Press, Jimmy MacDonald of *The New York Times*, and Stoneman of the Chicago *Daily News*, still grumbling and griping about the world in general, as well as many others. But the taking of the Remagen Bridge had cost the life of one of the correspondents, a big bluff man from a British paper, mortally wounded when a jeepful of reporters tried to follow the first troops who had seized the structure.

From Stolberg, the First Army headquarters, it was an all-day trip through battered Düren, shattered Euskirchen, down to the Rhine at Remagen and back again, without time to do more than look at the bridge before we headed back to reach Stolberg by nightfall.

It was as lengthy a trip the next day to Cologne, taken by the 104th Infantry Division, the Timberwolves, which Terry Allen had formed into a hard-hitting junior edition of the veteran Fighting First. As I passed through the streets, which were still mostly blocked by rubble and saw the cathedral, luckily only holed by a few shells, I could not help thinking of the other German cities I had seen, Aachen, Düren, and Euskirchen, and reflecting that the Germans were really learning how vast the payment for the war on which they had embarked so lightly back in September 1939. Everywhere

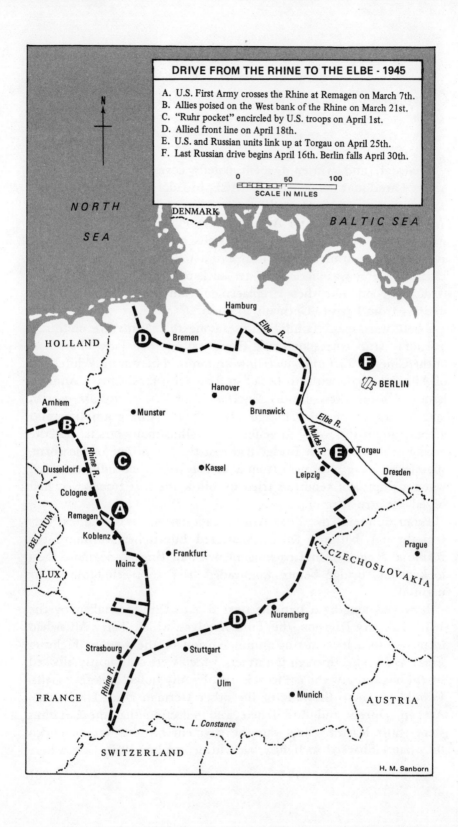

DRIVE FROM THE RHINE TO THE ELBE - 1945

A. U.S. First Army crosses the Rhine at Remagen on March 7th.
B. Allies poised on the West bank of the Rhine on March 21st.
C. "Ruhr pocket" encircled by U.S. troops on April 1st.
D. Allied front line on April 18th.
E. U.S. and Russian units link up at Torgau on April 25th.
F. Last Russian drive begins April 16th. Berlin falls April 30th.

SCALE IN MILES
0   50   100

N

NORTH SEA

DENMARK

BALTIC SEA

Hamburg

Elbe R.

HOLLAND

D Bremen

Arnhem

B

Hanover

Munster

Brunswick

BERLIN

F

Elbe R.

Mulde R.

Dusseldorf

C

Rhine R.

Kassel

E Torgau

Cologne

Leipzig

Dresden

BELGIUM

Remagen A

Koblenz

Frankfurt

Prague

LUX

Mainz

CZECHOSLOVAKIA

D Nuremberg

Strasbourg

Stuttgart

FRANCE

Ulm

Munich

AUSTRIA

Rhine R.

L. Constance

SWITZERLAND

H. M. Sanborn

there was that smell of cement and brick dust that had grown so familiar to me in the London bombings, the smell of St.-Lô and Warsaw as well as every other city pulverized by war.

The reporters' situation improved slightly when the First Army headquarters moved to Euskirchen, and we settled some miles east of the city in the low barracklike buildings that housed a wrecked radio transmitter.

But to reach the Rhine at Remagen was still a long drive when roads were jammed with trucks and tanks. Some of the reporters stayed at Bad Neuenahr, a village on the Ahr River only a few miles from Remagen. But my transmitter was back at our main press camp. If I were going to broadcast, I could not remain often at Bad Neuenahr. One of my recollections of that period is driving at night without lights along the dark roads to get back in time.

A couple of times I took Jim Rugg and the little Jig Easy Sugar Queen transmitter across the pontoon bridge our engineers had constructed at Remagen and from a hilltop made the first American broadcasts east of the Rhine.

It was a symbol of the fact that we were now reaching the heart of Germany.

We had moved four divisions into the bridgehead across the Rhine almost immediately. But the main bridge, after serving its initial purpose, one day collapsed and fell into the river. It had been weakened by some of the demolition charges the Germans had succeeded in exploding, and a lucky shell from a German cannon had weakened it still more. By that time we were depending on our pontoon bridges, and at night the Rhine was noisy indeed with the depth charges and shells fired into the river to keep Nazi frogmen from swimming down to cut the light floating bridges loose in an effort to isolate the troops we had passed into the bridgehead. Several of the frogmen were caught or killed in the attempts, and none succeeded in his task.

The Germans sensed the danger of the bridgehead and crowded more and more troops in to try to contain it. But the terrain was not good for fighting. Just as one crossed the bridge, one ran into a high bank shooting up into the air only a few yards from the water, and all over the bridgehead were little hills and woods so that movement was very constricted. Going up the road toward Honnef or Königswinter, one felt like a painter walking along scaffolding hanging on the side of an office building, with the river on one side and the little hills rising sheer on the other.

General Courtney Hodges's problem was to expand his bridge-head enough to get elbowroom for a sufficient number of divisions so that when he broke out, he could hit hard and keep going. But his progress seemed slow—a few hundred yards here and a few hundred there—at a time when south of us Patton had leaped across the Moselle.

Between the Moselle and the Rhine were hundreds of square miles of territory containing the forces which were blocking General Jacob Devers and his Franco-American Sixth Army Group, which had struck the Siegfried Line in that region and come to a jarring halt. Patton had struck behind the Siegfried Line and rolled up the forces in front of Devers by sheer surprise. Then, on the night of March 22, Patton's 5th Infantry Division crossed the Rhine at the village of Oppenheim eighteen hours before Montgomery crossed it far to the north after two weeks of bombing, shelling, and other preparations under cover of heavy ground smoke that fogged his entire front. There could have been no better comparison of the fighting methods of the two men. Both were successful in their objective, but Montgomery based his success on careful preparation and struck only when he was sure he had more forces available than he could possibly need in any contingency. Patton struck on the spur of the moment, and his risks seemed great. But he also succeeded.

Lieutenant Rugg had been complaining to me that he was going through the war without seeing any fighting or having any of the experiences the correspondents described since he was tied to the First Army headquarters. I thought this was a good opportunity to help the signal officer get a change of scenery.

The two of us and a driver set out in Rugg's jeep, south along the west bank of the Rhine through Sinsig and Andernach to Koblenz. We entered the city and heard the story of its capture from an officer who had taken part in the event. But south of Koblenz we had to move inland away from the bank of the Rhine, for the east bank was in enemy hands, and we would have been an easy target for a sniper across the narrow river.

That night we spent with a transport outfit made up entirely of black soldiers. They were a merry crowd stuck off in the deep woods with an MP unit at a fuel and supply dump that the Third Army had dropped on the way to the Rhine. We lined up for breakfast with the men next morning and got our pancakes from a cook whose broad grin and his quips to everyone he served put us in high good humor for the road to Oppenheim.

At a corps headquarters in Gross-Gerau we were told that the Third Army expected to take Frankfurt-am-Main that very day, so we hurried on. Before long we had reached the edge of the city, and there were the unmistakable signs of fighting. No traffic was moving, and there seemed a hush over the broad avenue, broken only by the chatter of a machine gun and the heavy bang of shells not far off. A soldier from a rifle company told us we had better leave our jeep and proceed on foot, for the city was still not taken and a vehicle might draw fire.

A squad of soldiers were peeking around the edge of a building. It was at the beginning of a broad bridge crossing the Main and entering the chief section of Frankfurt.

A lieutenant, when we joined him at the wall of the building, said, "This is all of Frankfurt we've been able to get so far, right here. The krauts are fighting like bastards for that bridge. They've got a couple of batteries of eighty-eights zeroed in on it."

"Have we got anyone across it?" I asked.

"We got most of a platoon across about five minutes ago," he replied, "but it's a rough deal. I don't know whether we'll be able to get anything more over unless we can find those goddamn eighty-eights. We don't know where they are yet."

We both peeked around the corner for a moment. I saw some figures running toward us.

"It's some of our boys coming back," the lieutenant said.

"It must be too hot over there."

We could hear the bang of explosion on the bridge. Then came louder bangs behind us and overhead, and I looked up and saw the black cloud of a couple of airbursts, shells exploded in air to kill soldiers on the ground beneath.

"All right, men," said the lieutenant, "let's get under cover in this house until it eases up."

We all went into the house, and some of the men who had run back across the bridge joined us, panting with their effort.

"Get through to company," the lieutenant said to one of his men with a walkie-talkie radio. "Tell them we need some support, and we've got to find out where those kraut guns are shooting from. Tell them it may be on the other bank about three hundred yards upriver. Say we can get across the bridge all right if we have to, but the krauts are keeping it under heavy direct observation fire."

The house shook with the noise of the shelling outside. I said, "I didn't mean to give you such a close bloody view of the war, Jim."

The men waited, not talking, only listening. They were the riflemen, the men who do most of the fighting and suffer most of the casualties. I always felt very respectful in their presence.

It is seldom known to people who have not lived intimately with the combat divisions that only about 3,000 of the 16,000 or 17,000 men in each combat division are the men with the rifles who form the actual spearhead. Each of these riflemen is supported in the division by perhaps five others, gunners, machine gunners, tankers, drivers, signalers, and clerks and cooks. But when a division is mentioned as having suffered a couple of thousand killed, wounded and missing, it is usually 2,000 of the 3,000 riflemen who are really involved.

In a combat theater each of the riflemen is backed by perhaps 15 other men, and if one were to take a whole military establishment, perhaps 30, 40, or 50 men are in some way thought to be necessary in order to get 1 man with a rifle out at the tip of a combat division. And when we speak of, say, ten divisions fighting, 200,000 men with the corps and army establishments, the commander knows that what he means is some 30,000 men, continually fighting, continually dying, and continually being replaced.

After half or three-quarters of an hour the shelling stopped, and Rugg and I went outside. The street was strangely still again. On its broad expanse, as far as I could see, nothing moved. A jeep was burning, but it was not ours, which we had left nearly a mile away.

Suddenly the street began to look familiar.

"Jim," I said, "I think I know this street."

I looked at the street sign, Forsthausstrasse—the only street in Frankfurt whose name I knew. My thoughts flew back just ten years to the time when Frank Mitford, Al Weinrich, and I, Oxford students on a Continental vacation, spent some happy days at the house of a German girl Hertha Passavant on that same street—that was it—91 Forsthausstrasse.

I tried to remember where number 91 was as we crossed over and walked along, the only people on the street. Where I had believed it was, there was a big gap in the row, the house entirely demolished. With relief, I saw I had been mistaken and that the number 91 was on the next gate.

As we went up the steps, an American soldier came to the door.

306

"For Christ's sweet sake," he said, "come on inside. Those damn airbursts have knocked out all our vehicles."

"Is the family, the Germans who live here, in the house?"

"There are some civilians down in the cellar. Have a look at them if you want."

I went down the cellar steps, down into the darkness. I groped along in the blackness, calling, "Herr Passavant. Frau Passavant. Are you there?"

There was no answer. I heard a shuffling noise and struck a match. I saw a man's face. He spoke no English, and I tried my German.

"I am looking for Herr Passavant or Frau Passavant. Are the Passavants in the cellar?"

He shook his head and called a woman. She shuffled through the darkness to me as I lit another match.

"No Passavants here," she said in German. "They left here several years ago."

"Do you know where they are?"

"No, I think they left Frankfurt."

Well, that was that, I thought. At least they had not seen their home city broken up or had to huddle in the cellar while the artillery dueled overhead.

Before we left, I looked out at the back garden where in that long-ago summer of 1934, ten years before, I had often dined in the open air with the Passavant family with Al Weinrich, and with Frank Mitford, now lying somewhere in the Libyan desert, perhaps killed by one of the same German boys we had known in the same garden.

I thought that it was a hell of a life to be living, coming to a place I had so much enjoyed, as a member of a conquering army, with death and destruction accompanying me. Not that I thought the Germans did not deserve everything they received in the war, for if any people were ever guilty of calling down the fury of war upon themselves, it was the Germans, with their stupid worship of power, their conviction that they had to bully the rest of the world into submission, and their unreasoning readiness to place their fate in the hands of warped and vicious leaders bent on conquest.

Why was it, I thought, that individually the Germans were quite all right, especially if you transplanted them to America or some other country, when in the mass they were impossible, subject to weird psychological impulses, capable of incredible cruelty and equally incredible sentimentality? With their energy, industry, cleanliness, and other minor virtues, they should have been good neighbors for the civilized community. Yet their boorishness and their disregard of the feelings of other peoples were matched only by their conviction that they must impose their mastery on the rest of the world, by force of arms, if necessary. A strange people, bearing an inferiority complex as big as a house that turned them into brutal master or abject slave depending on the situation. Thinking of the destroyed cities, I wondered if this time at least the Germans would not learn the lesson of war.

Chapter 28

My New York office was getting regular reports now not only from SHAEF and the Seventh Army, but from the Ninth Army, the Third Army, and the British Twenty-first Army Group. When I went on the air, I could often hear the reports that David Anderson, Red Mueller, Roy Porter, Bjorn Bjornson, and Ed Haaker were sending. Occasionally I could take a night off and spend it with the tanks or the infantrymen who were leading the procession, with Terry Allen and his PRO, Lieutenant Mort Kaufman, of the 104th Infantry Division, or Captain Max Zera, PRO of the 1st Division.

I remember approaching the marshlands of the Weser River with the 104th Timberwolves through obscure villages named Trendelburg and Gottsbüren and crossing the river on a pontoon bridge that engineers had to put up under fire from the opposite side, for there were still German units that were fighting.

One strange character arrived in our press camp. He was a Tass correspondent, and he was a major in the Soviet Army, a Guards unit, he said, although with his short figure and nearsighted eyes peering through steel-rimmed spectacles, he hardly was the equivalent of the British Guards. He spoke French but no English. Since I was one of the few American reporters who spoke French, I took him with me two or three times on my news-gathering expeditions.

On one occasion I brought him into Brigadier General Doyle Hickey's 3rd Armored command post and introduced him to the general, who had taken command on the death of General Rose. We spent the night with some officers of an armored cavalry unit. One young lieutenant from Pittsburgh could speak a kind of Slavic, learned from his Croatian parents, and Major Ivan and he were able to carry on a conversation.

Afterward the lieutenant said to me, "You really know this guy is from the old country. He sounds just like my old man. They're bullheaded when they get an idea, and they just shake their heads and don't listen to you."

The roads were beginning to fill with slave laborers now set free.

Ivan delayed our travel by leaping out of the jeep every time he saw a group that he recognized as Russian. His face would light up, and he seemed like another man as he carried on a conversation with twenty or thirty of them, men or women, at the same time. There were embraces and excited talk. When I could finally tear him away, Ivan's face would slip back into the glum mask he usually wore in my company. But with prodding I could get him to tell me some of the tales the slave laborers had just imparted to him. That some were gruesome I could tell in advance, for he would be on the point of tears as he left the ragged group that had crowded around us.

But even Marburg was too far behind the front for me to do a good job of covering the war. I requested the service of Jim Rugg and the little Jig Easy Sugar Queen transmitter again. I told my CBS competitor of the moment that I was taking off with the mobile transmitter, but he preferred to rely on the surer method of the Press Wireless transmitter at the First Army headquarters. I also brought with me Lieutenant Strother "Strut" Jones of New York, a parachutist turned military censor. Strut was a debonair character who joyfully accepted the chance to get away from his desk at headquarters and back into some activity that recalled, however vaguely, his adventuresome earlier army career. Thus, with a censor and a means of communication, I was completely freewheeling.

For the next two weeks or so we lived entirely on our own. Some of my broadcasts did not get through, but those that did gave a direct picture of our advance that was more realistic and authentic than anything I could have done from army headquarters. We tried to keep up with the advance elements of the two or three leading divisions each day, scurrying quickly from one to another after we had left JESQ at a likely place, near a division headquarters, if possible, so that I would be able to get the latest information the division commander had before I went on the air at night. We usually slept in houses in areas cleared of civilians by one of our units. Each house had a dirty pallet by the kitchen stove or in some corner of the basement or attic for the slave laborer, the Czech or Pole or Russian who had done hard labor for the household and received food scraps in return. In many houses I discovered hanging on a convenient nail the cat-o'-nine-tails, the little bludgeon, or the handy-sized club which the household used for the correction of the slave laborer who spilled the soup or pretended to be too old

310

to work. I brought one such weapon home with me. It had a wooden handle, with a flexible steel core encased in rubber tubing. Some German had made the instrument with loving care, and the old-fashioned policeman would have admired the skill, for a Polish maidservant could be beaten half to death without any ugly cutting of the skin.

It amused me later in a ghastly sort of way to hear the Germans say they did not know what had happened in the concentration camps. What happened there was only a methodical enlargement of the treatment meted out to the slave laborers in the clean, neat little German homes where some Slavic man-of-all-work lived in stinking filth and received many blows and little food.

I was always surprised that the slave laborers did not turn and string their hosts to the rafters and burn down the neat little houses around them when the opportunity for freedom came. But there were remarkably few instances of this. In most cases, they simply wandered off and in a confused, cowed way began to move dumbly to the east or west, in whichever direction their homeland might be. On the whole the slave laborers did not loot any more than the American soldiers themselves.

At one of our temporary bivouacs an officer of the headquarters told me that an English correspondent who had been a prisoner of war had walked into camp and said that he knew me.

I hurried to find him. It was the Honorable Edward Ward of the BBC, a prisoner of the Germans since he had been captured in the North African desert three years previously. Eddy was haggard and gaunt from undernourishment. His mustache was more scraggly than ever, but there was a gleam in his eye when he shook hands and said, "It's nice to see you again, John, the first familiar face I have seen since the Americans overran our camp this morning." He might have been saying that he had seen me only last week.

I remembered the day five years before in England when Eddy— with his regal smile to the admiring populace of Yorkshire—had been mistaken for a member of the royal family and the sheriff of the East Riding had dismissed the throng gathered to greet the king and queen. I remembered our trips to Dover to watch the beginning of the Battle of Britain and the broadcast Eddy did for NBC and how, when the list of the nations was called and after each of the names of the countries overrun by Germany, there was only silence and the roll of muffled drums, until when it came to Britain there were Eddy's clear English tones saying, "Great Britain and the British Commonwealth of Nations—all present and accounted for."

It had been a long time since I had been so happy to see an old friend because, for years, I had not known whether he was alive or dead. I let him use my typewriter to write the story of his being set free. Then I interviewed him in my regular broadcast and told NBC to record a broadcast by Eddy and send it to the BBC. He left our camp next day for the British Army group headquarters and London, and I thought I had seen the end of him—at least for the duration of the war—but ten days later and ten pounds heavier, he was back with BBC recording equipment to cover the finals on the front of the American First Army, which had set him free.

Eventually our little caravan arrived in Naumburg, southwest of Leipzig, with the 2nd Infantry Division. We stayed with the 2nd Infantry as it moved on to attack Leipzig. For a time the Germans were able to keep us off. They held Weissenfels on the road to Leipzig, but then the 2nd Infantry, one of the best in the Army, slashed on into the city. The men were still fighting in the streets and had taken only the western sector when I brought Jig Easy Sugar Queen to the bridge across the Elster River that cuts through the town. From the bridge we tried to broadcast an eyewitness account of the fighting which we could see and hear around us. But the task was just too much for JESQ's gallant tubes and Jim Rugg's skill. As mentioned earlier, the army 399 radio had been constructed to send voice broadcasts for a maximum of 75 miles. Now we were trying to broadcast about 570 miles from Leipzig to London. My voice could be heard faintly by those listening there, but much was unintelligible. So I failed in the last big battle of the war.

The fighting in Leipzig that day took more toll of the First Army correspondents. Two French reporters accredited to the First Army enthusiastically dashed through the city to the Napoleon Monument with a couple of photographers. That section of the city had not been conquered, the correspondents were killed in the monument itself, and the photographers were taken prisoner temporarily.

By this time V Corps, under General Huebner, was in Naumburg. The correspondents were all there, and so was our Press Wireless transmitter. I knew there was a concentration camp just the other side of Leipzig on the outskirts of the city, and I decided to look for it in company with another correspondent. We discovered it without difficulty, for people on the street freely gave us directions, and before long we came in sight of the sentry towers and the barbed wire.

Beyond the wire was a terrible sight. Several low buildings formed the central area of the camp. These were partially burned down. Inside were masses of charred bodies piled near the doorways and windows. Outside on the broad concrete expanse were thirty or forty other bodies. But these men had not been burned to death. They had been shot. They were only skin and bones, living skeletons, and they lay in grotesque attitudes just as they had fallen when they had been shot. One was up on his knees and elbows, his hands clasped in supplication, stiffened in position as he had been shot down. All were facing the wire barriers. One lay with his hand outstretched toward the wire. Others seemed to have been shot as they reached the wire; their bodies hung stiffly, with spidery arms and legs outstretched on the wire strands. Perhaps they had been electrocuted there and shot for good measure.

Some were badly burned. Their striped prison clothing having been burned away, the emaciated state of their bodies was even more apparent. Their heads had been shaved. A great wave of pity for these fellow human beings swept over me, human beings who hardly looked human anymore. They might have been the carvings of some mad sculptor trying to show that all life is vanity and that death is represented by these oddly posturing figures of skeletons covered with skin, sightless eyes still staring at the last scene they saw on earth, the German guards laughing hyenalike behind their machine guns and automatic rifles.

A light, misty rain began to fall as I walked about the camp of death. All was silent. The gate to the camp swung open now that there was nobody to walk through. But I would not have been surprised had a guard with a tommy gun suddenly appeared on the ghastly expanse of the camp and shouted, "So we left some of you after all," as he opened fire on us. I had seen the gruesome scene of Buchenwald after it had been largely cleaned up, several days after the Third Army overran it. I had seen the lampshades made of human skin at the whim of the camp commandant's wife, and I had seen the great prison dogs that we killed on sight as they skulked in the woods and along the roads, dogs trained to spring for the testicles of a prisoner whom the Nazi guards wished to admonish and chastise. But this Leipzig camp was death alone—the property of the bodies piled in the ruins and the property of the man, hands clasped still as he had clasped them when he asked for pity, stiff on his elbows and knees, head bent up toward the last hope of safety beyond the barbed wire. It was death alone—and I wondered again what kind of people were these Germans who could do such things to other human beings.

The Nazi mayor of Leipzig had committed suicide with his wife and children as our troops entered the city, but he was not solely responsible. It was the German people who could do such deeds either because a superior had so ordered or because the individual German felt a lust for cruelty that surpassed anything the civilized Western world had experienced for many centuries.

The next day I heard that a women's concentration camp was also near Leipzig and that one of the women in it was American. I went there immediately and asked the women in their striped prison garb which one the American was.

With her white hair and lined face, I took her to be past middle age.

"Where do you come from?" I asked after I had identified myself.

"Massachusetts," she replied.

"And what is your name?"

"I married a Frenchman. I am the Countess Henri de Mauduit."

"Henri de Mauduit?" I said in amazement. "Henri de Mauduit—your husband? Why, I had dinner with him in Paris last month."

I had not realized what effect this statement would have on the American-born woman. She swayed on her bunk as though she had been hit by a rifle bullet. Then she broke out in uncontrollable weeping. Great sobs sounded through the room, and she fell over on the wooden bunk.

I patted her and talked to her gently for ten or fifteen minutes before she could again gain control of herself.

"I have not known since 1940 whether he was alive or dead," she said, sobbing. "Don't worry about my tears. They are happiness at knowing Henri is alive."

The countess had not seen or heard of her husband since as an officer with the French Army he had been taken to England at the time of the German victory of 1940. Henri had joined De Gaulle, and in spite of the fact that he was at least in his middle forties, he had become a parachutist. Henri was the brother-in-law of Jacqueline de Mauduit, of whom I have written from time to time.

Henri parachuted into his home province, Brittany, and helped organize the Resistance in that part of France. He ended the war on De Gaulle's staff and afterward was made governor-general of one

314

of the French colonies in the West Indies and French representative on the Caribbean Council.

I learned the story of his wife from her own lips as she sat on the narrow wooden bunk, which, until the Americans arrived, she had had to share with two other women.

Not knowing where her husband was, she had retired to their château in Brittany. After the United States entered the war, she became an important link in the underground chain through which our fliers who had been shot down were passed out of the country secretly. There was a secret hiding place between the floors where she placed the escapees when the Gestapo came looking for them. Often the Gestapo made surprise raids on her house, but she always had time enough to conceal the Americans or British who were under her roof.

At last the Gestapo knew a large batch of escaping men were in the neighborhood. They were certain they were in the Mauduit house, but although they raided it and searched it from top to bottom, they could find no trace of the men. In anger, they took the countess off to a concentration camp.

She was sent to the big women's camp of Ravensbrück, a hellhole. Women, whether of gentle birth or not, were stripped naked for inspection by the guards. The youngest and prettiest the guards took for their own temporary amusement. The women tried to make themselves as unattractive as possible to escape the attentions of their captors.

The countess, like others, had been sent out in midwinter to stand at stiff attention, clad only in a slip. When the woman swayed, she would be clubbed by the guards, until her ultimate collapse. Many died under this treatment, but always more came to be crammed into the camp. They were beaten at every turn by men or women guards, who seemed to enjoy the sadistic experience.

The Massachusetts-born countess was a comparatively young woman; but under the treatment she received at Ravensbrück, her hair went white, and her face began to show the effect of the years of detention.

Eventually, as the Allies began to push the Germans' back, she was transferred to the Leipzig camp. But the Americans were pressing on into central Germany. The guards announced that the camp had to be evacuated. Only the sick would be left behind. The Countess de Mauduit and many others pretended to be too ill to walk. The able-bodied were cleared out and started on a march toward eastern Germany. The guards had orders to kill the women left behind, a fact that the women learned from a friendly guard after the majority of the women had departed. But the oncoming American Army arrived too quickly. The first American units reached the camp soon after the inmates heard the artillery fire that meant freedom was approaching. By that time the SS guards had fled without carrying out their orders to execute the women who remained.

The Countess de Mauduit told me the story of the men's camp which I had seen with so much horror.

"We saw the fire across the field," she said, "and we were so happy we clapped our hands and shouted for happiness. We thought the men in the camp had set themselves free and burned the camp behind them. We watched the flames growing and dying for a couple of hours. Then two or three prisoners, terribly burned or wounded, came across the fields to our camp. We took them in and hid them, for although the guards who remained with us were bewildered and upset, we did not trust them.

"The men who had escaped told us the story. At the time the first artillery fire was heard in the distance, the guards announced that they were to be given a big meal—and after that they might be released. The men were so happy at the thought of a real meal. They crowded into the barracks. The doors were locked behind them, and the buildings were set on fire. The prisoners rushed in terror toward the doors and windows. That is why you found their bodies piled there.

"A few of the men flung themselves out through the windows. But the guards were posted around the buildings with machine guns. They shot the men trying to escape as they ran across the open space, many with their clothes in flames. Only a few reached the wire. And of the few who did, only half a dozen managed to throw themselves out through the wire, with the barbs tearing their flesh, to reach freedom. They had nowhere to go. Most of those who came out walked or crawled across the fields to us. They told us the story—and we hid them."

I talked with the American woman for a while longer, then left her with the promise that I would let her family know she was freed. In my message that night to America, I included a request that New York immediately ask Roy Porter in Paris to tell Jacqueline de Mauduit that her sister in-law, Henri's wife, was alive and well and I had talked with her that day. Jacqueline was thus able to give her brother-in-law, the count, the first news he had had that his wife was still alive.

It was while our First Army correspondents were based at Naumburg that we had a visit from two leading Soviet correspondents. One evening the two arrived in our camp with their interpreter, a White Russian American major named Ustinov. They had flown to SHAEF and had been sent to the premier American Army on a visit to meet their opposite numbers, the cream of the American war reporters. One was Konstantin Simonov, author of the best-selling book *Days and Nights*, and the other was a reporter named Krivitsky from the Red Army paper *Red Star*.

Simonov was a lieutenant colonel in the Soviet Army. He was dressed in a beautifully tailored uniform with his rank on his shoulder boards, a tall, handsome young man with a clipped mustache and a look of aristocratic arrogance that told all whom he met that here was a man who had enjoyed the best of life and was convinced that he deserved it. His colleague was a major, blond and bespectacled.

In fact, Simonov had had a lovely war. He was the equivalent of a top Hearst correspondent or the chief war reporter of one of the major British newspapers with the added advantage of having government backing for everything he did.

Simonov lived in a spacious apartment in Moscow. He told us how he could press a button and the concealed bar would open up and show its variety of liquors, in similar fashion to one belonging to any Hollywood star. When he wished to go to a war front, a private plane was ready to take him to the nearest headquarters. At the airfield a command car and chauffeur met him. After he had looked over the situation a few days—at Stalingrad, for instance— he had only to mention that it was about time he returned to Moscow, and a plane picked him up and bore him away within a few hours. Everything he wrote was front-page news. If he wanted to go to Leningrad, or Vladivostok, or central Germany, or anywhere else in the world, he had only to express the wish, and it was accomplished. Between campaigns he could luxuriate in his apartment with his actress wife.

Simonov impressed me as one of those reporters who have no fixed opinions of his own, but if he does, he is glad to subordinate them to the exigencies of his employer. Simonov was clever, sophisticated, and, I thought, essentially shallow. He knew on which side his bread was buttered, and he was not going to miss any of the butter by writing something that might irritate his employer, the Soviet state. I had seen many exactly like him in America, men of talent who used their talent to cater to the prejudices of their employers, figuring that life is short and money is important.

We spent two or three hours putting questions to Simonov and Krivitsky, although Simonov did most of the answering. They told us of their work and their lives. Simonov kept insisting that he was a completely free reporter. His theory was this: The Communist party represented the mass of the workers of Russia. Any opposition to the state was opposition to the working people.

Certainly criticism of the war effort was permitted in Russia, but no one could criticize the basic aims of the war, the protection of Russia and the necessity to beat the Germans. Since the mass of the people approved the government, any opposition party would be opposition to the basis of the Soviet state, and that, as treason, could not be countenanced. Only a few fascists, sympathizers with the Nazis, had ever opposed the state, and it was the duty of the people to get rid of these characters. Simonov wanted to know how we could explain American toleration for such publishers as Hearst and McCormick and others who, he argued, were obviously doing the work of the Nazis in America. Were they not subversives? Should they not be prevented from expressing their ideas, which were so obviously aimed at reducing the whole Allied war effort?

Simonov gave us a hard time. We argued that a sufficiently strong country could afford all types of ideas and criticisms and that not everyone had to agree on the correct way of winning a war.

"But," said Simonov, "when you know that your publisher or your opponent is expressing ideas that give aid and comfort to the enemy, should you not eliminate him? Should you allow him to go on propagating ideas that are treasonable? That makes no sense to a Soviet correspondent."

Neither Simonov nor we Americans made much progress in explaining our different points of view. His sounded reasonable—except that all of us were convinced it was not compatible with individual freedom.

The Soviet correspondent must have looked on us with a certain amount of disdain. We were dressed in odd bits of uniform, and a more slovenly lot of semimilitary men could never have come to his notice.

After two or three hours of our questioning Simonov said, "There is one thing that amazes me about American correspondents. They

318

are apparently quite different from the Soviet correspondents. Is it possible that they never take a drink?"

We had been so interested that nobody had thought of a drink; but within three minutes we had brought in a case of bourbon from somewhere, and the glasses were out.

Sometime past midnight Simonov and Krivitsky sang us the song of the Red Army correspondents. The Red reporters' hymn it was, a long one, and Simonov sang solemnly in a clear baritone, translated by Major Ustinov. Before they began, we had drunk many times to *Russki correspondyents* and *Amerikanski correspondyents*.

"In our battered jeep," the song went, "we go into the villages ahead of the infantry. We risk our lives—and for what? For our scoop. We go without weapons ahead of the tanks, and where the fighting is hottest, there you will find us. Our motto is—get the story or die."

Now these were the sentiments that any correspondent might feel personally, but an American would die rather than voice them in public. It was quite stirring, however, and we secretly wished that we had thought of writing some such song so that the others could sing it about our own exploits.

When Simonov finished, he looked at us expectantly. "Have the American war correspondents no songs?" he asked.

We looked at one another in dismay. There was only one song which we all knew and which we jokingly called the "Hymn of the First Army Correspondents." It was a British Army song that somehow we had all learned. We used to sing it often when we happened to be dining or drinking together at our First Army press corps headquarters. One of us would start and in a moment we all were bellowing it out. There was nothing for it now. We had to sing something, and this was the only choice.

Hal Boyle and Don Whitehead and Jack Thompson and I began it—that bawdy ballad which went:

"Monday I kissed her on the ankle. Tuesday I kissed her on the knee. Wednesday—success, I undid her dress. And Thursday her chemise, gorblimey! Friday I put my hand upon it. Saturday she gave me balls a tweak. Woo-woo! And on Sunday after supper, I shoved the old boy up her. Now I'm payin' her seven and six a week. Gorblimey!

"I don't want to join the Army. I don't want to go to war. I just want to hang around Piccadilly Underground, living off the earnings of a highborn lydy. Don't want a bullet up me arsehole. Don't

319

want me bollocks shot away. I would rather stay in England. Jolly, jolly England. And fornicate me fuckin' life away. Hey, hey. And fornicate me fuckin' life away."

Simonov's face was quite a study as we sang this song of the First Army reporters and it was translated line by line into Russian by Major Ustinov. The Soviet reporter was too well bred to comment, but he was completely amazed. Here were American war correspondents, not talking about their exploits, but singing that they didn't want to go to war but would rather live on the money earned by a lady in the Piccadilly Underground. I tried to explain afterward that this was a kind of joke we had among ourselves, but polite though he was, Simonov obviously did not understand.

It was about half past three when I weaved my way off to bed. Simonov and Krivitsky and three or four of ours were still hard at it. The next morning one of our reporters who had stayed on paid tribute to the Russian reporters. They had kept on to the end around dawn and gone off to bed when it was obvious that the two or three of our men who were left wanted nothing so much as to drop dead on their cots or in the nearest chair.

It was an interesting experience. Far apart as we were with our songs, we could still understand Simonov to a certain extent, for we all had seen American reporters who resembled him. He was the special reporter par excellence, the feature writer whom the great paper or the syndicate sent to do a particular job in a particular place. He was highly paid and lived a life of luxury. In fact, he was at the top of his profession. If he ever had any doubts about the regime, there was no point in his writing them, for nobody would print his comments. He was valuable because he could express the thoughts of his bosses better than they themselves could. And many an American reporter had won fame and fortune with a similar talent. If tomorrow the regime changed, the new government would still need talent of Simonov's type, and Simonov would be there to write what they wanted without mussing a hair of his well-groomed head. I had known several counterparts in New York, Washington, London, and Paris. Who were we to condemn him for being cynical and making the best of the only world in which he could function?

Chapter 29

The great war drama which had begun with the plunge of the German panzers across the Polish border was now approaching its end. Our divisions closed rapidly to the Mulde River, but they were forbidden to cross it except for very limited patrolling. The Elbe River had been set as the dividing line between the Soviet and American armies, and as yet, none knew whether the Russians had reached the Elbe or had advanced beyond it.

I decided to stay with my friends of the 2nd Infantry Division, feeling that if any group made first contact with the Russians, it would be this distinguished and experienced fighting unit. General Robertson, the commander, was fretting with impatience to win the honor of having his division become the first to make the contact. Farther north, General Terry Allen of the Timberwolves was equally anxious to be the first.

I lived with Major Kenneth BeLieu, chief signal officer of the 2nd Division, and wanted as much as anyone to have the 2nd Division win the glory. To all of us, the war would not be over until we had actually seen the Russian soldiers. I was not to see BeLieu's face again for nine years, when he appeared on the nation's television screens in the dispute between the United States Army and Senator Joseph McCarthy of Wisconsin. By then BeLieu had lost a leg in Korea and as a colonel had become military assistant to Secretary of the Army Robert Stevens.

The 2nd Division's radio operators were able to hear the approaching Russian units talking among themselves. We got Major Ivan, the Tass correspondent, to join us one day in a serious attempt to talk to the oncoming Red Army.

The Russian radio signals had become very loud and clear, and we knew they were not many miles away. We set a 399 transmitter up on a hill overlooking the Mulde, and at intervals all day long, with the set tuned to what we believed was a Red Army frequency, Ivan would broadcast: *"Shlooshety. Shlooshety."* In Russian, this meant "Listen. Listen." Ivan would identify himself, major of a Guards division attached as a Tass correspondent to the American

First Army. He would explain we were anxious to meet the Russians, and they should send over a patrol to meet us on or near the Mulde.

At one point we saw tanks moving in the far distance across the river and saw the smoke of a village burning from gunfire. We believed the tanks were Russians, for at that time their radio signals were so loud that we realized some Red unit was only a few miles off. But although Ivan talked until he was hoarse and some operators with a knowledge of Russian listened on frequencies they thought the Soviet Army men might employ, we never did hear the Russians reply to us.

In the period I spent with the 2nd Division, I toured up and down the Mulde, checking other units, but none had made contact with the Russians. I visited Colditz prison, just across the river, on the afternoon it was liberated. The prisoners were still milling about, waiting for someone to tell them what to do. But a handful whom the Germans thought especially important, a relative of Winston Churchill's and sons or nephews of other prominent Allied statesmen, had been spirited off deeper into Germany. We feared they might be used as hostages during what we thought would be the German last stand in some mountain fortresses around Berchtesgaden.

Came April 25, and at five-thirty in the afternoon a report reached me at 2nd Division headquarters that American soldiers had met the Russians—not the experienced 2nd or Terry Allen's 104th, but the 69th, one of the new divisions which had hardly been blooded before it reached the Mulde. The faces of the 2nd Division men fell. The 69th had done what all the rest had hoped to do, and in fact, in another day or so, I was sure, the 2nd would have sent a patrol out to the Elbe against all orders, so impatient had the officers become at the trancelike state to which the Supreme Headquarters had condemned them. But I had no time to commiserate with Major BeLieu and the rest. It was off with the old love and on with the new—in ten minutes our luggage was thrown aboard the jeep, and I was off up the road to 69th Division headquarters.

Perhaps the best way to give the flavor of the events which followed is to give the text of a broadcast I made on April 27, 1945, from the First Army press camp at Naumburg. This is the way we all felt on that great moment of the meeting of the two armies:

"This is John MacVane in Germany.

"I saw American and Russian soldiers meet. I saw them meet and

322

Russian and American troops meet at Torgau on the Elbe River. WIDE
WORLD.

323

embrace, swap trinkets, drink toasts—and it still didn't seem as though it could be really true.

"I had waited for days on our front line—heard their voices on the radio. To meet them, I crossed thirty miles of ground that hadn't been occupied by us or by the Red Army. I rowed twice across the Elbe River in a skittish racing rowboat to go to the Russian command post.

"But to shake hands with those Russian fighting men seemed an experience too incredible for belief.

"Remember last January? The Russians were back on the Vistula some three hundred fifty miles from Torgau on the Elbe. The American armies were tangled up in the Bulge—back in Belgium—three hundred fifty miles this side of Torgau on the Elbe.

"I saw our two armies together at Torgau on the Elbe. In three months, our combined armies had covered seven hundred miles, cut Germany in two, and shattered the last German hope. From Stalingrad and Pearl Harbor—we have come a long way.

"It is a fine-looking army—the Red Army. Men of medium height, clear-eyed, alert-looking. They dress well and hold themselves proudly. You get the idea that here are men who are sure of themselves and their ability—inferior to none.

"I had always heard that the Russians were secretive, that American reporters weren't allowed to visit their front lines. Well, we visited their front—from our front—and we got a greeting so honestly glad and warm that even though we didn't use the same words, we knew we were speaking the same language in our hearts.

"I had been roaming up and down the American front lines on the Mulde River for several days, waiting for the Red Army to arrive.

"It was a great thrill when—from our hilltop above the Mulde—we saw Russian tanks and vehicles, saw German villages under Russian shell fire. And when we established contact with their tank radios, it seemed very close—the meeting of the two armies. But the Russians who came to a hill three or four miles from the Mulde were only on patrol, and they pulled back to the Elbe.

"A sudden tip sent us speeding from one division sector to the neighboring American Sixty-ninth Division area. Our own patrols weren't supposed to penetrate too far, but a couple of adventuresome young lieutenants, Lieutenant Albert Kotzebuhe of Houston, Texas, and Lieutenant William D. Robertson of Los Angeles became slightly deaf, or didn't hear the radio or something, and met the Russians at Triesa and Torgau at one thirty-two and four o'clock on the afternoon of Wednesday, April 25.

"I got the news at about five-thirty and hustled to the Sixty-ninth. So did twenty or thirty more reporters, collecting like flies from nowhere.

"There we learned that the patrols had evidently upset Supreme Headquarters plans about as much as the Remagen bridgehead had done. The idea seemed to have been that a sedate meeting would be staged sometime. Then a couple of brash young lieutenants went off and reported back that they had made contact.

"Later that night we saw Lieutenant Robertson. He's a slight fellow with a wispy blond mustache. With him were some of the Russians—come back with him to arrange a more formal meeting.

"His story was exciting. He didn't have any recognition flares, and the Russians fired the wrong one. Robertson yelled, '*Tovarich—Kamarad*,' and there was some more shooting at him. Then the whole thing began to get straightened out. He met a Russian soldier sitting on the sloping girder of a wrecked bridge. They pounded each other's shoulders in comradely fashion. Then Robertson shinnied over to meet the Russian division commander. They gave him wine, a can of sardines, chocolate, and biscuits. Then they insisted he have a drink of German schnapps. Robertson traded watches with the Russian captain. It was like a meeting of friends anywhere. You get over the language difficulty by smiling and saying, 'Good,' and taking a drink together and wishing like the devil you could express what you feel.

"Robertson was a typical American boy. One of the Russian officers must have been about his age. He looked more intense than the American, but both gave us that impression of youth, the period before things get too complicated.

"Lieutenant Robertson found the Russians were a little suspicious because, the day before, some krauts had waved the American flag at the Russians and yelled that they were Americans. When the Russians started coming toward them, the Germans opened fire and killed all the Russians. Some Germans were killed, but it left the Russians with a healthy skepticism.

"One of the Russian officers said he and his soldiers were overjoyed, so glad and astounded that they didn't know whether to invite the Americans to go for a jeep ride with them, have a drink of vodka, or go attack the Germans together. They compromised on the vodka.

325

"All this got the correspondents quite excited. Colonel C. M. Adams of Houston, Texas, commander of the Two Hundred Seventy-third Infantry Regiment, was going next morning to meet the Russians. We decided to follow.

"We crossed the Mulde and headed east. We started out in four cars, but we picked up eight or ten more, with an obliging officer and a thirty-caliber machine gun.

"Only the patrols had passed that way. The territory had not been occupied by either army. Warm sun, dust rising from the jeep wheels, and green fields was your impression. The country seemed strangely empty. We didn't know anything about it except that a patrol had been over the road the previous day, and probably another in the early morning.

"You didn't know where the Germans were, whether they would show fight if you met them, or what you could do about it if they did. Our own lines seemed a long way away—and so did the Russians.

"Some of the villages seemed desolate, windows shuttered. But on the roads was a stranger, more motley stream of human beings than you could find anywhere else in the world. Hansom cabs, fiacres covered with bedding, filled with household belongings and the families walking or riding. Twelve million people from all over Europe, the slave laborers, drafted by Germany to till her fields, keep her war industries going—under the lash. That's literal. In almost every house I've been in, you find a rawhide lash. In one house I found a flexible piece of rubber-covered iron tubing—with handle.

"Now the twelve million were going home, Czech and Serb, Frenchman, Dutchman, Belgian, women and children, all on their way. Our drive has also freed thousands and thousands of war prisoners. Uniforms of every Allied nation are on the road. The Indian Sikhs were the most smart in their salute, the most rigid at attention as we swept by.

"The Germans in that no-man's-land between the Mulde and the Elbe are also on the move. Fear of the Russians or forced evacuation by the Nazis put them on the road. We stopped them at the Mulde, so they were going in two directions. Add to this mixture German soldiers, some still carrying their weapons. German patrols still pass through the territory. Other thousands have quit, thrown their rifles away, and headed down the road to surrender.

"Many of the German villagers waved at us. They thought we

were coming to take over the territory, and in their minds at this last minute of the last hour, we have suddenly become popular—at least, in comparison with the Russians, the lesser of two evils.

"An average village would have a bunch of Germans out in the square waving to us and pointing the way, a few British Tommies waving, some French soldiers on bicycles going through, some Russian prisoners of war cooking on the bank by the roadside, some Germans or slave laborers moving along the road, pushing carts or baby carriages full of bedding and belongings, and some farmers driving their oxcarts to the fields.

"You wave and are never sure to whom you are waving, ally or enemy.

"Our road ended in the woods—at a roadblock. Logs across the way formed a barrier, and we had been told a patrol had been here only the day before. Trees without bark gleamed white. Branches were off all around the block, signs of heavy artillery fire against just this point. Shell nose caps lay on the ground.

"We turned, went back, and took another road.

"Torgau seemed empty. We went through one empty street after another. A town looks very dead when you take out the people. We went into a small empty square and stopped. Suddenly Russians, a few and evidently an outpost, appeared in all the doorways.

"We ran to them, pounded them on the back, and said unintelligible things. We were glad, and they were glad. That was the main thing.

"The Red Army men told us their command post was on the other side of the river Elbe. Down at the bank of river, it looked something like a miniature Coney Island. The Russian slave laborers were getting ready to go back to their own country. They were collecting on the bank. One civilian was playing a Russian tune on the accordion to some of the Red Army men. Women and children were scattered about, calling to each other.

"The Germans had blown the bridges, and their spans had fallen into the stream. The Torgau Rowing Club was being emptied of boats to provide ferries. Racing shells, clinker-built craft, pairs, eights—the Russian laborers were carrying them down and loading aboard, then off, paddling with sixteen-foot oars in the rushing stream. Some carried bicycles, carts. About the only thing I didn't see in the frail craft were jeeps.

"At the edge of the river I met Lieutenant Nikolai Bogush from Minsk. He's in the Guards division with whom we made contact.

I had been saving some German brandy to offer the Russians. But he took one look at the bottle and said, '*Deutsch?*—German?' I said, 'Yes,' and he shook his head. '*Nichts gut*' and drew his finger across his throat, laughing. '*American gut. Deutsch nichts gut*,' he went on, and shook his head again.

"Three of us pulled out a boat, fitted oars, and set out. I rowed and managed to get across to where I wanted to go.

"The American colonel had been negotiating a meeting of the division commanders. The division commanders would negotiate a meeting of the corps commanders and so on up through army until it reached a meeting of General Bradley and Marshal Koniev, or maybe higher. That's military etiquette, and the Russians are sticklers for etiquette.

"Since we were probably the first British and Americans to see a Russian front line, we looked them over carefully. They looked tough, competent, and well equipped. Their guns were good and skillfully emplaced.

"The officers and men dress up in a way that our more easygoing Army doesn't. The Russians wore all their medals and stars, plenty of them. One officer, a colonel, told us he never would allow the variety of dress that you find in our Army, and the slapdash, individualistic dress of the correspondents may have shocked him. Most of us felt like going and getting our Class A uniforms to wear whenever we meet the Russians again.

"I thought I had found a Red Army woman fighter, khaki uniform, Guards insignia, and medal of merit on her bosom. She told me she was a nurse, but she carried an automatic pistol in the holster at her hip. She had been at the front for two years, but she blushed even quicker than an American girl might have when we paid her a compliment.

"In the officers' mess, all was somewhat confused, with reporters milling around, some lunching with the Russian officers on captured German food, others trying to carry on interviews with those who spoke some other language but Russian. With the rest, it was a strange pidgin language, '*Tovarich—tovarich*,' over and over and things like 'me *kamarad—Russki*—Red Army—Stalin—gut—Germany *fini*—' But the real language was our smiles.

"Lieutenant Dimitri Ebert spoke pretty good English, but he said we were the first Americans or English he's ever talked with. He asked me to tell what I saw, to try to describe the happiness of the Russian officers and men. They were happy all right. Breakfast had turned into lunch. Bottles of vodka and white wine were getting emptier as toasts were drunk in the Russian fashion, bottoms up, to both our armies, to allies, to Marshal Stalin, and to the late President Roosevelt.

"The food was German Army food, and it was hard to get out of the room without eating or drinking too much. The Russian officers and men, the Guards division, had chests filled with decorations and stars. They looked more tough and military than German officers who look in real life like Erich von Stroheim playing German officers. The difference was that there was no swagger or affectation about the Russians. They looked like men who had done a good job and knew it and felt they could beat the Germans any time they met them. I felt very glad they were our allies.

"You can't spend ten minutes with an army without knowing a good deal about it. The Russian Army looked good. Our own Army will look good to the Russians because it is obviously so good. When our men met the Russians, they remembered Stalingrad, the defense of Moscow, the Crimea, and all the other campaigns that have made the Red Army what it is—and we met as equals.

"The men of the two armies were matching weapons. There would be a bang, and it was an American trying out a Russian antitank grenade or a *Panzerfaust*. A burst of machine-gun fire, and it was a Russian handling one of our grease guns.

"Meanwhile, on the bank of the Elbe, that miniature Coney Island was going on, accordions playing, Russian families opening picnic baskets, people laughing as they tried to paddle the overloaded boats across the Elbe and got carried down in the swift current, far down the opposite bank.

"Yet by the antitank guns, camouflaged with green branches, Russian gunners stand watchfully, for German units are still moving about in nearby territory that we haven't had time to clear. One unit, that very night, had offered to surrender, then opened fire on the Russians who advanced to take the surrender. The German unit was wiped out to the last man, but the Russians are still watchful and careful.

"You wondered how many green riverbanks, how many covered with snow and ice, the Russian men of that Guards division had stood upon since June of 1941. For us, there had been hundreds in less than a year, the Vire, the Ouse, the Seine, the Roer, the Rhine, and all the rest.

"One officer said to me that in '41 and '42, no Russian man hoped to live. He only hoped to kill a lot of Germans before he died. Few of the original unit are left, but now the rest can hope for peace soon, opportunity to rebuild their country, and the frank cooperation of their great world neighbor America.

"He pressed me to take a glass of white wine and, lifting it, he said, 'To both of us—and to the future.'

"I thought of that as I rowed back across the Elbe in the afternoon sunshine. The future. We can all think of that now." That was how my broadcast ended on April 27, 1945.

Chapter 30

When I arrived on the near bank of the Elbe, the first person I saw was Lieutenant Jim Rugg.

"I brought Jig Easy along," he said. "I thought some of you might want to try to broadcast."

So Jig Easy Sugar Queen had gone all the way from Normandy to the Elbe. It had done much more than the Army, or its makers, Hallicrafters, had ever expected. But Jim knew as well as I that to call upon it to reach London from the Elbe was an impossibility. The covered truck, into which I had climbed so often to talk to all America, looked incongruous among the Russians and the displaced persons and the Americans wandering about. I felt a little twinge of sadness when I said, "Jim, there isn't any censor here, and we don't know what the Army will let us say about this meeting with the Russians. We'd better go back and find out before we try to do any spots." I felt that I had broadcast from Jig Easy for the last time, and it had gone all the way with me in some of the most exciting moments of my life. If one can have an affection for a machine, I felt about Jig Easy almost as I might have felt about a horse that had served me faithfully and well, and now was the time to put it out to pasture, perhaps to act as a sire for other Jig Easies that would go on serving the Army in the years to come.

It was on April 28, I believe, that General Hodges went to lunch with General Jardov, commander of the Fifth Guards Army, which had made first contact with us. At least I remember having a hangover on the twenty-ninth, my thirty-third birthday, and I think the Jardov party was the reason. Age twenty-seven to age thirty-three, six years of war and nothing else, I thought. Six years of never seeing a city lit up at night. Six years of never knowing whether I or my family might not be killed tonight or next week.

At first it seemed that the Hodges-Jardov meeting might not take place, for Jardov did not want any correspondents to attend. But General Hodges told him that he would not come unless the First Army reporters could come with him, and Jardov yielded.

It was a wild affair, on a big country estate, some ten miles behind the Elbe, which served Jardov as his headquarters. We ate at long tables extending down a huge room. The generals were at the T at the top of the room with their chief staff officers.

I was between two colonels of the Red Army, and I had to drink a toast with first the colonel on my right, then the colonel on my left. The tables were strewn with ornate dishes of cold meat, cold game, cold fish, and cold fowl. The fowl had been boned, and their heads were turned and tucked under their wings. We ate and drank for more than two hours, and we Americans thought that the Russians were providing a very fine cold buffet for our lunch.

Then someone said, "Now we shall have lunch." In came the soup, and next the entrée, and then the dessert, and with each course came an assortment of wines.

Afterward we settled down to drinking and watching the entertainment that the Fifth Guards Army provided, dancers, singers, instrumentalists of all kinds with a great amount of talent.

Eddy Ward of the BBC had rejoined the First Army, and he had his recording equipment taking down the songs and the music. I suggested that he might let me record a short piece for my own network, and he gladly turned over the microphone to me.

After a while I handed back the microphone and wandered back to my seat at the table. Eventually people started to leave. I noticed one of our higher officers going out of the room between two aides. His toes were touching the ground from time to time, but only from time to time. Where a Soviet general had been sitting, only an empty chair remained. I did not think of looking under the table. That might have been construed as impolite. We moved outside. I noticed some recumbent figures on the lawn, lugged there by some willing soldiers. I was glad to see that about half were Russians and half Americans. They were slumbering peacefully in the last light of the setting sun. I had no idea of the time. They played "The Star-Spangled Banner" and the Soviet national anthem. We stood the whole time at salute. The next day a friend told me I got straighter and straighter until I was bending over backward at almost a forty-five-degree angle. He thought that if the music had continued another bar or two, I would have gone all the way. I was not aware of this; but in any case, the music stopped in time, and we clambered aboard our jeeps. Somehow most of us seemed to get back to our headquarters in Weimar, where we were staying at the time, although one or two correspondents fell out on the way and arrived bloodied but with bones intact. The rest of us had learned to sleep sitting up in a jeep, swaying mechanically in the right direction as we went around corners.

The next day about noon I looked up Eddy Ward and asked to hear the recording I had made. It sounded awful. The climax came when I said, "An' this l'il gal yur listnen to—this li'l singer from the steppes—soun's 'stho' she came right outta a nigh' club—is a sergeant, a sergeant in the AMERICAN ARMY."

I said to Eddy, "I guess we won't send that one along to London."

"I understand," Ward replied. "I recorded all afternoon, and only the first third is usable at all. But wasn't it a wonderful party?"

After the party there was little to do. Fighting on our front had ceased. There was some farther south in the Third Army area, but that was the concern of the Third Army reporters, not us. Once in a while we would visit Torgau, where a battalion of Russians and a battalion of our 69th Division were stationed.

The next event of importance was the party that Marshal Ivan Koniev, the Red Army group commander, gave for General Bradley on May 4.

This time we were more prepared and all resolved to be careful with our drinking. General Bradley himself took a swallow of mineral oil before he started out on the road to Koniev's headquarters.

The château that Koniev had chosen was, if anything, more magnificent than the one which housed his subordinate, General Jardov. Koniev looked like any top general the world around. There was a commanding look on his square face, and one had no difficulty in picturing him in an American or British uniform, looking at home in either. If it had not been for that martial air of command, he might have been a schoolteacher or the owner of a midwestern factory or a Hollywood character actor who preferred playing the part of the father to the young star.

The party itself was on a very high level, and it was incredibly sedate in comparison with our first brawl at army level. The singers and dancers were obviously professionals in uniform.

The tables were scattered through two or three rooms, and I could see the principals only from a great distance. It was notable that in spite of the number of toasts, nobody was doing bottoms-up with the glasses. The first party had demonstrated the natural exuberance of the combat commanders. In contrast this was the restrained festivity of protocol-minded group commanders. I heard that Koniev himself drank only sparingly because of a stomach ailment, and his action naturally set the tone for his staff, while the Americans meticulously followed suit.

As we walked out, I felt as though my feet were sinking in the luxurious carpeting. Mirrors with gilt borders covered the walls and made the building seem like a Hollywood dream of a house.

One familiar face was among the group of smartly uniformed, shiny-booted Russian officers—Solodovnik. I blinked in surprise, for he was dressed in the uniform of a Soviet major general. When I had known him in North Africa, he was a Tass correspondent, a reporter like any of the rest of us, accredited to the British Army. Well, I thought, that was as good a way as any for the Russians to get firsthand knowledge of what Montgomery was really doing, a major general turned into a reporter.

"Hello, Solly," I said. "I'm John MacVane. Don't you remember, I met you at Thibar with Dudley Forwood and we sat around one night drinking Pilkington's Scotch in the hotel?"

Solodovnik was fair-haired, not a great deal older than I, and I thought he looked somewhat embarrassed. "Of course, my dear fellow," he said. "Those were good old days in the desert, weren't they?"

I remembered how Forwood, a British captain, used to boss Solly around. I think now that the British must have known exactly who Solodovnik was and why he was assigned as a correspondent. It may have pleased Forwood's puckish sense of humor when he tugged his great mustache and said, "Oh, bloody Solly, won't you ever learn anything about warfare? Now this is how you read a map."

"How do you fellows get a château like this?" I asked. "My generals seem to live in barracks and schools all the time. Nothing as soft as this."

Solodovnik laughed. "We believe in comfort, old boy. After all, if you're a Red Army marshal, you don't need to live in a tent— not if there are places like this around."

Officers of both nations were milling about on the lawn, which stretched away for half a dozen acres to a grove of trees. A Russian GI led a fine-looking black horse up and down. Koniev beckoned to Bradley, and they both patted the horse while Russian officers with cameras began flickering their flashbulbs.

One of our photographers came up, dragging a plate out of his pocket. "Geez," he said, "these guys are on the job. They'd do all right on the run from quarantine up the bay."

Koniev made a speech and shook hands with General Bradley while more pictures were taken. Bradley gave Koniev an American jeep with a gift inscription painted on it. The jeep had an American carbine in a sheath.

A Russian officer whom I had met at dinner came up to me. He spoke some French, and he said, "Your general has given my marshal a carbine, but he forgot to include the bullets."

"That's easy," I said. "We wouldn't want anything missing on this occasion." I went down our line of correspondents' jeeps and got half a dozen clips of carbine ammunition. "Here. Happy target practice to the marshal."

Richard C. Hottelet of CBS came up. "How do you like settling international crises?" he asked. "Let's get out of here. I feel these Russians are all right at a party, but I still wouldn't like to be around them after the party is over."

We picked up Victor Bernstein of the now-defunct New York newspaper *PM*; Bob Reuben, an American who worked for the British news agency Reuters; and Jack Hansen, one of our press officers. As we started down the long driveway, someone said dreamily, "I wonder if we turned left instead of right at the road, we could go all the way to Berlin."

We knew that we had been forbidden by SHAEF to go to Berlin, but if we got lost and eventually found ourselves in Berlin, who could blame us? Nobody ever took a decision, but at the bottom of the drive the driver turned the jeep to the left, although a little Russian girl soldier waved her flags to the right and stood open-mouthed, looking after us when we disregarded her.

We went along for miles. I followed as best I could our route on the map, but we had not known exactly where the Koniev headquarters were, and all signs seemed to be in Russian. At last a German sign read, Berlin. 22 kilometres.

By this time I had begun to worry, for we had no idea of the situation behind the Russian lines, how much ground they had occupied or whether fighting was still continuing.

"Literally, we're all right on the SHAEF order," said Hottelet. "The order was not to cross the Elbe except in an official party. Well, we came in an official party. We got lost and suddenly find ourselves in Berlin. Can we help it?"

General Bradley presents Marshal Koniev with an American jeep and a carbine. (MacVane was there.) WIDE WORLD.

The road we were traveling on was an ordinary-looking road, but there was something strange and repellent about it. Only when I thought for a few minutes did I discover the reason. There should have been people on the road, other vehicles moving along, and people outside the houses we occasionally passed. Instead, we saw no one at all. The road was deserted, and the undamaged houses, the road without people gave us an impression of one of those unreal Dali paintings, as though the whole scene were hung in some empty other world.

I abhorred empty roads in wartime, and it was with real relief that we saw an occasional sign in Russian, reassuring us that at least the Soviet Army had once passed this way.

At last we came to a village which was filled with Russian soldiers and some Germans. A line of American-made Red Army trucks was filing into the village by one road, turning a corner and passing out another road toward Berlin. Most trucks were drawn up in the square, and in an open field soldiers were cooking a meal.

"I know this town," said Hottelet. "It's Grossbeeren. We're just south of Berlin."

Hottelet had lived in Berlin as a student. Later he had worked there as a reporter. Vic Bernstein had also worked in the city for a year or two.

On the corner a Russian girl in uniform, skirt, blouse, and beret was directing traffic with signal flags. She waved us to join the truck column. As we got opposite the pleasantly rounded blouse, she suddenly looked at us again—in surprise this time—and in one continuous motion tucked the flags under her arm and threw us a snappy salute. A moment later she was back with her flags waving at the traffic.

We ran along, between two Russian Army trucks, through the suburbs of Berlin. At one point a bridge had been blown. The truck column turned, ran through some fields, down a steep bank into a dry gully and up the other side.

Bernstein said we were near Tempelhof Aerodrome, and soon we could see it, pitted wtih shells and bombs and with some wreckage of planes around the edges.

The air over the city was thick with smoke. No Germans appeared on the streets. On the outskirts, the houses and other buildings did not look badly damaged, but no faces appeared at the windows as we went by.

We left the truck column and branched off on our own, with Hottelet giving the directions. "We'll stay at the Adlon," he said. "I heard it isn't damaged."

"Nothing but the best," I said. "The Adlon it is."

As we approached the central part of the city, the damage got progressively worse, and the signs of war multiplied. On one street corner stood a German Tiger tank, its turret blown clear off by a shell. Down another street, three Russian tanks about the same size as the German had been knocked out by antitank fire.

The sight of the center of the city did not shock us. We had seen too much total destruction for that, the fantastic collections of debris that had once been St.-Lô and Caen. Berlin was too large for total destruction, by any weapon we then knew. Parts of the city contained block after block of houses or factories that seemed undamaged, except for occasional bomb gaps or blown windows. But it was only when we stopped in the center of Berlin and beheld the hundreds of acres of ruins that we began to realize what damage our bombing had caused.

Smaller streets were choked with ashes and bits of buildings, and for block after block the debris lay as far as we could see. On the main thoroughfares, the Germans had been able to keep open lanes for traffic, but that was all that had been done to rehabilitate the city after our bombing.

Apartment houses had been sheared through as by a giant cleaver, and once again I saw the incongruous sight of a bathtub held by its piping high up on a wall which had been stripped of everything else but fireplaces.

I looked for the effects of the big blockbuster four-, six-, or ten-ton bombs that the Royal Air Force had carried to Berlin. I could mark where they had fallen by the complete leveling of areas 100 yards or so in diameter, splashes of total destruction among blasted walls, gutted interiors, and piles of broken stone.

Berlin was still burning, for, as we found out later, the Russians had entered the center of the city only the previous day. Flames from a great warehouse type of building crackled and flared against a column of smoke that joined the general layer of smoke that wavered and eddied over the city.

As we passed one street, Hottelet said, "Good God. That's the Chancellery, and there's the balcony Hitler used to appear upon."

The windows gaped empty. A door was blown off its hinges. The

338

Bomb-blasted Berlin. WIDE WORLD.

inside looked like a shambles, but the walls remained intact.

Across the street the Propaganda Ministry was burning, and the thick black smoke made us cough when a gust of wind sent it billowing across the roadway. Some Russian cars were collected in front of what had been Goebbels's headquarters.

I said, "This is a sight I used to hope I would one day see back in the days and nights of the London blitz—Berlin in flames."

To Dick Hottelet and Vic Bernstein, the whole scene was incredible, the spacious, clean city of Berlin where they had lived and worked reduced to a heap of rubble.

We stopped in front of the Adlon Hotel. It had lost a piece of its structure, and bomb blast had cleared the interior.

"And that's where I used to have cocktails," said Bernstein wonderingly.

"Well," I commented, "whoever told Dick the Adlon was all right certainly hasn't been here to look for himself."

We kept driving around the center of the city with Hottelet and Bernstein picking out buildings they had known. In one great open space Bernstein said, "Wait a minute. I'm lost."

He recalled the name of the street we had come along and the number of corners we had passed, and suddenly he exclaimed, "It must be the Potsdamer Platz, the Times Square of Berlin—and I didn't recognize it."

As we passed under the Brandenburg Gate, a column of Russian troops were moving in on trucks. We had our driver take our picture, standing in front of the great gate, holed by the Red Army's shell fire.

At each street corner Russian military policewomen were directing traffic. Soviet staff cars whirled by in a flurry of dust. Here and there bulldozers and captured German soldiers with shovels were clearing a path through some blocked street.

Occasionally we saw Russian tanks placed at points where they could cover the approaches to some Russian headquarters.

Turning one corner, we nearly ran into the biggest tank we had ever seen. It was mammoth, and I figured that if the American Sherman tank was thirty-two tons, and the German Tiger tank fifty tons or better, this Russian monster must be ninety tons. The gun that jutted from its turret was a six-incher or larger, at least the equivalent of our 155-millimeter Long Tom field guns. The ponderous giant clanked down the street past us, and as we turned aside, we

Correspondents Reuben, Hottelet, Bernstein, and MacVane in Berlin, May 4, 1945.

realized something of the power of the Russian force that had driven the German Army backward over so many hundreds of miles.

We went hunting for the house of an uncle of Hottelet's, who, he believed, might still be in Berlin. We picked our way along the street with broken glass crunching under our tires. When wreckage stopped us, we proceeded on foot. The house, when we found it, was partially wrecked, and nobody remained within. This whole section of the city seemed deserted. A few groups of working prisoners were all the Germans we saw, except for a civilian once in a while walking along by himself and looking as much of an anachronism as some aged prospector in a ghost mining town of the old West.

Before we realized it, dusk had caught up with us. The streets became completely deserted. Only an occasional Russian sentry at a doorway showed where Russian command posts had been established or Russian units billeted.

"I don't like this," I said. "We'd better go to the Russians and try to get a bed for the night. It's no use trying to get back to our lines in the darkness. We don't know the language, and if the Germans didn't shoot us, the Russians would."

"I'd rather park in some doorway and spend the night in the jeep," said Hottelet. "We might get in trouble with the Russians."

"Not for me," I replied with some emphasis. "Here we are in a city we don't know. We don't know how many German SS and soldiers are still knocking around hidden in these ruins. We'd be so easy to knock off in the darkness that we'd be foolish to spend the night outside. Once we get with the Russians we know we'll be safe. After all, we're allies. So we have a good sleep and we go back home in the morning."

"I don't see anything safe about the Russians," said Hottelet. "They don't know us. We shouldn't be here. These Russians would as soon shoot us as eat—if they thought we were spies. Allies or not— they don't give a damn. I've heard stories about them."

"So have I," I replied, "but I'd just as soon take a chance with the Russians."

"We could post a guard," said Bernstein, "take turns staying awake if we slept in the jeep."

We brought our driver and the young public relations officer into the discussion, and finally, it was settled by Reuben's saying, "If it's a choice between sleeping in a bed and in a jeep, give me the bed every time."

342

We cruised along slowly and pulled up near the first doorway in which we spotted a Russian sentry.

"You guys stay here," Hottelet said. "I'll find someone who talks German and fix the whole thing up."

Chapter 31

The time was past ten o'clock, and the night was dark. Berlin had become a city of mystery. Somewhere in the ruins were Germans with weapons. Of that I had no doubt. I wondered whether they came out at night and tried to slither through the Russian lines to rejoin whatever fragments of the German Army still existed as cohesive units.

No sound broke the stillness. In the distance the fires of the burning city rose and fell against the sky.

Suddenly nearby came a clatter of heels on the sidewalk, and a voice said something to us in Russian.

"*Amerikanski—Amerikanski,*" I replied.

Two faces appeared at my elbow. "*Amerikanski?*" said the faces. The Red soldiers pointed to themselves and said, "*Russki,*" and laughed. "*Amerikanski soyuzniki,*" they said, and patted us as you might pat a friendly dog.

"I don't know what you guys are saying," commented our driver, "but have a cigarette anyway." He shoved a pack toward them.

"*Papyrosen,*" said the Russians. They pulled packs of cigarettes from their blouses and offered them to us. We all smoked.

Another Russian, evidently an officer, loomed out of the darkness. "Come here," he said in German.

"Our friend. American officer. Where is he?" I asked in German.

"Come. Come," the Russian reiterated.

I pointed at the jeep. "Where? Here?"

"Yes. Here."

That was the only communication we had, an enemy's language that neither of us knew.

We followed the officer through the doorway, with Reuben saying, "I wonder what they're going to do with us and what happened to Hottelet."

We entered the black doorway and went down a narrow hall. A door in front of us opened.

We were in a small sitting room. A table nearly filled the little room. Candles were the only light. They occupied the center of the table with a half dozen bottles of different shapes and sizes. Four or five officers sat near the table. They rose when we came in.

The officer who had come with us said in German, *"Amerikanski—* eat. Drink. *Gut."*

The officers who were in the room introduced themselves with names that blurred at once in my memory.

I said, "MacVane. Officer. Correspondent."

The Russians made places for us at the table. At my place was a water glass filled two-thirds full with a brownish liquor. All the officers rose and with eyes in my direction, or so I thought, offered a toast: "Marshal Stalin." All drank.

I knew that it was considered etiquette to drain the glass, but with my first mouthful I realized I was drinking fiery, cheap German schnapps. And I could not stop drinking. I felt as though I had been booby-trapped. Ever since Prohibition I had been unable to gulp down straight liquor without gagging. But this time I gulped down the liquor without breathing. I could feel my stomach tie into an agonizing knot.

I placed the glass on the table and tried to smile, but the effort was torture. Every muscle in my stomach, chest, neck, and face was strained in the effort to keep from vomiting there at the table.

A cold sweat stood out on my forehead. I looked at the nearest American, but by chance he had been given only a small wineglass of liquor, so the toast had been no hardship.

All sat down. I looked straight across the table. I could not have spoken if my life had depended on it. A Russian across the table raised his glass and smiled. I nodded and pretended to look at the food as I fought minute by minute to keep control of myself, for I realized that if I gave in, I would not have enough time to reach the open air. Finally, I began to win the battle, and my stomach muscles began to relax.

We had evidently come to the Russian officers' regular evening meal. A soldier brought in a huge bowl of ravioli, squares of spaghetti dough filled with finely minced meat and served in a tasty cream sauce. Around the table were plates of sliced wurst. I was hungry, and the food began to make me feel normal, except for the glowing warmth that now spread from my stomach.

To prepare for the next toast, I casually pulled a wineglass from the center of the table and filled it from a bottle of white wine I had marked out.

A Russian officer then stood up to toast "President Roosevelt."

My nearest neighbor poised a bottle of colorless schnapps or vodka over my water glass. But he stopped when I smiled and pointed to my full wineglass.

Again we drained our glasses, but this time I was too slow. My neighbor filled my empty wineglass with schnapps, filled his own, and proposed: "President Truman."

The jolt of the liquor gave me a quick, gasping sensation; but it passed after a few seconds, and I hastily filled my glass with wine.

Then Hottelet came in the door with a Russian officer. "Everything is fine," he said. "This fellow speaks good German. We're in a regimental command post evidently. I think this is the headquarters company mess. I've been having a couple of drinks with the colonel. He wanted me to stay, but I told them I had to join you.

"We've been having some drinks here, too," I said grimly. "I had to down a whole water tumbler of schnapps, and I almost shot my cookies."

A place was made for Dick, and he stood up and said, "Marshal Zhukov and the Red Army," in German. Again we all drank.

My neighbor leaned over and said, *"Amerikanski gut. Harasho. Amerikanski Russki soyuzniki."*

"Russki army okay," I said.

"Harasho. Harasho," said the Russian.

"Harasho," I replied.

The Russians all smiled and said, *"Amerikanski harasho."*

I tried the phrase I had learned in preparation for the Russian meeting, a Russian greeting, *"Sdravtsvouytyeh tovarich."* They all laughed and raised their glasses.

Reuben said, "I get that *harasho* business. It means okay, in Russian. But what's *soyuzniki?"*

"It means allies," I said.

The dinner and the drinking went on until early morning. The party ended up in a happy blur of good fellowship with one of the Russians, weeping with joy, trying to kiss me on the cheek.

An officer took me to a dark room and showed me a bed, empty. Three or four Russian soldiers were sleeping in the same room on couches and chairs. After I lay down, a Russian soldier came in, coughing asthmatically. I had a feeling he was the man I had deprived of a bed. No windows were open. The room was close and airless. I rolled off the bed and opened the door to the hallway, to try to get at least that amount of air. In three or four minutes a

346

soldier got up, sleepily clumped over to the door, and shut it, muttering to himself the while. I tried to open the window a crack at the top, but as soon as I was back in bed, another soldier banged it shut. I gave up and went to sleep.

When I woke up, light trickled into the room, and my wristwatch showed half past eight in the morning. I got off the bed, stuck my feet in my boots, and walked into the hall. The living room at the end of the hall had been cleared of the bottles and litter of the previous night. I hardly recognized it. In the kitchen a couple of Russian soldiers were making coffee in a saucepan. They offered me a cup, and I drank it gratefully. They said, *"Amerikanski. Harasho,"* and touched me on the shoulder in friendly fashion. I thought they were just like two GIs making morning coffee in their billets.

I asked them the way to the toilet in German, French, and English and finally had to pantomime, saying at the same time, *"Psss-psss."*

The soldiers laughed. One led me down the hall to a door which we found to be locked. He patted me and motioned me to stay by the door. In a few moments he was back with a Russian lieutenant. The lieutenant tried the door, knocked on it tentatively, and waited. Nothing happened. The officer beckoned me to follow him up the stair.

I had already realized we were in part of a large tenement house. The windows had been blown out and covered with cardboard or cloth. On the second floor the Red Army officer knocked on a door. A woman opened it. I could see a man inside and another woman cooking.

In German the Russian officer said, "Please. The bathroom door is locked. Could you open it for us?"

The woman seemed to show no fear whatever of the Russians. "You Russians are always wanting something," she grumbled. "It's always do this, do that. I don't know where the key is. I'll have to ask Frau Weiss."

She called, "Frau Weiss. The Russians want the key to the toilet. I suppose if we don't give it to them, they'll move us into the street. Just like them. Old women who never did them any harm."

She got the key and went down the stairs, still scolding the Russians. The Russian winked at me behind her back. She opened the toilet door, took the key with her, and returned up the stairs.

I was amazed by this byplay. If our own American Army had taken over the building, we would never have allowed civilians to remain in it. But the Russians had taken over the downstairs and left the

Germans undisturbed in the upstairs apartments.

I asked the Russian officer later why this policy was followed. "Well, they have to live somewhere," he said, "and we don't need all the rooms."

Nor could I envisage Americans letting the woman keep the key to the toilet, so they had to ask her permission each time they wished to use it. We Americans would either have taken the key in the first place—or kicked in the door.

I had heard the Russians treated the Germans with harsh discipline, but this did not look like it. The way the old woman scolded showed she knew they were not going to harm her. The Russian had seemed to take the business as a huge joke, laughing and looking a little sheepish under her berating.

In the living room the Russian officers were beginning to assemble. Reuben, Hottelet, Bernstein, Jack Hansen, the American public relations officer, and our driver came in, all looking a little bleary-eyed.

"The barber will be around in a minute," said one of the Russians. The officers were beginning to assume identities to me now. The thin-faced man with the big mouth was, to give him a fictitious name, Lebedev. The captain with the pronounced Slavic features and narrow eyes was Tulov. And names and faces began to come together for the others.

"We shave every day," said Tulov. "It is good for the morale of the Army to be clean."

The barber, a little private, unpacked his kit and stood expectantly with his cloth beside a chair. The officer beckoned to me to be first.

With one sweep the barber encircled my neck with the cloth and with another slapped lather on my face. He paused, gave my face a calculating look for a fleeting second, then darted at it with a naked razor.

It was the quickest shave, and it may have been the best, that I ever received. The razor went over my face in great sweeps, but as lightly as a feather. Hot towel, cream, shaving lotion, powder, and I was through. The treatment could have been no more thorough in one of New York's best barbershops, but he had completed the shaving of all of us within half an hour.

When he finished, we Americans started to say our good-byes, and Lebedev's face fell. "We have arranged a breakfast for you. It will be very short. You cannot go on an empty stomach."

Two Russian soldiers brought in armfuls of bottles and glasses and began setting them up on the table.

"We must have a toast. To victory."

The first toast was hard on our stomachs. The second was more kindly. Hors d'oeuvres were spread on the table. Soup, roast lamb, the breakfast was a full-scale banquet.

Someone began swapping insignia. My bronze war correspondent shoulder pieces I had worn since my days with the British Army went for a Red Star cap badge and a couple of silver shoulder stars. The rest were doing the same thing.

Lebedev left the room and came back with an accordion. "It is yours," he said, and dumped it in my arms.

"But I have an accordion."

"It is yours."

I gave him an Eversharp pencil, and we embraced.

Tulov presented an old-fashioned watch on a thick chain. A tiny little girl's locket was entangled in the chain. I was caught, for everyone was watching me expectantly. With a flourish I unbuckled my chronograph wristwatch and buckled it on Tulov's wrist.

"*Sdravtsvouytyay*, Tulov," I said. The Russians shouted and clapped me on the back. We got outside and climbed into the jeep.

Suddenly Lebedev shouted and ran back into the building. He re-appeared with the accordion, beaming, and threw it into my lap.

"You forgot it," he said. "*Amerikanski gut. Russki gut. Nimyets——Deutsch—nicht gut.*"

While the seven or eight Russian officers smiled and waved, we sped away.

That day there were German civilians in the streets, both men and women. The fires that had been burning the previous day seemed to have been put out except for a few ruins that were smoldering.

At one point we stopped at a street corner to watch some German civilians clearing a path along one of the sidewalks. A Red Army soldier stood nearby, a submachine gun slung on his shoulder.

A woman in a mink coat came up the street, a mink coat the first week of May! She had a spoiled, petulant face, and her blond hair was done up in black lace. She would have appeared more at home in the Waldorf-Astoria or Twenty-one than in the ruins of Berlin.

The Russian sentry looked at her and jerked his thumb toward the group of civilians clearing the pavement. The German woman pretended not to notice and started to hurry past. The Red Army man touched her on the arm, pointed at some brooms and shovels, then at the working civilians. The woman began to expostulate. The sentry uttered a command in Russian and pointed again toward the work crew. The woman picked up a broom and sulkily began to brush the sidewalk. She looked as though it were the first time she had ever touched a broom. The Red Army man looked on as impassively as a Sphinx.

Reuben said, "I never thought I'd see a woman in a mink coat sweeping the sidewalk."

"Let's find out how the Russians are treating the German women," I said. We had heard many stories about how the Russian soldiers raped all the women in the towns they entered. I wondered why they needed to rape them, for all of us had seen the German women lined up along the autobahns beckoning to us as we drove past.

They would beckon and gesture, even out in the depths of the country. Since the Russians were loaded with German marks, which to them were just so much paper, there was little need for them to do any raping. If it was not given away, they could buy it.

We spent a couple of hours talking to the civilians of Berlin. Both Dick Hottelet and Vic Bernstein spoke fluent German. We picked women at random on the streets, told them we were Americans, and asked them how the Russians were treating them.

The first reaction was that the Russians were treating them terribly. They had made them work. They had moved into the houses, and there were few enough houses left in Berlin, and everyone was crowded. The Russians were just animals. They did not know how to act. They were brutal.

But did they actually harm you? To be frank, did any try to rape you?

Well, no. Not exactly. But they looked as though they might.

Did you know anyone who had been raped?

Oh, yes. Frau Schultz had said that she knew someone out in such-and-such a district who said all the women out there were raped by these beasts of Russians. It was horrible. Horrible.

But did you know anyone yourself who was actually raped?

No, but Frau Schultz knew someone who knew someone who was raped. Killing and raping and looting. That was what the Russians were doing.

We heard this same story time after time. We picked some attractive women who might have been expected to receive the attention of the brutal and licentious soldiery of any nation. Not a single one had been raped or personally knew anyone who had been violated by the Russians.

Whether the occupation troops that came along later misbehaved themselves, I do not know. It is an old tactic of the woman to cry rape if she thinks she has been underpaid. But I am as certain as I can be that the front-line Russian troops who did the fighting and took Berlin did no raping there. Inevitably we would have found at least one case in our search. We found a lot of rumors, but not a single instance of fact.

I thought I deduced the reason for the correctness of the Russian behavior from something one of the officers had said during our party of the previous night. I had asked him whether there was much fraternization between Russian soldiers and German women.

"No," he said. "The Army has ordered there shall be no fraternization of any kind."

"What if a Russian makes love to a German girl?" I said.

The Soviet officer looked at me, smiled grimly, and drew his finger across his throat in the gesture familiar to every land. Enough said. What American GI would risk going into the bushes with one of the German women if it meant standing up against a firing squad as the result?

By this time we had come to the square near the Chancellery and the Propaganda Ministry.

A Russian officer with a thin, humorous face and bright blue eyes looked at us curiously. On his shoulder he wore the single large star of a major, and around his neck was slung a movie camera. There was something about him and about us that made recognition inevitable.

A reporter can almost always go into a room full of people and pick out another reporter, by a kind of instinct.

"Are you correspondents?" he asked in English.

We introduced ourselves. The major said, "I am Roman Karmen, correspondent for *Izvestia*. I also write for *The New York Times*. Just this morning I had a cable from Moscow telling me that the American papers gave a big play to my stories of our fight into Berlin. Are there any other reporters with you?"

"No. I think we're the first to get here since you took the center of the city. I heard a couple of other correspondents had come while you were still fighting on the outskirts."

"Did you get any permission?" Karmen asked.

"No. We took a wrong turn and found we were near Berlin and

came on in. We were at Marshal Koniev's party yesterday."

Karmen laughed. "A good party, huh? This is quite a sight, isn't it? Come with me. I have brought a bottle of champagne a thousand miles, from Stalingrad, and I made a resolution I would save it to drink in Berlin with the first Americans I met."

We followed him to the front of the Chancellery. He had built a wooden structure around the back of his jeep so that he could use it as a darkroom for developing his pictures. He leaned inside, and from out of the welter of cameras, equipment, and boxes of film, he brought tin cups.

The Pommery 1928 opened with a loud pop, and the wine foamed out.

Karmen said, "To our common victory," and we drank the wine of luxury, the wine of weddings and tailcoats and orchids and muted music at the Ritz, standing there among the ruins, seven men in grimy uniforms with tin cups. The champagne tasted better than we had ever believed possible.

Roman Karmen said, "Do any of you know an American correspondent named Wright Bryan?"

"Yes. Yes. What do you know about him?"

"A tall man, wounded in the leg. We overran his prison camp a short time ago. He is thin, but alive, and we sent him right off to Moscow for medical treatment."

It was the first I had known that Wright was still alive, and I could have kissed Karmen for bringing us the good news.

Someone said, "Where's Hitler?"

"I don't know," Karmen replied, "but we can ask."

We all walked over to the Chancellery and to one of the sentries on guard. The sentry saluted and pointed out his commanding officer, a lieutenant colonel. Karmen interpreted our questions and the answers.

"Can we go in the Chancellery?"

"I regret that that will be impossible. The Chancellery has not yet been taken. We have cleared the upper floors, but underneath lie deep shelters and catacombs. Several hundred German officers who do not know that Berlin has been captured are down there. They are holding out, and my men will have to go down and smoke them out with flamethrowers and grenades. In the meantime, I am under strict orders to let no one into the building except a high officer with direct written authority from Marshal Zhukov."

I could imagine the German officers waiting in there, deep beneath the ground, perhaps too deep to realize the noise of battle had passed away westward. They would be hoping for a rescuing German army that would never come and wondering why their communication lines gave no answer to their appeals.

"Where's Hitler? Have you found any trace of him?"

The Russian colonel grinned. "We have found the bodies of three men who look like Hitler. We have examined them as carefully as possible, but we do not think any one of them is really Hitler. There will be further tests, but we are sure that Hitler was either destroyed completely or escaped. He was here in this building almost to the end. But even up to a few hours before we fought our way here, the Germans were getting in and out by lightplanes that landed in the street. I personally think Hitler got away on one of those planes and now is probably off to Spain or Argentina."

"Do you mind if we walk down between the buildings along the side of the Chancellery?" Major Karmen asked.

"As long as you don't go in, it will be all right. But don't go wandering around inside. It is very big, and it has not yet been really explored. You might get into trouble."

We went to the side entrance, past the sentry. The great doors were open. By the steps lay a young German soldier of an SS regiment, the tall, blond, fanatic type that Hitler liked for his bodyguards. The soldier's eyes stared emptily at the blue sky above. Beside him some Russian soldier had placed a bronze bust of the Führer. Scattered over him were Nazi war medals, dozens of them, their ribbons making bright splotches against his gray uniform.

I thought that this was the end of the Third Reich. Where now was the lust for conquest and war? The glory had ended like this, a shapeless thing in shapeless gray mingling his flesh with the dirt and the man he had followed, a crazy bust on the ground. The soldier had enough Hitler medals now, one even in his stiffened jaws. I touched the bust with my foot.

The mustached face with the familiar dangling lock of hair fell over in the dirt. Two sightless stares, the soldier and the marble bust. That was how Germany had ended.

We went inside and walked through the rooms nearest the entrance. Piles of medals, cases of medals were strewn in the helter-skelter of broken furniture. The loft walls were scarred with bullets and the blast of bombs. It reminded us of walking about in a mausoleum from which the bodies had been removed. We picked up a few medals for souvenirs and came into the open air.

Out in the Wilhelmstrasse, we started to say good-bye to Major Karmen. But before we left, the *Izvestia* correspondent wanted us to see snapshots of his wife and little girl.

"I'm tired of war. It's such a long time since I have seen them," he said. "I'm tired of all the blood and living like this and all the ruined cities from Stalingrad to here. I just want to get out of uniform and spend the rest of my life in Moscow. And if I have to take a picture or write a story, I don't want to go farther away than the suburbs, and I want to be back home for supper and kiss my little girl good night."

He was saying what we all felt to some degree or other. We had had enough of war, and the sight of Berlin depressed us. As we passed under the Brandenburg Gate, Russian soldiers were already dumping lumber on the street, lumber that was to make the stands for a triumphal Red Army victory review.

Many years later Roman Karmen was the chief producer of a series of films shown on U.S. television entitled *The Unknown War*, which described the Soviet Union's Army in action from the first German attack in 1941 to the end in Berlin in May 1945.

Chapter 32

Hottelet said, "On the map, it's easier if we take the autobahn straight westward out of Berlin. It will be quicker than going back to Torgau."

I argued that we should go back the way we had come. We knew that way was safe, and we had not the slightest idea of the situation west of Berlin. For all we knew we might run into a major battle. Or all the roads might be mined, the bridges blown. But Hottelet, Bernstein, and Reuben argued against me. In an ordinary campaign excursion I might have carried the day, being much the senior in combat experience. But in Germany, with the war won, Hottelet and Bernstein with their thorough knowledge of German and their previous experience in Germany were able to outweigh me. So we took the autobahn.

As we sped down the broad six-lane ribbon, we passed a column of horse-drawn carts heading for Berlin. Each cart was loaded with boxes, crates, stoves, blankets, all the paraphernalia of any army. It was the Red Army on the march.

Civilian Russian women, possibly refugees the army had picked up in its passage, perched on some of the carts. On each cart a Russian soldier handled the reins. Some vehicles carried a mixed load of civilians and soldiers.

The officers in Berlin had told us that as the Red Army overran prisoner of war camps, they freed the Red Army prisoners, gave them rifles, and incorporated them at once into combat units. Many Russian civilians who had been used as slave laborers by the Germans had attached themselves now to the Russian Army and were doing auxiliary work for the soldiers.

I wondered how these long horse-drawn supply trains could keep up with the speedy advance of the Russian armor. Probably they did not. From what I had seen it seemed to me that motor transport carried the shells and other vital supplies, moving along with the tanks, and the horse vehicles brought up nonessential materials that the Army could do without for varying periods of time during an advance.

The weather that May afternoon was clear, with a languid warmth in the breeze that brought back memories of peacetime when weather was not so much of a military secret.

Five miles outside Berlin, our autobahn ended in midair. The retreating Germans had blown up the whole road at the point where it mounted over a small river. Back we had to go all the way to Berlin to get onto another autobahn going in the same direction. Unfortunately our passage was interrupted for the second time a few miles outside Berlin. The reason was the same, a blown bridge. I thought bitterly that by this time, if my advice had been taken, we would have been well on the way to Torgau.

We paused in disappointment. Bernstein was driving an aged Mercedes he had picked up, and Hottelet and I were in the jeep. Just then an American lieutenant and an American sergeant roared up beside us in a racy two-seater Mercedes, the type the SS officers used to drive. The lieutenant introduced himself as an Eighth Air Force pilot who had got a "slight case of flak" over the Ruhr and had had to bail out.

"The *Russkis* overran our prison camp last week," the lieutenant said. "We been having a wonderful time. The sergeant speaks some Russian he learned from his folks. The Russians gave us a car and food and liquor, and we have just been tearing around ever since, living on top of the world."

I told the American we were trying to get to Potsdam and move westward.

"I don't think I'll go back to our side of the fence for a while," said the lieutenant. "I'm having too good a time here. And are these Russians fast men with a drink! But I know the way to Potsdam, and you can follow me. We may run into trouble. The last Russians I talked with told me some SS units are giving them a party out around Potsdam."

He turned the Mercedes and sped off like a racehorse leaving the barrier. We tried to follow, but he was out of sight before we had covered two miles.

We took what we thought was the right turnoff and finally hit the autobahn again some miles west of Potsdam, where the fighting was taking place, as we found out later. We had a couple of punctures on the way, and night was gathering as we sped past Ziesar, Theessen, and Burg and approached the Elbe River.

I was quite jubilant at our nearness to the river and was ready to admit Hottelet had been right and I had been wrong. But at that moment we came to a barrier of sticks across the road. We got out to look. The road ended right there in midair. Before us stretched 200 yards of the river, without a bridge in sight. The roadway had been completely destroyed.

"I'm sorry," Hottelet said. "It's my fault."

We told him none of us could know the bridge was blown. The map showed a nearby village, which, as I remember, was Hohenwarthe. We drove to it in the dusk. It turned out to be a couple of dozen one-story houses. Some chickens were pecking about in the dirt of the only street.

We tried to question a passing Russian soldier, but he spoke no German. When we identified ourselves as Americans, he grinned and pointed to one of the houses.

At that particular minute one of the last remaining four tires on the jeep chose to expire with a sigh.

"Now we really have to get some help," Reuben said. "We can't go far on three tires."

We walked into the barnyard where a young Russian sentry was standing, tommy gun slung on his shoulder. He took us into the parlor of the house, low-ceilinged and musty-smelling. On one wall was the tinted photograph of a German peasant and his wife, dating from the last century. On another was a print of a castle by a lake. Two Russian lieutenants were sitting by the table. One had a square Slavic face with suspicious eyes. The other, younger and more alert, was talking on a field telephone. We waited until he had finished; then Hottelet, after we found the younger man spoke some hesitating German, began to explain our plight. Dick asked for a mechanic to fix our tires or for tools to remove the rim and put on a patch.

The Russian nodded but said, "We have nothing like that here. At headquarters they will be able to help you. But first you must eat with us. We were just going to supper."

"We really ought to be on our way at once," Dick said. "We have come a long way and we have far to go."

"But we can do nothing here. You will have to go to headquarters. They will send someone to tow your car to a garage. By tomorrow you will be all ready to leave. Driving at night is dangerous. You never know when you may meet Germans who will still shoot. Eat with us, and you will feel better about it."

We went outside with them to another one-story house. A table was set for two, but a soldier brought more plates and cutlery. He came in with a big platter of fried eggs, another big platter of

German sausage, a loaf of dark bread, and two pitchers of beer. The fresh food reminded me how tired we all were of food from cans. Our army seemed to live out of cans, and the Red Army obviously lived on what it found in the countryside.

The younger officer ate quickly, slipped out of the house without explanation, and returned in ten minutes.

"Headquarters is sending a car down for you," he said. "Everything will be fixed there. You can explain to them, and they will take care of you."

Less than half an hour later a car roared full tilt into the village and stopped with a squeal of brakes in front of the door. An officer was driving. A soldier sat beside him, holding a tommy gun. The officer beckoned us to get in; then shot away, rocking from side to side, with lights full on.

"Deutsch! Nimyets! Krieg!" I shouted in the officer's ear. The officer shrugged and gestured at the soldier, who had his tommy gun poking out the window. Then he slapped his own tommy gun on the seat beside him. Well, I thought, it is a comfort to know our Russian friends will put up a fight if we are ambushed.

At a certain point in the road the driver switched his headlights on and off twice. A light ahead blinked an answer, and we shot forward. Suddenly our driver stamped on the brakes.

We had halted in front of a large three-story house. The silent officer driver motioned us to follow, through a dark hall, up the stairs. All at once we were in a smoky lighted room.

We were blinking in the light when a voice said, "Take it easy, Greasy. It's a long slide home."

We could have been no more astonished if we had walked into the room and found Louis "Satchmo" Armstrong singing "Beat Me, Daddy, Eight to the Bar."

Six or eight Soviet officers were standing or sitting in the small room. The officer who had addressed us wore the one star of a sub-lieutenant, the lowest commissioned rank. Above the collar of his immaculate uniform we saw a red-cheeked, boyish face and round, appealing eyes. He would have looked quite at home at any New York debutante party or dancing at the Four Hundred in London with the daughter of some county family up for the season.

We Americans all started to laugh. The youthful officer looked puzzled, then started to laugh with us.

"What can I do to help you, sirs?" he said.

I said, "We were laughing at the phrase you used. It's American slang, and we didn't expect to hear it here."

"Oh, that," the officer explained. "It was one of the questions on my test at the interpreters' school at Moscow. But you are the first Americans I have ever talked to. Can you understand me without difficulty?"

"Hell, you speak better American than half the people in New York," said someone.

The officer's pink cheeks became pinker with pleasure.

When we started to explain our plight, he said, "We have heard about it. The officer at the village telephoned. Permit me to introduce myself. I am Vsevelod Altaev. But my friends call me Willy. Some of my Russian friends can speak English, and they gave me this English nickname."

We introduced ourselves with our war correspondent assimilated rank as captains.

Willy looked puzzled. "I am looking for your badges of rank. See. We have pictures of them, but I do not see you are wearing any." He showed us pictures of American officers' insignia on a colored chart with descriptions in Russian.

Dick tried to explain that we had swapped insignia with some Russian officers in Berlin. Willy still looked puzzled. An older officer, a major, spoke to him in short Russian phrases.

"I am sorry," said Willy, "but my major suggests I should look at your identification. You understand, of course, it is only a formality."

Willy sat at a table. The major was beside him with pen and paper. I gave them my adjutant general's office card.

Willy said, "What does 'assimilated captain' mean?"

I started to explain that it meant I had the privileges of a captain but was not a part of the Army.

"But you are captains, are you not? You are in uniform and so part of the Army?"

"I am a correspondent, subject to Army discipline, part of the Army, but—oh, hell. It just means I am captain but I do not fight. Instead, I write."

Willy translated. But his superior did not look very convinced.

Finally Willy said, "Good. Now we must eat. Tonight we have a good time. Your car will be fixed, and tomorrow you can go."

We thanked him and explained how eager we were to return to our camp. The food and drink came in in great profusion. The major thawed a little under the drink, and we found he was chief of staff of his unit. But when someone incautiously asked him what unit or what kind of unit it was, the major's face froze at once into hard lines.

I quickly changed the conversation and asked why it was that German civilians were permitted to live in the same buildings as Russian Army men. I said our own practice was to clear every civilian out of any buildings or areas taken over by the Army.

The major thought a moment. "There are two ways to treat the Germans," he said. "We could kill them all. That would perhaps be the proper punishment, for they killed many, many of our people.

"The other policy is to punish the Nazis who got the Germans into the war and treat the rest of the Germans with kindness so that they will appreciate our example and learn to be democratic. Then they will not wage war. That is the difficulty. We have to live beside them. We must teach them democracy so that they will not attack us and the rest of Europe again."

The major could understand English when it was spoken slowly, and his own English was not bad, although he fumbled for words like someone who had learned the language at school but had had no opportunity to practice speaking it in recent years.

The major went on: "It is for this reason, the need for kindness to the ordinary Germans, that we do not turn all the people out of a house. We leave them some rooms so they can live, for if we turned them all out, where could they go?"

"What do you do when you capture a town?" I asked. "How does your military government work?"

The major said, "We enter the town with a list of the chief Nazis of the area. These we try to find and arrest. We get rid of them.

"The others, we call together and say, 'Elect a *Bürgermeister.* You can elect anyone but a Nazi.' When the *Bürgermeister* is elected, he runs the town. Of course, he must have our approval, but we try not to bother him unless he does something we think is undemocratic. We feel the Germans must learn how to govern themselves, for we cannot govern them forever. The time for them to learn self-government is right now."

I said I thought that was much the same as our own system. We, too, entered each area with a list of the most important Nazis. These we also tried to catch. I did not go into ways of getting rid of the Nazis, which I could well imagine. But I said that we usually appointed the *Bürgermeister* because we did not think the time had

360

come for the Germans to start holding elections. In fact, I wondered whether the Russians were not overoptimistic dividing Nazis and non-Nazis, like sheep from the goats.

The party continued until past three o'clock in the morning. Willy offered to take us to our beds. At the door he stopped. I beckoned him to go ahead.

"Oh, no," Willy replied. "You are a captain, and I am only a lieutenant. You must go first."

"We don't pay much attention to that sort of thing in our Army," I said. "I have been calling you Willy for three hours. Why don't you call me John, instead of Captain?"

"I couldn't do that," said Willy. "In the Red Army you can never call your superior officer by his first name. That would not be respectful. It would not be right. The same with your lieutenant. I must call him Lieutenant because he is a first lieutenant and I am only a sublieutenant."

I had noticed the formality between officers. Yet between Russian officers and men there seemed even more equality than in the American Army. Soldiers and officers were billeted in the same buildings, even in the same rooms. Enlisted men treated officers with a familiar directness that seemed even more American than the Americans. The soldiers joined in officers' conversations and offered opinions without waiting to be asked.

I thought it was all very puzzling—but interesting. And that was what I was pondering when I pushed the counterpane to the bottom of the bedstead and drifted off to sleep.

Chapter 33

The next morning we came outside to find the sky blue overhead and the birds singing in the nearby fields. We were in a small village. One section had been blocked off with wooden poles that were let down across the streets and could be raised for cars to go in or out. It was undoubtedly some kind of headquarters area.

There were German civilians in the streets, and they looked curiously at us walking along with Willy, the Russian. Willy, we found out, did not understand German, so Hottelet and Bernstein talked to some of the civilians. They were extremely voluble. Later Hottelet said he had asked most of them how the Russians were acting. They replied they did not like the Russians, but none had any tales of rape or pillage.

"The strangest thing," Hottelet said, "was their eagerness to know when the Americans were coming. They have listened to Goebbels so long that they expected us to start fighting the Russians as soon as our armies met. They were puzzled to see Americans on friendly terms with a Russian officer, and they thought we might be prisoners."

We told Willy that we wanted to get away back to our lines. He replied that the jeep would be ready after lunch. "I am so sorry," he said, "but the mechanics could not work on your jeep until this morning. But do not worry. They will complete it this morning and everything will be—okeydokey. The officers want to give you a big luncheon. The *polkovnik*, the colonel himself, is coming."

The thought of another party made us wince. The two previous days and nights had left our stomachs feeling as though they were filled with feathers.

We ate at a big table, covered with white linen. The bottles stood up like spines on a cactus all over the table.

The colonel—the *polkovnik*—was a heavy square man. He had eyes like agates, and his face could have been carved from granite. He looked very, very tough indeed. I could imagine him at Stalingrad, where, in fact, he and his regiment had fought. I could imagine

362

him making love or ordering 5,000 Germans shot without any flicker crossing his features in either circumstance.

As we drank toasts, the *polkovnik* only touched a glass of beer to his lips.

Willy apologized. "The *polkovnik* does not drink," he said. "He is doing you a great honor coming to lunch with you."

I could have done without the honor. I felt that the *polkovnik* was appraising us carefully and coldly, and I saw not a trace of friendship in his icy gaze.

The *polkovnik* left the luncheon party early, and with his departure the junior officers visibly loosened up. The luncheon went with a swing, with Willy making swift translations of the toasts and the banter.

It was nearly half past three in the afternoon when we managed to tear ourselves away. I asked one of the captains whether the Red Army always ate and drank in such plenty.

The captain explained that in battle the Red Army ate what it could. Sometimes men fought for days on a few pieces of bread and a bit of cheese and cold meat.

"Our supply system depends on where we are," the captain went on. "If one of our divisions is in territory where there is plenty of food, the supply headquarters sends it very little rations. If the division is in barren, foodless territory, all its food will be sent to it by the Army. The supply people try to do the easiest, most practical thing. Sometimes they make mistakes, and a division or a corps finds no food in an area that the supply headquarters believed was filled with food. Then we may go short of food for a few days."

The captain laughed. "But now we are not fighting, so we eat and drink very well. Can you think of anything better to do?"

We all continued down the lane. At one point a herd of perhaps a hundred horses were grazing in a field. The captain winked and said, "The mechanized transport of the Red Army."

Eventually came the time for our good-byes. I said, "Well, Willy, it's been a lot of fun, but now we must get our cars and be on our way."

Willy's pink cheeks got even pinker. He looked down at his shiny black boots with the air of a schoolboy caught cheating in class. "I am very embarrassed," he said. "I am terribly afraid it will be impossible for you to leave us right now."

"What's the matter? Isn't our car fixed?" We all wanted to know.

"Yes. Both tires are fixed. You have plenty of petrol. But, you see, last night the headquarters reported to Marshal Stalin that you had arrived here."

"Marshal Stalin!" we chorused. We were stupefied.

"What will happen now?"

"I am so embarrassed," said Willy. "My colonel pointed out that you were not here on official business. The headquarters had to tell Marshal Stalin. Marshal Stalin will probably send a message to President Truman. Then President Truman will probably inform General Eisenhower. General Eisenhower will inform General Bradley. General Bradley will say that you are all right, and President Truman will tell Marshal Stalin. Marshal Stalin will inform our headquarters with a message, and soon you may go."

"If we don't die of old age first," someone commented.

"Oh no," said Willy. "You will not die of old age. That would be absurd. Perhaps a few hours. Perhaps a day. I have a feeling that everything will be all right tomorrow."

Knowing the length of time messages took in going through channels of the American Army and assuming that the Russian Army was equally lethargic in such matters, I could see us staying there for months with no one in the First Army knowing what had become of us.

"Serves us right for coming around with two flat tires and no insignia and asking where the nearest bridge was," said Hottelet.

Reuben said, "Bradley is going to be sore as hell at us for giving him all this trouble." We could imagine the effect on the Twelfth Army Group of a message from SHAEF or Washington that a bunch of American reporters was giving the Russians trouble. We could see our war correspondent credentials taken away and ourselves, perhaps, sent as privates to Alaska.

"We have a nice little house for you," said Willy hopefully. "It is just outside the headquarters area. You will be all by yourselves. If you like, I can stay with you. And we are arranging a party for you tonight."

We found the jeep waiting, and Willy directed us through the road bar to a house about a quarter of a mile down the road.

It was a neat little cottage. Three German women were near the door, talking to a Russian soldier. One of them owned the house, and she complained to us about the haste in which she had had to move out. She said they were staying with friends, who would now be very crowded. The woman asked us how long we would be needing her house.

Hottelet said, "We hope for not more than a day or two," and the woman said, "*Gut. Gut,*" and walked away.

When we got inside, Willy began to sing "Pistol-Packin' Mama." It was incongruous to hear a sublieutenant in the Red Army singing "Pistol-Packin' Mama. Lay that pistol down. Lay that pistol down, Mama. Lay that pistol down."

Willy explained that he had some girl friends in Moscow who spoke English, and they had learned the song from some American Air Force officers stationed on a Russian airfield. The girls had taught Willy the words and music.

Willy bustled about like a mother hen, making sure we had enough blankets on the beds. A Red Army barber arrived and shaved us. A soldier entered with an armful of Rhine wine and brandy.

Willy said, "I think I can get some girls for the party tonight." We followed him a short way up the street to a large building. Some girls in uniforms came out and talked to Willy. He explained they were nurses. But just when things seemed to be going swimmingly, an older man in major's uniform bounced out of the door and talked to Willy in peremptory tones. He shooed the girls inside and followed them. Willy came back with downcast face.

"They wanted to come, and I had the *polkovnik*'s permission; but their major refused to let them join us. He said they had work to do." Willy brightened up a little as he added, "At least, a Hero of the Red Army is coming, and the major and two other officers."

Soon sparkling white tablecloth, silver, and plates arrived and were set up in our little cottage. The guest came shortly afterward. The meal began with hors d'oeuvres and continued with small broiled chickens.

Two Russian privates with accordions entered and were invited to join us.

I was cutting at my chicken when I happened to notice the Soviet major break off a drumstick and hold it in his hands.

He saw me looking and, somewhat defiantly, said, "This is the way we Russians eat chicken." He acted as though he felt I might not think he was using the proper Emily Post etiquette.

I said, "That's how we Americans eat chicken also," and I picked up a wing in my hand and began to gnaw at it.

The major laughed, clapped me on the shoulder, and everyone rose to his toast: "The American Army."

The Hero of the Soviet Union was a lieutenant colonel of infantry, somewhere in his early thirties, with cropped hair and a windburned complexion. He reminded me of some young professional American Army officers I knew. He wore his Hero medal and with it the second highest bravery decoration, the Order of Lenin medal.

The hero refused to talk about the specific deed of valor which won him his medal, the equivalent of our Congressional Medal of Honor. He had spent sixteen years in the Army, several of those as an enlisted man. Since Stalingrad he had commanded a Guards battalion, a crack unit.

The hero was interested in American military tactics and asked questions about the liaison between our infantry and our support planes and our use of armor to support infantry. He explained Russian methods which had developed along the lines similar to our own. He was especially eager to hear of the big airborne actions of the Americans and British—the dropping of whole divisions on the Cherbourg peninsula before D-Day and the drops at Nijmegen and Arnhem.

I told him that some of our infantry officers thought that mass airborne attacks were not the most effective way of using airborne troops.

I said, "We hear you drop your parachutists and gliders in small numbers ahead of your infantry to cut enemy communications and confuse them."

"That is right," the hero answered. "But in our Army we are coming to the conclusion that the mass airborne attack is probably the best. We have found that our system costs us heavy casualties in our highly trained elite airborne troops, and the system of dropping them in small units behind enemy lines does not bother the enemy sufficiently to warrant the losses we sustain. In Russia, of course, the situation was quite different. There our small detachments of parachutists worked with the local partisans behind German lines and completely disrupted German communications."

"I suppose, back at Stalingrad, you thought we Americans were never going to get started."

"That is right. We were very impatient. When we were in Stalingrad, I did not think of your bombing of Germany as being very important. Since I came to Germany, I have changed my mind. In the cities my battalion entered, I noticed how oil plants and tank factories were destroyed by bombing, and I knew then why the Hitlerites could not send their masses of tanks and planes against us as they used to do. Believe me, I appreciate what your bombing did."

I asked the hero what had been the most valuable lesson in warfare that his experience had taught him.

He pondered a moment before replying: "That is very difficult. There are so many things. But one of the great things we learned was the need to decentralize our administration. When the war began, all administrative problems had to be referred to Moscow. This wasted time and administrative battles cost us battles—and many lives."

"What did you do about it?"

"Finally Moscow learned that everything could not be decided by Moscow—if we were going to win the war. So each marshal was given a large share of the responsibility for his own area. He was free to make decisions that previously he would have had to ask Moscow about. Asking Moscow and getting a reply necessitated waiting hours, perhaps days without action. It was only when the administration system changed that we began to win battles."

His comments seemed to prove something that I had thought was indicated by Soviet diplomatic policy, the fact that many of the delays and contradictions lay in the necessity for referring all decisions to Moscow. I thought the administration must be even more centralized than France's, and I had seen how red tape had fouled up France's bureaucratic activity. If the presence of a few obscure Americans behind Soviet lines had to be referred to Moscow, I wondered what a welter of minuscule administrative details must be flooding into the Kremlin.

The two accordion players had finished eating, and they brought out their instruments. One was a captured German piano-accordion; the other, a Russian instrument with bewildering banks of buttons.

The music was wild and earthy. Folk music, Cossack dances, and the songs of the Red Army followed one another, with Willy explaining the titles and the meaning to us. These were people who lived on music. The soldiers sat swaying with sweat running down their faces, as first one, then another picked up the melody or accompaniment. It sounded as untutored and as moving as the music of the Highland war pipes in my ears.

I asked for the piece known in Britain and America as "The March of the Red Cavalry." It was not one of their more popular Army songs, but they knew it under a Russian name that meant something like "Meadowland."

The musicians even played some American songs, "Yankee Doodle," "Dixie," and "My Country 'Tis of Thee."

The major, who was chief of staff of the regiment or the battalion, I was never able to ascertain which, felt the brandy and the heat of the night more than the rest of us. He sat, with his glass in his hand, listening to the music. He gazed fixedly at me at one point and said, "Do you really think we are uncultured Russian barbarians with no manners?"

"Tovarich Major," I said, "we think your hospitality is as warm and your manners as fine as any nation we have seen. We only hope that when you visit us, we can give you as fine a welcome as we have had from the Red Army."

We clicked glasses and drank. In the light of the flickering candles, with the sweating Red Army soldiers, drawing the wild music out of their accordions, and the officers breaking into snatches of song as the glasses were filled once again, I felt as though I were living a page out of Tolstoy. I knew I would never again read of a Russian dinner or a Cossack celebration without thinking of the scene that night in the German cottage.

It was three o'clock in the morning before the music finished and the guests departed. As they left, Willy said, "Our sentry will stay on duty all night outside. We are outside the headquarters area, and it is best we have protection." So we were really in protective custody. We were being protected. But we were being prevented from doing anything rash such as trying to take off for our own lines. We might, in fact, have felt nervous without a guard, for the war was not ended, and we had no idea of what German units might be still left in the neighborhood or whether some of the SS might not be ready for a final thrust against a Russian headquarters. But the fact that we could look out the door and see a Red Army sentry with his submachine gun slung ready under his arm meant that with the utmost politeness, we had been made prisoners. I do not think any of us was afraid. At most we expected a few days or even weeks of being held immobile by the Russians. We did not imagine that anything worse could befall, not with the treatment we had been given.

Chapter 34

We stayed with the Russian unit for three more days. Each day we would ask Willy whether any word had come for our release. Each day Willy would shake his head and apologize. His answer was always: "Perhaps this afternoon" or "Perhaps tomorrow."

We were treated as honored guests. We ate magnificent meals. We talked with whomever we wished and went wherever we wanted, provided it was in the immediate neighborhood of the headquarters.

We had no MVD guardians among these front-line troops. They would come later. Our only guardian was our indispensable Willy, nineteen years old and a proud sublieutenant. He had been in the Army two and a half years already, as private, cadet, sublieutenant, then as interpreter-candidate at the Moscow Army School for Interpreters. He translated quickly both our questions and the replies, the jokes of the soldiers when we sat down with a group of them, and all the little asides that add spice to a conversation.

We were the first contact that most of the Russians had ever had with Americans. They asked us questions about the New York skyscrapers, about the factories that made the Red Army's best trucks, and the film stars, some of whom we had almost forgotten, stars of yesteryear, such as Buster Keaton, who, I took it, were still the stars of the latest American films being shown in Russia.

Not once in the numerous conversations over several days did I hear any officer or man mention communism. They talked of their country and their eagerness to return to it. They talked, as American soldiers would talk, of army matters, the food, weapons, tactics, and battles. When they spoke of women, it was of their own wives and girl friends, and they showed pictures such as any soldier carries.

The Red Army men seemed filled with combined exultation and amazement that they had been able to drive the Germans from the Volga to the Elbe. To them, the German had always been the *nimyets*, the foreigner, who from immemorial time had sought to conquer or exploit them. The fact that they had been able to beat this traditional foreigner almost seemed to raise their status in their own eyes, as though they had been expected to lose and suddenly discovered that the traditional tables had been turned and they had become the conquerors.

One of the officers told me vehemently that ever since the days of the Mongols foreigners had entered Russia only to become the masters and exploit by trickery the Russian people. His pride at beating the Germans could have been tinged with the feeling that his generation at last had been able to meet and defeat the would-be exploiters of the Russians on equal terms.

It surprised me that the Russians seemed to feel that they were citizens of a democratic state, free citizens of a democracy. They called their press the "freest in the world," for, said they, it was written and published by men who write and think democracy.

As with Simonov, I tried to explain that in America we tolerated differences of opinion as the highest good.

"We also believe in differences of opinion," said the officer with whom I was talking. "We have much criticism of the various ways of accomplishing the ends we all desire, liberty and justice.

"But there can be no difference of opinion about the fundamental basis of our lives, democracy. The fascists who attacked that basic truth all have gone, and now the people take democracy for granted. It has proved to be the best way of life, and through education, the children and the older people have learned that this is so."

He seemed as proud of the democratic way of life in Russia as any American politician making a Fourth of July speech at home. It was apparent that we were using the same words and speaking about quite different concepts. My arguments for tolerance of opposition and allowing even the basis of the state to be questioned seemed to make no sense at all to him, no more sense than such sentiments made a few years later to certain American political figures. Nor could I see how any intelligent person, and many of the Russians were as intelligent as their American counterparts, could be happy and content living in a centralized police state.

As I talked with more and more of the Russians, it seemed to me that they resembled Americans in their quick changes of mood, their eagerness, their ready friendship, the way gloom and exultation followed each other in the same minute, and their bluntness of address. They certainly resembled us more than they resembled the English or the French, whose ideas so often ran in the deep channels of tradition.

The Russians seemed like Americans of only a few generations ago, men who could howl louder, jump higher, and fight better than any man in Sangamon County. Like the Maine fisherman, their way of showing their welcome was to pile your plate with more food than you could eat. They were a little like the raw westerner who struck it rich in the mining camps and now, half-contemptuously, half-admiringly, is trying to pick up the proper way to dress and act at a string musicale or a formal dinner.

Their admiration for Americans seemed to be admiration for things that it was no longer fashionable to admire in America—our tremendous industrial civilization. They admired Americans for technical accomplishments that they were convinced they could someday equal. We all took our factories and our assembly lines for granted, and spiritually, we had passed on to other things. But the Russians got quite as enthusiastic about the thought that they also were engaged in great construction projects, turning out trucks and planes, dynamos and turbines.

But they also appeared to be haunted by the conviction that the rest of the world did not want them to achieve this objective. They kept harking back to the fact that most of the civilized world had tried to stop their progress from the time it began, after World War I, when the Communists came to power. They recalled that the armies of Britain, the United States, Germany, Japan, and half of Europe had tried unsuccessfully to crush them. They did not think it could happen again. They believed that during the new war they had shown too much strength. But the fear that an attempt against them might be made one day still lurked. The fear brought suspicion of the foreigner, but it also seemed to strengthen them in the belief that cooperation with other right-thinking nations was as necessary for them as it was for the rest of the world.

"As long as the Soviet Union and the United States work together," was their refrain, "another great war can never happen."

One sunny morning, May 8, Willy returned from headquarters with face wreathed in smiles. "It's okay," he said. "Word has come in that you are all right, and you may go."

"It's about time," Hottelet said. "How did Marshal Stalin take it?"

"I don't know," said Willy seriously. "I'm only a sublieutenant. They would never tell me. But I can assure you everything is all right, and they are letting me go to the river with you to show you the way."

We had our last lunch, and this time the colonel also attended.

But it was a different *polkovnik* who sat with us trying to make un-accustomed jokes. At times a flicker of a smile tried to rise to the surface of his iron visage. He apologized for our long wait and said he hoped we would understand and he hoped also that his officers had treated us well. Then he brought out some bottles of cham-pagne to drink the final toasts.

But I was not sorry to see the last of it all as, with Willy leading us in his jeep, we started out of the camp, waving good-bye to all the privates, the sublieutenants, the *leetnants* and the *stashi-leetants*, the *tovarich Kapitäns*, and the *tovarich* majors, and even the grim *polkovnik*, to whom we threw a brusque final salute.

Near the river we came to a convoy of about twenty big Amer-ican trucks, driven by as many tall American blacks. A motley col-lection of Americans, Canadians, and British in every type of clothing and uniform packed the trucks.

When they saw our American jeep, they began to yell, "We're prisoners going home. Help us get the hell out of here."

Their prison camp had been overrun by the Russians. Then, for days, nothing had happened. That morning twenty American trucks had arrived out of nowhere, but the Russian camp commandant had received no orders to release them. So he told them that if they jumped in the trucks while his back was turned, he could not force them to stay, but he had no orders to send them back across the Elbe. They would have to take their chances.

Now the whole convoy was held up by an excited Russian colonel at the Elbe, who was kicking up a fuss because they had no Russian or American Army orders to pass through his territory. The pris-oners' interpreter, a Canadian officer of Russian extraction, was trying to persuade the colonel to let them pass through.

At that moment a huge cream-colored Opel limousine rolled up beside the colonel and the Canadian arguing in the roadway. A tall man in gleaming boots and smart uniform, with three big gold stars shining on his gold shoulder boards, sprang out.

Willy snapped to rigid attention, whispering, "That's my lieu-tenant general."

The general was black-haired. With his thin face and hawklike nose, he might have been a fifteen-years-younger edition of General Patton.

Without bothering to acknowledge the colonel's salute, the gen-eral stepped in front of him, placed his hands on his hips, and began to talk. He spoke for three or four minutes, then jumped into his car and sped away. During his stay, not a Russian in sight had moved from a position of stiff attention.

The colonel seemed to have wilted as the general departed. He started giving quick orders.

The Canadian officer came over to us. "I never heard anything like it," he said in awed amazement. "It was brutal. That general called the colonel things I wouldn't call my worst enemy. He said what did the colonel mean by letting an American convoy block the roads. He had better get it to the American side of the river or the general would have the colonel's blood—but quick. That colonel would have been better to get a beating with cat-o'-nine-tails. It would have been easier."

A Russian major came half running to the convoy, sprang into the lead car, and beckoned the others to follow.

We followed the convoy to the river. Opposite Magdeburg at the approach to the bridge, the convoy halted. The bridge had been blown. The freed prisoners piled out and stood in the road, cursing.

An American flier said, "It's V-E Day today."

"How do you know?" I asked.

"We heard on the camp radio yesterday that the Germans have surrendered, and Churchill was going to make a broadcast today announcing that V-E Day has arrived officially today."

I asked a Russian soldier how he felt. "It probably won't make much difference. I'll probably have to go to Japan before I ever get back to Moscow. I haven't had any leave in two years." This seemed to be the consensus. All thought they would have to get ready for Japan in two or three months, without time for leave.

A Russian officer said he had heard the rumor of V-E Day, but he could not tell if it was true because Moscow had not yet announced it.

The prisoners and one of the Russian officers crawled across the river on the wreckage of the bridge. We asked Willy where we could find a bridge, for we could not leave our cars. A Russian major spoke to Willy.

"My major says I must stay and interpret for the truck drivers until we can send the trucks back across the river tomorrow. I am sorry. I can go no farther with you. But I think there is a bridge down the river at Schönebeck."

We looked up the point on our maps. The tall black boys crowded around the slim young Willy. They were the first blacks he had ever seen, and he smiled in sheer delight.

From the jeep I heard him say, "You soldiers must stay here until tomorrow. Then we will send you across the river. Now I am going to get you plenty to eat—"

"Yeah, man. I sure can use it," came the comments.

"—And plenty to drink—"

"Oh, boy. Couple good drinks. Hit me again, son."

"—And I'm going to try to introduce you to some nice Russian girls."

The black soldiers started to shout. They were still cheering when our jeep went around the first corner and they and Willy were lost to view.

Within two hours we found the American pontoon bridge down the river. A Russian sentry saluted as we went out on it. It was dusk. A couple of signal flares arched into the sky over the American side of the river. Some GIs from an engineering unit were at the other terminus of the bridge.

We got from them the confirmation that the flares meant V-E Day had really come.

A soldier said, "Come around to the kitchen. We've got a little straight alky and grapefruit juice to celebrate with."

Our stomachs winced, but we went ahead.

When I got on the army telephone and got through to the First Army public relations, the officer at the other end said, "I don't know where you have been. But if you have been to Berlin, don't tell anyone. Two correspondents who just came back saying they had gone to Berlin got their credentials taken away, and they were sent home. An officer disappeared at the same time you reporters did. If he went to Berlin, he will be court-martialed. I thought you ought to know all this before you come back to camp. SHAEF is plenty sore."

"Thanks," I said. "Thanks very much."

We reporters held a consultation. Who knew whether we might not need war correspondent credentials for the Pacific war? And the officer. We did not want him crucified at a court-martial, for the responsibility had been ours, and he had simply come along for the ride.

We made an agreement on the spot that we would say only that we had spent a few days with a Russian Army unit and we would not mention Berlin in our reports and broadcasts. I said I would perhaps do two broadcasts on life with the Red Army, and the others said their reports would be the same, but none would mention

Berlin to our fellow reporters, the public relations officers, or the public.

That was what we did, and as far as I know, this is the first time an account has been written of what happened to the only American reporters who actually saw Berlin at the moment of its conquest, in flames.

Index

382